BEING HUMAN

BEING HUMAN

AN HISTORICAL INQUIRY INTO WHO WE ARE

J. Andrew Kirk

WIPF & STOCK · Eugene, Oregon

BEING HUMAN
An Historical Inquiry into Who We are

Copyright © 2019 J. Andrew Kirk. All rights reserved. Except for brief quotations in critical publications or reviews, no part of this book may be reproduced in any manner without prior written permission from the publisher. Write: Permissions, Wipf and Stock Publishers, 199 W. 8th Ave., Suite 3, Eugene, OR 97401.

Wipf & Stock
An Imprint of Wipf and Stock Publishers
199 W. 8th Ave., Suite 3
Eugene, OR 97401

www.wipfandstock.com

PAPERBACK ISBN: 978-1-5326-6419-9
HARDCOVER ISBN: 978-1-5326-6420-5
EBOOK ISBN: 978-1-5326-6421-2

Manufactured in the U.S.A. 01/17/19

Contents

Preface | vii
Acknowledgments | xi

Prologue | 1

Chapter 1
Initiating the Inquiry | 5

Chapter 2
Human Life in Renaissance Humanism | 21

Chapter 3
Human Reality in the Thought of John Locke | 57

Chapter 4
The Humanism of the Enlightenment | 93

Chapter 5
**David Hume and Denis Diderot:
Two Prominent Figures of the Enlightenment** | 115

Chapter 6
**Diagnosing the Human in the Thinking
of Karl Marx and His Followers** | 140

Chapter 7
The Human Species According to Charles Darwin | 166

Chapter 8
Friedrich Nietzsche and the Human Predicament | 194

Chapter 9
Sigmund Freud and Human Pathologies | 236

Chapter 10
Human Existence in the Thought of Secular Humanism | 275

Chapter 11
The Nature and Destiny of Humanity and the Messianic Hope | 310

Chapter 12
The Gaining of Wisdom? | 356

Bibliography | 385
Index | 399

Preface

ANYONE ENCOUNTERING THE TITLE of this book may be amazed that one individual has undertaken to give an account of some of the principal observations made over the last five hundred years on the theme of the humanity of humans. Such a venture could be interpreted as a major example of personal conceit on my part. Perhaps it is, for how is it humanly possible to cover the ground at all adequately within a fairly short space of time, using only my own faculties? Surely it requires several life-spans of one person to do the subject a little justice, or else the single life-span of many people contributing to an encyclopedia on the vast amount of material available to be considered. Conceivably it would help to allay fears that this project is bound to be lightweight, or even unreliable and misleading, if I were to attempt to convey what I have set out to achieve and what I have not intended to attempt.

I have been guided by the supposition that no one has yet endeavored to set down in one volume what I have called an historical inquiry into what, over the course of nearly six centuries, a few prominent contributors to the foundations of Western culture have offered as their opinion about the complex reality of human existence and experience. The criterion of selection has been the influence they have exerted over many aspects of human life in what is now broadly known as the Western world.

The main problem has been how to distill from their writings, and from the comments that specialized students of their thought have made, their musings on being human. The most that I think I have been able to achieve in each case is a short survey of their suppositions, ideas, reflections, and judgments, culled from their most important writings, or in the case of the Renaissance, also from their art forms. As the reader will discover, I do not pretend in any way to have arrived at some form of comprehensive distillation of their core convictions, nor come to definitive personal conclusions about their sets of beliefs.

I do trust, however, that I have been able to offer an accurate account of what characterizes their main lines of thought in a way that does justice to what they held to be true. This is obviously crucial, for a substantial misreading of any person's views will cause even the most limited endeavor to miscarry. It would be possible to defend oneself by arguing that the content of all the beliefs cited has been open to various interpretations and that, therefore, the accusation of misinterpretations is simply one more interpretation. I assume, however, that in each case there exists sufficient consensus to make the whole undertaking worthwhile. I have, therefore, attempted to avoid promoting a partisan promotion of just one version of the thought being described.

The reader may detect an emphasis on the basic assumptions that guide each person's convictions and the historical context in which they developed their thought. This procedure is particularly important when it comes to assessing their perceptions. In this regard, it is just as crucial that I declare my own, since I am pretending that this is an inquiry (i.e., a critical engagement with other people's opinions from my point of view). After many years of reflection and intellectual and existential engagement with distinct worldviews, both religious and nonreligious, I am still of the conviction that three key sayings sum up the principal sources of our knowledge and understanding of all reality:

"In the beginning God created the heavens and the earth" (Gen 1:1);
"God created humankind in his image" (Gen 1:27);
"To honor the Lord is the beginning of wisdom" (Ps 111:10).

Each of these sayings needs much filling out and defending against challenge and denial. The main reason for claiming these convictions is that they are true in the sense that each one reflects reality exactly and produces a coherent account of the whole of human experience in ways that no other set of fundamental beliefs are able to match. I will give a summary of the reasoning behind the convictions at the end of various chapters and in the last two chapters, and invite those of totally other persuasions into a dialogue on the contentious issues.

I am, so far, convinced that these three statements give a more solid basis for understanding the fundamentals of the totality of existence than any other attempt to produce a similarly consistent, reasonable, and intellectually satisfying solution to the many conundrums of life. This particular inquiry has tended to confirm the convictions, thereby setting human beings within a framework that makes sense of all their experience and gives it all the tools necessary to interpret it judiciously.

I trust the readers will perceive that I have opened myself fully to the reasoning of those who strongly contradict my views. I also affirm that I am open to being convinced that what the convictions convey could be wrong. In other words, I am not claiming absolute certainty, which would point to some horrible vices such as presumption, condescension, and arrogance. I am, however, maintaining a strong probability that the convictions are most likely to be true, in comparison with all the alternatives.

In the long run, the whole discussion is aimed at offering credible and convincing responses to such questions as, "How did it all begin?" "How did we happen to be here?" "What kind of a creature are we?" "What kind of a life should we pursue and why?" "What does the future hold for each person?" After all, unless we can give competent, well-reflected replies to these questions, and others like them, and the reason why we are the only living creature who asks them, I surmise that we will never be fully satisfied in ourselves. So, with this introduction, I invite you to take part in this immensely significant debate about who we are.

J. Andrew Kirk,
August 2018

Acknowledgments

LIKE MOST AUTHORS, I am indebted to too many people who have helped and encouraged me with the completion of this book to be able to name them all. However, there is one person in particular who has generously given me of his time to peruse carefully three of the chapters, where his expert knowledge and understanding of the material (in the field of the philosophy of the mind) have been invaluable. The chapters are the ones on Nietzsche, Freud, and Secular Humanism. His name is Pablo Lopez-Silva. He is an Adjunct Professor in the School of Psychology in the Faculty of Medicine and Professor of Post-graduate Studies in the Institute of Philosophy in the Faculty of Humanities of the University of Valparaiso, Chile. His comments on the chapters have been invaluable and most of his suggestions have been incorporated into the revised text.

I would also like to thank my publishers, Wipf and Stock, and in particular Matt Wimer, its Assistant Managing Editor, for being willing to take on this project and bring it to a conclusion in published form. The publishing house has an excellent reputation for its expertise in the wide range of books that it has published and promoted. I would also like to thank all the team who have been involved on the editing, production, and marketing sides. This is the first book that I have had published directly in the USA (other books have been published in the USA, after first seeing the light of day in the UK). They have all guided me well through the slightly different process adopted on the other side of the Atlantic "pond."

Andrew Kirk

Prologue

THERE ARE A NUMBER of signs that the remarkable achievements of Western societies over the last half millennium are under threat of disintegration. The history of human communities in all parts of the globe has been characterized by the rise and fall of compact civilizations. Western civilization, since the first stirrings of thought and action challenged the autocracy of the Holy Roman Empire at the time of the Renaissance and the Reformation in Europe, has been in the ascendency for the past 500 years.

    Gradually, but not without many reverses, freedom of conscience, speech, and practice came to be recognized as integral parts of the justified entitlements of both individuals and groups. The language of human rights arose at the beginning of this period and slowly and cautiously gained strength against the self-declared authority of rulers to control most aspects of their subjects' lives. A fresh understanding of the nature of the human being in relation to the universe, and consequently to political and ecclesiastical power, began to be articulated. An increasing confidence in the exercise of reason, a developing view of the uniqueness and autonomy of the human person and the impact of the evidentially-based natural sciences became powerful instruments in helping to liberate individuals from the controlling influence of tradition and the excessive intrusion of the state in their affairs. The authority and control of both religious institutions and civil governments over social affairs and moral judgments were curtailed, step by step.

    Up to the time of the devastation and desolation caused by the First World War, the peoples of Europe and the United States rode on the back of a mood of optimism that progress to an increasingly free and morally enlightened society would be a permanent feature of present and future ages. The self-assurance of Western civilization in its effortless superiority was carried throughout the world in the colonial enterprise of conquering foreign territories and imposing Western-style institutions on indigenous populations. Such idealistic confidence tended to ignore the many signs of unenlightened thinking and uncivilized practices still evident in Western nations, such as multiple deprivation, excessively harsh punishments for minor offenses, lack of participation in political decision-making, and the inferior state and status of women at all levels of society. The peoples subjugated by the superior technology of Western military force might well have responded to their new rulers by saying, "physicians first heal yourselves, before you can pretend to cure us of our ills."

The so-called "great war" ("the war to end all wars"), marked a huge watershed in the history of Europe. The destructive consequences of the slaughter and the harsh settlements imposed on the vanquished were responsible, in considerable part, for the rise of two of the most vicious and malignant, ideologically-driven regimes that human history has ever witnessed: Communism and Nazism. Although eventually, at great cost, both were overcome, the fact of their existence and the havoc that they wreaked should have severely dented the belief of Western nations in their preeminence and sense of "manifest destiny" in bringing their moral, political, and economic convictions to the rest of the "backward" (or to use a less emotive, but more patronizing designation, "developing") peoples of the world.

In the three-quarters of a century since the end of the Second World War, there is not much evidence that the opinion-formers and ruling elites of the West have become more humble and circumspect in their claims to represent the best for the future of humanity. In the latter part of the twentieth century, and into the twenty-first, the Western "coalition of the willing" has continued to see that one of its duties is to intervene directly and unilaterally in parts of the world of which it has minimal understanding: the Middle East (in the Israeli-Palestinian conflict, Lebanon, Iraq, and Syria), Vietnam, Central America, Afghanistan, Libya, Somalia, Pakistan, etc. Only a blinkered person would have the temerity to suggest that the situations in these countries have been greatly improved as a result of Western interventionism.

If accumulating evidence appears to show that Western nations are now struggling to maintain any semblance of moral supremacy in either their foreign policies or their domestic rules and regulations, there does not seem to be another civilization ready to supplant them and take on the burden of guiding the nations into a less violent, confrontational, and self-serving future. At present, the West is absorbed by its conflict with various manifestations of Islamic fanaticism, which in part it has helped to fuel. Whether or not this amounts to a clash of civilizations,[1] the West so far has singularly failed to understand Islam's challenge to its declining ability to live on the basis of a coherent, sophisticated, and transforming worldview.

In general terms, the West has a problem of major proportions. It is my view, already expressed at some length in a project that analyzed the basic convictions underlying the trajectories of modernity and postmodernity,[2] that the West, by abandoning its roots in a refined understanding of its Christian heritage, now has no credible, critical foundation for assessing its past, reviewing its present, and establishing a convincing project for its future. As Tolstoy put it eloquently,

> "(advocates of secularist humanism) are like children who see beautiful flowers, grab them, break them at their stems, and try to transplant them without their roots."[3]

Crucially, what seems to have happened is that Western societies are becoming increasingly confused about the explanation and meaning of being human. The reigning anthropology appears to be rather shallow and inadequate to the task of establishing a robust set of criteria for understanding the fullness of what it means to be human. It relies too heavily on the most recent findings of scientific research, which are quite likely to be overturned within another few years. It tends to repudiate any notion of a fixed and abiding human essence, in spite of the championing of human rights that presuppose just such a given nature. It is somewhat reductionist, tending toward an increasingly mechanistic interpretation of human thought, motives, and emotions. It is dominated by a naturalistic worldview which asserts, without evidence, that the universe is closed to any nonmaterialist cause or influence.

In this book, therefore, as a response, I intend to grapple afresh with the notion of being human by exploring some of what has been said in the West about the nature of human life in these 500 years of immense changes to religious convictions, moral foundations, political arrangements, scientific discoveries, technological innovations, international relations, economic growth, increasing inequality and poverty, and much

---

1. See Huntington, *Clash of Civilizations*; Kirk, *Civilisations in Conflict*.
2. Kirk, *Future of Reason, Science and Faith*.
3. Tolstoy, in Pojman, "On Equal Human Worth," 295.

more. How do we understand ourselves? Naturally, space imposes strict limitations on how much can be said from within a vast field of possibilities. I have to be selective. However, I have endeavored to uncover some of the main contributions to reflection on the nature and place of the human being in the grand scheme of things. Although not everyone will agree with the choice, there should be enough material here for a fascinating, and hopefully enriching, excursion into our own humanity as we ask: "Who are we?"

CHAPTER 1

Initiating the Inquiry

Asking Questions, Searching for Answers

NEVER BEFORE HAS THE human species been subjected to so much interest and analysis from such a diverse collection of disciplines as it is today. We are, quite rightly, fascinated by who we are within the vast array of living creatures that inhabit planet earth. Such natural curiosity is one of the distinguishing marks of homo sapiens. Humans are inclined to ask many questions about themselves in relation to previous history, the environment, their amazing ability to reason, reflect, discuss, and debate. Sometimes, although probably not that frequently, they will ask genuinely fundamental questions about their existence: How have human beings arrived on earth? From where have they come? How should they live? What constitutes right and wrong action? Do individual lives have an inherent purpose, or can people simply invent their own? What should one believe about religious claims, suffering, life beyond the grave? How can we justify the assertion that "all human beings are born free and equal in dignity and rights,"[1] seeing that such a pronouncement does not seem to accord with real life? Why do human beings have so many different, and often contradictory, beliefs?

More often, however, humans ask comparatively mundane questions. Most are not inclined to explore deep philosophical issues. They are immersed in the day-to-day round of actual living. Their questions are more likely to focus on earning enough to support themselves and their family: to secure adequate housing, food, clothing, access to medical

1. United Nations, *Universal Declaration of Human Rights*, Article 1.

care, and a satisfactory education for their children. If they are parents, they will probably ask many questions about the best ways to nurture their offspring, so that the latter become fully mature adults. If their children are being bullied at school or intimidated on social media, they are more likely to ask "How may this be overcome?" rather than "Why does it happen in the first place?"

Nevertheless, despite the ordinariness of daily life, with both its struggles and joyful moments, there are more fundamental matters that do exercise many people. General questions about economic life and how either growth or stagnation is going to effect one's long-term financial prospects, such as job expectations, are prevalent. Many are concerned about environmental matters such as climate change, the effect of human exploitation of natural resources on the continuing existence of many animal and plant species, the health risks associated with atmospheric pollution, or unsustainable population growth in some parts of the world. There are questions about terrorism and the use made of gratuitous violence for perverted ideological, political, and religious ends. The increase in corruption, fraud, cheating, forgery, double-dealing, and any other kind of dishonest means to deceive people and take advantage of their ignorance, weakness, or distraction, worries many, particularly when it affects the use of electronic technology. In recent years, the increase in migration and its effects on native populations has become a divisive issue.

Whatever the question, whether intellectually profound or practically urgent, human beings are searching for answers. Humans are distinguished by their need and ability to discover, where possible, explanations for many of the events that happen in their lives. As far as can be ascertained, not even the most advanced primates have the capacity to deliberate on life's enigmas or wish to be satisfied by the solution to simple or complicated challenges to existence. Humans are questioning creatures. In this they are entirely distinct and unique within the animal kingdom.

Distinguishing Features of Being Human

The Process of Learning

Human beings are complex entities. If one were, for example, to keep a detailed record of the development of a baby into a child and to compare his or her progress with that which is exhibited by any other young mammal, enormous differences would soon be noted. Physically, the baby takes much longer to grow into full adulthood, when it can become independent of its parents. The reason for this is clear: people need an extended time to learn to take responsibility for their own lives. They are brought into a world of enormous variety, where they need to acquire knowledge and understanding to be able to make responsible choices about their own lives and how they are going to relate to other people. The situation of all other mammals is quite different. They have a limited capacity to learn what is required to survive in the wild and to reproduce their kind. Certain habits will be passed on by the parents to their offspring, such as how to avoid danger or where to find food appropriate to their species. Largely, however, the learning is by instinct; they are born with an innate awareness of how to fit successfully into their environment.

On the other hand, humans learn through close interaction with other humans who have already gained information, intelligence, and discernment through their various experiences of life. This interaction happens through the medium of language, by which young children begin to express themselves and pick up interpersonal skills. Just because children have so much to understand about themselves, the situation in which they live, and what is required for them to attain a healthy, well-integrated personality, a long period of guidance has to take place. In the first place, parents are responsible for instructing, training, and counseling their children. At a certain stage, formal education in a public institution we call school is also involved. The value of the school is largely threefold: children learn how to act and react in a social context among those they encounter initially as strangers; they have begun a journey toward an eventual separation from the close supervision of their father and mother and begin to make crucial choices for themselves; they interact with a wider world of adults, which will undoubtedly bring an enlarged and distinct perspective to the learning process.

From an early age, then, humans grow in knowledge and understanding through their mental ability to think and ask questions about their lives in relation to the circumstances in which they find themselves. Of course, this is not a straightforward, uncomplicated, upward progression, as any parent well knows. Children hover between an innate desire to follow their own inclinations and desires and dependence on the care and oversight of older people who are better able to know what really leads to their well-being. The result is quite often a clash of wills, whose resolution is in itself part of the learning process. How adults deal with these altercations will directly influence the child's emotional and psychological well-being.

Self-Consciousness

In describing this process, we are now quite far removed from the way in which the rest of the animal kingdom grows to maturity. The main reason for this is that humans possess uniquely a consciousness of themselves as individuals. The progress from childhood to adulthood is one in which this self-awareness is shaped by how the person interacts with the circumstances of their life. Through this interaction, a certain identity is formed. It certainly is not a smooth path. The onset of puberty and adolescence are turbulent years, in which young people are discovering more about themselves physically and emotionally. They are beginning a more intense period of separation from the control of their immediate family, whilst at the same time trying to build appropriate relationships with their peers. In spite of a certain amount of bravado, teenagers are still remarkably vulnerable to a loss of self-confidence. They are in the midst of trying to discover who they really are, a process made more difficult by the many discordant theories and ideas to which they are increasingly exposed.

Moral Values

At this juncture, humans are trying to come to terms with what they should believe about right and wrong behavior, and why. From infancy, humans begin implicitly, and later explicitly, to recognize within themselves a certain moral compass that we call the conscience.[2] This is perhaps most obvious in a child's innate championing of fairness and in the ability to appreciate the need to deal with others on a reciprocal basis (i.e., to treat them as you wish to be treated yourself). In other words, a child can understand that there is no justification for asserting that they should be made an exception to the "golden rule," or that rules which

---

2. For example, Paul Bloom, in his research into how very young children, even those of less than one year, react to examples of moral goodness and badness, incline him to believe that moral discernment is innate from the beginning of a child's existence. See Bloom, *Just Babies*.

they approve for other people (e.g., bullying is not tolerated) should not also apply to them. Whether or not conscience is directed in a selfless or self-centered way is another matter, which we will have to consider in more depth throughout this study.

The predisposition to ask questions, the existence of humans' self-consciousness, the reality of an innate conscience, and the gift of language are common to all human beings. They are distinguishing marks. There are other characteristics that make humans stand out from the rest of the natural world, although these may vary much more in relationship to culture, personality, inheritance, age, and belief systems.

Aesthetic Appreciation

Most, if not all, people have an inborn sense of beauty. There are events in the world that people will spontaneously call beautiful: the exquisite mixture of colors of a sunrise or sunset; a favorite piece of music; a striking landscape; an intricate movement in sport; the grandeur of wildlife like a pride of lions, a polar bear with her cubs, swans in full flight, and many more; an arrangement of flowers; a painting; certain architectural features; the flowers of trees like magnolia, jacaranda, bougainvillea, and ornamental cherries; a smile of contentment, and so on. The point is not that all humans agree about what should be termed beautiful, but that all have the capacity to appreciate beauty of one kind or another.

Reasoning

Humans, in normal circumstances, have the power to reason. Intelligence may differ owing to genetic inheritance or mental stimulation from an early age, but everyone[3] can think, work out solutions to problems, refer to the past for clues to the present, reflect on possibilities in the future, and plan for their realization. All possess a sense of time beyond the mere chronology of hours, days, months, and years. Humans appreciate the reality of timing (i.e., of taking hold of a particular moment as an opportunity for progress or change). All have the ability to think rationally

---

3. People whose mental capacities have been severely impaired through the process of birth, genetic inheritance, illness, or an accident, are obvious exceptions to this rule. This, emphatically, does not mean that they cease to be human beings.

about aims and objectives, the means to reach them, and how to remove obstacles that may be in the way.

Giving and Receiving Love

Above all, perhaps, human beings flourish most when they receive disinterested love from others, especially from those they most admire or on whom they most depend. Love is translated as care, compassion, consideration, forgiveness, encouragement, stimulus, perseverance, and fairness. It holds others to high ideals, but is understanding and supportive when those ideals are not reached. Humans blossom, when they receive recognition, appreciation, and admiration. They wither when they are ignored, shown ingratitude, despised, abused, or turned into means purely to satisfy other people's desires.

Perceiving and Experiencing a Nonphysical Reality

Finally, and perhaps more controversially, humans have an innate sense of transcendence. This concept is difficult to specify, being somewhat intangible. However, it may be detected through a number of manifestations. Keith Ward, in a recent book, has argued the case for a dimension of life that goes beyond the material.[4] Fundamentally, the notion of transcendence springs from the conviction that what we know about ourselves cannot be reduced to "collections of physical particles accidentally arranged in complicated patterns."[5] The mind, thought, and reason transcend the physical operations of the brain. The intuition that lives must have some greater purpose than the daily routine of fulfilling mundane, short-term tasks indicates that humans are not satisfied by the notion that existence is intrinsically meaningless.[6]

Feelings of compassion, grief, empathy, and self-sacrificing, altruistic deeds that take us away from a preoccupation with self, cannot be explained on the basis of the need to survive at all costs. The apprehension that all human beings have an unconditional worth, not dependent on their character or achievements, seems to denote a claim on us to treat others in ways that go beyond merely pragmatic considerations. The idea

---

4. Ward, *Evidence for God*.
5. Ward, *Evidence for God*, 1.
6. A sentiment expressed cogently by the author of Ecclesiastes in the Bible.

that something called rights (or entitlements) adhere to every human being, irrespective of their situation or station in life, and that they are not conditional on human-created laws or conferred by government decree, appears to require some transcendent source for their existence.

Then, there is a near-universal sixth sense that a reality beyond time and space and what can be measured and quantified exists. This reality may be conceived in the vaguest of terms or with some specific detail. It may be experienced as a deep dissatisfaction with the routine obligations of ordinary existence or the trivialities of much entertainment, or as a longing for the assurance that somehow justice will be done and good will be vindicated by an authority higher than fallible human judgments. Many people speak of an encounter with a divine being that they find deeply satisfying, not least because such a being would explain the many enigmas of life in the universe.

The point here is not to be too specific in identifying the nature of the transcendent. To make the point that human beings generally have an instinctive perception of something that calls them to see and experience reality through a dimension that transcends pure physicality, one does not have to name it god or God. It is enough to recognize that this perception is characteristic of humans alone. Perhaps one of its most supreme manifestations is the urge to know whether life in some form will continue after death and whether each individual will be required to give an account of their earthly life. With this uncertainty comes a trepidation in the face of one's own death. As far as we know, no other animal species is perturbed by the thought of death.

I accept that the evidence for a transcendent dimension to life does not convince all people. There are a minority of committed atheists, who adhere to a wholly materialist philosophy of life. They find the language of transcendence unwarranted, superfluous, and delusional. Still, I would also want to assert that there is plenty of evidence that these people do not, because they cannot, live consistently by their materialist philosophy. However, such an allegation takes us, for the time being, in a different direction. A discussion of the strengths and weaknesses of a full, materialist worldview will be taken up at various points in the ensuing study.

The Origin of the Human Species

If the above characteristics of human experience distinguish human beings from all other higher creaturely existence, how did humanity come to be within the world as we know it? By what process did such an extraordinary and unparalleled creature emerge to take its place among all other living beings? We will confine ourselves to attempting answers to these questions that fit with a sophisticated, scientifically-informed sensibility specific to modern societies.[7] Within these terms of reference, there seem to be three distinct alternative explanations: first, that the universe, life, and human existence have originated and evolved through some kind of impersonal, self-generating mechanism that had an explosive beginning at the dawn of time; second, that the universe and all that is in it has its origin and subsequent unfolding through specific, individual creative acts of one supreme, eternally-existing, personal, divine being; thirdly, that the universe was created by this personal divine being and has subsequently evolved by means of mechanisms built into the very fabric of the universe's constituent parts. If one were to give the three theories provisional names, the first might be called "chance evolution," the second "intelligent design," and the third "theistic evolution."[8] Here we will look only at the bare bones of each theory, exploring the merits and defects of each at later stages of the study (particularly in the chapter dedicated to Charles Darwin).

"Chance Evolution"

The title given to this theory arises from the conviction of those who propose that the expansion of the universe and the growth of life on earth is not guided by any intentional plan nor does it possess any inherent purpose. The theory assumes that the only and final reality in the universe is matter. How matter came into existence in the first place remains an enigma. However, the theory rules out *a priori* any resort to an extramaterial entity as the cause of all things existing:

---

7. This means that mythological or legendary accounts of origins, peculiar to some religions, will not be considered.

8. I recognize that these terms lack precision, being open to different interpretations. However, for the sake of not multiplying categories unnecessarily at this point, I will stick with these three options for the time being. In later chapters, I will seek to introduce more carefully conceived nuances into the discussion of origins.

According to this paradigm, evolution is driven by chance. Chance mutations affect one or a few nucleotides of DNA per occurrence. Bigger changes come from recombination, a genetic process in which longer strands of DNA are swapped, transferred, or doubled. These two processes, mutation and recombination, create new meaning in DNA by lucky accidents. According to the prevailing paradigm, this is the mechanism behind evolution.[9]

The theory in this form posits that a process of natural selection acting upon random mutations is a wholly sufficient explanation for the emergence of all new forms of life, as well as for the impression that living forms manifest some kind of intentional design. In essence, this paradigm constitutes what is known as the Neo-Darwinist synthesis: a combination of Darwin's evolutionary ideas of adaptation through natural selection and Mendel's genetic thesis concerning biological inheritance. Neo-Darwinism is a particular way of explaining how units of evolution (genes) combine with the mechanism of evolution (natural selection).

Inherent to this theory is the claim that the evolution of all forms of life has proceeded by constant small changes from one single beginning over an enormous period of time. The theory has come to be known as "gradualism"; it defines a process of macroevolution from exceedingly simple beginnings to astonishingly complex organisms. The theory relies in part on an analogy being drawn between macroevolution (evolution that occurs at a level greater than that of individual species) and microevolution (evolution within species). It is said that the same mechanisms apply, but occur over different ranges of time. Macroevolutionary theory is often referred to as the theory of common ancestry.

---

9. Klyce, "Neo-Darwinism," para. 5.

"Intelligent Design"

The second theory of change and development springs from a few considerations: firstly, the difficulties of accepting that the neo-Darwinian synthesis is based on adequate biological and paleontological evidence;[10] secondly, the new discoveries in genetic coding; and thirdly, the ability to account for the appearance of purpose underlying biological processes.

According to intelligent design theorists, the final (although not only) reality in the universe is not matter but information. They argue that the hypothesis that the only reality is material is a metaphysical claim, not a scientific one. Thus, in the search for the origin of the universe and life on planet earth (especially human life), a materialist philosophy will discount, by its reductionist presuppositions, consideration of other possible mechanisms that could give a better explanation of how everything happens to be. In a recent book,[11] William A. Dembski, the doyen of the intelligent design thesis, sets out a sophisticated (and highly intricate) set of arguments to demonstrate the plausibility of information theory. He argues, with many examples, that "the attempt to understand the world in terms of their material properties, leaving no remainder for anything non-material"[12] does not do justice to the complexity of life and does not give an adequate explanation of the full experience of being human:

> If the only legitimate way we have to make sense of the world is in materialist terms, then many of the things we value most go by the board or become dim reflections of their former selves. Here we may include such famous triads as God, freedom and immortality as well as truth, beauty and goodness.[13]

Moreover,

---

10. A number of eminent scientists have disputed the neo-Darwinian account of evolution, though not necessarily all evolutionary theories. For example, Lynn Margulis, author of *Symbiotic Planet: A New Look at Evolution*, says, "This is the issue I have with neo-Darwinists: They teach that what is generating novelty is the accumulation of random mutations in DNA, in a direction set by natural selection . . . Natural selection eliminates and maybe maintains, but it doesn't create . . . . [N]eo-Darwinists say that new species emerge when mutations occur and modify an organism. I was taught over and over again that the accumulation of random mutations led to evolutionary change—led to new species. I believed it until I looked for evidence" (Teresi, "Discover Interview," paras. 6, 9.).

11. Dembski, *Being as Communion*.
12. Dembski, *Being as Communion*, 3.
13. Dembski, *Being as Communion*, 4.

> Materialism ... raises a self-referential paradox: how can knowing subjects composed only of matter know that they are only composed of matter? Matter, it would seem, has no intrinsic capacity to produce agents that think, much less that can form representations about the world, much less that can know that these representations are true.[14]

Nowhere in his book does Dembski discount the possibility of some form of evolution. What he and his colleagues strive against is the dogmatic insistence by some scientists on what is termed "methodological naturalism" (i.e., the restriction of all explanations in the natural sciences to purely material factors). What he advocates is a scientific method that is open to the possibility of nonmaterial impulses bringing about change and diversity in the material world. Intelligent design theorists believe that this is the only way that a fully adequate description of observed reality is possible. In the last analysis, the controversy over this main proposition is a metaphysical, not a scientific question. To say that intelligent design is not a scientific theory is only true if science is defined according to metaphysical materialist assumptions. It presupposes that only a materialistic concept of science has the right to pronounce on the status of truth claims.[15] This is not the place to enter into a full-scale discussion of the pros and cons of the intelligent design hypothesis. However, we will need to return on a number of occasions to the debate about origins if we are to try and make sense of who we are.

Theistic Evolution

In recent years, a number of Christian scientists, philosophers, and theologians have argued strongly for a view of evolution that accepts the basic neo-Darwinian paradigm of a gradual, cumulative progression of all living organisms, from the simplest to the most complex, through the dynamic process of natural selection working on the variations produced by adaptive mutations. They accept, therefore, the current consensus that the incredible variety and diversity of living beings have arisen over

---

14. Dembski, *Being as Communion*, 7.

15. The highly critical article on intelligent design in Wikipedia is full of caricatures and misleading information on what intelligent design does and does not claim in its relationship to other theories of origins and to claims made for evolution in general. Such misinformation (for example, to confuse it repeatedly with "creationism") does nothing to promote intelligent debate.

millions of years by a series of continuous, small changes. They agree that the changes that can be observed within species through selective breeding can, by analogy, be extrapolated to include all species, given an enormous amount of time for the changes to have taken place.

These scientists, philosophers, and theologians are not, however, materialists. They disagree with the two main metaphysical assumptions that people who hold to a materialist philosophy start with. Firstly, they deny that science, as an enterprise in exploring, mapping, and applying knowledge of the universe and the earth, has the only reliable and exhaustive understanding of reality. As Keith Ward argues,[16] science reigns supreme in its sphere of operation, but there is much more to experience than the physical world. He cites the examples of the axiology the principle of intentionally causing something to happen with a future purpose in view and the human mind. A materialist philosophy cannot give an adequate account of minds that "have intentional thoughts, and act in intentional ways."[17] Minds are irreducible components of reality. They cannot be fully explained in purely physical terms. It is wholly logical to infer from what we know about ourselves as intelligent, thinking beings that within the processes of evolution, a rationally purposeful mind is operating to bring about preconceived ends. In other words, a theistic interpretation of the whole of reality, the legitimate field of a wide variety of scientific disciplines, is a better explanation than a materialist one.

Secondly, they deny one of the supreme premises of a materialist account of evolution, namely that the existence of the universe and human life within one tiny planet in an insignificant solar system, within one relatively small galaxy, cannot be assigned to any preordained plan, design, or purpose: to use Dawkins's famous description, "there is . . . nothing but blind, pitiless indifference . . . DNA neither knows nor cares. DNA just is. And we dance to its music."[18] On the contrary, the view that everything that exists implies a "somebody" who brought it into being is a perfectly reasonable and indeed elegant, comprehensive, and simple hypothesis, superior as an explanation to a "whole battery of separate mathematical laws and forces and fields like gravity, inflation, electric charge, spin and so on, which have no obvious connection with one another."[19]

16. Ward, *Evidence for God*, 67–75.
17. Ward, *Evidence for God*, 71.
18. Dawkins, *River Out of Eden*, 133.
19. Ward, *Evidence for God*, 73.

The problem with the materialist account is that, though it is said to be based solely on scientific evidence, in fact it emerges from an unscientific premise. Mikael Stenmark clarifies the situation in this way:

> Let us grant, for the sake of argument, that it is true that the existence of human beings is a wildly improbable event given the information that is accessible to scientists through the use of biological methods; but how can we from this information alone conclude that we are not intended by God or something like God to be here? . . . We need an extra premise to make the argument valid because it is quite possible that things could exist for a purpose even if evolutionary biologists were unable to discover it.[20]

In other words, Dawkins's musings on the purposelessness of the existence of life are not a conclusion derived from his scientific research. They are based on the "extra premise" that is smuggled into the discussion, namely the philosophy of materialism as an alternative to theism. Both are equally based on a core background belief, and not susceptible to demonstration or refutation by the means of scientific methodology. Theistic evolutionists believe that the purely materialistic account of human origins is unreasonable. Due to its host of anomalies, unresolvable on the basis of its core belief, it is highly unlikely as an explanation. In its place they posit a rational development of forms of life guided and implemented by a personal, informational-generating mind, imagined from before the beginning of the universe, and working through appropriate material conditions.

Credible Answers to Complex Questions?

Controversy over the origin of the universe, life on earth, and the human species is not likely to diminish quickly. This is due not so much to the lack of conclusive evidence of the process by which organic life emerged spontaneously from inorganic matter,[21] as it is to the consequences of

---

20. Stenmark, *How to Relate*, 160.

21. Many attempts have been made to provide a credible conjecture as to how animate organisms came to exist. One of the latest is set out in the book by Nick Lane, called *The Vital Question*. However, in his complex discussion of the reactive potential of alkaline hydrothermal vents, the author seems to substitute the conditions necessary for organic life to subsist with the cause of their existence: "the physical structure of alkaline vents—natural proton gradients across thin semi-conducting walls—will

coming to particular conclusions about the biological history that has brought us to where we are. Human beings are used to looking at the world as a massive collection of external objects that can be analyzed, classified, ranked, and graded. So, we separate the entities into species and subspecies and give them complex Latin names. We are in control of the methods, systems, and techniques. We may make scintillating discoveries, such as identifying a new species or reclassifying some living object by understanding more about its morphology. Nevertheless, though it may advance knowledge in significant ways, it does not affect us existentially in the core of our being. The subject-object distinction is maintained. The object has no intrinsic power to prevail over our interests.

However, the situation changes dramatically, when we begin to treat ourselves as objects. When we are asking questions about human life and behavior, we are dealing with issues concerning identity, for we alone of all the species are self-reflective. For example, when seeking the causes of certain quite common illnesses such as diabetes, heart problems, and certain types of cancer, we take note not only of possible directly physical causes outside our control, but also ask ourselves about our lifestyles (i.e., the choices that we make, which may contribute to our ill health). So, we become to ourselves not only objects of medical science to be diagnosed, as though the illness was wholly external to ourselves, but also subjects. To what extent might the illness in question have been caused, at least in part, by the kind of choices that we have consciously made, and for which we are responsible?

At this point, we begin to feel uncomfortable, because we may be implicated at a moral level in the adverse physical or mental situation in which we find ourselves. In other words, our deteriorating health condition may well be the result of our own poor choices, such as overeating or overdrinking. It is quite reasonable, in these circumstances, to ask whether people suffering from illnesses they have largely brought on themselves should expect a health service, with limited resources, to spend vast sums of money on restoring them to health again. So, we use

---

(theoretically) drive the formation of organics" (*Vital Question*, 120). The fundamental question which this theory does not answer is how inanimate nature, on its own, can possibly supply the vast amount of information needed to build an entity (the first living cell) capable of reproduction. What needs explaining is the origin of information. All theories of self-organization fail to account for the moment of transition from relatively simple nonbiological structures to complex, information-based, genetic organizations of living organisms. Is Professor Lane, perhaps, unwittingly confusing necessary conditions for life with sufficient conditions?

the language of culpability, blame, and desertion; language that would be wholly inappropriate in a veterinary surgeon's practice.

The likely outcome of this type of reflection is to continue to treat the afflicted person, but at the same time to make clear to the patient that unless they take steps to alter their life choices the medical profession cannot treat them indefinitely for recurring problems. Such a conclusion will then lead to deeper questions about what drives a person to overeat, overdrink, take little or no exercise, experiment with dangerous drugs, or deliberately engage in highly risky, life-threatening ventures, such as climbing at high altitudes or exposing oneself for long periods, without adequate protection, to the sun's rays.

Now we are becoming increasingly the objects of our own subjectivity. A rigid subject-object distinction is breaking down. We may force ourselves, or be urged by others, to begin to ask questions about purpose in life, motivations, self-respect, and personal relationships. These are all questions that hover around the fundamental concern about who we are. As already intimated, current secular culture, with its propensity to reduce complex reality to well-worn shibboleths, slogans, and simplistic remedies, its tendency to turn its back on the wisdom of the past, its refusal to acknowledge a reality that goes beyond the material, and its belief that most, if not all, problems have physical causes, does not help to provide adequate answers to the enigma of what it means to be human. It seems reasonable, therefore, in the light of recurring, unresolved puzzlements about who we are, to look again at some of the key responses that have been given over the last half-millennium within the European tradition of thought to see whether perhaps our present generation, by accident or by choice, has overlooked relevant clues.

For reasons that will be explained in the next chapter, I intend to begin with the period known as the Renaissance. I will then explore some of the most influential voices that have shaped European thought about the human condition in the Reformation, in the Enlightenment, in the controversies aroused by Darwin's theory of descent (or ascent?), in the thinking of the denominated "masters of suspicion" (Marx, Nietzsche and Freud), and in a range of secular humanist thought of the last fifty years. The inquiry will conclude with chapters dedicated to some of the most significant twentieth-century Christian thinkers on the subject of human nature.

I realize that this is an ambitious study; also, that it is not in any way comprehensive. However, I believe that the inquiry will touch on the main beliefs that have been put forward in this five-hundred-year period. There is also, of course, the fundamental challenge of doing justice to the chosen protagonists, some of whom wrote many works relevant to the main question. So, this inquiry will be an exercise in distilling the primary thoughts of the chosen witnesses in as fair a way as is possible, given that I, like all other humans, bring certain considered convictions to the table that are bound to influence both the search and conclusions to be drawn from it.

In the final chapter, I will attempt to bring the enquiry to an opportune close by asking which understandings of the meaning of being human appear to give the best explanation of the wide variety of human experience. I write from the perspective of what may be described as a mainstream Christian set of beliefs; not one, I hasten to add, that has been unaffected by the various stringent critiques made against these beliefs by a variety of people who reject them in favor of a general humanist approach to the knowledge of ourselves. I have followed the discussions over many years, and have already written on aspects of the challenges. Here I am attempting a more comprehensive survey of the answers given to the riddle of the human state in the hope, at least, of clarifying the alternatives on offer for shaping our present and future.

Questions

1. In comparing human beings with the highest group of mammals (apes and monkeys), what do you think are the most significant distinguishing features (from the most to the least distinctive)? If challenged to produce an order of importance, how would you respond?

2. In your experience, what are the most fundamental questions about being human that your contemporaries are asking? What kind of answers are they receiving?

3. In what ways, if any, does the question about the origin of life and the human species impinge on present everyday existence? How would you defend the thesis that ultimate reality is material or, alternatively, nonmaterial?

4. In what ways, if any, does a process of self-examination, in which you become the object of your own exploration, benefit your growth into maturity?

Chapter 2

Human Life in Renaissance Humanism

Introduction

IN ATTEMPTING TO CONSIDER a subject as broad as the significance of being human through the eyes of Renaissance humanists, in the limited space of one chapter, I will need to make some assumptions. Firstly, the actual period to be examined will not cover the whole history. The Renaissance, a movement that has come to be associated with a rebirth of literature, the arts, philosophy, religious reform and political structures, together with the expansion of wealth through trade, new inventions, and geographical explorations, is said to have extended from the early fourteenth century to roughly the third decade of the sixteenth, a span of nearly three hundred years. It would be invidious to try to cover such a length of time in just a few pages. I will, therefore, confine the survey to what is sometimes called "the High Renaissance," a period stretching for a century, from about 1430 to 1530. This is a time when most classical works associated with the rebirth were produced.

Secondly, I will have to be selective with regard to the sources that are handled. Bearing in mind that the purpose of the inquiry is to discover what people of different epochs thought about human nature, either explicitly or implicitly, as deduced from their writings or practices, I will refer only to a few, and those considered key figures and who most clearly indicated their beliefs.

Thirdly, I will endeavor to include some evidence that may be distilled, not only from "high culture," such as the paintings and sculptures of renowned figures like Donatello, Michelangelo, Leonardo, Raphael, and Holbein, but also from daily urban life, which was shifting and changing in the expansion of the recently established city-states, particularly in Northern Italy. In other words, I accept the assumption that convictions about human nature may be deduced from patterns of living in a given environment, not only from works of art and the writings of literary giants.

Fourthly, this study needs to assume that the Renaissance can be coherently and legitimately described as a real historical event. As this has been disputed, I will need to list briefly some of the reasons that justify this assumption.

Characteristics of the Renaissance

That a particular historical period has been, and continues to be, known by one well-worn epithet suggests that something was happening in society that distinguished it from what preceded and followed it. By and large, historians are still content to point to a number of distinctive features that separate it from the "late Middle Ages" and from the period following the early Reformation. What, then, are these features?

Why Renaissance?

The term *rinascita* (rebirth) appears to have been coined first by the Italian author Vasari in his book, *The Lives of the Artists*, published in 1550. As the word suggests, it points to the rediscovery and appropriation of the merits of a past age that had been lost in the mists of time. Whereas in what identifies a typical modern consciousness human history is seen as a gradual, upward progression to an ever-greater understanding of what makes for a good society, accompanied by technological advancements of every kind, at the time of the Renaissance, human life was not experienced as an inevitable ascension toward an increasing knowledge of the truth. Rather, the march of time was often interpreted as a regression to a period of greater obscurity, pain, and violence. The strong notion of time indicating a linear process on a path always from an inferior to a superior phase of existence came to dominate Western consciousness at a later date. Life, during the earlier period, was measured still by the repetitive cycle of the seasons, which suggested recurrent rotation rather than forward movement.

It is for this reason that some writers sum up the general ethos of the Renaissance as the pursuit of the new by a return to the best examples of what the old had to offer:

> Paradoxical as it may seem, the Renaissance movement was a systematic attempt to go forward by going back—in other words, to break with the medieval tradition by following an older movement, that of the ancient Greeks and Romans.[1]

A Turn to the Past

The Renaissance was characterized by the avid collecting, critical editing, imaginative annotating, and careful translating of scores of Latin manuscripts rediscovered in libraries across Europe, and of Greek manuscripts, many of which were brought by Greek scholars fleeing to the West from the military conquests of the Ottoman Empire after the capture of Constantinople in 1453. A whole new world was opened up: not so much a world of future possibilities as one of the past, a glorious age of philosophical reasoning, moral thought, political and legal development, literary innovation, and architectural magnificence. Add to this new birth of interest in the Greek language, a discovery of the New Testament, the church's foundation document, in its original language, and one can imagine the enthusiasm with which contemporary fifteenth-century students pored over the manuscripts to rediscover a long-lost heritage. For that generation, renewal of society was much more likely to come from engaging with the glorious beginnings of Western civilization than by pretending that it had been superseded by developments that occurred during the meantime. In its understanding and experience, human societies were just as likely, and perhaps more likely, to degenerate as they were to improve.

Nevertheless, the Renaissance period was also one that witnessed innovation. The study of the ancient manuscripts, both Christian and non-Christian, can be viewed as the initiation of a critical approach to texts of the past. The translators and commentators paid attention to the subtleties and nuances of language, to style, to original contexts, and authorial intentions—in other words to historical distance—as well as the application of the written content to the realities of their own age.

---

1. Burke, *Italian Renaissance*, 1.

The Renaissance in Painting

When thinking of the Renaissance, the first image that generally comes to mind is that of the magnificent paintings of Michelangelo in the Sistine chapel or Leonardo's enigmatic portraits of women such as *The Mona Lisa*, *Lady with an Ermine*, or *Virgin of the Rocks*, or his portrayal of the Last Supper on the wall of the refectory in the Church of Santa Maria delle Grazie, Milan. The period of the High Renaissance is replete with exquisite works of art also by other artists such as Botticelli, Titian, Tintoretto, and Veronese in Italy, but also by Flemish artists such as Jan van Eyck and Pieter Bruegel the Elder. Their paintings broke away from the generally stylized, devotional religious paintings of a previous age in a number of ways. Although they continued to paint religious themes, the *Adoration of the Magi* being a familiar scene, they also explored the non-Christian world of Greek mythology. The Northern European tradition incorporated the portrayal of ordinary everyday life, without any necessary religious motif, although the artists may have intended to convey symbolic meanings through their paintings.

In the medieval period, the portrayal of the human figure tended to be as an icon, pointing away from individual human characteristics toward the evocation of deep, universal, spiritual truths. It was important to the sensibilities of the time that the painting should not distract from what the image represented by being too lifelike or by enabling the viewer to identify recognizable contemporary people.[2] The Renaissance artists had different ideas. Their paintings included thinly disguised contemporary figures. Thus, Gentile and Giovanni Bellini's painting of St. Mark preaching in Alexandria (1504–1507) included in the crowd a group of Venetian gentlemen and another group made up of Oriental figures, including Moors, Ottomans, Persians, Tartars, and Ethiopians. Although St. Mark wears clothes appropriate to the first century, the garments of the audience are recognizably from the early sixteenth century. Here is a case of intermingling the period of the Roman Empire with that of contemporary Europe and comparing its world with that of its trading partners to the East.[3] Botticelli's *Adoration of the Magi* (1470s) casts the three wise men as Cosimo Medici and his two sons, Piero and Giuliano. Guido Ruggiero calls it "an intriguing Medici crowd scene" and concludes that

---

2. See Ruggiero, *Renaissance in Italy*, 328.
3. See Brotton, *Renaissance*, 20–22.

"all the Medici in this group portrait (which included Lorenzo) seem to be carefully constructed works of art."[4]

Of all the many famous (and more obscure) paintings of this period, perhaps the one that most focuses on the characteristics of the Renaissance is Hans Holbein's *The Ambassadors* (1533). Of the many features in the painting, redolent of Renaissance ideals and realities, we may mention the book, placed in a prominent position on the desk, which is a manual instructing merchants on how to calculate profit and loss in their businesses. Behind the book stands a globe that represents travel, exploration, and trade. On the map, the continent of Europe is given a single name, "Europa," signifying a landmass that possesses a common identity.

The painting speaks eloquently of the politics of the time. The ambassadors were sent by Francis I, king of France, to Henry VIII in an attempt to prevent the latter's rupture with Rome over his marriage to Anne Boleyn. They were also entrusted with the mission of establishing a new political alliance between Francis, Henry, and the Ottoman Sultan, Suleyman the Magnificent. For this reason, it is suggested, a rug positioned on the top shelf of the painting is of Ottoman design and manufacture, heralding a belief that somehow the Ottoman empire was also part of the European rebirth that was underway. Although Europe is shown at the heart of the world on the globe, there is much evidence in many of the objects in the painting of the impact of the East on European political and economic life, culture, and trade.

All in all, the painting summarizes the remarkable changes that were taking place at the time; changes that have led subsequent historians to herald this age as one of rejuvenation:

> Objects in the bottom part of the painting reveal facets of the Renaissance: humanism, religion, printing, trade, exploration, politics, empire and wealth and knowledge of the East. Objects on the upper shelf point to new scientific instruments, mostly invented by Arab and Jewish astronomers and that came to the West brought by travellers by boat from the Middle East.[5]

All the seven liberal arts, considered the basis of a formal education at the time, are represented by the objects: grammar, logic and rhetoric (known as the trivium), and arithmetic, music, geometry, and astronomy

---

4. Ruggiero, *Renaissance in Italy*, 346–47.

5. Brotton, *Renaissance*, 2–8. I am indebted to Brotton's book for this interpretation of Holbein's painting.

(known as the quadrivium). These collectively constituted the humanities, from which was derived the original use of the word "humanism." A good grounding in these subjects was indispensable to anyone who wished to pursue a successful career in the societies of that time.

Although the Renaissance is often associated with great works of art, the paintings themselves often depict a wider world of political, commercial and social realities, and therefore offer an insight into the context in which the art flourished. Were it not for an unprecedented accumulation of wealth, the artists (often from a lower strata of society) would not have received the patronage they needed to free them for their creative impulses. Were it not for a new impetus for trade beyond Europe, facilitated by the maritime city-states, such as Venice and Genoa, there would not have been such a growth in wealth. Sea trade itself profited from the recent discovery of maritime instruments, such as the compass and the mariner's astrolabe, that allowed a more prolonged season of sailing on the Mediterranean, through the Bay of Biscay and on through the English Channel to Northern Europe.

The Turn to the Individual

For the purposes of this inquiry into the meaning of human life according to a broadly conceived Renaissance humanism, one of the interesting characteristics of the period is what we might call, "the turn to the individual." Ruggiero, for instance, argues cogently that in the century roughly between 1425 and 1525, "the individual became a more and more carefully considered cultural construct . . . Many portrayals tended increasingly to reflect, draw upon, and reinforce the artfulness of being an individual."[6]

The Risk of Anachronism

This latter may indeed be a significant feature of the changes that were taking place. However, the historian, in assessing the most indicative aspects of the period, needs to be aware of reading the age selectively through the preconceptions of his or her own context and interests. This may have been a fault of the first detailed reflection on the recent

---

6. Ruggiero, *Renaissance in Italy*, 326–27.

explosion of artistic talent, written by Vasari, *Lives of the Most Excellent Painters, Sculptors and Architects* (1550, second edition 1568).[7]

He focused on the individual genius of a series of artists, culminating in Michaelangelo. In trying to explain the clustering of so many outstanding creative individuals in a relatively short period of time, Vasari suggested three factors that encouraged artistic innovation in Florence: freedom of thought and criticism; necessity of hard work to earn a living; and the pursuit of honor and glory. This opinion may be the result of a certain hagiographical intention in his writing.[8]

The shaping of the Renaissance in the image of a later generation came to full fruition in the nineteenth century. Many modern writers on the Renaissance consider that one popular view that has interpreted it as a great leap forward from the obscurity of the so-called "Dark Ages" of medieval Europe to a new, cultivated, and refined stage in civilization, is no more than a romantic rewriting of history that reflects their own much later age. For Jerry Brotton, the two main protagonists of this "invention of the Renaissance as a powerful myth"[9] are the French historian, Jules Michelet,[10] and the Swiss writer, Jacob Burckhardt.[11] According to Michelet, "man re-found himself"[12] in the exciting new discoveries being made by explorers and scientists. For him, the new findings and inventions heralded the beginning of modern science and technology. They originated in a fresh, bold, and enterprising approach to the natural world, unaccompanied by the baggage of superstition and mystification that characterized the world of religion. According to Burckhardt, the Renaissance proclaimed the "rebirth" of the classical virtues of literary purity and aesthetic beauty, questioned religious authority, and promoted a new spirit of artistic experimentation and scientific curiosity. In other words, for both of them, the Renaissance was a direct forerunner of the Enlightenment and of modern, secular humanism.[13]

---

7. See Cast, *Ashgate Research Companion*.
8. See Burke, *Italian Renaissance*, 32–33.
9. Brotton, *Renaissance*, 11.
10. In his *History of France*, originally published in 1855.
11. *Civilization of the Renaissance*, originally published in 1860.
12. Brotton, "Myth of the Renaissance," 10–11.
13. Brotton, "Myth of the Renaissance."

William Caferro[14] alleges that Burckhardt stressed the individualism of the Renaissance, because he saw it as the first sign of a movement toward the emergence of modern humanity and the modern world. In distinction from the collectivist attitude to life that characterized the Middle Ages, the "spirit of the Renaissance"[15] emphasized an individualism that represented a dedication to self-interest and freedom from authority, both moral and political. John Symonds's magnum opus[16] also equated the Renaissance with the emergence of modernity, the birth of liberty, political freedom, the power of self-determination, a recognition of the beauty of the outer world and the body through art, the liberation of reason in the scientific enterprise and conscience in religion, and the restoration of culture to intelligence.[17]

Peter Burke asserts that these nineteenth-century, romantic rereadings of the Renaissance were highly selective in the historical records they chose to consult. They were anachronistic. He argues, for example, that "romantic notions of the spontaneous expression of individuality were not available to him (Botticelli)";[18] for artists generally did more or less what they were paid to do.

The "Grand Narrative" Interpretation of the Renaissance

The Renaissance used to be studied as part of a "grand narrative" of the rise of modern Western civilization at a time when many leading writers and statesmen had assured themselves of the superiority of Western culture, its role as a standard for progress, and its position in the vanguard of artistic and intellectual life and political, economic, and scientific advance.[19]

No longer burdened with the need to defend and promote a particular vision of the steady development of European civilization, more contemporary interpreters are sceptical of the claims made by their illustrious, but noticeably partial, forebears. One example of an exaggerated

---

14. Caferro, *Contesting the Renaissance*.

15. Caferro, *Contesting the Renaissance*, 27.

16. Symonds, *Renaissance in Italy* (7 volumes) (Hall Press, 2009; first published in 1900).

17. Caferro, *Contesting the Renaissance*, 6.

18. Burke, *Italian Renaissance*, 2.

19. See, Burke, *Italian Renaissance*, 32.

misreading of history is the alleged disjunction between the medieval world and the rebirth that followed, linking the former to intellectual stagnation and the latter to innovative progress. However,

> the link between medieval and modern is even more marked. Prominent among the early physicists ... were Roger Bacon (d. 1294) and Thomas Bradwardine (d. 1349), whose work provided a basis for the scientific advances of the seventeenth century. Indeed, from the point of view of the natural sciences, the Renaissance, with its emphasis on the arts and humanities, was a period of regression, interrupting the development of experimental techniques and disrupting the process of accumulating knowledge about the nature of the physical world.[20]

The Origin of and Stages in the Perception of the Renaissance

Bearing in mind that "periods are merely useful, heuristic devices for gathering together central aspects of society and culture of particular times," [21] it may still be productive to consider a certain schematic division of the Renaissance phenomena into loosely conceived phases. Some have postulated three stages that mark sequential, although certainly overlapping, features of the period.[22] There was an age of passionate longing to learn more about classical cultures and, where fitting, to appropriate their approach to civic living. This stage is connected especially with the writings of Petrarch and Boccaccio.[23] A second age was characterized by the acquisition and accumulation of manuscripts, many of which had lain unknown or unappreciated in libraries throughout Europe, or had been brought from Greece after the fall of Constantinople. The third and final age that marked the boundaries of the Renaissance was that of the scholars who translated and annotated these ancient authors and had their works printed in one or another of the new printing houses.[24]

20. Lockyer, *Hapsburg and Bourbon Europe*, 79.

21. Ruggiero, *Renaissance in Italy*, 590.

22. See Symonds, "Beginning and Progress."

23. Symonds, "Beginning and Progress," describes the latter's conception of human existence as "a joy to be accepted with thanksgiving, not as a gloomy error to be rectified by suffering the form of semi-pagan gladness. He proclaimed the beauty of the world, the goodliness of youth, and strength and love and life, unterrified by hell, unappalled by the shadow of impending death" (7).

24. The works of Virgil were printed in 1470, Homer in 1488, Aristotle in 1498, and

Another way of dividing the Renaissance into distinct periods is suggested by Ruggiero. He detects two main forms of urban civilization: a first, lasting from about 1250 to 1450, was centered on cities in the center and North of Italy and manifested the culture and values of a new urban-centered elite (the *popolo grosso*), made up largely of people engaged in the merchant world of banking and trade that supplanted the older, rural, feudal elite; a second, which lasted for roughly another one hundred years, was marked by the emergence of an aristocratic and courtly society. The two forms of urban existence coalesced around the notion of virtue, which "stressed reason, moderation and self-control, sliding toward cunning and ... cleverness ... essentially the values of an urban elite that could be shared widely in an urban environment."[25] This virtue, it was claimed, was in direct line with the behavior expected of the leaders of Greek and Roman civic life.

However one conceptualizes the different stages of the Renaissance, public life was severely traumatized by the occurrence of the "Black Death" (or bubonic plague[26]) that first affected Europe in 1346, lasting until 1353, and then recurring at regular intervals for several hundred years. In the initial pandemic, around 45 to 50 percent of Europe's population perished. One of the effects of this devastation was to hasten a process of urbanization: as the workforce in the cities was depleted, it was supplemented by migration from rural areas. Labor was scarce, so its value increased. This in itself affected the demographic constituency of the cities and brought new elements into the cultural mix of urban populations. By the time of the beginning of the High Renaissance, populations had stabilized and recovered considerably from the initial destruction of the disease.

Plato in 1512.

25. Ruggiero, *Renaissance in Italy*, 16.

26. The actual cause of the plague and the way in which it was spread are still disputed amongst experts in medical archaeology. The rats and fleas thesis, made popular at the end of the nineteenth century, is now questioned, although it may have been one factor. Death on such a scale would probably have been spread by human contact (as is the case with ebola) and may have been caused by some form of pulmonary disease. See Cohn, *Black Death Transformed*.

The Social and Political Context of the Renaissance

The Impact of Encounters with "New Worlds"

Jerry Brotton has emphasized that "The Renaissance has to be set within a wider world of trade, finance, commodities, patronage, imperial conflict, travel and inter-cultural exchange."[27] Many historians have assigned a great significance to the ending of the continent's isolation, just at a time when the term "Europe" was invented to name the entire Western peninsular of the Asian land mass. Fresh ideas and accumulated experience were not only engendered internally by a rediscovery of Europe's past, but, perhaps just as importantly, by encounters with unfamiliar cultures and ways of thinking. Peoples who lived beyond the eastern end of the Mediterranean had many possessions that proved highly desirable to the emerging city-states of Europe, not only precious commodities and exotic goods, but scientific and technical knowledge, artistic techniques, and business experience. Peoples who lived at the far end of the Atlantic seaboard presented a new challenge to European adventurers and to Christian belief: Were these people as fully human as Europeans imagined themselves to be? After all, in complete seclusion from "the old world," this "new world" had produced remarkable civilizations, particularly in the fields of governance and architecture.[28]

The government, the church, and academic institutions in Spain during the second quarter of the sixteenth century were engaged in a fierce debate about how the indigenous peoples of the Indies should be treated by the colonial power:

> The impact of the encounter with new races of people, unlike any familiar to the Europeans hitherto, was keenly felt by the church. Up to 1492, the only people known outside Christendom were Jews and Muslims. Now the church had to recognize and deal with people whose religious way of life was not remotely comparable to its own. It became engaged, then, in a highly significant debate about the human status of the indigenous peoples of the Americas, the legitimacy of slavery, the nature

---

27. Brotton, *Renaissance*, 19.

28. Pizarro, the conqueror of the Incas, was much impressed by the rebuilt capital of the Inca empire in Cuzco. In a letter to the king of Spain, he said, "this city is the greatest and finest ever seen in this country or anywhere in the Indies . . . We can assure your majesty that it is so beautiful and has such fine buildings that it would be remarkable even in Spain." See Gonzalez and Gonzalez, *Christianity in Latin America*, 18.

of salvation, the means of evangelization, freedom of religion, self-determination and human rights. It is largely to the credit of the Dominicans of Salamanca and the tireless efforts of the Dominican, Fray Bartolome de las Casas, that new theological ground was broken in response to this novel situation.[29]

He reversed the general attitude to the Indians: the conquistadors saw them as people to be exploited for what could be extracted from them; Las Casas saw them as people, created by God as equals, to be the privileged recipients of the good news of a salvation which would enhance their humanity. In his thinking, the only justification for the presence of the Spanish in the Americas was the divine commission to share the good news of Jesus Christ.

In his magisterial *Apologetica Historia* (Apologetic History),[30] de las Casas expounds reasons for accepting the ability of the Indians to exercise rational judgment, comparing their laws and customs favorably with those of the Greeks and Romans and "even our own Spaniards of Cantabria."[31]

> He further disputes, at some length, the use of the epithet "barbarian" to describe the original inhabitants of the Americas. He sets out the four characteristics of the meaning of the word and concludes that ... the Indians qualify as barbarians in two senses lack of a written language and lack of belief in the one, true God ... He concludes that, if it is legitimate to refer to the Indians as barbarians in the sense of having no proper government or laws of their own, it is because the Spaniards have made them so. As a result of the Spaniards' encounter with the Indies, it may be said that some of their theologians and experts in law became the first to elaborate a theoretical basis for human rights, derived from the Scriptures and the writings of previous divines, pointing to equality and liberty, freedom of religion and a democratic society. It is regrettable that in many discourses on the origin of these beliefs due acknowledgment is not given to these first pioneers. They were ahead of their times. Had their voices been listened to and acted on, the whole history of colonialism would surely have been vastly different.[32]

---

29. Kirk, *Church and the World*, 123–24.
30. de las Casas, *Obras Completas*.
31. de las Casas, *Obras Completas*, 264.
32. Kirk, *Church and the World*, 124–25.

The Impact of Wealth-Creation

The importance of wealth-creation by merchant entrepreneurs cannot be overestimated. The capital accumulated was reinvested in expanding businesses, and profits were spent on the commissioning of paintings, sculptures, and architectural masterpieces:

> The profits of finance were added to those of trade, and the entrepreneurs who were the principal beneficiaries of this process were also among the major patrons of Renaissance scholars and artists . . . They demonstrated their awareness (of the virtues of civic life) by supporting and encouraging artists and men of letters, as if to show the world that only in a climate of republican liberty could intellectual and artistic creation flourish . . . Mercantile wealth had created in these cities a leisured class outside the Church-university nexus, and the individual, provided he was rich and talented enough, was free to develop as he thought fit.[33]

City-states gained greater impetus and power at the conclusion of the Italian Hundred Years' War. The peace of Lodi in 1454 divided Italy among five great powers: Venice, Milan, Florence, the Papal States, and the Neapolitan kingdom. This peace, which brought a certain political stability not experienced for a long time past, lasted for forty years (until 1494) and may be a crucial factor in the depiction of this period as the high watermark of the Italian renaissance.[34]

The Position of Women in Society

William Caferro has written a chapter of his book on the Renaissance with the intriguing title of "Gender: Who was the Renaissance Woman?" In it he portrays the prevalent sexual discrimination practiced at that time. Women were limited in terms of their role in society by legal restraints, accepted attitudes, and inherited traditions. Whereas men could play a public role as acknowledged providers for their families, women were confined to domestic and family matters. Whereas traditions of male honor demanded of men loyalty, bravery, honesty, integrity, and good craftsmanship, female honor was mainly confined to maintaining chastity. Women's power lay in the threat of opting for some sexual indiscretion

---

33. Lockyer, *Hapsburg and Bourbon Europe*, 81, 82.
34. See Ruggiero, *Renaissance in Italy*, 203–4.

or other form of improper behavior. These, at one level, could upset the governance of a state, and at another, destroy the reputation of an entire family. Male honor, therefore, was conceived as a positive attribute, whereas the female's was understood negatively. In other words, womens' allure was regarded as highly risky. This justified their virtual removal from the public sphere, not being allowed either a proper education or employment. Women were seen primordially as temptresses; a view confirmed by the alleged teaching of the Bible and the opinion of Plato (in his *Timaeus*) and Aristotle (in his *Politics*).[35]

Nevertheless, some women did exercise considerable influence in society, even in the face of cultural and religious restrictions. Making the most of their opportunities, they became renowned for what they contributed to the intellectual, artistic, and religious environment of the time. One such woman was Isabelle d'Este, the duchess of Mantua, nominated by some writers as the first lady of the Renaissance. She was well-educated, being fluent in Latin and Greek, accomplished on the flute, and an enthusiastic patron of the arts, whose circle of acquaintances included Leonardo, Raphael, and Titian. After her husband was captured in war, she ruled Mantua, and even led armies into battle.[36]

> She participated in the visit and coronation (of the emperor Charles V in Bologna in 1530) as a widely recognized, powerful figure on a par with the male leaders of Europe and ... a number of the leading women as well. Her glory was evident to all. She had fashioned it over the course of her life with her patronage and cultural leadership; with the power she had cultivated in the Church, via her cardinal son and her close relationships with many of its leaders; with her significant ties to the emperor; and with the ongoing brilliance of her family's court in Mantua.[37]

Counted among other leading ladies were Caterina Sforza, the widow of Giovanni de Medici and a ruler in the city of Forli, Catherine de Medici, the Queen Regent of France, and, in a totally different sphere of influence, Teresa of Avila, a member of the Carmelite order, a writer of profound spiritual and devotional material, who also founded seventeen new houses for the order.

---

35. Caferro, *Contesting the Renaissance*, 63.
36. Caferro, *Contesting the Renaissance*, 62.
37. Ruggiero, *Renaissance in Italy*, 385–86.

Renaissance Humanism, Depicted in Art

What is Meant by Humanism?

Although a commonly used expression, the humanism of the Renaissance, often paraphrased by the epithet, "Renaissance man," is open to confusion. Since the time of the Enlightenment (as we shall see in later chapters) the word humanism has come to mean something rather different. Over the course of time, the use of the term has changed dramatically. Humanism, at least in European secular culture, is held as a default description for all who seek to live almost exclusively by faith in reason and the tenets of scientific methods of explanation. It excludes the relevance of God from human discourse. It tends to view religious beliefs as not only false (and delusional), but harmful, for

> they distort reality, provide false hopes, justify harmful practices and often hinder what humanists conceive to be moral advancement . . . Human beings are alone in the universe. They are, therefore, responsible to themselves alone. They have to resolve their problems on their own.[38]

This is the kind of humanism that Charles Taylor describes as "imminent and exclusive."[39] It encompasses perhaps the most radical intellectual and cultural shift that the modern world has witnessed; indeed, it defines modernity. God is viewed as an unnecessary hypothesis. Human beings live in a silent universe, broken only by the chatter of their own voices. Humanism, in this sense, advocates what Taylor calls "closed world structures." Humanists believe they have shifted the burden of proof "on to those who wish to claim that there is another reality beyond the material that impinges directly on the physical one . . . God has been replaced by nature"[40] (often spelled with a capital "N").

When speaking about the Renaissance period, the danger is that this latter understanding of humanism is read back into the writings and artifacts of Renaissance authors and artists. We have already encountered something of this in the reconfiguration of the Renaissance in the studies of Michelet and Burckhardt, as they interpreted the phenomena through the intellectual spectacles of post-Enlightenment fundamental

---

38. Kirk, *Church and the World*, 300.

39. Taylor, *Secular Age*, 19, 542.

40. Kirk, *Church and the World*, 305–6.

beliefs. Symonds is, in part, guilty of the same kind of historiography. In his study of the Renaissance, he sums up what he conceives to be the underlying spirit of the Renaissance:

> But with the dawning of the Renaissance, a new spirit in the arts arose. Men began to conceive that the human body is noble in itself and worthy of patient study . . . He studied from the nude; he drew the body in every posture; he composed drapery, invented attitudes, and adapted the action of his figures and the expression of his faces to the subject he had chosen. In a word, he humanized the altar-pieces and the cloister-frescoes upon which he worked. In this way the painters rose above the ancient symbols, and brought heaven down to earth. By drawing Madonna and her son like living human beings, by dramatizing the Christian history, they silently substituted the love of beauty and the interests of actual life for the principles of the Church . . . Finally, when the classics came to aid this work of progress, a new world of thought and fancy, divinely charming, wholly human, was revealed to their astonished eyes. Thus art, which had begun by humanizing the legends of the Church, diverted the attention of its students from the legend to the work of beauty, and lastly, severing itself from the religious tradition, became the exponent of the majesty and splendour of the human body. This final emancipation of art from ecclesiastical trammels culminated in the great age of Italian painting. Gazing at Michaelangelo's prophets in the Sistine Chapel, we are indeed in contact with ideas originally religious. But the treatment of these ideas is purely, broadly human . . . Titian's Virgin received into Heaven, soaring midway between the archangel who descends to crown her and the apostles who yearn to follow her, is far less a Madonna Assunta than the apotheosis of humanity conceived as a radiant mother. Throughout the picture there is nothing ascetic, nothing mystic, nothing devotional. Nor did the art of the Renaissance stop here. It went further, and plunged into Paganism. Sculptors and painters combined with architects to cut the arts loose from their connection with the Church by introducing a spirit and a sentiment alien to Christianity. Through the instrumentality of art, and of all the ideas which art introduced into daily life, the Renaissance wrought for the modern world a real resurrection of the body, which, since the destruction of antique civilization, had lain swathed up in hair-shirts and cerements within the tomb of the medieval cloister. It was scholarship which revealed to men the wealth of their own minds, the dignity of human thought, the value of

human speculation, the importance of human life regarded as a thing apart from religious rules and dogmas . . . The Renaissance opened to the whole reading public the treasure-houses of Greek and Latin literature. At the same time the Bible in its original tongues was rediscovered. Mines of Oriental learning were laid bare for the students of the Jewish and Arabic traditions . . . With unerring instinct the men of the Renaissance named the voluminous subject-matter of scholarship "Litteræ Humaniores"—the more human literature, or the literature that humanizes.[41]

This kind of reader response (or viewer response) to the literature and art of the Renaissance appears to confuse two approaches to the existence, significance, and implications of God's presence in the world, and to the way in which the self-designated guardians of faith had chosen to interpret and implement that faith in practice. This is a huge subject which cannot be tackled adequately in this particular study. Suffice it to say that disillusionment with, and criticism of, established religion did not infer a rejection or marginalization of the Christian faith, but rather an attempt to purify it by rediscovering the authenticity of the original proclamation and practice, as we shall see in the cases of Erasmus and Luther. Thus, Roger Lockyer asserts correctly that

it might seem from the example of Valla that the Renaissance was anti-Christian and skeptical to the point of atheism, and it has often been assumed that the revival of the ancient world meant the revival of paganism. But such an impression is a long way from the truth. Critical methods were valued not because they would undermine the foundations of Christianity but because they would reveal them in all their strength . . . The humanists . . . were determined to separate the grain from the chaff, on the assumption that Christianity, since it was undoubtedly true, had nothing to fear from the removal of erroneous practices and doctrines, however hallowed these were by time.[42]

Having made this point, it is nevertheless true that a new belief in the power and productive potential of the human being came to the fore at this time. We have already alluded to the extravagant symbols of the Renaissance view of the world in Holbein's painting, *The Ambassadors*.

41. Symonds, *Beginning and Progress*, 18, 19, 20.
42. Lockyer, *Hapsburg and Bourbon Europe*, 89.

Here we can see a certain amount of ostentation, whose aim is to communicate a certain impression of a new age in the making:

> The purpose of humanism was to create a universal man whose person combined intellectual and physical excellence, capable of functioning honorably in virtually any situation.[43]

One of the symbols of this universal man taken from ancient biblical history was the youthful David, who was to become king of Israel. As an historical figure, he combined in his person a number of virtues admired by both the aristocracy and the upwardly mobile new class of business pioneers: his knowledge and experience of agricultural life; his musical skills; his ability to write exquisite poetry; his leadership qualities; his military prowess; his administrative competence; his honesty and contrition when confronted with his sins of adultery and manslaughter. It is not surprising, therefore, that David evoked two of the most famous statues ever constructed. The first was created by Donatello. The image was that of "the Florentine ideal of the young male figure of the day."[44] The date of its construction is uncertain. However, if it is intended to pay homage to the youthful Lorenzo de Medici ("the Magnificent"), then a date in the 1460s would seem to be appropriate. Outwardly, the statue recalled the triumph of the teenage David victorious over Goliath; it was a depiction of the glorious and highly unlikely conquest of overwhelming might and adversity by a young lad, whose physical immaturity was offset by his immense courage and resilience:

> A figure like David triumphing over Goliath perfectly associated ... (an) exterior beauty with precocious strength and courage, and perhaps suggested an inner beauty and grace that would remain beneath the more masculine body of an adult. In this context, a David that in the early 1460s suggested the youthful beauty of a Lorenzo— ... then in his teens—was a virtually perfect symbol of all the promise of his and the Medici's future.[45]

Michelangelo's statue of David, carved in marble rather than the bronze of Donatello's, was commissioned in 1501 by the wool guild in Florence to be one of the Old Testament prophets that would adorn the roof of the Cathedral. The finished work (1504) is considered by many as

---

43. Hause and Maltby, *History of European Society*, 245–46.
44. Ruggiero, *Renaissance in Italy*, 337.
45. Ruggiero, *Renaissance in Italy*, 308, 309.

one of the greatest statues ever made. Unlike Donatello's, it depicts David as a fully grown man, before the combat with Goliath, with his sling over his shoulder, but without a sword. David is taut, ready for the fight, but also relaxed. He is looking slightly over his left shoulder in anticipation of the conflict to come. Apart from the fact that this David symbolized the struggle of Florence against its enemies and anticipated the victory of the weak, who trusted in God, over the strong, who trusted in their own power, he also epitomized in a general way the perfection of male strength, beauty, and excellence. Some historians have suggested that the real model was not the biblical David at all, whom he does not seem to represent, but rather Hercules, the archetypical hero, able to undertake and fulfill the most improbable challenges. The tradition of Hercules's twelve labors was later reinterpreted as the successful struggle of humanity against every kind of threat, including the threat of evil desires. If the mythological tales were in part an inspiration for Michelangelo, it would further confirm the conclusion that his David was intended to be a token and image of the triumphs open to humanity, including his own as an artist.

It would be a failure of this inquiry if it did not mention the immense symbolism of Michelangelo's painting of the newly created Adam on the ceiling of the Sistine chapel. Edith Sichel, in her study of the Renaissance,[46] says that this depiction of the pristine beginning of human life might be taken as a symbol of the Renaissance, a time when man (in particular) was conceived as being more glorious than before. His body is naked (like David's) and unashamed. His arm is stretched out toward light and life. According to her (just as in the case of the first Adam),

> It was a revival of man's powers, a reawakening of his consciousness of himself and of the universe.[47]

The human body was no longer considered a necessary enemy of the human spirit.

Renaissance Humanism, Depicted in Literature

Our final port of call in attempting to infer beliefs about being human from selected figures, influenced by the rebirth of education and learning,

---

46. Sichel, *Renaissance*; first printed in 1914 and republished many times since.
47. Sichel, *Renaissance*, 7.

fresh trends in philosophical and theological thinking, new discoveries in scientific disciplines and technological inventions and firsthand acquaintance with unfamiliar and unusual cultures to the East and West of Europe, are one or two of the most distinguished scholars of the age. I have selected four of the most well known, whose influence did not end in the immediate aftermath of their own lives, but has continued to intrigue and provoke many subsequent generations: Marsilio Ficino, Leon Battista Alberti, Giovanni Pico della Mirandola, and Desiderius Erasmus. I will not attempt a mini biography of each character, for these may be found in any reputable encyclopedia, but rather concentrate on their thinking about human life, expressed both in their writings and in their own careers.

Ficino[48]

His thought has been described as eclectic, in that Ficino had several aims in writing his discourses. The thinking, therefore, does not always display an inner cohesion and consistency.[49] One of his principal intentions was to defend the immortality of the soul against any form of materialist philosophy. If the human being is merely mortal, then there is no animal more miserable. If the human being's desire for a continuing existence after death were to be an illusion, the desire would be unfulfilled and the whole of life would be futile.

Thus, he spends much time and intellectual effort to convince the readers that the human being is a special creation within the natural world. The one wholly unchanging reality in (and outside) the universe is God, and from this flow a number of important consequences. The ultimate reality behind all the myriad, distinct elements of material existence is intelligence. Deriving much of his philosophical underpinning from Plato's theory of the forms, he concludes that the ever-changing

---

48. His most well-known writings are: *Liber de Christiana religione* (*Book on Christian Religion*, 1474); *Theologia Platonica* (*Platonic Theology*, 1482), and *De vita libri tres* (*Three Books on Life*, 1489).

49. As this brief summary of Ficino's most characteristic thought focuses on his understanding of the reality of the human condition as a created being in a material world, I have not thought it necessary to delve into his controversial speculations about the occult, which he explores in the third book of *The Three Books of Life*. Such an exploration would take us too far from the purpose of this inquiry. However, a fuller treatment of his thought would have to take it into account.

movements of things in the realm of the senses are representations of unvarying patterns held in the mind of God. These are perfect expressions of the changing and distinct qualities of any material object. Human beings are able to reflect on both the unchanging form and the changing features of everyday entities, for they, through the existence of their mind and soul, stand between the eternal and the transitory.

A second consequence is that a fundamental differentiation exists between being and becoming. As far as the human is concerned, they possess an essence that is constant and stable. What they may become, due to individual choices and circumstances, will vary. However, their essential constitution remains determined, fixed, and secure. They partake both of the eternal form of human nature and the changing reality of individual lives. This view of human nature is profoundly significant in the history of Western philosophy. It has been both upheld and vehemently challenged many times in recent history; in particular, the challenge has come from mid-twentieth-century existentialist philosophy and postmodern thinking.

A third consequence of Ficino's metaphysical thought is that it underpins the essential dignity of humanity. Possession of a soul gives humans a privileged position in the hierarchy of being. The human being links the higher and lower orders of living entities. Humans share qualities with both and is drawn to both simultaneously. They are charged with the governance of the physical world, being responsible for its welfare. As they are destined for eternity, they are also born for the contemplation of the one who inhabits eternity, the divine being. This places humans in a unique relationship to the visible and invisible worlds.

A fourth consequence derives from Ficino's body-spirit dualism. The soul cannot fulfill its highest destiny because it is locked into a body that frustrates its desire to soar beyond the restrictions of physical existence. Through the senses, the soul is assaulted by many and various violent impressions. It is led astray into thinking that nothing can be real that is not material. There is a gulf fixed between the nature and aspirations of the soul and its subjective experience when joined to the body. This leads to a kind of common-sense materialism, which causes a profound misunderstanding about what is ultimately real and, therefore, worthy of being followed.

One of Ficino's aims was to show that ancient traditions in philosophy (particularly the Platonic) did not oppose Christian faith, but could be used as tools to bring further understanding of the latter's deep truths.

Thus, for example, he saw salvation in terms of the ascent of the soul from out of its transient and trivial existence in the material world, to an ever-greater union with God. Evil occurs in the world just because humans accord far too much prominence to material existence, which, to some degree, is shadowy and unreal. Whilst trapped in the prison of their bodies, humans remain restless and anxious. They long for a place of rest, which is achieved by both the discovery of the distinction between the ephemeral and substantial aspects of existence, and the pursuit of the latter.

Alberti

One of the main reasons for including Alberti as a protagonist of what we have loosely described as Renaissance man is that he incorporated that description in his own being. He combined in himself the achievements of being an architect, artist, author, cryptographer, linguist, moralist, philosopher, and poet. Moreover, he was a priest in the church. To say the least, he was versatile and eclectic in his interests. He has been commended as the principal pioneer of Renaissance art theory, as both the foremost theorizer of Renaissance architecture and one of its leading practitioners. He created the first grammar book of the Tuscan language, comparing it favorably with Latin as a regular *lingua franca*, and therefore worthy to be a medium of written communication, on a par with its ancient predecessor.

In his book, *On the Art of Building* (published posthumously in 1485, although it was finished in 1452), he furthered the knowledge of engineering handed down from antiquity, and he discussed a wide range of subjects from practical topics like town-planning to more theoretical themes like the nature of historical study and the essence of beauty. In his work, *I Libri della famiglia* (*The Books of the Family*), he discourses on what it means to be a virtuous member of a family. In spite of the fact that he himself was an illegitimate child, who felt betrayed by his family in the matter of inheritance, and that he was not married himself (his ordination required celibacy), he brought his theoretical understanding of practical virtues, as expounded by the philosophers of ancient Greece and Rome, in contact with the daily concerns of his society. So he conversed, in dialogue form, on topics such as handling prosperity and adversity, friendship, family relationships, education, and service of the common good.

In the name of reason, common sense, and nature, he endorses a traditional, engendered view of family roles. Women, being weaker than men, deserve to be protected. They should not be over-exposed to the cut and thrust of civic and business life. On the other hand, they have the gift, given them by nature, of nurturing the young and being the stabilizing agent for the continuing well-being of the family, whilst the husband attends to the wider affairs of society and trains his male progeny to take their place within the community. In effect he echoes, in an idealistic way, the common Renaissance virtues embodied in successful child-rearing for the sake of enabling good civic order to overcome the immorality of the rather chaotic cities of the period.

Pico della Mirandola

Perhaps the most often-quoted words that have come down to us from the foremost thinkers of the Renaissance occur at the beginning of Pico della Mirandola's famous treatise, *Oratio de hominis dignitate* (*Oration on the Dignity of Man*), published in 1486 together with a series of theses (900 in total) which he believed contained a summary of what was necessary to imbibe in order to discover the roots of all knowledge:

> I was not fully persuaded by the diverse reasons advanced for the preeminence of human nature; that man is the intermediary between creatures, that he is the familiar of the gods above him as he is the lord of the beings beneath him; that, by the acuteness of his senses, the inquiry of his reason and the light of his intelligence, he is the interpreter of nature, set midway between the timeless unchanging and the flux of time; the living union (as the Persians say), the very marriage hymn of the world, and, by David's testimony but little lower than the angels. These reasons are all, without question, of great weight; nevertheless, they do not touch the principal reasons, those, that is to say, which justify man's unique right for such unbounded admiration. Why, I asked, should we not admire the angels themselves and the beatific choirs more? At long last, however, I feel that I have come to some understanding of why man is the most fortunate of living things and, consequently, deserving of all admiration; of what may be the condition in the hierarchy of beings assigned to him, which draws upon him the envy, not of the brutes alone,

but of the astral beings and of the very intelligences which dwell beyond the confines of the world. A thing surpassing belief and smiting the soul with wonder. Still, how could it be otherwise? For it is on this ground that man is, with complete justice, considered and called a great miracle and a being worthy of all admiration.[50]

And so, the greatness and uniqueness of the human species is founded on God's intention to create a being like himself, with whom he could converse, endowed with a free will, to see what he would make of his surroundings:

> We have given you, O Adam, no visage proper to yourself, nor endowment properly your own, in order that whatever place, whatever form, whatever gifts you may, with premeditation, select, these same you may have and possess through your own judgment and decision. The nature of all other creatures is defined and restricted within laws which We have laid down; you, by contrast, impeded by no such restrictions, may, by your own free will, to whose custody We have assigned you, trace for yourself the lineaments of your own nature. I have placed you at the very center of the world, so that from that vantage point you may with greater ease glance round about you on all that the world contains. We have made you a creature neither of heaven nor of earth, neither mortal nor immortal, in order that you may, as the free and proud shaper of your own being, fashion yourself in the form you may prefer. It will be in your power to descend to the lower, brutish forms of life; you will be able, through your own decision, to rise again to the superior orders whose life is divine.[51]

Pico della Mirandola ends this first tribute to the status of the human person with a doxology to the Creator for taking the risk of allowing his progeny such freedom to use their individual gifts and circumstances as they see fit.

> Oh unsurpassed generosity of God the Father, Oh wondrous and unsurpassable felicity of man, to whom it is granted to have what he chooses, to be what he wills to be![52]

---

50. Pico della Mirandola, *Oration on the Dignity*, 17.
51. Pico della Mirandola, *Oration on the Dignity*, 19–20.
52. Pico della Mirandola, *Oration on the Dignity*, 20.

It is not surprising that later generations, brought up on the diet of a different kind of humanism, should focus on these words, in particular as a summary of what leading Renaissance thinkers believed about the essential nature of what it means to be human. Thus, many subsequent interpreters of the Renaissance have taken these words of homage as a charter that defines the preeminent standing of humanity within all living creatures. In particular, in accordance with much later thought, they emphasize both the dignity accorded to humans and their freedom to shape their own destinies. No wonder that the *Oratio* has been declared a, if not the, key text of Renaissance humanism—a kind of manifesto, indicating the potential achievements of which humans are capable.

One wonders, however, to what extent those who concentrate on the beginning of the *Oration* have gone on to read it to its conclusion. Unlike a later view of the uses to which the gift of freedom can be put, namely to declare one's complete autonomy from traditions, dogmas, and self-declared authorities, in order to shape one's own life anew, Pico della Mirandola saw it as a precondition and stimulus "to pant after the highest things."[53] He did not follow a later illusion that all external restraint is inevitably inimical to personal preference and choice:

> So, we should not abuse the gift of a free option, but disdain mediocrity . . . Let us disdain things of the earth . . . and . . . hasten to that court beyond the world, closest to the most exalted Godhead.[54]

Freedom was never intended to enable humans to indulge their physical desires and cravings. Rather,

> by refraining the impulses of our passions through moral science, by dissipating the darkness of reason by dialect, thus washing away, so to speak, the filth of ignorance and vice, may likewise purify our souls, so that the passions may never run rampant . . . Then we may suffuse our purified souls with the light of natural philosophy, bringing it to final perfection by the knowledge of divine things.[55]

He evokes the picture of Jacob's ladder with angels ascending on it to heaven. We cannot, he says, touch the ladder with muddied feet or soiled hands. We need moral philosophy to cleanse us from accumulated

---

53. Pico della Mirandola, *Oration on the Dignity*, 23.
54. Pico della Mirandola, *Oration on the Dignity*, 23.
55. Pico della Mirandola, *Oration on the Dignity*, 26.

dirt, so we can ascend by means of philosophy to reach the bosom of the Father. Natural philosophy, he believes, will reduce the conflict of opinions and the endless debates which from every side vex, distract and lacerate the disturbed mind.

Pico della Mirandola clarifies what he means by natural philosophy. It is the combined wisdom of all humanity, from wherever it may come. He claims (by the age of 24) to have "ranged through all the masters of philosophy, examined all their works, become acquainted with all schools."[56] This he believes is the only adequate path to ascertaining the truth about human life:

> It seems to me that by the confrontation of many schools and the discussion of many philosophical systems that "effulgence of truth" of which Plato writes ... might illuminate our minds more clearly, like the sun rising from the sea.
>
> We have proposed a harmony between Plato and Aristotle ... We have, in addition, adduced a great number of passages in which Scotus and Thomas, and others in which Averroes and Avicenna, have heretofore been thought to disagree, but which I assert are in harmony with one another.[57]

At this point, Pico della Mirandola introduces his *piece de resistance*, the mystical tradition of Cabala, which he takes to be the final word on the wisdom needed to ascend into the heavenly realms. Cabala, which in Hebrew means "reception," was the secret law and wisdom imparted first to Moses as a truer explanation of the law than that written down in codes. It was handed down orally and secretly to successive high priests. Only those initiated into the knowledge of its truth could be entrusted with its transmission. Eventually, according to Esdras, it was written down by seventy scribes after the release of the captives from Babylon and the restoration of Jerusalem:

> In these books ... resides the springs of understanding, that is, the ineffable theology of the super-substantial deity; the fountain of wisdom, that is the precise metaphysical doctrine concerning intelligible and angelic forms; the stream of wisdom, that is the best established philosophy concerning nature.[58]

---

56. Pico della Mirandola, *Oration on the Dignity*, 44. He mentions specifically Christian theologians, Muslim scholars, and Greek philosophers.

57. Pico della Mirandola, *Oration on the Dignity*, 46, 48, 49.

58. Pico della Mirandola, *Oration on the Dignity*, 57–58.

Pico della Mirandola was nothing if not an extraordinarily self-confident young man. His claims are immense:

> What labor was mine, what difficulty was involved, in drawing out the secret meanings of the occult philosophy from the deliberate tangle of riddles and the recesses of fables in which they were hidden . . . I have wanted to make clear in disputation, not only that I know a great many things, but also that I know a great many things that others do not know . . . Let us now, with the prayer that the outcome may be fortunate and favorable, as to the sound of trumpets, join battle.[59]

In fact, the disputation, for which the 900 theses were written and for which the *Oratio* was a preface, never took place. The Pope, Innocent VIII, stopped the debate and appointed a commission to look into the orthodoxy of the theses.

It appears, therefore, that the divine gift of freedom to choose which path in life to pursue was intended by God, according to Pico della Mirandola, to move humans to search for the liberation of the soul from the constraints of physical existence through moral transformation, intellectual research and absorption into the final reality, which for Christians is the Trinitarian God, but for followers of other faiths may be comprehended through other names.

In his understanding of the human condition, Pico della Mirandola appears to believe that some people are destined to be the privileged interpreters of the meaning and ultimate purpose of existence through having received an entrance into the mysteries of the universe. These are recorded in a secret tradition, originally given as a kind of second revelation to Moses and subsequently passed on from generation to generation to those willing to open their minds to such wisdom. It is not surprising, perhaps, that some of the theses were rejected by the papal commission as heterodox, as they appear to make claims about secret knowledge similar to those of the first-century gnostics, condemned by the early church as perverters of the doctrine of Christ.

Erasmus

Although declared to be "the prince of humanists," Erasmus's vocation and pursuits were of a different nature from those of other leading figures

---

59. Pico della Mirandola, *Oration on the Dignity*, 60, 61, 62.

of the Renaissance. He was a fiercely independent thinker, not reliant on the patronage of leading political figures of the time, or even of the ecclesiastical hierarchy. He was unafraid to court controversy for his views on such matters as reform of the church, pacifism, the views of Martin Luther, education, the place of ancient philosophy in the renewal of learning, the fundamental importance of the Bible in shaping Christian faith, and the relationship between human free will and divine grace.

That he is considered to be perhaps the foremost champion of humanistic learning at the time is due to his profound scholarly interests, his early advocacy of the potency of education to shape character for the common good,[60] his promotion of the virtues of moral philosophy as inherited from ancient sources, his refusal to be drawn into an ultra-polemical denunciation of much of the current teaching and practices of the church, and his desire to conciliate between factious views in some of the major controversies of his day. Nevertheless, it appears that toward the end of his life, he was much less sanguine about the power of education to guide and reform people's moral life and much more inclined to accept the limitations of human free will.[61] Of all those categorized as Renaissance humanists by later commentators, Erasmus is probably the most unique in his views.

He developed his own form of Christian spirituality, presented in his treatise, *Enchiridion* (1st edition published in 1503; final edition in 1518), influenced perhaps by Jean Vitrier, the reform-minded warden of a Franciscan convent in St. Omer, who introduced him to the writings of the apostle Paul and early Greek fathers. He may also have been guided by the lives and teaching of the Brethren of the Common Life with whom he was in contact during his early education in their school at Deventer in The Netherlands. In informal lay communities, they practiced a simple devotional life, centered on following the way of Christ as revealed in the Scriptures. They did not engage in elaborate rituals, being highly critical of the current emphasis on the external, conventional ceremonials of the church at the expense of an inner life transformed by the direct action of the Spirit of Christ. He found this interpretation of Christian devotion to be the most authentic and compelling.

---

60. Encapsulated in his treatise, *On Education for Children*, written in 1509 (although not published until 1529).

61. In a frank letter to Thomas More, he confessed that, "If I follow Paul and Augustine, very little is left to free-will" (Tracy, *Erasmus*, 231).

In one of his most celebrated writings, *In Praise of Folly*, Erasmus, in a brilliant satirical expose of the numerous stupidities of contemporary life and thought, voiced in the words of Folly herself, shows his indebtedness to the convictions of the Brethren. The essence of the essay is to show the absolute absurdity of attempting to defend the numerous examples of folly he elaborates upon, and in particular those committed by representatives of the church:

> (On the folly of the religious and monks). A greater part of them are farthest from religion ... They do not endeavor how they may be like Christ, but how they may differ among themselves ... A great part of them build so much on their ceremonies and petty traditions of men that they think one heaven is too poor a reward for so great merit.

> (On the folly of contemporary preaching). You see how much this kind of people are beholden to me (i.e. Folly), that with their petty ceremonies, ridiculous trifles and noise exercise a kind of tyranny among mankind, believing themselves to be very Pauls and Anthonies ... They are impudent pretenders to religion, which they haven't."

> (On the folly of popes, cardinals and bishops). They are ambitious of their dignity; if there be anything of honor or pleasure, they take that to themselves ... Scarce any kind of men live more voluptuously or with less trouble ... As if the Church had any deadlier enemies than wicked prelates ... (They) murder him (Christ) by the evil example of their pestilent life.[62]

It is clear that, in this *tour de force*, Erasmus, in a not-too-subtle way, has begun his offensive against the absurd and half-witted operations of the official church. Its leaders are out of touch with the way educated people observe it. Above all, it upholds a *modus vivendi* that, when it refuses to put its house in order, opens it up to the threat of schism.

That threat became a reality when a German Augustinian monk nailed ninety-five theses to the main door of a church in Wittenberg on October 30th, 1517. Erasmus's relation to Luther and the Reformation, which his action initiated, is ambiguous. Nevertheless, the controversies that transpired later indicate something of Erasmus's views on the human condition.

---

62. Erasmus, *Praise of Folly* (translated by Guerrero), 120.

It is not surprising that, in Erasmus's first comments on Luther's reforming zeal, he showed appreciation. He agreed that many of the reforms of the church that Luther was so strongly advocating were indeed urgently required. In early correspondence, Luther reciprocated by praising Erasmus for his tireless efforts on behalf of purifying the church from its many corruptions. Both in the *Enchiridion* and *In Praise of Folly*, Erasmus had set his face against religious formalism in all its manifestations. When Luther published his fierce condemnation of the Church of Rome in his tract, "On the Babylonian Captivity of the Church" (1520), Erasmus refused to condemn it, even though he believed that Luther's polemic would do more damage to the cause of reform than it would achieve. As a result of a continuing desire to bring about conciliation between the two antagonists through reasoned debate, Erasmus was accused by many in the church (in Louvain, where he was living at the time,[63] in Paris, and among members of religious orders in Spain and Italy) of both being the cause of Luther's theological deviations and of encouraging him in them.

However, in 1524, he showed his disagreement with Luther on one central point of belief about the status of humanity: that of free will. In that year he had his famous treatise, *De libero arbitro* (*On Free Will*) published. In it he sought to lay out in an irenic spirit how he understood the relationship between the work of divine grace and human response in salvation, perhaps the key theological issue in the growing dissension between the reformers and the church. He claimed to base his convictions wholly on the Bible's teaching, uncovered through a meticulous exposition of the meaning of the original texts in their contexts. His stated intention was only to accept what is clear from a well-grounded reading of the relevant passages. In this way, he hoped that some kind of rapprochement could be achieved with others who accepted a similar approach to the text.

He concluded that the extent or limit of human free will was not set out in Scripture in such a way that there was only one possible interpretation. He believed that the question could not be settled with absolute certainty. The best one could attain was a high degree of probability, because the Bible, as a whole, was ambiguous on the subject. There were texts which inclined one to a view in favor of a liberal interpretation of free will, and others which seemed to point to a human being's incapacity to

---

63. He moved to Basel in 1521, where he lived for eight years until the city turned fully Protestant.

make free choices. Erasmus adopted a method of study which today we would call inference to the best explanation (i.e., the testing of a range of possible, alternative solutions to the problem, to discern which was most likely to be correct). He came down on the side of the capacity of humans to choose freely in certain circumstances as this was the view that had the most biblical and patristic support in its favor.

His dispute with Luther concerned the question of how much the fallen state of human beings (i.e., their settled inclination to think and do evil) affects their freedom to choose unrestrainedly to accept or reject God's offer of salvation through Christ. The fundamental dispute was posed around the question of whether salvation is appropriated by means of a human's weakened will cooperating with God's gracious call to trust his word, or as the result of God's work alone, apart from any human effort. Erasmus defined free will in this way:

> By free choice in this place we mean a power of the human will by which a man can apply himself to the things which lead to eternal salvation or turn him away from them.[64]

He uses an illustration to try to show, in ordinary, everyday terms, how the sovereign initiative of God relates to the human capacity to decide on a course of action. Suppose a father is looking after his injured son, and in order to encourage him and show his care, he offers him an apple. The son is so disabled that grasping hold of the apple would be beyond his own individual ability. So the father gives him all the help he can, apart from actually placing the apple in his hand. The son's part, says Erasmus, is to rely "with all his powers on the one who offers it."[65] However, the child could have refused the outstretched apple; he had to decide to cooperate with the father's initial action. In this decision, he acted freely; there was no external compulsion. Analogies, however, tend to offer less than perfect illustrations. In this case, Erasmus concludes,

> I will readily allow that less is due to our industry in following after eternal life than to the boy who runs to his father's hand.[66]

The implication of Erasmus's view seems to be that God offers the gift of the one and only way of salvation, and God's grace draws human beings toward the gift. However, the offer may be declined by the person's

---

64. Erasmus and Luther, *Discourse on Free Will*, 26.
65. Erasmus and Luther, *Discourse on Free Will*, 92.
66. Erasmus and Luther, *Discourse on Free Will*, 92.

free choice; receiving the offer is, therefore, by the person's own decision. This way of looking at the relationship between grace and free will appears to exalt the individual's participation and lower the effect of God's action.

Erasmus rejects what he considered Luther's pessimistic doctrine of humanity's total depravity inherited from the effects of Adam and Eve's first sin. After the fall, the human will was weakened: "obscured, but not totally extinguished,"[67] says Erasmus. Although human beings' reason is impaired, it is still functioning. They have the ability, therefore, to do some good by their own choice. However, this does not, affirms Erasmus, enable them to merit salvation through their good works:

> There is a will in some way ready for the good, but useless for eternal salvation without the addition of grace by faith.[68]

Erasmus speaks of three different types of grace: common grace, which restrains the worst effects of evil in humans and provokes works of goodness in them; peculiar or stimulating grace, which arouses the sinner to see the folly of his ways and draws him toward repentance; and effective grace. When individuals have had their minds changed and their wills enabled, this third grace will complete their salvation.

Luther's reply, written in 1525, "*De servo arbitrio*" ("On the Bondage of the Will"), was highly polemical. Luther was not in the mood to offer any kind of concession to his own uncompromising views on how salvation is appropriated. So, he accuses Erasmus of all kinds of deficiencies in his understanding of the gospel. According to Luther, he fails to distinguish between law and gospel, and he has no proper understanding of the doctrines of election, regeneration, and renewal. Above all, he fails to understand the nature and effects of original sin. In their natural state, the whole constitution of humans is hostile and opposed to God, not just the mental and volitional parts, but the spirit as well. They are so blind that they cannot see their own corruption. In their unregenerate state, they like to think they are free creatures, but this is not the reality of life. They are deceived. Saving faith is not a first step toward reconciliation with God that humans can take on their own, and for which they are rewarded by God. It also is a pure gift of God's unmerited grace. Erasmus, according to Luther, wishes to defend the human's role in salvation. He is a humanist and therefore needs to exalt humans in some way.

67. Erasmus and Luther, *Discourse on Free Will*, 94.
68. Erasmus and Luther, *Discourse on Free Will*, 30.

What should one conclude from this vitriolic exchange of views on human free will? In the fundamentally changed environment of the twenty-first century, it may seem abstruse and esoteric. However, there is much to be said for Steven Orment's opinion:

> [The debate between Luther and Erasmus being] seemingly narrow and obscure, actually involved the most fundamental discussion of human nature and destiny.[69]

At the time of the debate, Erasmus had an optimistic view of the potential of human endeavor, "since by the use of reason (as long as it was accompanied with humility and devotion) man could hope to attain a knowledge and understanding of God."[70] He was an advocate of the power of education to strengthen and elevate the noble aspects of human nature. He did not agree with, or perhaps he misunderstood, the concept of the total corruption of human nature caused by humanity's willful decision to defy God's counsel.

Looked at empirically, human beings, as well as performing unspeakably evil acts, are capable of virtuous deeds. It would seem, therefore, that those who had a sensitive conscience toward the distinction between good and evil would be capable of responding to the absolute justice of God by the light of their own moral standards. Looked at, however, from the perspective of a person's relationship to God, human achievements are sullied by people's desire to be independent of God's demands, or at least to claim freedom to interpret them to their own advantage. In this situation, the categorical words of the apostle Paul, quoting the Psalms, seem authentic: "there is none who is righteous, not even one . . . there is no one who seeks God . . . All have sinned and fall short of the glory of God" (Rom 3:10, 11).

Perhaps part of the difference between Erasmus and Luther sprang from a failure to recognize the distinction between evil and sin clearly enough. Erasmus could admit that human beings were flawed; they quite often chose the wrong path. At the same time, they were capable of honorable thoughts and righteous actions. Above all, they could discern where they had failed, repent, and ask for mercy and forgiveness. For Luther, the human dilemma centered on the reality of sin. Human beings are in a state of perpetual rebellion against God, because they do not wish to submit their lives to God's control. They are ingenious in the ways

---

69. Ozment, *Age of Reform*, 290.
70. See Lockyer, *Hapsburg and Bourbon Europe*, 101.

they imagine that they can gain God's protection, whilst at the same time continue to keep God at arm's length. Their will is warped, out of shape, and they are totally incapable of putting it straight again. Only God can do that through creating in them a new nature, which is sensitive to the leading of God's Spirit and attentive to his word.

Toward the end of his life, Erasmus had become more pessimistic about the capabilities of human nature. He conceded that reason too is corrupted by sin. He recognized that Paul's use of the word "flesh" (*sarx*) refers to all of a person's faculties, not just the lust of physical appetites. In his final treatise, *De purite tabernaculi* (*On the Purity of the Tabernacle*), published in 1536 (the year of his death), he expressed serious doubts about the ability of human beings to be educated into a morally good life apart from God's grace. Without the direct action of God, humans were helpless to overcome sin in their lives. Studying alone the best tenets of moral philosophy was inadequate to repair the damage caused by human beings' decision to take total control of their own lives.

Ultimately, perhaps, Erasmus and Luther were not as far apart on the question of the freedom or bondage of the will as the highly contentious disputation of the mid-1520s would suggest. The two were undoubtedly separated by different temperaments and styles of argumentation. Erasmus was probably more concerned about Luther's willingness to heighten theological rhetoric, stir up dissension, and take irrevocable steps to break up the unity of the church, than with his reading of Scripture. Luther complained that Erasmus was unwilling to follow his own theological logic, in his critique of the church, by separating himself from untruth. The differences between them on the question of the human condition concerning freedom and enslavement continues, quite rightly, to be debated. It is a crucial consideration, given the amount of energy that has been expended in understanding and protecting humanity's alleged freedom. This subject will reappear a number of times during the course of this inquiry.

Review

The European Renaissance can legitimately be considered a distinctive period in human history. It has been the subject of various, and often contradictory, interpretations. Commentators belonging to subsequent generations have often been tempted to read the period through the eyes of their own historical epoch, finding the origin of what they regard as social and political progress in changes that were occurring at the earlier time. It requires a balanced assessment to avoid reading back into past history trends and emphases that belong to a later context.

The search in Europe for the meaning of human existence was being challenged by a number of developing situations occurring during the fifteenth and sixteenth centuries. There was the impact caused by encountering new worlds beyond Europe. The peoples of the continent were outgrowing the confines of the Mediterranean basin, to the East and to the West. Explorers, traders, adventurers, and colonizers were meeting cultures they found strange and perplexing. There was the impact of trade. Commerce with overseas merchants and the plundering of the wealth of the Americas brought a notable growth of wealth in the old world. In part, this wealth brought a remarkable artistic flourishing: painting, architecture, sculpture, engraving, wood carving, and so on. This blossoming of talent was also enabled by a relative political stability (in Italy at least) toward the end of the fifteenth century. Undoubtedly, artistic creators working in different mediums produced imaginative interpretations of how they saw the unfolding of human life in the light of the new questions being raised by the recurrence of the bubonic plague, urbanization, scientific discoveries, religious turmoil, and political upheaval.

Then, there was the impact of a number of distinguished scholars of the age who, thanks largely to the invention of the printing press, were disseminating their thoughts throughout Europe. Contrary to many later interpretations, on the whole, these writers were not so much celebrating the dawn of a new, advanced civilization, as extolling the virtues of a rediscovered past which was both pagan and Christian. Also, counter to some historical reconstructions, there is little evidence that a basic and tenacious adherence to the Christian faith by the peoples of Europe was being subverted and loosened by this new explosion of knowledge and experimentation. Underlying cosmological and ontological assumptions remained firmly rooted in the Christian tradition of belief. Nevertheless, it is true that important aspects of the Catholic Church's teaching, rites, ceremonies, and structures were being criticized and denounced from inside and eventually from outside established ecclesiastical order.

Probably the most significant debate concerning human nature coalesced around the question of human free will. This involved a number of subsidiary issues: To what extent does unconstrained human choice contribute to a person's salvation? What is the place of God's grace (his initiative and empowering) in bringing people to authentic faith? What role do the church's sacraments, dispensed by a priestly order, play in mediating this grace? How far are human beings in the grip of sin? Does it merely weaken human beings' resolve to do good? Or does it so corrupt their whole being that even their best endeavors are contaminated by self-serving motives? Is it only the human will that is affected by the perpetual predisposition to look after one's own interests first? Or, is human reason also molded and bent by the innate inclination to defend one's own views, whatever the arguments and evidence? The fundamental questions about human liberty, independence, and emancipation will journey with us through subsequent inquiries.

Questions

1. To what extent do you think it is legitimate to deduce people's fundamental beliefs from their artistic creations? Can you think of clear-cut examples from the time of the Renaissance where such a deduction is obvious?

2. From your study of the Renaissance, up to what point do you think the term "Renaissance humanism" is a helpful description of a particular movement of belief and formation?

3. To what degree do you think the encounter, at the time, between the peoples of Europe and those of the East and the Americas, might be properly described as a clash of civilizations?

4. How would you assess the significance of the debate between Erasmus and Luther concerning human free will? Give reasons for and against, considering that the issues they contested are still important today in assessing human nature.

CHAPTER 3

Human Reality in the Thought of John Locke

Introduction

"JOHN LOCKE REMAINS, AFTER over 300 years, a central figure in philosophy and a key thinker for an understanding of the culture and categories of modern society."[1] "John Locke is one of the great figures in the history of Western philosophy. He is one of the dozen or so thinkers who are remembered for their influential contributions across a broad spectrum of philosophical fields . . . he was a seminal thinker in the rise of the modern intellectual world."[2]

The quotations in praise of the achievements of this remarkable man by subsequent and current philosophers, political scientists, ethicists, and theologians could be multiplied several times over. Locke, whose life spanned over seventy years of one of the most turbulent political and intellectual periods of the last 500 years (1632–1704), was a thinker whose intellectual interests ranged over a wide spectrum. At the same time, through various friendships and his formal employment as physician (1667–1675) to Lord Ashley, the first Earl of Shaftesbury and the subsequent favor that he enjoyed during the reign of William and Mary (1689–1702), Locke became involved in high-level political affairs.

From the time of his return to England from exile in the Netherlands in 1689, caused by his alleged involvement in a plot to kidnap Charles II

---

1. Rogers, *Locke's Philosophy*, 1.
2. Mack, *John Locke*, 3.

and his brother, James,[3] till his death, he was engaged in a number of official duties, most particularly as a Commissioner of the Board of Trade. This latter occupation brought him directly in contact with the affairs of the British colonies of North America and caused him to reflect seriously on various moral and political issues to do with relations between the new settlers and the indigenous populations.

Locke is not remembered particularly for his political activities, except insofar as they influenced his political thinking. He is recognized more for his far-reaching and penetrating convictions about a number of significant philosophical, political, moral, and religious questions. However, at the time of his writing there was no appreciable divide between theoretical academic studies and their application and implementation in the public realm. His main writings, in order of their publication, were *A Letter Concerning Toleration* (1689), *Two Treatises on Civil Government* (1689), *An Essay Concerning Human Understanding* (1690), *Some Thoughts Concerning Education* (1693), *The Reasonableness of Christianity* (1695) and *A Commentary on the Epistles of St. Paul* (1705). Most of these works went through a period of gestation and revision, and more than one draft, before their final publication. This has led Locke's commentators to attempt to discern how his thought developed and matured over an approximately forty-year period.

My present interest in John Locke's thought is focused on what he believed about the nature and features of human reality. This is not necessarily an easy task, since Locke apparently never set out to produce a succinct statement of what he considered to be the meaning of being human. Rather, anyone interested in understanding his views on this subject will have to deduce them from his various writings. This is a complex procedure, as they will be required to discern what is and is not relevant to the task.

Obviously, to try to cover all of Locke's diverse thinking on a multiplicity of subjects would be impossible over the course of one chapter. Thus, aspects of his thought, which are highly significant in their own right, will have to be put on one side. Where, however, implications of his philosophical reasoning for his views on human reality appear to be applicable, they will be acknowledged.

Due to the limited space available to treat such an important subject, I will have to work with a number of assumptions. Firstly, Locke

---

3. The Rye House plot (1683). See Rogers, *Locke's Philosophy*, 1.

engaged with substantial philosophical topics, but he was not what today we might recognize as a professional philosopher, a person dedicated largely to teaching, research, and publishing in one philosophical discipline or another. This may be a worthwhile pursuit, but it was not one with which Locke involved himself:

> He was a very practical person, not at all tempted to speculate but, at the same time, concerned to identify and challenge the philosophical assumptions of his age.[4]

Thus, for example, although heavily criticized by some other contemporary philosophers (most notably Gottfried Leibnitz and George Berkeley), subsequent to their publication, his writings were not independently peer-reviewed before publication, as they would be today.

Secondly, Locke's thinking ranged across what today we would consider different disciplines, not only philosophy, but science, political and economic theories, moral philosophy, and theology as well. Many of his considered opinions, such as those on toleration, rights, identity, language, and freedom of conscience, were culled from a cross-fertilization process involving two or more of these areas.

Thirdly, although not to the liking of some of Locke's modern interpreters, his overarching worldview or core beliefs were firmly anchored in the Christian faith. Even though some detect in his beliefs the seeds of a secular outlook on life, he would not have understood how convictions about freedom, equality, rights, and responsibilities could possibly have stood on intellectually compelling grounds apart from a belief in a personal creator and redeemer, as he envisaged such. His belief in toleration, for example, did not extend to atheists or those he deemed religious deviants (such as Roman Catholics).

Fourthly, even though some find in Locke's writings a number of examples of inconsistency and contradiction, I will assume that the major lines of his reasoning are coherent. This does not imply that they never changed. He himself acknowledged, either openly or tacitly, that they did. I presume that, if the contradictions were many and flagrant, his thought would never have made the impact that it undoubtedly has.

---

4. Thomson, *On Locke*, 4.

From His Theory of Knowledge

An Essay Concerning Human Understanding was Locke's most theoretical work. In it he explores the nature of knowledge and how it may be obtained. The purpose was to discover how the human mind works through the processes of experience, introspection, reasoning and reflection and how the activities of the mind relate to perception of the external world:

> My purpose is to inquire into the original, certainty and extent of human knowledge; together with the grounds and degrees of belief, opinion and assent . . . All we need for my purposes is to consider the human ability to think.[5]

This is Locke's major contribution to the subject of epistemology. It is his attempt to unravel the complex procedures by which humans may come to know the truth, by being able to distinguish between certain and probable belief and opinion.

Although Locke's essay often proceeds by means of abstract thinking about theoretical concepts, such as ideas, qualities, substances, nominal and real essence, identity, and volition, he is not given to speculation. Indeed, he discourages needless speculation beyond all human capacity to know.[6]

Locke was guided by a fundamental conviction that had sprung from his acceptance of the reliability of the biblical account of the origin and design of human life in the world. Human minds have been created with all the faculties needed to live in God's world as God intended:

> Men have reason to be well satisfied with what God has thought fit for them, since he has given them whatsoever is necessary for the conveniences of life, and information of virtue; and has put in reach of their discovery the comfortable provision for this life and the way that leads to a better one.[7]

So the gaining of knowledge was for practical ends: how to enjoy and live the good life according to the way the Creator has ordered his creation.

---

5. Locke, *Essay Concerning Human Understanding*, I.1.2.
6. Thomson, *On Locke*, 12.
7. Locke, *Essay Concerning Human Understanding*, I.1.5.

Ideas

There are two main sources of our knowledge: sense-perception of the external world, and introspective reflection of the inner world of our thought processes. The two come together through ideas. Ideas are mental images or pictures of the objects of our senses. Perception of objects is transmitted through these pictures in our mind, which are a kind of mental analogue of what our senses are receiving from the world outside the mind. As Locke notes:

> (Ideas are produced in us) by the operation of insensible particles in our senses.[8]

The visible properties of the idea (or mental image) resemble visible properties of external objects which we see by the aid of ideas that they produce in us.[9]

From this brief outline of Locke's theory of perception, we can deduce one or two conclusions. First, Locke believed that all knowledge originated directly from the two sources of external objects and internal reflection. He completely dismissed the notion that humans are born with innate ideas, already hardwired into our minds from the time of our arrival in the world. We do not possess inherent knowledge. However, we do possess a natural disposition or faculty that gives us the capacity to acquire knowledge. Secondly, as a consequence of this initial belief, all knowledge is derived from experience. External objects have the power to produce certain ideas in our mind. This power resides in the primary qualities of the object. It is because of this belief that Locke has been categorized as an empiricist. So, thirdly, we perceive external objects, but not directly, for we can only directly perceive ideas in our mind. Fourthly, therefore, Locke's epistemology is a representative, indirect realism. Ideas are bridges to or windows on reality, and are necessary antecedents to understanding what the senses transmit from outside.

Locke has been accused of sustaining a rather confused notion of perception giving rise to knowledge, since he appears to be saying that we can only possess a first-order experience of the workings of our mind. Nevertheless, in book IV of the essay, he tries to clarify his understanding of reality by affirming, against all skeptical notions, that knowledge of everything outside of the workings of our mind is real:

---

8. Locke, *Essay Concerning Human Understanding*, II.18.13.
9. See, Lowe, *Locke on Human Understanding*, 38.

We are "invincibly conscious" of the effects on us of the external world, and the supposition that it might all be a dream is either pointless or manifestly improbable.[10]

This statement is assumed, rather than argued, on the pragmatic ground that a thoroughgoing skepticism is impossible to live by in practice.

Language

Book III of the essay is devoted almost exclusively to Locke's theories on language and the place of words in interhuman communication. He was well aware of the way in which words can be used cheaply and misused. For Locke, language was an ambiguous and perilous facility,

> in being liable to abuse by those more concerned to persuade us by the force of their rhetoric than by the cogency of their thoughts.[11]

He identifies the tendency of humans to use language with vague or obscure meanings as one of the chief obstacles to good communication:

> Vague and insignificant forms of speech, and abuse of language, have so long passed for mysteries of science; and hard and misapplied words, with little or no meaning, have, by prescription, such a right to be mistaken for deep learning and height of speculation, that it will not be easy to persuade either those who speak or those who hear them, that they are but the covers of ignorance, and hindrance of true knowledge.[12]

Nevertheless, language is indispensable for communication, and a cogent theory of language is necessary for good communication.

Locke begins his discussion with a reference to God as the explanation of why, of all the creatures on earth, human beings alone have a sophisticated verbal means of communication:

> God having designed man for a sociable creature, made him not only with an inclination and under the necessity to have fellowship with those of his own kind, but furnished him with language which was to be the great instrument and common tie

---

10. Locke, *Essay Concerning Human Understanding*, IV.2.14.
11. Lowe, *Locke on Human Understanding*, 143.
12. Locke, "Epistle to the Reader," 13–14.

of society, man therefore had his organs so fashioned as to be fit to frame articulate sounds which we call words.[13]

A plausible theory of language needs to be able to explicate the interconnections between thoughts, things, and the words used to express them. The relationship between thoughts and objects in the world is the most difficult, precisely because the way in which words are used as a medium of communication lacks a certain precision.

Locke, having stated that language as verbal communication is a unique feature of human beings and is indispensable for meaningful social discourse, proceeds to explicate his beliefs by assuming that

> words, in their primary or immediate signification, stand for nothing, but the Ideas in the mind of him that uses them.[14]

In other words, we can only be sure of the exactness of the use of words to signify our own ideas. In order to communicate these ideas to other people, we need to assume that the words we utter correspond in meaning to the ideas that other people have when using the same words. For this to be possible, we need some account of how interhuman discourse works publicly, otherwise we cannot be certain that ideas in the minds of two distinct people are sufficiently aligned to make understanding of the other's thought transparent.

At this point, Locke's thought appears to mystify what should be a relatively straightforward presentation of the requirements needed to ensure that the hearer interprets correctly the idea that the speaker wishes to convey. According to Lowe, Locke does not think that success or failure requires the production in the hearer's mind of ideas similar to those in the mind of the speaker. Communication can be adjudged successful when an idea produced in the mind of a hearer is relevantly related to the idea of which given words are signs in the mind of the speaker. Whether the ideas and perceptions of both people are similar is irrelevant. In the case of describing, for example, a bunch of red carnations to someone who cannot see them, what is required is that the other person should associate with the description "a bunch of red carnations" an idea that would correspond to her perception of the flowers were she able to see

---

13. Locke, *An Essay*, III.1.1.
14. Locke, *An Essay*, III.2.2.

them, irrespective of whether that idea corresponds to how the speaker imagines them.[15]

If this is how Locke envisages interhuman communication then, in the case of a bunch of red carnations nothing much may be lost. What the speaker has communicated is what the hearer sees in her mind as a bunch of red carnations. However, if that were true for all interpersonal communication, there would be little confidence that the speaker had really communicated something concrete to the hearer. The hearer would only have registered her own interpretation of what the speaker was saying.

It is not certain that Locke is consistent in his theory of language. According to Locke's own criticism of the abuse of language, some precision in the meaning of words used would seem to be a *sine qua non* for successful communication. Such precision surely demands commonly accepted definitions; otherwise how can one person be sure that they have entered as far as is possible into the thought processes of another? Locke tends to complicate issues of comprehensible communication by attempting to distinguish carefully between the signification, meaning, and definition of words:

> A definition is nothing else, but showing the meaning of one word by several other not synonymous terms. The meaning of words, being only the ideas they are made to stand for by him that uses them; the meaning of any term is then showed, or the word is defined when by other words, the idea it is made the sign of, and annexed to the mind of the speaker, is as it were represented, or set before the view of another; and thus its signification ascertained.[16]

In much less complex language, Locke is saying that a definition shows the meaning of a term, and the meaning of a term is explicitly identified by Locke with the idea that the term signifies.[17] I suppose that, if every time one used a word or concept (let us say "cow" or "justice") one was analyzing introspectively the exact mechanics of what was going on in the mind, it might be possible to distinguish terms in the way that Locke asserts. However, in ordinary conversation that is not happening. One uses words to make observations in the knowledge that they have a common meaning or definition in the language of use. Were this not

---

15. Lowe, *Locke on Human Understanding*, 153.
16. Locke, *An Essay*, III.4.6.
17. Losonsky, "Locke on Meaning and Signification," 125.

so, translation from one language to another would be too convoluted to proceed smoothly. If there is any doubt that in a conversation, group discussion, teaching session, speech, or other form of communication, words were being used in unfamiliar ways, the speaker would be asked to interpret her meaning by explaining in what way she is deviating from a standard definition.

The problem with Locke's theory of language is his insistence on the priority of ideas. As Michael Losonsky specifies,

> The source of Locke's problem of communication is that ideas are "peculiar" to the person having those ideas and that we have immediate knowledge only of our own particular ideas, and this peculiarity is compatible with a non-representational theory of ideas.[18]

A. C. Grayling believes that Locke's account of the use of language confuses two things: the public sense of a term and the psychological associations that might be aroused in the hearer. He argues that whatever contributes meaning cannot be the relation of signification to private ideas.[19] If Locke has genuinely confused two aspects of language in this way, then to return to a representational theory of language and communication would mean reversing the priority of ideas and public meaning.

Whenever a misunderstanding in communication occurs either because the speaker is using language in an idiosyncratic way or because the hearer is imagining a false understanding of the speaker's thought, the misunderstanding can only be cleared up through the medium of clarifying what is meant by a careful attention to definitions. Locke, in the last analysis, seemed to recognize that there had to be a process of rectification leading to mutual understanding if it were ever going to be possible to be assured that the ideas of different people were mutually intelligible. Thus, he affirms the ultimate priority of the definition of language over individual ideas to make possible a clarity of communication. We must endeavor to ensure that our words signify,

> as near as may be such ideas as common use has annexed them to.[20]

---

18. Losonsky, "Locke on Meaning and Signification," 133.
19. Grayling, *Philosophy*, 500.
20. Locke, *An Essay*, III.11.11.

From His Political Philosophy

The maxim, "What touches all must be approved by all" (*quod omnes tangit ab omnibus approbari debet*) was reinforced by Locke's incursion into political theory as a fundamental principle of law. He thoroughly shifted thinking about the foundation of political power from self-appointed authority to consent. He assumes that individual subjects are moral agents presumed to be the ultimate judges of how they wish to control their property, meaning not only their material goods, but also their lives and their freedoms. Nevertheless, they are not isolated individuals, accountable only to themselves. For mutual benefit and for their own well-being they will form themselves into social communities to protect what is rightly theirs:

> All being naturally free, equal, and independent, no one can be deprived of this freedom etc. and subjected to the political power of someone else, without his own consent. The only way anyone can strip off his natural liberty and clothe himself in the bonds of civil society is for him to agree with other men to unite into a community, so as to live together comfortably, safely and peaceably, in a secure enjoyment of their properties and a greater security against outsiders.[21]

Locke's account of the origin of stable government follows a logical sequence. It springs first from his foundational belief that all humans come into the world as equal beings. As equals, no one person (for example, an absolute monarch) or group of people has the prerogative to curtail the freedom of others by an arbitrary grasp of power. This implies that a limitation on freedom can only be given by the consent of the individual. Clearly, for an ordered and civilized society, some restraint on freedom is necessary if all people are to be guaranteed a measure of security to enjoy a freedom that is open to all. It is for this reason that individuals have agreed to come together to set up laws and institutions to enhance and protect the well-being of all. As not all can govern, the majority of a society will agree to hand over the authority to be governed to a group of representatives. However, the representatives have to earn their right to rule through being worthy of respect. If they abuse their power by threatening peace and good order or by failing to administer the law impartially, the subjects have a right to resist. Here in a nutshell the main elements of Locke's theory of political warrant are contained.

21. Locke, *Second Treatise of Government*, II.8.95.

Locke quite specifically outlines his understanding of the meaning of equality and the reasons why he believes that all are born equal:

> A state of equality, in which no-one has more power and authority than anyone else; because it is simply obvious that creatures of the same species and status, all born to the same advantages of nature and the use of the same abilities, should also be equal one amongst another without subordination or subjection to anyone else.[22]

Locke further clarifies his understanding of equality (which is not about individual capacities or even circumstances in life) and the extent and limits on freedom:

> The equality that all men have in respect of jurisdiction or dominion over one another ... the equality that is relevant to the business in hand, namely the equal right that every man has to his natural freedom, without being subjected to the will or authority of any other man.[23]

A man's freedom, his liberty of acting according to his own will, is based on his having reason, which can instruct him in the law he is to govern himself by, and to make him know to what extent he is left to the freedom of his own will[24]:

> He takes equality to be a self-evident fact of the natural order of things. He also accepts a long tradition in Western legal thought that accepted a doctrine of original equality.[25]

Locke firmly believed that the doctrine of natural equality could only be derived from the reality of God's existence as creator and sustainer of the world:

> In Locke's account, the shape of human, the way in which the extension of the predicate human is determined, is not in the end separable from the religious reasons that Locke cites in support of basic equality ... Someone in denial of or indifferent

---

22. Locke, *Second Treatise of Government*, II.2.4.
23. Locke, *Second Treatise of Government*, II.6.54.
24. Locke, *Second Treatise of Government*, II.6.63.
25. For example, in the writings of Nicholas of Cusa (1401–1464), who discusses the need for the German emperor to gain consent of the people to rule, based on "the common equal birth and the equal natural rights of all men" and in Richard Hooker's *Laws of Ecclesiastical Polity* (see Sigmund, *Selected Political Writings*, 306–8).

to the existence of God is not going to be able to come up with anything like the sort of basis for equality that Locke came up with.[26]

The Case of the Amerindians[27]

Locke's understanding of equality lacks a certain coherence in theory (which we will consider later in the chapter) and consistent application in practice. In 1696, Locke was appointed Commissioner of Trade and Plantations. This brought him into close contact with the situation in the colonies of North America. This, in turn, induced him to write his thoughts on the rights of the settlers with regard to the acquisition of property and co-extensively the status of the Amerindians as the original inhabitants of the land.

Locke made two big assumptions, both of which to differing degrees allowed him to justify the expropriation by the settlers of land used by the native peoples before the colonization period. Firstly, he assumed that these people lived still in what he called a "state of nature," that is a situation where there was no formal, contractual agreement to belong to a political community bound by communal laws and administered by representatives of those who have acquired a franchise to vote. Locke called this state "individual popular sovereignty."[28] It is characterized by every member of the community having the right to administer justice. The grounds for distinguishing between right and wrong and for punishing offenders are firmly rooted in natural law:

> By breaking the law of nature, the offender declares himself to live by some other rule than that of reason and common fairness (which is the standard that God has set for the actions of men, for their mutual security); and so he becomes dangerous to mankind because he has disregarded and broken the tie that is meant to secure them from injury and violence. This is an offence against the whole human species, and against the peace and safety that the law of nature provides for the species.[29]

---

26. Waldron, "God, Locke and Equality," 314, 318.

27. This section on the Case of the Amerindians is indebted to the following essay: James, "Two Treatises and Aboriginal Rights," 165–81.

28. James, "Two Treatises and Aboriginal Rights," 165.

29. Locke, *Second Treatise of Government*, II.2.8.

Locke concludes that this "state of nature" is a primitive form in the context of a worldwide historical development. One of the tasks of the colonizers was, therefore, to bring to the "First Nation" peoples a more ordered form of government in which there would be a "democratically" and accountable system of law-making, which would set commonly agreed rules and regulations for civilized living.

Secondly, Locke assumed that productive powers within a political society were derived from labor power and, therefore, the fruit of labor belonged to the person who added value to the products. However, unlike in the state of nature, ownership had to be regulated by civil society to avoid the unjust appropriation of another's labor. According to Locke, there were three outstanding defects in the state of nature: the lack of

> an established, settled, known law, received and accepted by common consent as the standard of right and wrong . . . a known and impartial judge, with authority to settle all differences according to the established law . . . a power to back up and support a correct sentence, and to enforce it properly.[30]

Moreover, the state of nature is inadequate, because of the "corruption and viciousness of degenerate men."[31]

Based on these two assumptions, Locke argues that it is perfectly legitimate for the colonizers to expropriate land formerly used by the native peoples for acquiring fruit, hunting deer, and growing corn. He adds three more considerations to his argument. Firstly, recognized, legal ownership of land (and presumably capital goods) is a necessary consequence of the growth of populations and the consequent scarcity of land and natural resources. In a quite peculiar line of reasoning, Locke states that

> All the fruits (the world) naturally produces and the animals that it feeds . . . belong to mankind in common . . . But they were given for the use of men; and before they can be useful or beneficial to any particular man there must be some way for a particular man to appropriate them . . . If any one of them is to get any benefit from fruit or venison, the food in question must be his and his (i.e. part of him) in such a way that no-one else retains any right to it.[32]

---

30. Locke, *Second Treatise of Government*, II.9.124–26.

31. Locke, *Second Treatise of Government*, II.9.128.

32. Locke, *Second Treatise of Government*, II.5.26.

The first and second parts of this statement do not seem to be logically connected. However, Locke was keen to establish the right of private property. This seems to be the fundamental consideration from which follow both his theory of added value (when he takes something from the state that nature has provided and left it in "he mixes his labor with it, thus joining to it, something that is his own, thus making it his property"[33]) and his theory of political societies.

Secondly, from the concept of added value he deduces the right of expropriation (without consent) of what he considers to be land that is unproductive; all land that is not under active cultivation is said to be vacant. Therefore, anyone who is able to use it in such a way that it produces enough for many more people (added value) than the producer's own family is justified in claiming title to it.

Thirdly, a settler's right of ownership is guaranteed by his successful defense of his expropriated land against the aggression of the original people's attempt to recover land taken without any formal pact or contract. According to Locke, such militancy violated natural law, allowing the settlers' right to defend themselves and avail themselves of the rights of war.[34] Expropriation (not permitted in Europe) was justified on the basis of there being huge tracts of uninhabited land in North America, which were more than sufficient for both the original inhabitants and the emigrants from Europe, and as long as no one was impoverished as a result.

Eric Mack has provided a helpful summary of the basic tenets of Locke's political philosophy. Each individual possesses natural rights of life, liberty, and property. For each, individual rights define boundaries of a domain within which individuals may do as they see fit. Individuals' rights to the fruit of their labor and what they acquire in exchange for the fruits of their labor flow from their rights over themselves and their labor. The legitimate function of government is the articulation and protection of individuals' lives, liberty, and property. Governments derive their legitimate authority from the consent of the governed. Political rulers who infringe upon or systematically fail to protect individuals' rights may be rightly resisted and replaced. Political authority does not extend to matters of deciding on religious beliefs. Respect for the rights of

---

33. Locke, *Second Treatise of Government*, II.5.27.
34. Tully, "Two Treatises and Aboriginal Rights," 172.

each individual and voluntary associations of individuals requires broad religious toleration.³⁵

Rights

> Locke stands as the historically most salient expositor of a rights-oriented classical liberalism because of his case for liberalism and its protection by a narrowly circumscribed government and for resistance against tyrannical government propelled by his contentions about rights.³⁶

Certainly, John Locke's exposition and defense of natural rights has contributed much to his prominence as a Christian moral philosopher. According to Paul Sigmund,³⁷ there were two main pictures of the human moral condition abroad at the time of Locke. Firstly, some held to a firm deontological moral position in which God gives binding laws to all, based on his prerogative as creator with a comprehensive plan for the well-being of his creation. Human creatures have a duty to treat other humans well. Breaches of this moral duty are wrongs committed, in the first place, to God, and only derivatively to the others. So, rights of third parties were based on the duties owed to God. Thus, for example, liberties would be protected because humans have a duty owed to God to implement the freedom to act, without which justice and injustice would cease having any meaning. In this first view, the language of rights is not prominent, being only a byproduct of obligation.

Secondly, whilst God remains the creator, planner, and lawgiver, the ends promoted by God's law are detachable, so that law is more for us than over us. Law facilitates human ends, as these are decided, not just by a strict interpretation of ancient law codes, but through conscience and reason. In this view, humans are seen less as creatures of God with responsibilities derived from his will and purpose, and more like fellow creatures, equals in every respect, to be taken seriously in and for themselves. So, duties are regarded as owed to others, not just in respect of

---

35. Mack, *John Locke*, 4. What Locke's whole discourse on the "state of nature," political government, property, and the justification of war in "self-defense" says about his view of human reality, I will endeavor to summarize in the conclusion to the chapter.

36. Mack, *John Locke*, 4.

37. Sigmund, *Selected Political Writings*, 286–90.

others. According to this account, rights come into much sharper focus, based on the individual's independent worth and the dignity of being one's own person. This emphasis leads quite logically to the pressing of all sorts of claims concerning one's entitlements.

Sigmund believes that Locke embraced both positions simultaneously, sometimes emphasizing one, sometimes the other. It is perfectly intelligible for moral duties to be owed both to God and other people (the two chief commandments of the law are to love God and one's neighbor). The two parties hold corresponding moral rights: God, because he is creator and lawmaker; humans, because each person is equal in being a rational and purposive being. The natural characteristics of human nature point to the sanctity of life, with a reciprocal freedom to plan one's life without interference from some self-appointed guardian of morality.[38] In due time, the second position gained the ascendency in ways and for reasons I will explore in the next chapter.[39]

For Locke, then, rights are grounded both in God's claims as creator and in natural human capacities. The theory may be much easier to articulate than the practice, for Locke, in devising policies in the real world, was quite often not as consistent as his moral assumptions would lead one to believe. We have already recounted how certain pragmatic arguments allowed him to justify the expropriation of utilized land in North America, even though he defended theoretically the equality of all peoples, their right to be free from harm, their individual dignity, and their natural right to own the means of preservation. Locke also defended the right of taking people as slaves as long as they were the aggressors in war and those wronged conquered them in a just cause, using just means, even though he declared (theoretically) that

> the natural liberty of man is to be free from any superior power on earth.[40]

He himself was involved in the African slave trade, although he did make an exception in the case of forcing the Amerindian peoples into

---

38. At this point, the argument touches on Locke's view of toleration. This will be reviewed more fully in the next section.

39. For the time being, it is enough to cite Charles Taylor's summary of the reasons for a gradual drift toward an individualistic interpretation of rights in his study, *Secular Age*, 170–71.

40. Locke, *Second Treatise of Government*, II.4.22.

slavery.[41] Clearly, as is still the case today, neither moral philosophers, nor society at large, have yet worked out how to deal with conflicting rights.

Toleration

In his preface to Locke's "A Letter Concerning Toleration," William Popple, who translated it from the original Latin into English, declares that "absolute liberty, just and true liberty, equal and impartial liberty is the thing that we stand in need of."[42] He is referring to freedom of religion within any nation, but particularly within England.

Locke disagreed with Thomas Hobbes's position on the relation between citizenship and religion expounded in his *Leviathan*. The latter believed that an outward uniform confession of the same religion was the key to a smoothly-operating civil society. Locke took the opposite view, arguing that, by permitting more religious groups, magistrates were likely to lessen civil unrest, because attempts to interfere in religious practices actually increased confrontations. Locke's primary goal was to distinguish exactly the business of civil government from that of religion. He sought to persuade the reader that political government and the church have quite different functions. The former is instituted to promote material interests, relating to the general welfare of the whole population, while the latter exists to promote spiritual concerns. Because the two have independent roles, they must be considered separate institutions:

> The whole jurisdiction of the magistrate reaches only to these civil concernments . . . and that it neither can nor ought in any manner to be extended to the salvation of souls.[43]

> [Ecclesiastical authority] ought to be confined within the bounds of the church, nor can it in any manner be extended to civil affairs; because the church itself is a thing absolutely separate and distinct from the commonwealth. The boundaries on both sides are fixed and immoveable.[44]

---

41. See, Farr, "So Vile and Miserable," 374–79.
42. Popple, "To the Reader," 125–26.
43. Sigmund, *Selected Political Writings*, 130.
44. Sigmund, *Selected Political Writings*, 138.

Here, Locke is establishing strongly the principle of the entire separation of church and state. He gives a number of powerful arguments in favor of this position.

Firstly, the unity of Christians is not the same as uniformity. According to Locke, there is an irreducible essence to Christian belief which all Christian groups share, and then there are distinct beliefs and practices, based on historical circumstances, divergent traditions, and fanciful speculations, which are emphasized by different groups. Problems arise when politically more powerful Christian institutions insist on the whole nation adhering to one interpretation of what are called adiaphora, or secondary matters, about which a latitude of belief ought to be permitted. These are would-be beliefs and practices over which the church has never come to a unified, settled mind.

Secondly, Locke, taking as an assumption the nonexistence of innate ideas (i.e., universally intrinsic, intuitive knowledge) argues that certainty about any matter is not attainable. Therefore, the church should not regard as inerrant any dogma that it may wish to proclaim, and even less should civil authority insist on the absolute necessity, on pain of punishment, of confessing such beliefs. For, if we have no warrant for our claims to absolute certainty, nor have we the right to condemn others for differing beliefs.

Thirdly, the magistrate's only concern is to maintain peace among citizens by upholding those laws in which he has competence; clearly in matters of doctrine and religious practice the magistrate has no more authority than any other member of the church, and may have less. Therefore, he is not qualified, simply on the basis of his office, to impose his own opinion:

> For all these opinions, except such of them as are apparently destructive to human society, being things either of indifferency or doubt, and neither the magistrate nor subject being on either side infallible, he (the magistrate) ought no further to consider them then as the making laws and interposing his authority in such opinions may conduce to the welfare and safety of his people.[45]

Fourthly, and this is probably the most powerful argument, belief that is coerced ceases immediately to represent a faith that is personal to the individual:

---

45. Rogers, *Locke's Philosophy*, 5–6.

> The care of souls cannot belong to the civil magistrate, because his power consists only in outward force: but true and saving religion consists in the inward persuasion of the mind without which nothing can be acceptable to God. And such is the nature of the understanding, that it cannot be compelled to the belief of anything by outward force.[46]

In spite of these arguments in favor of freedom of belief in a society that still attached great importance to national unity through (at least outward) conformity, Locke was not prepared to allow tolerance to extend to ideas that, in his opinion, have antisocial consequences. Thus, he held that atheists' beliefs should not be tolerated:

> Those are not at all to be tolerated who deny the being of God . . . Promises, covenants, and oaths, which are the bonds of human society, can have no hold upon an atheist. The taking away of God, though but even in thought, dissolves all. Besides also, those that by their atheism undermine and destroy all religion, can have no pretense of religion whereupon to challenge the privilege of a toleration.[47]

This is an interesting argument. Locke assumes that those who deny the existence of God cannot be trusted to keep their word. He does not say why. One can only presume that he thought that such people, having abandoned the ultimate guarantor of all truth-telling and justice, would have no compunction in breaking their pledge, if it suited their self-interests. Nor did Locke say what should be done about atheists in the kind of society of which he approved.

The second class of people Locke would not tolerate were those who, through their religious convictions, owed their first allegiance to a foreign power. Although he does not mention them by name, he was clearly thinking of Roman Catholics (papists):

> That church can have no right to be tolerated by the magistrate, which is constituted on such a bottom that all those who enter it, do thereby, *ipso facto*, deliver themselves up to the protection and service of another prince. For by this means the magistrate would give way to the settling of a foreign jurisdiction in his own country.[48]

---

46. Sigmund, *Selected Political Writings*, 130–31.
47. Sigmund, *Selected Political Writings*, 158.
48. Sigmund, *Selected Political Writings*, 157.

Locke assumes in this case that Roman Catholics are bound to work for the imposition of a Catholic monarchy in England, who, he also assumes, would be bound to work for the conversion of the nation back to the Catholic faith.

Locke's views on toleration are an attempt to settle a perplexing question: Just how far can diverse views be tolerated in a society? He probably raises as many questions as he answers. The question is still very much part of a continuing debate about the extent of freedom of belief, expression and action. Locke seems to suppose that beliefs can be divided into those which affect issues of personal salvation and those which concern the public affairs of society. So on the one hand he emphatically rejects the power and authority of civil society to dictate the terms on which people believe certain doctrines and renounce others. On the other hand, he says (equally emphatically),

> No opinions contrary to human society, or to those moral rules which are necessary to the preservation of civil society, are to be tolerated by the magistrate.[49]

The major problem, which today an increasingly secular society does not appear to know how to handle, is the attempt to draw a rigid distinction between private conviction and public consensus. Ultimately, all moral rules necessary for the preservation of civil society are based on private beliefs, whether of a religious or secular nature.[50]

Freedom of the Will

In the previous chapter, in the acrimonious debate between Erasmus and Luther, we saw the importance of the nature and extent of peoples' free will to choose, resolve, and act according to their purposes. In that context, the altercation was conducted largely on theological grounds. In the case of Locke, the examination of the issue takes a more philosophical bent. The matter is made complex by the fact that Locke's many interpreters do not agree about what he believed. In part, this may be due to the fact that he was not himself consistent. Nevertheless, his thoughts on the

---

49. Sigmund, *Selected Political Writings*, 156.

50. This is a debate that exceeds our present discussion. Locke was optimistic about the possibility of settling the issue in such a way that private beliefs would by and large coincide with public morals. For a contemporary review of the question, see Trigg, *Equality, Freedom and Religion*.

subject contribute enormously to his overall view of human reality. He believed, for example, that humans' ability to control or manipulate their own wills through procedures in which they voluntarily engage in practical reasoning is a distinctive feature of human (as opposed to animal) agency, importantly connected to notions of freedom and responsibility.[51]

His view of freedom is an appropriate place to begin his train of thought. In his terminology, freedom occurs when a person has the power to act, or not act, according to what the mind directs. It means having a choice as well as choosing. So a person is free when they are able to do something because they chose to do it, or, alternatively, to refuse to do it or to do something different. Freedom does not require an action to be free of external causes. A person's willing or choosing may be strongly influenced by outside factors, such as others' opinions, advertising, family traditions, laws, religious convictions, and so on. These factors, however, do not determine a person's decision to act in a certain way, in the case that they have acted freely.

On the other hand, all involuntary actions are necessary, whether they are bodily functions done instinctively, such as facial expressions, or forced on one by a superior power. In the latter case, actions are necessary when the agent cannot avoid doing them, because either internal or external constraints prevent alternatives from being taken.

Locke equivocated on the question of whether the will is free. In an earlier version of his thoughts, he proposed that the will is not free, only that the agent is free. He thought the question as to whether a person is at liberty to will was absurd:

> The absurdity lies not in the question itself, but in an affirmative answer to it; that it consists in some sort of viciously infinite succession of wills; and that it arises from the idea of . . . willing to will . . . (This is) an argument of the *reductio ad absurdum* form.[52]

In a later edition of his work, he recognized that there could be situations (which often occur in real life) when the will, as such, is free. These concerns those occasions when the subject suspends her decision on some matter. The will is free, because the person can will to choose a particular action or not to choose it. A person may desire to follow a course of action and could say to himself, "I will do it," and he does it.

---

51. See the discussion in Lowe, *Locke on Human Understanding*, 134.
52. Chappell, "Locke on Freedom," 108.

Equally, the same person could suspend a decision about the case, saying "although I greatly desire to implement this decision, I need to think more carefully about whether the decision is wise." So, he forebears from accomplishing it, at least for the moment. Locke sums up the conclusion he eventually came to in this way:

> In most cases a man is not at liberty to forebear the act of volition; he must exert an act of his will, whereby the action proposed, is made to exist, or not to exist. But yet there is a case wherein a man is at liberty in respect of willing, and that is the choosing of a remote good as an end to be pursued. Here a man may suspend the act of his choice from being determined for or against the thing proposed, till he has examined, whether it be really of a nature in itself and consequences to make him happy, or no.[53]

In 1702, Locke wrote a letter to his friend Philipp Van Limborch, which seems to clarify his final position on the freedom of the will:

> In my opinion a man is free in every action, as well of willing as of understanding, if he was able to have abstained from that action of willing or understanding . . . Where he was able to will or not to will, he is free.[54]

Identity

Locke seems to have been the first philosopher to address the problem of personal identity in anything like its modern form. Indeed, it was he who was responsible for setting the terms of the modern debate, and his views on the issue remain highly influential.[55]

Locke begins his discussion by distinguishing between a human and a person: a human is a member of a particular species; a person is a distinct, intelligent, thinking being that considers itself as itself. Most importantly for Locke, the characterization is used as a forensic term:

> Person, as I take it, is the name for this self. Wherever a man finds what he calls himself, there I think another man may say is the same person. It is a forensic term appropriating actions and

---

53. Locke, *Essay Concerning Human Understanding*, II.21.71.
54. Chappell, "Locke on Freedom," 119.
55. Lowe, *Locke on Human Understanding*, 102.

their merit; and so belongs only to intelligent agents capable of a law, and happiness or misery.[56]

In other words, a person is a rational being, responsible morally in law for what he thinks and does.

Forensic finds its use in contexts in which questions of responsibility (i.e. praise and blame, punishment and reward) are uppermost.[57] A person (or self) is constituted by consciousness:

> Personality extends itself beyond present existence to what is past only by consciousness, whereby it becomes concerned and accountable, owns and imputes to itself past action, just upon the same ground, and for the same reason that it does the present.[58]

Locke links the concept of person with consciousness in respect of past and present thinking and actions, and with moral and legal accountability with respect to right or wrong action. Locke's understanding of consciousness allows him to separate off the two spheres of inner mental processes and outer sensations. Thinking, contrary to Descartes's idea, is not identified by Locke as the essence of the mind, but as one of its operations.[59]

Locke appears to say that consciousness is an inner awareness or sensibility that an individual has of being the same self now as at earlier times, and will be in the future, and this is the substance of his or her identity:

> There is something, himself, that he is concerned for and wants to be happy; and that this self has existed continuously for a period of time and therefore may exist for months and years to come ... and thus may be the same self carried by consciousness into the future.[60]

This would seem to link closely consciousness, identity, and memory. However, in Locke's thought there is some ambiguity about the role that memory plays in a person's self-identity. Identity seems to require a continuity over time as a subject of experience. In the case of each individual

---

56. Locke, *Essay Concerning Human Understanding*, II.27.26.
57. See Stawson, *Locke on Personal Identity*, 4.
58. Locke, *Essay Concerning Human Understanding*, II.27.26.
59. See Sandford, "Introduction."
60. Locke, *Essay Concerning Human Understanding*, II.27.25.

this comprises a unique set of experiences about which only the person concerned can reflect. This must assume a continuity of consciousness by which a person recognizes themselves today to be the same person as they were yesterday. And yet, consciousness is not the same as memory, for in the case of one's autobiography, one may be able to remember a fact that was pertinent to one's being at a particular moment, without being able to recall how one felt about it at the time.

The problem for Locke is how to give an account of his personal continuity in terms of his understanding of consciousness. He sets out his thesis thus:

> Consciousness always accompanies thinking, and makes everyone to be what he calls self and thereby distinguishes himself from all other thinking things; in this alone consists personal identity, i.e. the sameness of a rational being; and as far as the consciousness can be extended backwards to any past action or thought, so far reached the identity of that person; it is the same self now as it was then; and this present self that now reflects on it is the one by which that action was performed.[61]

Locke appears to be saying that a person is identical today with herself in the past by virtue of the fact that she still remembers the thoughts she had and the actions she performed at that time.[62] If this is so, then memory is a crucial part of consciousness over time. However, Locke also appears to believe that if the person cannot today recollect the past deeds and thoughts of some person, deemed to be the same, then she cannot be that same person who thought and acted in those ways.

This has, in his theory, serious implications in judicial cases, for Locke believed that a person should not be held accountable for deeds he has no recollection of performing in the past. A conviction could only be secured if the prosecution could prove that the defendant did have such a recollection. Conclusive evidence for a felony having been committed would then depend wholly on a person's internal conscious memory. It makes the case for identity of the same person completely subjective or, as Lowe argues, psychological. This is only one aspect of a person's identity.[63] Locke's view of consciousness, identity, and person-

---

61. Locke, *Essay Concerning Human Understanding*, II.27.9.

62. Lowe, *Locke on Human Understanding*, 104–5.

63. Locke's defense of his consciousness view of personal identity against the above objection, in *Essay Concerning Human Understanding*, II.27.20, is unconvincing. He simply reasserts his presupposition that an individual's identity as human and person

hood would immobilize the administration of justice, a conclusion that presumably he would not wish to reach as he considers "person" to be a forensic term. This test case probably means that his neat division of an individual into human (substance) and person is not sustainable. Identity has to be predicated on both realities.

Morality

The forensic account of identity summarized above brings us to consider what Locke thought about the moral life. Theoretically, he is obliged to concede that the issue of the good and the right cannot be settled empirically; it is a reality prior to experience, for it can be ascertained by deduction or intuition. To use the famous truism, what ought to be the case cannot ultimately be inferred from what is the case, without begging the question about the origin of the content of the good and the right.

For Locke, morality possesses three main characteristics. Firstly, what is right or wrong reflects a natural law. In other words, through reason it is possible to acquire knowledge about those beliefs and actions that maximize human beings' flourishing. As Locke rejects the notion of innate ideas, so he rejects the belief that moral laws are inherent to a human's constitution. Secondly, there are moral absolutes which are defined by being in accordance with the will of God. So, the good is defined by the laws that God has set down. Locke argues that the concept of obligation requires laws and a supreme lawmaker. Moreover, the reality of punishment for wrongdoing and reward for virtuous living ultimately presupposes an afterlife, for otherwise there would be no conclusive evidence that justice was ultimately achievable and completed. Thirdly, the main motivation for the moral life is the prospect of gaining pleasure and avoiding pain:

> Anything that is apt to produce pleasure in us we call "good," and what is able to produce pain we call "bad," just because it is apt to produce in us the pleasure or pain that constitutes our happiness or misery.[64]

This latter precept seems to contradict the other two, as it is based on a consequentialist account of morality that begs the question about

---

can be wholly distinguished, whereas the "I" in question partakes of both aspects of the individual's sameness.

64. Locke, *Essay Concerning Human Understanding*, II.21.42.

what is really good and bad. It is a matter of observation that something generally considered evil (such as torture) can induce considerable pleasure for the person who indulges in it. Here, Locke seems to betray an unwarranted optimism in his view of human nature and also appears to advocate an individualistic and relativistic view of how good and bad are to be judged.

Locke allows, up to a point, a certain evidentialist basis for moral conclusions: God's existence can be extrapolated from the manifestation of design in the natural world: through observation and reflection, God's particular purposes in creating humans can be inferred from the way they function best. The fulfilling of these purposes, codified in specific commandments, is the content of the good, and the thwarting of them, the bad. This account is often referred to as "rule-utilitarianism." Some interpreters of Locke find a certain amount of inconsistency in his account of the relation between the basis and the motivation of following the good and avoiding evil.[65]

Religious Faith

Although I have left it to the end, the part that Locke's version of the Christian faith played in his philosophical, political, and moral thinking is in many ways the most important aspect of all his great variety of ideas. Locke was brought up by his parents in a form of Calvinism, which undoubtedly influenced his thinking throughout his life. However, he did not allow himself to be bound by any particular contemporary Christian school of thought. His many interpreters have found it difficult to say exactly what his views were on certain key doctrines of the Christian faith, such as the Trinity and the atonement. It may be, of course, that he did not hold a consistent position on some of the main elements of the faith.

We have already seen how his political and religious views intermeshed and how he believed that human rights ultimately required the sanction of creation in the image of God to make any sense. Locke was a person who wished his theoretical thought to have practical implications; hence, he was not given to speculative beliefs. Nevertheless, in the two major works where he expounded his Christian beliefs more fully, he usually followed an orthodox line.[66]

---

65. See, for example, Simmons, "From the Lockean Theory," 286–90.
66. *The Reasonableness of Christianity* (1695) and *A Paraphrase and Notes upon the*

It is not, however, the intention of this study to do a review of Locke's beliefs about Christian faith, except insofar as they shed light on his understanding of the reality of being human. The main themes are the nature, effect, and overcoming of human sin, the possibility of knowing God through human reason, human beings as creatures of a personal creation, and the place of reason in adjudicating true belief.

Locke begins his treatise on the reasonableness of Christianity with a reference to the Christian doctrine of redemption and its counterpart in the fall of Adam:

> It is obvious to anyone, who reads the New Testament, that the doctrine of redemption, and consequently of the Gospel is founded upon the supposition of Adam's fall. To understand, therefore, that we are restored by Jesus Christ, we must consider what the Scriptures show we lost by Adam.[67]

In the current discussions of his time about the effect of Adam's original act of disobedience to God's clear command, whereby he overstepped the generous freedom that God allowed him in the garden, Locke takes a mediating position between what he saw as two erroneous extremes. On the one hand, he repudiated the notion that all people are already condemned to eternal punishment for Adam's transgression, seeing that without every individual's consent, he could not be their representative, and seeing that such a course would not be consistent with God's justice. On the other hand, he equally rejects the idea that God is so good and merciful that he would not need to provide redemption, and that therefore Jesus is not a savior but no more than the restorer and preacher of pure natural religion, a belief that, in Locke's opinion, does violence to the whole tenor of the New Testament.

According to some commentators, Locke abandoned the orthodox view of original sin. Thus Rogers says,

> Locke, in his later writings at least, was never committed to explaining human sin by the fall, merely by human nature ... (Locke's position) leaves no room for the imputation of Adam's sin and punishment to mankind.[68]

Epistles of St Paul (1687, published after his death in 1704).

67. Locke, *Reasonableness of Christianity*, para. 1.

68. Rogers, *Locke's Philosophy*, 26.

This is a mistaken view. Other writers have a more accurate description of the subtlety of Locke's position. Thus, Paul Sigmund emphasizes Locke's belief that

> because of the Fall it is difficult, although not impossible, for man to know the good, and even more difficult to do it. Human weakness can only be remedied by faith in Jesus as the Messiah and repentance for sin.[69]

Spellman rightly interprets Locke to state that people have lost both the state of immortality and original righteousness through the disobedience of Adam.[70] However, for Locke the doctrine of the fall was not just some kind of legal fiction, for humans have always and everywhere demonstrated their complete inability to live by the standards of God's holy law and thus to justify themselves in his sight by their righteous deeds. Though they can by reason know the requirements of the law, sin in the form of lust, inadvertency, and fearful apprehension has blinded their reason and, instead, they have turned to all kinds of polytheism and idolatry. Only the light that the Messiah has brought into the world can dispel the darkness of human perversion, and only his death and resurrection can bring reconciliation, forgiveness, and eternal life.[71]

How far, according to Locke, could human reason reach in knowing God? The position that Locke seemed to take made a big division between what should be the case and what in practice was the reality. Locke wrote,

> Though the works of nature in every part of them, sufficiently evidence a Deity; yet the world made so little use of their reason, that they saw him not, where even by the impression of himself, he was easy to be found.[72]

In other words, the existence of God is an obvious deduction from any purely rational observation of the universe in which we live, yet reason has let us down. It has been distorted by other factors that have intervened in our psyche:

> Natural religion in its fullest extent, was nowhere, that I know, taken care of, by the force of natural reason . . . Experience

---

69. Sigmund, *Selected Political Writings*, 361; emphasis added.
70. Spellman, "Locke and Original Sin," 364; italics added.
71. Locke, *Reasonableness of Christianity*, paras. 236–38.
72. Locke, *Reasonableness of Christianity*, para. 238.

shows, that the knowledge of morality, by mere natural light . . . makes but a slow progress, and little advance in the world. And the reason for it is not hard to be found in men's necessities, passions, vices, and mistaken interests; which turn their thoughts another way.[73]

Reason has a potential power, but the reality of human life demonstrates conclusively that it is corrupted, when it comes to issues of knowing God and the content of a righteous life. Jeremy Waldron sums up Locke's basic premise:

> In Locke's account, the shape of human, the way in which the extension of the predicate human is determined, is not in the end separable from the religious reasons that Locke cites in support of basic equality.[74]

Paul Sigmund agrees:

> The natural equality on which Locke based his political theory is neither hedonist, relativist nor secular. It is based on a belief in shared human nature, rationality and creation by God.[75]

Unwaveringly, Locke assumes that all human beings are creatures of a living, personal God; or, as he prefers it, his workmanship. He simply believes the teaching of the Judeo-Christian Scriptures at this point. The basic premise that shapes Locke's concept of human reality is that all are the servants of one Sovereign Master, sent into the world by his order, and about his business. We must, therefore, treat them as his property, whose workmanship they are, made to last during his, not one another's, pleasure. This being so, no human has the authority to destroy, harm, or exploit another. Someone in denial of, or indifferent to, the existence of God, is not going to be able to come up with anything like the sort of basis for equality that Locke came up with.[76] As we shall see in subsequent chapters, those who disagree with Locke at this point have had to invent another rationale for their concept of human nature. It is they who have created a notable watershed in the intellectual history of Western Europe.

Finally, we come to Locke's thinking on the relationship between faith and reason. Although reason is often inadequate to the task, as

---

73. Locke, *Reasonableness of Christianity*, para. 241.
74. Waldron, "God, Locke and Equality," 314.
75. Sigmund, "Equality, Legitimacy and Majority Rule," 313.
76. Waldron, "God, Locke and Equality," 318.

we have already shown, Locke believed that humans, by light of their reasoning powers, are capable of knowing certainly that there is a God. By reflecting on our own experience of ourselves, we must come to the logical conclusion that we could not exist as we are without there being an external cause, which like us is also personal, rational, knowledgeable, and willing. In other words, there must be a being, corresponding to us, more perfect than ourselves, that has produced us:

> Nothing cannot produce a being . . . If we know there is some real being (humans), and that nonentity cannot produce any real being, it is an evident demonstration that from eternity there has been something; since what was not from eternity had a beginning, and what had a beginning must be produced from something else.

This is as succinct an exposition of the cosmological argument for the existence of God, taken not just from an observation of the amazing nature of the universe, but from considering our own nature, as may be found. He continues:

> That eternal being must be most knowing. Again a man finds in himself perception and knowledge. We have then got one step further; and we are certain now that there is not only some being, but some knowing, intelligent being in the world . . . For it is as repugnant to the idea of senseless matter that it should be put into itself sense, perception, and knowledge, as it is repugnant to the idea of a triangle that it should put into itself greater angles than two right ones. This from a consideration of ourselves, and what we infallibly find in our own constitutions, our reason leads us to the knowledge of this certain and evident truth. That there is an eternal, most powerful, and most knowing being.[77]

Reason ought to be able to get us this far. Nevertheless, due to both the inherent limitations of reason and its propensity to go astray, human beings need to rely on another source of knowledge, namely revelation. Revelation is God disclosing truth that we could not know apart from his communication. This disclosure is set down in written form in the Bible. If humans do not heed scriptural revelation, they go astray. So faith discerns truth that goes beyond reason, but does not contradict it. Particularly in the area of right conduct (i.e. how we should live), humans

---

77. These quotes are taken from Locke, *Essay Conerning Human Understanding*, IV.10.1, 3, 5, 6.

cannot arrive at correct judgments by making deductions from what exists before their eyes. At the same time, reason, properly used, aids us in distinguishing between what is likely to be true revelation, and what false. So,

> When he illuminates the mind with supernatural light, He does not extinguish that which is natural . . . Reason must be our last judge and guide in everything.[78]

Locke is convinced that we have a duty to avoid error. To fulfill this duty, it is helpful to distinguish between belief, knowledge, and faith. Belief is the conviction that a proposition is true, knowing is justifying its truth, and faith is a personal act of commitment to its truth. This implies that evidence is an important part of knowledge and believing. Evidence may go beyond our immediate experience, as in the case of miracles, but it will never conclude that anything is true that is clearly absurd. Miracles may be unusual, quite often claims made for them may be fanciful and ingenuous, but there is no ultimate reason why they could not happen, given a rationally justifiable belief in a supremely powerful and free divine agent.

Locke sums up how he envisages the relationship between faith and reason:

> Reason . . . I take to be the discovery of the certainty or probability of such propositions or truths, which the mind arrives at by deduction made from such ideas, which it has got by the use of its natural faculties; viz. by sensation or reflection. Faith . . . is the assent to any proposition, not thus made out by the deductions of reason; but upon the credit of the proposer, as coming from God, in some extraordinary way of communication. This way of discovering truths to men we call revelation.[79]

Critical Summary

The breadth and depth of Locke's thinking about a wide variety of topics has, I hope, been shown in this brief survey of his interests. Not for nothing has so much interest been shown in his ideas and opinions by so many over such a length of time. Inevitably, his thought has been subjected to

---

78. Locke, *Essay Conerning Human Understanding*, IV.19.4.
79. Locke, *Essay Conerning Human Understanding*, IV.18.2.

much critical examination. In numerous instances, he has been defended against detractors; in other cases his reasoning and opinions have been found ambiguous, inconsistent, or just plain wrong.

As in all assessments of another person's beliefs, the evaluation will depend to a considerable extent on how much of the person's fundamental worldview the critic shares. Within the constraints of a basically mainstream Christian faith,[80] Locke was an original thinker. Locke was confident that a right understanding of God's revelation, transmitted through Scripture and the person of Jesus Christ, was a totally reliable guide to the ultimate truth about existence. Nevertheless, this understanding was not mere faith; even less credulity. Locke was opposed to what is called in the philosophy of religion, "fideism," namely a strong conviction about nonempirical realities that are ascertainable by faith independently of reason. A fideist is someone who argues that faith does not need to meet standards of evidence or proof, because faith is its own warrant and has to be the starting point for any rational view of the world to get off the ground.[81] Locke, on the contrary, believed that all claims to revealed knowledge, independently of experience, had to be substantiated by reason making judgments about the credibility of evidence:[82]

> Whatever GOD hath revealed, is certainly true; no Doubt can be made of it. This is the proper object of Faith: But whether it be a divine revelation, or no, Reason must judge; which can never permit the Mind to reject a greater evidence to embrace what is less evident, nor allow it to entertain Probability in opposition to Knowledge and Certainty.

> I think that this vaunting of faith in opposition to reason is a primary source of the absurdities that fill almost all the religions that possess and divide mankind... Credo, quia impossibile est, "I believe, because it is impossible," might in a good man pass for a slogan expressing his zeal; but it would be a dreadful rule for men to choose their opinions or religion by.[83]

80. For Locke, the essentials of Christianity were "the belief of Jesus of Nazareth to be the Messiah, together with those concomitant articles of his resurrection, rule, and coming again to judge the world, [is] all the faith required, as necessary to justification" (Locke, *Reasonableness of Christianity*, para. 151).

81. On "fideism," see further, Penelhum, "Fideism," 376–82.

82. Kirk, *Future of Reason*, 47.

83. Locke, *Essay Conerning Human Understanding*, IV.18.10, 11.

Locke's confidence in the power of reason to discern what is true and false in creedal statements about God and the state of humankind was derived firstly from his assurance that reason was a gift from God, and therefore could not contradict God's true revelation, and secondly from his ultimate belief that the world outside human perception matched our inner reflection upon it, both also being given by the creator. At the same time, he acknowledged both the limitations of reason, that there are matters which in principle the mind cannot know on its own, and the corruption of the mind by the effects of sin. In both cases, humans should be humble about how far reason alone can take us in understanding the complexities of our own existence.

I take it, therefore, that Locke did not oppose reason and faith. He sought for a proper and well-founded integration of the two. Faith is a necessary precursor to reason, for reason cannot establish its own supremacy by reason alone; some more fundamental assumption, which we might call "tacit knowing" [84] is needed to justify the importance of reason. For Locke, the ultimate bedrock for making sense of experience is the one personal God known supremely in the historical and post-historical figure of Jesus Christ. Human beings live *sub specie aeternitatis*.

Every human being has been created free and equal in the image of this creator God. For Locke, this conviction was the most basic reason for considering every individual as deserving of equal treatment. There are those who interpret Locke as advocating, at least in principle, universal suffrage in a representative democracy and equality of opportunity for women as well as men.[85] And yet, in practice he was by no means consistent with his belief. As we have seen, he defended the right to expropriate land without consent, suggesting that democratic principles of equality before the law could be set aside. He justified the slavery of black peoples (but not indigenous American inhabitants), suggesting that equality did not really extend to all races. One would have expected the essential theological tenet to have overridden his argument from the state of nature, seeing that the givenness of the *imago Dei* was prior to any historical human situation. In this respect Locke was an anthropological essentialist: nothing and nobody could efface the image of God engraved in the constitution of every human inhabitant of the earth, from the greatest to the smallest.

---

84. See, Polyani, *Tacit Dimension*, and Polyani, *Personal Knowledge*.
85. See, Butler, "Early Liberal Roots of Feminism," 379–85.

Locke's views on toleration were consistent, up to a point. He staunchly defended the separation of civil and ecclesiastical powers, allowing to each its rightful jurisdiction. Thus, the law of the land should not seek to impose uniformity of belief, touching as it would on matters of relationship to God, for religious faith ceased to be authentic when imposed by an external agent. Correspondingly, the church must not teach as imperative to belief any article of faith that would cause hostility and dissension within the body politic.

Locke followed and reinforced a view of toleration, pioneered before him by nonconformist religious bodies, that separated personal approval from permission to believe and act. Thus, to tolerate another person's or group's beliefs, opinions, and behavior means accepting their right to express them as they wish, even though others might thoroughly disapprove. It involves, therefore, a deliberate choice not to forbid, outlaw or hinder their openly declared views, expressed in either speech, writing, or conduct, even though one might have the power to do so. It is essential for the definition of tolerance that the beliefs and actions tolerated are ones that the tolerator considers either mistaken, unhealthy, or immoral. The roots of Locke's view of tolerance are to be found in his view of humans' intrinsic freedom and equality, his antipathy to a hierarchically structured society, his skepticism about claims to absolute certainty, and his advocacy of the democratic rights of citizens not to be coerced by the state. Unfortunately, this traditional view of tolerance has, in recent times, been virtually abandoned by some political activists and moral zealots.[86]

On the question of personal identity, Locke's ideas are curious. To the critique already presented, I would add the observation that identity is not solely a matter of introspection. Identity is formed not only in personal consciousness and memory, but in connection with external relationships. Locke's concept is almost solipsistic (i.e., wholly self-referential). However, another dimension to identity is added in the African aphorism, "I am, because we are." Using a different image, it is contained in the affirmation that "we are surrounded by such a great a cloud of witnesses."[87] In other words, my identity, whatever my consciousness may tell me, is shaped by all kinds of human and other interactions. The implications are important. In the case of an individual's loss of memory

---

86. For examples of the reversal of the original Lockean understanding of toleration, see Furedi, *On Tolerance*.

87. Heb 12:1.

or complete absence of a consciousness that ties that person to past events and memories (such as when suffering from dementia or accidental brain damage) that person is still identifiable, even though they may not know exactly who they are.

Finally, in his discussion of the freedom of the will, Locke considered his notion more from a philosophical than a theological angle. He did not, for example, give an opinion concerning the controversy aroused by the debate between Erasmus and Luther.[88] His interest was in the inductive procedure of understanding what are the conditions necessary for a person to choose, decide and act freely in most circumstances and when were those conditions annulled by irresistible external forces. He did not enter the deductive procedure of attempting to unravel what consequences an inherited corruption of the will might have on decision-making, especially on one's freedom or otherwise, to accept God's offer of salvation through Jesus Christ.[89]

Having said that, his general approach to Christian faith leaves one wondering whether he duly considered the nature of faith as an entirely unmerited gift of God's grace. Locke spoke of the need of reconciliation and forgiveness, yet he did not attempt to present a comprehensive doctrine of salvation from sin. His view of redemption follows from his conviction that it responds to whatever it was that humankind lost in the fall of Adam. This he summarizes as a fall from "the state of perfect obedience, which is called justice in the New Testament . . . he lost bliss (being turned out of paradise) and immortality (all men should die, and remain under death forever, and so be utterly lost)."[90] He saw, therefore, salvation in terms of restoration, of regaining "life and immortality."[91] Now he gives the impression that humans are capable of attaining that restoration by obediently following Christ's example through allowing themselves to be illuminated by his teaching and trusting him to grant them a resurrection from the dead.

It appears that for Locke, resurrection referred to life after death, what the creed calls "the life of the world to come." This belief, in Locke's thinking, was both an inspiration and reward for a virtuous existence in

---

88. See chapter 2.
89. The subject matter of the Luther-Erasmus debate.
90. Locke, *Reasonableness of Christianity*, paras. 2 and 7.
91. 1 Tim 1:10.

life before death. Near the end of his treatise on the reasonableness of Christianity, he writes these words:

> The view of heaven and hell will cast a slight upon the short pleasures and pains of this present state, and give attractions and encouragements to virtue, which reason and interest, and the cares of ourselves, cannot but allow and prefer. Upon this foundation, and upon this only, morality stands firm, and may defy all competition. This makes it more than a name; a substantial good, worth all our aims and endeavors; and thus the Gospel of Jesus Christ has delivered it to us.[92]

However, he missed the emphasis of the New Testament on a resurrection before death,[93] which the gospel of Jesus Christ declares to be the inner power for attaining a life of virtue.[94]

Questions

1. John Locke has been called the father of modern political liberalism. Why do you think this is so? Are there any reasons to question this claim?
2. How did Locke relate the use of human reason to religious faith?
3. Locke is also credited with developing the notion of human rights. What in particular was his contribution to its understanding?
4. What difference to Locke's thinking about human nature did the Christian understanding of original sin make?

---

92. Locke, *Reasonableness of Christianity*, para. 151.

93. Set out most passionately in chapter 6 of Paul's letter to the Romans.

94. This may be due to the fact that he gave only a secondary status to the occasional letters of the apostles as witnesses to the truths necessary for salvation, privileging the Gospels and Acts of the Apostles as the primary witnesses.

CHAPTER 4

The Humanism of the Enlightenment

How consoling for the philosopher . . . is this view of the human race, emancipated from its shackles, released from the empire of fate and from that of the enemies of its progress, advancing with a firm and sure step along the path of truth, virtue and happiness.

—Marquis de Condorcet, *Sketch for a Historical Picture of the Human Mind*

History in general is a collection of crimes, follies and misfortunes, among which we have now and then met with a few virtues, and some happy times; as we sometimes see a few scattered huts in a barren desert.

—Francois-Marie Arouet de Voltaire, *Essays on Manners and Spirits of Nations*

Introduction

TO ATTEMPT TO COMPRESS some of the thinking about the human condition made by people associated with eighteenth-century Enlightenment into one chapter is, to say the least, ambitious. Even to characterize a period of history as "The Enlightenment" is open to serious challenge. In the first place, historical reconstruction, if it is to do justice to the diversity of events, thought, culture, international relations, social, political, and economic developments, religious controversies and many other interests happening within less than one century, must attempt to address the widest possible context. Much occurred within this time span that was untouched by the agenda proposed by those linked to enlightenment ideas. Although some of the more radical proposals for change influenced the political upheavals of the French Revolution, those who advocated them were unrepresentative and socially marginal.[1]

Secondly, it is impossible to trace one coherent set of propositions, principles, or programs for action that could collectively be enrolled under the banner of the Enlightenment. There were both common opinions and strong disagreements[2] among those who ascribed to the general view that human thought should be liberated from the constraints of past tradition, political ideologies, religious dogmatism and superstition, custom, and state coercion. Some enlightened thinkers were hugely optimistic about the probability that the future would usher in a new era of human achievement in every sphere of endeavor, such as Condorcet. Others, among whom were Voltaire and skeptics like Pierre Bayle, were generally pessimistic about the faith being placed on reason and the new scientific developments to engender and promote a fresh beginning for humankind, free from the multiple errors of the past.

Thirdly, subsequent opinions, given by a diverse group of historians, philosophers, cultural analysts, political theorists and others, about the true nature of the Enlightenment are diverse, quite often contradictory, and sometimes highly contentious. There are those, for example, who believe that the very notion of an historically concrete Enlightenment (with a capital E) is a creation of later historians.[3] It is supposed that it suits their contemporary worldview to paint a cohesive picture of emancipation that established foundational principles for the continuation of a progressive spirit that would leaven the lump of human social existence. Thus, for example, Anthony Pagden sees the Enlightenment as the source of most modern, liberal, tolerant, undogmatic, and secular understandings of politics, and as the intellectual origin of all modern forms of universalism and humanist sentiments.[4] For him, the Enlightenment witnesses to his own self-assessment as one who distinguishes himself as being "modern, forward-thinking, tolerant, generally open-minded," a group of representations which he believes characterizes "the enlightened."[5]

---

1. See Israel, *Democratic Enlightenment*, 15.

2. "At the time of the Enlightenment, there was radical disagreement on the nature of the universe, first causes, teleology, the basis of freedom, toleration and human rights" (for example, in the correspondence between Turgot and Diderot; Israel, *Democratic Enlightenment*, 18).

3. See Robertson, *Enlightenment*, 10.

4. Pagden, *Enlightenment and Why It Still Matters*, viii.

5. Pagden, *Enlightenment and Why It Still Matters*, vii.

Others, for example the German philosophers Max Horkheimer and Theodor Adorno, to the contrary, writing immediately after the rise and fall of Nazism, portray the Enlightenment as the source of "a new kind of barbarism," in which control over nature has been sublimated into control over human beings, using ever-more-sophisticated technological means.[6] The Enlightenment has been criticized because its incipient secular perfectionism has anticipated the social messianism of modern totalitarian movements, and because its ideal of an autonomous self has led to isolation and a solitary existence, full of human rights' entitlements, and unencumbered by obligations and duties to social groups.[7] Nevertheless, in spite of these reservations about the legitimacy of identifying a specific "Age of Enlightenment," there are sufficient common traits within the philosophical, social, and political culture of the eighteenth century to be able to use this characterization meaningfully.

What is the Enlightenment?

The Enlightenment is a fairly loosely determined period in which thinking about substantial religious, moral, political, economic, and social issues were being redefined. In a broad sense, many beliefs that had for centuries been taken for granted were now being challenged by a diverse group of writers. They were eager to herald a new era of uncensored philosophical and political ideas that would lead to profound shifts in social conditions.

These authors shared a number of assumptions. At a fundamental level, they believed that the time had come to replace tradition, custom, and religious faith with unassisted human reason. They believed that a thoroughgoing, rational approach to life, aided by the birth of modern science, would eradicate debilitating superstition and thus free humanity to engage with the true nature of reality, hitherto obscured by pure ignorance. They attacked old sources of authority, such as the hierarchy of the church and the Bible as containing the revelation of a sovereign God, monarchy, and the established nobility. In theory, but not always in practice, they advocated a defused democracy in which the people (or at least some of them), through a social contract, would decide who governed,

---

6. See Horkheimer and Adorno, *Dialectic of Enlightenment* (original, *Dialektik der Aufklärung*, published in 1944).

7. See Kramnick, *Portable Enlightenment Reader*, xxi, xxiii.

in whose interests and with what policies. The famous refrain, "government of the people, by the people, for the people shall not perish from the earth,"[8] may not yet have been articulated in exactly these words, but its sentiment was already being anticipated. However, a number of the writers were deeply suspicious of the ability of the masses (particularly women) to choose political representatives and policies wisely.

At the least, they advocated freedom of conscience in matters of faith, freedom of speech to criticize those in authority, and freedom of association to organize in opposition to those who held power. There was a marked turning from understanding one's human identity in terms of belonging to communities to a pronounced individualism. Adam Smith, the Scottish philosopher, moralist, and economist, for example, promoted a sophisticated self-interested individualism. Every individual, he stated, quite naturally seeks to better his or her own condition in life, by the operation of a mysterious "hidden hand": the combination of every individual's economic self-seeking drove forward economic growth.[9]

The chief end of human life was drastically revised. Whereas once it had been defined as "to glorify God and enjoy him for ever" (i.e., to enjoy all the gifts he had given, for the purpose for which they were given, in communion with God), now it was being secularized as the pursuit of happiness through the cultivation of pleasure. Such was the basis for a utilitarian ethic of the greatest good (maximum pleasure and minimum pain) for the greatest number.

This epoch saw a subtle, but also profoundly influential, shift from a person's presumed place in the scheme of things, with its obligations and duties, to the language of equality and individual human rights. Emphasis was being placed on the common identity of all human beings (including people of other races)[10].

Finally, the writers were, for the most part, convinced that the new thinking, combined with the improvements being brought about by the

---

8. The final words of Abraham Lincoln's short oration delivered on November 19, 1863, at the consecration of the National Cemetery at Gettysburg.

9. "By directing that industry in such a manner as its produce may be of the greatest value, he intends only his own gain, and he is in this, as in many other cases, led by an invisible hand to promote an end which was no part of his intention . . . By pursuing his own interest he frequently promotes that of the society more effectually than when he really intends to promote it" (*Wealth of Nations*, taken from Kramnick, *Portable Enlightenment Reader*, 509).

10. However, although considered equal in principle, few Enlightenment authors recognized in them an equality in terms of civilized and civilizing achievements.

technological ingenuity of human experimentation, would lead to perpetual progress in the human condition, both in the external world of sufficiency for all and in the internal world of reasonable decision-making, the overcoming of enmity and violence, and the healing of disturbed emotions. According to Jonathan Israel, the Enlightenment is not just a story of ideas, but the interaction of ideas and social reality. The main intellectual effort was directed toward the betterment of this world, not an emphasis on the recompenses to be received in a mythical next. Human amelioration would arise quite naturally once the means of progress in human society were better understood. This would come about by challenging accepted values through the transformation of people's thinking, attitudes, and ideas.[11]

Aspirations

One major feature of those who believed that a new Age of Reason had dawned was optimism. Many proponents of enlightenment believed that the goals of a thoroughgoing intellectual, moral, and social revolution were achievable.[12] Condorcet, for example, hoped for the abolition of inequality between nations, a progress toward equality within each nation, and the true perfection of mankind:

> Will all nations one day attain the state of civilisation which the most enlightened, the freest and the least burdened by prejudices, such as the French and the Anglo-Americans, have attained already? . . . The real advantages that should result from this progress, of which we can entertain a hope that is almost a certainty, can have no other term than that of the absolute perfection of the human race.[13]

Joseph Priestley, a renowned scientist and religious dissenter, conjured up a utopian vision of a new society based on the prospects forged by the American and French revolutions:

---

11. Israel, *Democratic Enlightenment*, 5.
12. See Jordan, *Enlightenment Vision*, 18.
13. Quote from the tenth and final stage of his *Sketch for a Historical Picture of the Human Mind* in Kramnick, *Portable Enlightenment Reader*, 27, 32. Branded a traitor by some of the revolutionaries after the French Revolution, he was arrested in 1794, imprisoned, and two days later found dead in his cell, having either been murdered or committed suicide.

> These great events ... make a totally new, a most wonderful and important, era in the history of mankind ... It is a liberating of all the powers of man from that variety of fetters by which they have hitherto been held ... Together with the general prevalence of the true principles of civil government, we may expect to see the extinction of all national prejudice and enmity, and the establishment of universal peace and goodwill among all nations.[14]

Immanuel Kant also, at first, believed that the French Revolution marked a sign of humankind's changed moral disposition to engage enthusiastically in the collective construction of a moral ideal, namely the defense of liberty and individual rights. He believed that it revealed a faculty in human nature for permanent progress toward a society capable of ensuring liberty, peace, mutual security, and rights, not only within nations, but also between them. The birth of an age of enlightenment brought the promise that humankind would eventually move to a moral level that would leave behind the struggle for power through violence:

> His view of the Enlightenment led to a general view of the Enlightenment as a cultural practice, a political myth, a progressive ideology, a perennial philosophy of man as master of his own destiny, a utopia to be realized, the emancipation of man by man.[15]

By and large, the aspiration that a total and formal recognition of the equality of status and opportunities between men and women would be one outcome of enlightenment thinking was not fulfilled. However, there were a few exceptions:

> Condorcet affirmed woman's equal humanity on the grounds of reason and justice. While never entirely dismissing the influential case for women's difference, Condorcet refused to accept this as an impediment to their equal enjoyment of civil and political rights. He attributed women's limitations, to the extent

---

14. Priestly, in Kramnick, *Enlightenment Reader*, 382–83, 384.

15. The references to Kant are taken from Ferrone and Tarantino, *Enlightenment*, 7–10. As the events of the French Revolution unfolded, Kant was forced to change his optimistic perspective. In spite of his hope that the revolution could herald a new, permanent and balanced conjunction between the exercise of power, the rule of law and freedom and individual rights, he saw the distinct signs of a return to barbarism in the actual effects that transpired.

they existed, not to their sex but rather to their inferior education and circumstances.[16]

Attitudes toward the nature and social place of women during the period of the Enlightenment is a matter of great controversy in contemporary debate.[17] However, it was during this period that the most notable championing of women's equality with men was first asserted. Mary Wollstonecraft wrote *Vindication of the Rights of Women* in 1792. Her main complaint about the way in which women were treated in a male-dominated society focused on the utter waste of talent that was the result of the position in which women were traditionally placed. Instead of contributing, on an equal footing with men, to the common good of society, women were expected to be the servants of men. She knew, from observation and personal experience, that women, were they allowed to develop their aptitudes, would enrich society in hitherto unimaginable ways:

> Women then must be considered as only the wanton solace of men, when they become so weak in mind and body that they cannot exert themselves unless to pursue some frothy pleasure, or to invent some frivolous fashion... Women might certainly study the art of healing and be physicians as well as nurses... They might also study politics, and settle their benevolence on the broadest basis... Business of various kinds, they might likewise pursue, if they were educated in a more orderly manner... The few employments open to women, so far from being liberal, are menial... How many women thus waste life away the prey of discontent, who might have practised as physicians, regulated a farm, managed a shop, and stood erect, supported by their own industry.[18]

Mary Wollstonecraft also criticized women for conniving in a state of affairs in which they expected to be supported by their husbands in exchange for carrying out domestic duties. This situation, she argued, demeaned women, deprived society of the outlook of half its population, and made women less able to fulfill their unique capacities as wives and

---

16. Landes, "History of Feminism," para. 2.

17. See, for example, Knott and Taylor, *Women, Gender and Enlightenment*.

18. "Of the Pernicious Effects Which Arise from the Unnatural Distinctions Established in Society," Chapter IX of Wollstonecraft's *Vindication of the Rights of Woman*; the text comes from Kramnick, *Portable Enlightenment Reader*, 624, 626, 627.

mothers, and men theirs as husbands and fathers, and both as fully recognized citizens:

> Would men but generously snap our chains, and be content with rational fellowship instead of slavish obedience, they would find us more observant daughters, more affectionate sisters, more faithful wives, more reasonable mothers—in a word, better citizens. We should then love them with true affection, because we should learn to respect ourselves.[19]

Beliefs

Bearing in mind what has already been said about the diversity of intellectual stances and practical ideas, it is worth noting in a little more detail some of the main convictions which the defenders of enlightenment shared. In this way, it may be possible to acquire a greater insight into the thought processes which drove these people to be confident that they were in the process of making European culture turn the most significant corner of its history. They genuinely believed that, leaving behind obscurantism in all its forms, it was possible to embrace a new vision of humanity's potential to order life more rationally in tune with the reality of the natural world.

Progress

"Everything tells us," says Condorcet, "that we are approaching the era of one of the grand revolutions of the human race."[20] What is the evidence for such a bold claim? Well, for Condorcet, a major part was invested in the expanding achievements of the natural sciences. He believed that the constancy of the laws of nature would secure future progress. As the pseudo-knowledge of a mythical world was gradually eroded, advancement would be due to improved knowledge of the real world through the universal language of the sciences and by international commerce. For example, evidence was beginning to accumulate that improvement in medical practices would eventually mean the end of both infectious

---

19. Kramnick, *Portable Enlightenment Reader*, 628.
20. Kramnick, *Portable Enlightenment Reader*, 394.

and hereditary diseases and illnesses, leading to a growth in the average lifespan of the human race.

Educated people now possessed the tools to dispel ignorance, error, and prejudice, and arrive at the truth of existence through a thorough sifting of experience. The human mind itself could be oriented toward a new kind of social perspective by the guidance and training of the informed, literate, and cultivated *avant-garde*, the *cognoscenti* of their age. One might call the ambition, not unfairly, a case of indoctrination into the values of a self-evidently superior class. As Vincente Ferrone puts it, the works of the Enlightenment were informed by specific ideological and philosophical stances, among them the idea of a stage-by-stage development of civilization that enabled humankind to believe in progress. Although the language of dialectics and evolution were not yet coined and developed (these concepts were given a full expression later in the thinking of Georg Hegel, Karl Marx, and the theories of Charles Darwin), there was an assumption that within the movement of history itself there is a progressive unfolding of an absolute reality:

> What we know and what we can achieve are the result of the attainments of the philosophies, arts and sciences of the past depositing their cumulative wisdom into our present. Philosophy discerns a dialectic process through which historically rooted concepts would, in the course of changing times, come into conflict with opposing concepts and become resolved into an ever higher synthesis, until an absolute system is achieved . . . The thesis of an end to history is a meta-historical view about the nature of the development of human societies. It rests on the belief that history is both cumulative—i.e. that it constantly takes into itself the former contradictions which have been overcome and progressive.[21]

Progress is understood to have reached its zenith at the time when "mankind has achieved a form of society that satisfies its deepest and most fundamental longings."[22]

---

21. Kirk, *Future of Reason*, 144, 146.
22. Fukuyama, *End of History*, xii.

The Autonomy of the Individual

Kant's response to the question of what enlightenment is is well known. It has become a kind of manifesto for the validity of the opinions of individuals, arrived at by their own processes of thought and understanding:

> Enlightenment is man's release from his self-incurred tutelage. Tutelage is man's inability to make use of his understanding without direction from another... *Sapere aude!* "Have courage to use your own reason!"—that is the motto of enlightenment.[23]

Kant, in his short essay, was advocating a process whereby the individual human being breaks free from slavishly following the advice of those who have appointed themselves as his or her guardians. They are to take responsibility for their own reasoning and decisions. Diderot, a little earlier, had exclaimed that the true philosopher is one who,

> Trampling underfoot prejudice, tradition,... authority... dares to think for himself... to admit nothing save on the testimony of his own reason and experience.[24]

For enlightenment thinkers, it was self-evident that in order for an individual's self-belief in his or her capacity for making rational choices to increase, without the intervention of the commanding authority of the state or the church, it was necessary that they had the freedom to dissent from the moral and legal control of external institutions. They did not need to seek permission to think for themselves and to come to conclusions that might have seemed outlandish to the conventional norms of the society of the time. *Sapere aude* was a formidable challenge to the collective ideas of traditional wisdom.

The Rights of Man

On the 27th of August, 1789, the French National Assembly issued "The Declaration of the Rights of Man and the Citizen." It "recognizes and proclaims, in the presence of the Supreme Being," certain "natural, inalienable, and sacred rights" pertaining to all human beings:

> Men are born and remain free and equal in rights... the natural and inalienable rights of man (are) liberty, property, security

---

23. Kramnick, *Portable Enlightenment Reader*, 1.
24. Quoted in Taylor, *Sources of the Self*, 323.

and resistance to oppression . . . no-one is to be disquieted because of his opinions, even religious, provided their manifestation does not disturb the public order established by law . . . free communication of ideas and opinions is one of the most precious of the rights of man; consequently, every citizen may speak, write and print freely, subject to responsibility for the abuse of such liberty in the cases determined by law.[25]

According to the eminent French historian Georges Lefebre, the Declaration stands as a tributary of the great stream of ideas that constituted a common ideal that summarized the evolution of Western civilization. It recognized the eminent dignity of the human person as such, and pronounced, therefore, the unity of all human beings. It was, he says, a set of moral principles, rather than a tightly drawn legal code, an ideal to be realized, a declaration of intent.[26]

Two years later, Thomas Paine, who was born in England but became an American citizen, supported both the American and French Revolutions, and was known as a political philosopher, theorist, and activist wrote a long tract with the title, *The Rights of Man*. This was his response to Edmund Burke's critique of the French Revolution (published in 1790), *Reflections on the Revolution in France*. Paine's work swiftly was considered one of the most radical promotions of individuals' all-inclusive rights that had been articulated. Rights possess four characteristics: they are natural to human beings, he declared, by virtue of their being human; they are distributed equally by virtue of humans' common creation by the one maker of all things (Paine declared himself to be a Deist); they are inalienable due to the fact that all are born into the same human race; and they are sacred, because of their origin in the purposes of God.

Paine believed that the implementation of universal rights would bring a renovation of what, after all, was the natural order of things. Human rights would become the great foundation for moral and political happiness and national prosperity.[27] Paine, despite his scathing attack on orthodox Christian faith in his book, *The Age of Reason*, at least under-

---

25. Kramnick, *Portable Enlightenment Reader*, 467–68. I have quoted just a brief selection from the Declaration. There are, in fact, seventeen clauses which also cover topics like the nature and power of the state and its laws, the consequences for public office of the absolute equality of all citizens, the dispensing of justice, the creation of a public force to guarantee citizens' rights, and a tax to pay for it.

26. Lefebre, "Declaration of the Rights," 126–28.

27. See Paine, "Rights of Man," 18–24.

stood that the notion of universal human rights required a foundation in the belief of a personal deity who was the original creator of all things.

Atheism and the Birth of Exclusive Humanism

Whether merely a legend or not, the reported dialogue between Napoleon and the French scientist Pierre-Simon Laplace sums up one of the main reasons for the decline of any belief in a personal God:

> Napoleon, "You have written this huge book on the system of the world, without once mentioning the author of the universe."
>
> Laplace, "Sire, I had no need of that hypothesis."

Rejection of belief in a divine being was not a new phenomenon at the time of the Enlightenment, although it was not particularly common. The rise of modern science, with its ability to increase knowledge and decrease reliance on speculative beliefs, appeared to give evidence-based answers to many of the enigmas of the natural world. Laplace's reply to Napoleon, whether fact or fiction, sums up an attitude to human life in the world that saw no necessity to account for natural phenomena by appealing to the direct intervention of God.[28] So God, if he did exist, was pushed to the margins of the universe.

Increasingly, philosophers and scientists adopted a mechanistic interpretation of reality. Everything had been set in motion (possibly by a divine being) and allowed to run, as it were, under its own steam. The logic of a first cause was appreciated by many thinkers, including Voltaire and Paine, even though they disassociated themselves from organized religion. However, they saw little relevance in ascribing to this belief:

> not that I call in question the existence of a supreme being; on the contrary it seems to me that the greatest degree of probability is in favour of this belief. But since the existence of this being does not prove that one form of worship is more necessary than any other, it is a theoretic truth with very little practical value.[29]

For La Mettrie and many like him, this being was indeterminate and remote.

---

28. Laplace himself probably professed a deistic belief in a supreme being.
29. Julien Offray de la Mettrie, *Man a Machine* (1747) in Kramnick, *Portable Enlightenment Reader*, 208.

The move from belief in an active God, ceaselessly immersed in the life he had created (theism), to deism, the denial that the deity had any active role in worldly events, marked a major shift in the background understanding of what it meant to be human. God had, as it were, his uses. He guaranteed the rational structure of the universe. He also endorsed the equality, freedom, and intrinsic entitlements of all. He could be called upon to explain why there appeared to be an orderly design to nature. Importantly, he underwrote a teleological interpretation of history and ensured that justice would finally be accomplished, at least in a judgment of all sin and evil at the end of this life.

Whereas most supporters of enlightenment probably subscribed to some form of deistic belief, the Enlightenment period also witnessed an upsurge in atheism. This sprang from a sense that the God hypothesis, when it came to giving a satisfactory explanation of the whole of reality, was completely redundant. In place of theology, certain influential philosophers began to develop a materialist ontology. Helvetius was the first to make a clear statement of materialism. He based it on an approach to knowledge that held that perception of the world came through sensations created in the mind (sensationalism):[30]

> The philosophical theory of perception and the external world's essential tenet is that propositions about material objects are reducible to propositions about actual and possible sensations, or sense data, or appearances.[31]

Our physical senses alone are the ultimate sources of the true knowledge of nature. Human mental, volitional, and affective phenomena are wholly bound up with matter that is self-explanatory. Human beings are the thinking part of nature, which is the final horizon of all that we can know or contemplate. Materialism (or naturalism) was developed into a complete response to all forms of theism, deism, mind-body dualisms, and spiritualisms. Belief in God was interpreted as an affective reaction to the feeling of helplessness felt in the presence of the intimidating powers of nature.[32]

The most systematic treatment of an atheistic philosophy came from the pen of Baron d'Holbach (Paul Henri Thiry). He expounded his

---

30. Also known as phenomenalism.

31. *Encyclopaedia Britannica*, https://www.britannica.com/topic/epistemology/The-history-of-epistemology#ref309085.

32. See Hunter and Wootton, *Atheism from the Reformation*, 274–76.

materialist theory most forcefully in the book, *Systeme de la nature*.³³ d'Holbach asserted that humans always deceive themselves when they abandon experience for imaginary systems. They are wholly a work of nature, submitted to her laws. They cannot step beyond them:

> It is vain that his mind would spring forward beyond the bounds of the visible world . . . there exists nothing beyond the great whole of which he forms a part . . . Let man cease then to search, out of the world he inhabits, for beings who can procure him a happiness that denies him . . . Let him submit without murmuring to the decrees of a universal necessity, which can never be brought within his comprehension nor ever emancipate him from those rules his essence has imposed upon him.³⁴

The ultimate reality is matter in motion. This accounts for the universe, for the existence of animate and inanimate phenomena, for the development of species, for the birth of language and the rationality of humans:

> The universe . . . offers everywhere but matter and motion . . . The sum total makes what we call NATURE.³⁵

In sum, d'Holbach has substituted Nature (all in capital letters) for God. Here is born a totally impersonal order. Nothing exists beyond what the senses perceive or are able to deduce:

> the very time that a word or its idea does not furnish any sensible object to which one can refer it, this word or this idea is derived from nothing, is void of sense; one should banish the idea from one's mind, and the word from the language, since it signifies nothing.³⁶

Charles Taylor, in his celebrated study, *A Secular Age*, refers to this way of thinking as "the birth of exclusive humanism."³⁷ The main condition which accounted for its birth was the disappearance of belief in a

---

33. Published in 1770 under the pseudonym "Miraboud." There is a substantial extract from the book in Gay, *Enlightenment*, 373–82. Gay believes that he was "undoubtedly the most consistent and most articulate atheist among the *philosophes* . . . To him and his associates, changing the general way of thinking would be a success only when mankind had cast aside all religions of all descriptions" (372).

34. Gay, *Enlightenment*, 373, 374.

35. Gay, *Enlightenment*, 378, 379.

36. See Hunter and Wootton, *Atheism from the Reformation*, 281.

37. Taylor, *Secular Age*, 19–21.

personal God intimately related to, and interested in, the world he had created. Gradually, human beings were emancipating themselves from the notion of a spiritual world distinct from the material reality with which everyone was familiar. This intellectual movement has been aptly named, "disenchantment." It was based on a conscious reduction of the parameters of human life. God was not needed to account for the motion of the planets. When it came to accounting for humans' highest spiritual and moral aspirations, he was also redundant. The human race was learning to stand on its own two feet. It now understood what would make for human flourishing, quite apart from religion. It believed that the necessary moral and spiritual resources were imminent within the world, not dependent on a transcendent power:

> The discovery/definition of these intra-human sources of benevolence is one of the greatest achievements of our civilization, and the charter of modern unbelief.[38]

Having rejected orthodox theism, the catalysts of enlightenment were left with an imminent, impersonal order, one which screens out all phenomena that does not fit into this procrustean framework. This imminent order is self-contained; it can be grasped and fully understood independently of any special relationship with a personal God. This way of thinking and living marked an amazing revolution. It was nothing less than a new way of inhabiting the world, in which the human being was alone at the center of existence.

Christianity, in calling for a dedication to more than human flourishing, was considered to be the implacable enemy of the human good and a stumbling block in the way of recognizing the dignity of a self-sufficient humanist identity. The Christian proclamation of humanity's need to be restored to an original, but now lost, goodness was rejected. Enlightenment thinking broke the hitherto dominant religious and metaphysical consensus that had been the default worldview of Europeans for more than a millennium:[39]

> The Enlightenment represented a specific attitude of mind that was dedicated to human reason, science and education as the best means of building a stable society of free men on earth. Suspicious of religion, hostile to tradition and resentful of authority

---

38. Taylor, *Secular Age*, 257.

39. For a full view of Taylor's interpretation of Enlightenment culture, see ch. 6 ("Providential Deism") and ch. 7 ("The Impersonal Order") of *Secular Age*.

based on custom or faith alone . . . secular in orientation . . . It sought to construct human community out of natural materials alone.[40]

The Moral Order

This shift to exclusive humanism had inevitable consequences in the realm of defining the good and motivating people to follow it. Francis Hutcheson (d. 1746), a leading representative of what came to be called the "moral sense (or sentiment) school," believed that there is

> in human nature a disinterested ultimate desire of the happiness of others, and . . . our moral sense (implanted by God) determines us to approve actions as virtuous which are apprehended to proceed . . . from such a desire.[41]

However, d'Holbach, who rejected any idea of an inborn moral sentiment, and aware of the weakness of any universally valid feeling of benevolence, believed that the "solidity" of morality must rest on the one constantly observed fact about human beings: that they are in love with their happiness, occupied with their own preservation. Moral sensibilities, therefore, can only be based on the self-interest of individuals, who live together in society that they may with greater facility attain (their) ends.[42]

A moral idealist might find d'Holbach's opinion somewhat cynical. However, for one who believed passionately that there was nothing more to existence than matter in motion in an impersonal order, moral good and evil were, objectively, meaningless categories. The universe is devoid of any moral qualities. It cannot be praised or blamed for anything that happens. It just is. Hence, there is a fundamental problem of speaking about virtue and vice, of laying a basis for behavior and apportioning praise or blame. If human beings are genuinely turned in on themselves in a silent universe, their only recourse for modeling a civilized existence must come from within themselves ("the proper study of mankind is

---

40. Anchor, *Enlightenment Tradition*, ix.

41. *An Enquiry into the Original of our Ideas of Beauty and Virtue*, quoted in Cooper, *World Philosophies*, 277.

42. *Systeme de la nature*, quoted in Schneewind, *Moral Philosophy*, 437–45.

man"[43]). It is not surprising that humans must therefore be content with a working ethic of prudence and expediency.[44]

The best that could be achieved with regard to the source of moral consciousness was probably a direct intuition of the good, a self-sufficient justification for the content of acceptable moral views and behavior. So, there arose a belief that people were somehow endowed with a natural feeling of sympathy for others, related to sympathy for one's own well-being. Altruistic impressions came to be expressed largely in utilitarian terms: the morality of acts depends not on the acts themselves, nor on the motivations with which they are performed, but simply on the consequences that were produced.[45] The measuring rod became the promotion of the greatest possible happiness or pleasure for the greatest number.[46]

The Human Condition

So how did the human world look to those who adopted the stance of exclusive humanism? They now lived in a world in which they were the highest being. Either God was an invention of people who needed to lean on a superior force, hoping to gain divine favors in exchange for ritual observances, or God showed no particular interest in people's daily lives. From now on, humanity was obliged, due to its own rationalist deliberations, to live entirely by its own inner resources.

The Enlightenment has been called the age of "the Rise of Man." He was in the process of being released from the bonds of superstition and suffocating, human-constructed traditions. Both were arbitrarily sanctioned by a powerful organization, the church, in league with the state, and in the name of a supreme, all-powerful being who delighted in punishing perverse humankind.

So in this new horizon of thought, humans were placed firmly in the center of existence. Their main task was now one of redefinition, encompassing the whole question of religion and the social, political, and

---

43. Pope, *Epistle* ii.1.1 (1733; also, Charron, Pierre, "La vraye science et le vray etude de l'homme, c'est l'homme," *De la Sagesse*, I.1 [1601]), in "Essay of Man," 255–56.

44. Hibben, *Philosophy of the Enlightenment*.

45. Dupre, *Religion and the Rise*, 34.

46. Dupre, *Religion and the Rise*, 144. I will review the moral dilemmas that Kant faced in his critique of practical reason in the section on Kant as an enlightenment figure.

economic order.[47] On the whole, the *philosophes* did not carry through their dreams into practical political programs; there was too much opposition. Through the dissemination of their conviction that peoples were being called to fulfill a new destiny, they began to change people's perception of their fundamental identity as individual subjects possessing equal dignity, inherent rights, and independence to think and act on their own behalf.[48] They set themselves the task of speaking up for the interests and aspirations of ordinary people.

In point of fact, some of what they professed was highly rhetorical. Few proclaimed a literal equality for all individual people: some continued to advocate the practice of slavery, keeping slaves themselves;[49] different races were still catalogued in a hierarchical order of superiority;[50] women were, by and large, still considered an inferior species who did not have the abilities needed for public life; universal suffrage was still a long way off, and voting rights were confined to males who owned a certain amount of property. Many Enlightenment figures benefited from the patronage of aristocrats and monarchs and enjoyed the privileges that European society continued to offer males of their education and class.[51]

Helvetius, in his *A Treatise on Man*,[52] comes close to a kind of solipsism, as he seeks to discover what drives people forward in their lives. He begins the essay with a confident, definitive assertion:

> What is said here will be sufficient to convince the discerning reader, that every idea and every judgment may be reduced to a sensation.[53]

---

47. See Ferrone and Tarantino, *Enlightenment*, ix.

48. Ferrone and Tarantino, *Enlightenment*, xiv.

49. The most notorious example was Thomas Jefferson.

50. "I am apt to suspect the Negroes and in general all the other species of men . . . to be naturally inferior to the whites . . . There are negro slaves dispersed all over Europe, of which no-one ever discovered any symptoms of ingenuity" (Hume, in Kramnick, *Portable Enlightenment Reader*, 629); "All these savages have little feeling for the beautiful in moral understanding, and the generous forgiveness of an injury . . . is completely unknown as a virtue among the savages, but rather is disdained as a miserable cowardice" (Kant, in Kramnick, *Portable Enlightenment Reader*, 638).

51. See Burns, *Enlightenment*, xvii–xxiv.

52. Helvetius, *Treatise on Man*; Kramnick, *Portable Enlightenment Reader*, 287–97.

53. Kramnick, *Portable Enlightenment Reader*, 287.

This leads him to claim that the faculty of judgment emerges wholly out of the faculty of sensation. It is an effect of corporeal sensibility. The interest in making judgments is

> necessarily founded on our love of happiness (and) cannot be anything else than the effect of bodily sensibility, because there all our pleasures, and all our pains have their source . . . I conclude that corporeal pains and pleasures are the unknown principles of all human actions . . . Corporeal sensibility is therefore the sole mover of man.[54]

He then proceeds to show how the principles of pleasure and pain materialize in feelings of remorse, friendships, the love of power, sociability, and moral attitudes of sympathy and compassion. He concludes:

> The love of others is never anything else in man than an effect of the love of himself, and consequently of his corporeal sensibility.[55]

Only people who suffer misery and pain can truly empathize with other human beings who experience suffering themselves. They have to have felt it personally within their own bodies and, as they encounter the other, to bring it to mind as a physical sensation.

It may be said that Helvetius is not a typical representative of Enlightenment thought. Kant, for example, affirmed a very different basis for his moral philosophy, grounded on a different concept of what it means to be human.[56] If the best we can do, in relating to others, is to project our own love of ourselves, it is not surprising that the Enlightenment, as well as generating optimists, also produced radical skeptics.

Although the promoters of enlightenment had long since rejected the Christian doctrine of original sin, mainly because, in their opinion, it undermined the possibility of a steady improvement in the human environment and behavior, there were those associated with the movement who took a dismal view of the likelihood of human betterment. Pierre Bayle, for example, launched a scathing attack on human pretentiousness in believing it possible to solve metaphysical problems (like the existence

---

54. Helvetius, in Kramnick, *Portable Enlightenment Reader*, 288.
55. Kramnick, *Portable Enlightenment Reader*, 296.
56. See Kirk, *Future of Reason*, 55–56.

of evil) or the call of conscience by reason alone.[57] De la Mettrie declared, "let us conclude boldly then that man is a machine."

The idealism of Berkeley and Hume, summarized by Tomas Reid as the hypothesis that,

> nothing is perceived but what is in the mind which perceives it: That we do not really perceive things that are external, but only certain images and pictures of them impressed upon the mind, which are called impressions and ideas . . . So that upon this hypothesis, the whole universe about me . . . all things without exception, which I imagined to have a permanent existence, whether I thought of them or not, vanish at once[58]

causes a radical dichotomy between the human mind's assimilation of ideas produced by the senses and the concrete reality of the external, material world, whether perceived or not.[59] As a consequence, both men were considered to be skeptics, even though Berkeley was attempting to refute an absolute skepticism about knowledge, which left one bereft of any ground to believe any one thing rather than its contrary.[60]

Adam Smith believed that vanity was the cause of all tumult and bustle, all the rapine and injustice, which avarice and ambition have introduced into this world.[61] Voltaire, likewise, was sceptical about the ability of human beings to raise themselves above an inclination to pursue destructive ends:

> What makes, and will always make, this world a vale of tears is the insatiable greediness and the indomitable pride of men.[62]

These quotes are but a small sample of the way in which an original optimism was accompanied during the eighteenth century by an apprehension that humans were, after all, incapable of achieving their moral

---

57. See O'Hara, *Enlightenment*, 47.

58. Reid, *Inquiry into the Human Mind* (1764), in Kramnick, *Portable Enlightenment Reader*, 214–15.

59. Ronald Knox parodied this form of idealism in his famous limerick: "There once was a man who said 'God Must think it exceedingly odd, If he finds that this tree Continues to be When there's no one about in the Quad'" (Reed, *Complete Limerick Book*).

60. Kramnick, *Portable Enlightenment Reader*, 214.

61. Smith, *The Wealth of Nations* (1776) in Kramnick, *Portable Enlightenment Reader*, 514.

62. "Letter to Jean-Jacques Rousseau" (August 30, 1755) in Kramnick, *Portable Enlightenment Reader*, 377.

aspirations. For example, Antoine Prevost, in his novel (a cautionary tale) *Manon Lescaut*, dramatized the conflict between natural impulses and moral sensibility.[63] It is not surprising that the Age of Reason gave way at the beginning of the nineteenth century to a different characterization of human nature and its abilities:

> the Romantic instinctively reacts against the loss of freedom implied in a reductionist account of human nature. If rationalism provoked the end of a universally accepted belief in a personal creation as the act of a personal transcendent divine being, Romanticism substituted its own immanent creation, often in art-forms, in the hope of generating its own answers to the many enigmas of human experience.[64]

Enlightenment skeptics were surely right, in the face of the awful reality of evil, to be indecisive in their promotion of a gradual improvement in the moral transformation of human consciousness concerning the common good. They recognized an actual state of affairs, but had no adequate explanation from within their core beliefs for its origin and persistence. In giving an account of what it means to be human, this major concern has continued to baffle commentators of every ideological hue right up to the present day. I will continue to keep this dilemma under review, as I consider the ideas of other influential thinkers of the nineteenth and twentieth centuries.

Questions

1. The Enlightenment has often been referred to as the most profound watershed in recent Western culture. How would you characterize it as such?

2. One of the watchwords of the Enlightenment was "progress." What criteria would you use to define the meaning of the concept?

3. What were the main problems of the Christian faith for the champions of Enlightenment?

---

63. See Anchor, *Enlightenment Tradition*, 56–57.
64. Kirk, *Meaning of Freedom*, 114.

4. Enlightenment figures were divided in their assessment of the future between optimists and pessimists. Which group do you think were closer to reality, and why?

CHAPTER 5

David Hume and Denis Diderot: Two Prominent Figures of the Enlightenment

David Hume

THE SCOTTISH PHILOSOPHER AND essayist has been considered by historians to be one of the most influential thinkers of the Scottish Enlightenment. Tom Beauchamp, for example, believes that his *An Enquiry Concerning Human Understanding*,

> is, in some respects, the quintessential Enlightenment book. It incorporates a confidence in science, a daring attempt at new discoveries about the human mind, an opposition to superstition and fanaticism, an emphasis on human nature, . . . and a mood of reform and critique. However, the clarity of his relationship to some of the most central ideas of Enlightenment thought, especially on the European continent, remains in doubt.[1]

From the quotation above, the sentence "a restrained skepticism about traditional views of knowledge and belief" is omitted, in order to emphasize that he is not perceived as being particularly enthusiastic about some of the claims of the more radical enlightenment thinkers.

It is well known that Hume did not wax lyrical about the power of human reason to take civilization onto an ever-more-progressive path in which human nature itself would be transformed for the better. He was an empiricist, who limited understanding to what could be known on the basis of experience. He opposed the view that reason alone provided a

---

1. Beauchamp, *David Hume: Enquiry Concerning Human Understanding*, 10.

different way of gaining a perception of human reality. He dismissed the idea of innate, abstract knowledge:

> When we reason *a priori*, and consider any object or cause, as it appears to the mind, independent of all observation, it never could suggest to us the notion of any distinct object, such as its effect ... A man must be very sagacious, who could discover by reasoning, that crystal is the effect of heat, and ice of cold, without being previously acquainted with the operation of these qualities.[2]

So his approach to thinking about any subject was, in his own words, "to feign no hypothesis." In other words: to refrain from offering explanations of phenomena that could not be supported by experimental evidence. This method of intellectual working would have made him cautious about some of the rhetoric that was being used about the future possibilities of human societies. He distrusted unfounded assumptions.[3] His overruling question would always have been: Where is the evidence?

Hume's thought is complex, controversial, and, not infrequently, contradictory. He has been variously interpreted. It is not possible in a short space to evaluate his whole life's work. I will limit myself to portraying some of the essential points that he made about human nature, human behavior, and what he would have considered the human creation of religion.

Human Nature

In the introduction to his first major writing, *A Treatise of Human Nature* (1739–1740), he explained that his intention was to present an organized and comprehensive account of all the principal elements of human nature.[4] He hoped to discover laws concerning the inner world of perception, desires, and reasoning and how they worked.

---

2. Hume, *Enquiry Concerning Human Understanding* (4.13).
3. See Scott-Kakures et al., "David Hume," 209.
4. See Harris, *Hume*, 82.

The Mind

Through his own observation, he set out the faculties of the mind. All beliefs about the physical world and life are derived from impressions that humans receive from their environment. These are original perceptions that appear directly to the mind from daily experience. They are outer perceptions. The human mind also encounters inner perceptions, such as feelings of joy, sadness, anger, fear, and so on.[5] Ideas are secondary views based on impressions. To be meaningful, they must correspond to impressions. They must represent something real in the orbit of impressions. If not, they can be classified as inventions and fictions. Hume thought that if ideas were not traceable to impressions, they were meaningless. This was his way of distinguishing between truth and error.[6]

Ideas

According to Hume, there are three principles of connection that link ideas together: resemblance, contiguity and causation. Hume proceeds to give some examples of how these three principles work. In the case of resemblance, he suggests the connection between seeing a picture of a friend and having many impressions of her, as a result of the times of joy or sorrow that have been shared:

> Sensible objects have always a greater influence on the fancy than any other; and this influence they readily convey to those ideas, to which they are related, and which they resemble ... The effect of resemblance in enlivening the ideas is very common; ... in every case a resemblance and a present impression must concur.[7]

In the case of contiguity, distance diminishes the force of every idea, whilst the presence of an object or person clarifies it:

> The thinking on any object readily transports the mind to what is contiguous ... When I am a few miles from home, whatever

---

5. Hume, *Enquiry Concerning Human Understanding* (2.1–3).

6. Hume's opinion on this point was later developed into an empiricist theory of meaning: a term only makes sense if it refers to something that can be experienced or refers to ideas that can be analyzed into terms that can be experienced.

7. Hume, *Enquiry Concerning Human Understanding* (5.16).

> relates to it touches me more nearly than when I am two hundred leagues distant.[8]

Finally, with the case of causation:

> When I throw a piece of dry wood into a fire, my mind is immediately carried to conceive, that it augments, not extinguishes the flames. This transition of thought from the cause to the effect proceeds not from reason. It derives its origin altogether from custom and experience.[9]

Causation and Induction

Famously, Hume sees a problem with the common assumption that every effect must have an invariable, corresponding cause. He held that the causal nexus of things is never perceived, rather it is deduced from mental perceptions. Thus, the regularity of events in the natural world does not reflect a necessary state of affairs, only habits of the mind: we infer absolute causality from constant conjunctions that we perceive in our mind from the sensations that come from observation.[10]

Hume detected a real problem with the assumption that underlies inference of future events from past experiences of causation. Can we be sure that similar causes will have similar effects? We cannot know with certainty that nature is invariably uniform, so that the future will resemble the past and be conformable to it. It is possible that nature will change, or our understanding of it will prove to be incorrect, thus throwing into doubt the deductions we have made hitherto on the basis of what has appeared to be the case. The problem of induction is that it involves a circular argument:

> All inferences from experience suppose, as their foundation, that the future will resemble the past . . . If there be any suspicion, that the course of nature may change, and that the past may be no rule for the future, all experience becomes useless, and can give rise to no inference or conclusion. It is impossible, therefore, that any arguments from experience can prove this

---

8. Hume, *Enquiry Concerning Human Understanding* (5.17).
9. Hume, *Enquiry Concerning Human Understanding* (5.20).
10. Kirk, *Future of Reason*, 62–63.

resemblance of the past to the future; since all these arguments are founded on the supposition of that resemblance.[11]

In other words, in the premise of my argument, I have already assumed what I am setting out to demonstrate. Hume admits, however, that although this may pose a deep philosophical problem, for it seems to undermine an expectation that causal connections are necessary and therefore certain (i.e., an unbroken chain of cause and effect is always invariable), in real life there are no grounds for suspecting that something totally irregular and abnormal will occur next time.

Skeptical arguments about causation fail to convince, because they diverge from the experience of ordinary life. Physical objects are distinct from, and independent of, us. To know that a given sensation is due to the impression made on us by the material object, we must be able to observe the two separately (i.e., the observed and the observer) in order to notice the consistent conjunction between them. How we can observe the material object as something distinct from the sensation is precisely the question at hand.[12]

Moreover, we can be absolutely assured that petrol thrown on a fire will always cause it to blaze more fiercely and water will likewise always dampen it down. Our confidence is not only gained through constant experience, but also by an analysis of the respective chemical properties of fire, petrol, and water.[13] Hume, in a sense, posed a problem of his own making in adopting a subjectivist or psychological account of epistemology. Knowledge, as justified true belief, pertains to the objective world outside our thought processes, so that our beliefs can be shown to be correct or erroneous by comparing them to the given nature of things.

Human Behavior

It is intriguing to learn that Hume considered his essay, *An Enquiry Concerning the Principles of Morals* (1751), the work with which he was most satisfied, since, from a later perspective, its assumptions and reasoning appear to be quite confused. Hume was convinced that moral belief and action could not be based on abstract, rational principles, but only on sentiment or feelings. Rules of morality, he believed, are not conclusions

---

11. Hume, *Enquiry Concerning Human Understanding* (4.21; my emphasis).
12. See Urmson and Ree, *Concise Encyclopedia*, 141–42.
13. See Randall, *Career of Philosophy*, 649–50.

derived from reason, but emerge from a personal sense of what is right to approve, or wrong to condemn. Approval or disapproval, in turn, derive from our past experiences of the pleasant or unpleasant consequences that follow from our moral decisions. Reason has no power to motivate people to act. Only feelings and desires can motivate. Thus, moral conflicts do not happen between what is reasonable and what may be desirable, but between two different passions that may well pull in opposite directions.

A married person, for example, may believe that he has fallen in love with a colleague at work. His desire is to form a sexual liaison with that person. If the feeling between the two is mutual, then there is an overwhelming longing to commit adultery. Hitherto, however, he has had a contented marriage, and he knows that adultery represents a breakdown of trust between husband and wife and with his children, which may well be irreversible. So now he is faced with two irreconcilable desires: to have sexual relations with the colleague, or to keep the family intact. No wonder that many in this situation attempt to get what they may consider the best of both worlds by attempting to keep the relationship a secret.

However, Hume's moral thought, based on principles of what causes pleasure and pain, is shown to be incoherent in the (quite common) case cited above from experience. For the thought of adultery may give much pleasure (even its riskiness can add to the pleasure) and the thought of maintaining a stable marriage may also give pleasure. However, the fact that these two pleasures can only be sustained simultaneously by keeping the liaison clandestine will surely cause pain. How is it possible to be guided ethically in a situation like this by weighing the strength of the two kinds of pleasure or, if the decision is to keep the liaison, to balance the pleasure against the pain of having to conceal from one's family a major part of one's life?

If it is true that moral goodness or virtue is manifested when actions cause feelings of satisfaction or pleasure, it is not surprising that many criminals show no remorse when convicted, since they do not feel they have done anything wrong. Hume seemed to believe that many moral virtues, such as generosity, arise through the natural constitution of human beings. They possess a natural sympathy which allows them to identify with both the pleasure and pain of others. However, supposing that what gives some people pleasure is by abusing children or torturing others, causing both sets of victims immense pain, how do the principles of pleasure, pain, satisfaction, or dissatisfaction guide a moral response? In such cases, identifying with someone else's pleasure is a dereliction of moral principle. Whatever the person's individual satisfaction in pursuing them may be, child abuse and torture are just plain wrong, not on the basis of subjective sensations, but on objective precepts.

Hume was an advocate of a fairly extreme form of moral subjectivism. Its characteristics can be summed up in three propositions. Firstly, no justification for moral actions can be grounded in anything else than a person's particular desires and feelings. Secondly, there are no moral statements that cannot be reduced to statements about the desires and feelings of human subjects. Thirdly, there are no moral facts that cannot be reduced to subjective desires and feelings.[14] Hume appears to have been driven to this kind of conclusion by his initial observation that there is no logical argument from what is the case to how we should behave (i.e., from the description of a situation to how one ought to act in response to it). So, what is the case is the reality of the passions. The consequence is that Hume lacks any basis for obligation or duty. He is unable to say why anyone ought to follow a particular psychological state at any particular time.

In starting his discourse on the principles of morals by declaring that reason plays no part in justifying or condemning a passion, Hume commits a fundamental error. In his famous declaration that "'tis not contrary to reason to prefer the destruction of the whole world to the scratching of my finger,"[15] he appears to omit from consideration the fact that the destruction of the whole world would include himself, and thus he is counterbalancing his own death against a mere minor laceration of one of his limbs. Most people would conclude that such a sentiment is contrary to reason, for it makes no sense. It is perverse in the strict dictionary definition of that term: an idea, belief or action that is turned against what is reasonable or fitting.[16] In the case of the temptation to commit adultery, it is reason that will ultimately decide which course of action to take, for it will consider the probable consequences of being

14. For these three characteristics, see Scott-Kakures et al., "Hume's Moral Theory," 300.

15. Hume, *Treatise on Human Nature* (2.3.3).

16. Kirkpatrick, *Cassell's Concise English Dictionary*, 988.

swayed by passion alone. Hume's belief, therefore, that reason is and ought to be the slave of passions has to be reversed. Passions, feelings, and sentiments are no guide to distinguishing between what is a good or bad belief or action.

A wife who has been verbally and physically abused for years by her husband, may, in a moment of extreme provocation, lash out in a passionate action of fear and anger and kill her husband. Whilst such an action is fully understandable, it is not justified morally because it was committed in a fit of rage. The sentence may be lighter, because of the circumstances, but the judgment is that the murder was not the reasonable way to have acted; the only exception being in the case of self-defense against the likelihood of being killed herself (and even then there may be alternative ways of defending herself). The use of reason in making moral judgments is necessary; it is, of course, another matter to consider whether the use of reason is sufficient. That is a discussion that would take us too far away from our present purpose.

Another aspect of the vast subject of justifying or censuring moral beliefs and actions concerns free will and necessity. To what extent are we constrained into accepting certain beliefs? Are we being influenced by certain feelings to act in certain ways, to such an extent that we cannot be held responsible for those beliefs, feelings, and actions? Is there an immutable and irresistible chain of cause and effect, such that the individual is compelled to hold certain beliefs, to possess certain emotions, and to behave in certain ways? The chain may be the result of certain mechanical impulses that have come to bear on my nature, many of which I am unaware. Or, they may be the result of the way I have been nurtured from my infancy or the circumstances through which I have had to live. Or, they may be due to the way I have been created by a deity, so that the deity's will compels me to be the person I am:

> The ultimate Author of all our volitions is the Creator of the world, who first bestowed motion on this immense machine, and placed all beings in that particular position, whence every subsequent event, by an inevitable necessity, must result. Human actions, therefore, either can have no moral turpitude at all, as proceeding from so good a cause; or if they have any turpitude, they must involve our Creator in the same guilt, while he is acknowledged to be their ultimate cause and author.[17]

---

17. Hume, *Enquiry Concerning Human Understanding* (8.32).

Hume's response to the dilemma he sets out is interesting, and to some extent unusual.[18] On the one hand, he appears to endorse a fairly strict form of determinism: the thesis that every event is caused suggests that no choices or actions are free, in the sense that they could have been other than they are; the laws of nature cannot be violated. This conclusion suggests that people cannot be properly praised or blamed for what they do. On the other hand, he affirms that, although everything is determined, free will is possible.

Hume defends a variety of compatibilism. He defines "liberty" as the power of acting or not acting according to the determinations of the will.[19] Actions, therefore, are free, when a person wills them in the absence of duress, which either constrains or forces her to act against her will. So, on the one hand, we cannot transcend the laws of nature: if I jump off a cliff and I have no wings, I am constrained by the law of gravity from gently flying to the ground below. On the other hand, natural laws do not impel us to take certain actions. Unless I am pushed off the cliff by a superior force, I do not have to jump. Our decisions are caused by our own character. This is an internal, not an external, causation. The resultant actions, therefore, are ours, and we can be held responsible. An absolutely unbreakable chain of cause and effect, if it could ever be traced in its minute detail (by means of a super powerful computer, perhaps), would enable anyone to be able to predict how a person would act and react in any given circumstance. We know, however, from experience that although most people act with a certain amount of regularity that can be anticipated, at other times their actions are quite unpredictable; they choose to do things which we would never have expected.

Moreover, Hume argues, a state of affairs devoid of necessity would not make us free, for then every action would be arbitrary, random, and out of our control. Freedom is real when choices are made after much thought and within a certain framework of nature that delivers us from chance events which we have no means of understanding or foreseeing. Behavior can only be morally responsible, if it proceeds from the inner causation deriving from a person's character and disposition. In this sense, it is necessitated, but it is not compelled.

---

18. The following presentation of Hume's discussion of necessity and free will is based on the summary of ch. 8 of *Enquiry Concerning Human Understanding*, given in Beauchamp, *David Hume*, 38–43. The illustrations, however, are mine.

19. Hume, *Enquiry Concerning Human Understanding* (8.23).

On Religion

It is almost a truism to claim that the presence or absence of a belief in a personal God, who has created and sustains all things and has revealed his nature and his purposes, will substantially effect a person's view of what it means to be human. Although Hume counted amongst his friends Christian believers whom he respected, he was adamant that he could not personally believe in the existence of the God they acknowledged. He adduced several arguments in favor of atheism.

The most basic contention was that nothing should be believed except on the basis of convincing evidence, and that evidence had to be based on experience of the everyday world. Hume argued that the only possible experiential evidence for God's existence came in the form of either miracles or a providential ordering of the world. In the case of miracles, Hume dismissed all reports of their having happened as highly improbable:

> Miracles, by their nature, are events that run counter to invariable experience. If uniform experience was not the experience of everyday life, a miracle, as a break in that uniformity, would have no sense. However, experience amounts to certainty, whilst the testimony of a miracle can be no more than a matter of possibility. It is more prudent to believe the certainty... The assertion of miracles is based not so much on faith as on credulity. The presumption is always against their having happened.[20]

With regard to a theistic explanation of the universe, Hume rejects the assumption that mental order (intelligent design) gives a better account of the universe than physical order:

> The orderly universe that we find is only in greater need of explication than a chaotic one, because it is what we live in. Order is what we experience and there is nothing else by contrast that makes order more or less probable. Given the initial event of the universe, the result is the natural order we perceive. We do not need to hypothesise God to make sense of it. Random movements of matter could produce stable entities by a process akin to that of natural selection.[21]

---

20. Kirk, *Future of Reason*, 51–52.
21. Kirk, *Future of Reason*, 52; see also Gaskin, "Hume on Religion," 324–28.

Hume was simply not persuaded that the evidence of our senses pointed unmistakably in the direction of a benevolent deity who created all things well. He argues against this presumption in the following way:

> You (believers in the god or gods of creation) find certain phenomena in nature. You seek a cause or author. You imagine that you have found him . . . You imagine it impossible, but that he must produce something greater and more perfect than the present scene of things, which is so full of ill and disorder. You forget, that this superlative intelligence and benevolence are entirely imaginary . . . and that you have no ground to ascribe to him any qualities, but what you see he has actually exerted and displayed in his productions. Let your gods, therefore, O philosophers, be suited to the present appearances of nature: And presume not to alter these appearances by arbitrary suppositions, in order to suit them to the attributes, which you so fondly ascribe to your deities . . . Hence, all the fruitless industry to account for the ill appearances of nature, and save the honour of the gods; while we must acknowledge the reality of that evil and disorder, with which the world so much abounds.[22]

Thus Hume, with familiar arguments, seeks to demolish the argument for God's existence from design.

Hume's explanation of the origin of religious beliefs is quite conventional. He believed that human beings invented superior invisible powers in order to counterbalance their fear of irresistible natural events and their ignorance of the causes:

> These unknown causes, then, become the constant object of our hope and fear; and while the passions are kept in perpetual alarm by an anxious expectation of the events, the imagination is equally employed in forming ideas of those powers on which we have so entire a dependence.[23]

Whereas such an explanation may account for some primal religious beliefs and practices, it is totally inadequate as an explanation for all that might be considered under the category of religion.

As for Hume's arguments against miracles, it is now recognized that they are circular in character and question-begging:

---

22. Hume, *Enquiry Concerning Human Understanding* (11.15, 17).

23. From *Natural History of Religion* (1757) in Kramnick, *Portable Enlightenment Reader*, 113.

He assumes that a miracle is the equivalent of an event that has never been observed in any age or country.[24] His argument is that there could not be, in principle, any evidence available that should be sufficient to persuade us that a miracle has occurred. However, this is to beg the question. It is not good reasoning to rule evidence out of court before it has been examined.[25]

When Hume asserts that "a miracle is a violation of the laws of nature; and as a form and unalterable experience has established these laws, the proof against a miracle, from the very nature of the fact, is as entire as any argument from experience can possibly be imagined,"[26] he assumes what the argument is supposed to demonstrate. The statement is as dogmatic as the claim that a miracle has taken place, whatever the evidence may be. So, we could only know that experience refutes the possibility of miracles, if we already knew that all reports of them are false. Such a claim amounts to special pleading. It contradicts his exalted view of the importance of experience and the prior requirement to assess all evidence before coming to a conclusion.

Unfortunately, Hume's inadequate reasoning and his ineffective explanation of what has brought about the universe and human existence within it has led him to embrace a reductionist account of what it means to be human. His problem is that he will not admit that some knowledge, understanding, and wisdom about human existence could come from beyond what can be gleaned from observation or inferred from reasoning about experience. If no personal intelligence exists outside material reality, human beings are entirely left on their own to make sense of their life within the limits of the natural order, which is where they have situated themselves.

This is the arena in which Hume and a number of Enlightenment thinkers decided to try to forge a "science" of human nature. As a consequence, he rejected the Christian account of the essential dignity of human beings and their sinfulness. At the same time, he admitted that humans are aggressive and acquisitive animals, capable of cruelty, and often selfish and greedy.[27] Having dismissed the claim that human worth could only be safeguarded ultimately by the doctrine of the *imago Dei*, his defense of political rights and liberties falls short of an adequate

---

24. Hume, *Enquiry Concerning Human Understanding* (10.8).
25. Kirk, *Future of Reason*, 224.
26. Hume, *Enquiry Concerning Human Understanding* (10.12).
27. See Baier, *Pursuits of Philosophy*, 136–37.

foundation in what is true (not just expedient). Hume oscillated between a mild confidence that human beings naturally possessed enough virtues to forge communities of mutual respect and sympathy, and a fairly firm skepticism in the realistic possibility that gradual reforms of social wrongs was achievable by nonviolent means. According to Annette Baier, the second wise thing that Hume advocated was resignation to living in imperfect societies.[28] The extreme rhetoric of a Condorcet, Turgot, or Joseph Priestley were not for him.

John Randall sums up his life's work as typical of the spirit of the British Enlightenment, boldness in speculation with conservatism in practice. By and large, he complacently accepted the British establishment. Thus, for example, he was a staunch defender of the stability of owning possessions, whose transference to another had to be by consent. He believed that overall public utility was the sole basis for the exercise of justice and the pursuit of perfect equality was impracticable.[29]

Denis Diderot

For a variety of reasons, Diderot may be considered the eighteenth-century *philosophe* par excellence. He bore the main burden of editing the massive *Encyclopedie*, perhaps the most lasting monument to the Enlightenment: it contained 71,818 articles, submitted by 150 contributors; it stretched to seventeen volumes of articles and eleven volumes of plates. It was designed as a map that connected together as much knowledge of the world as was then available. Its purpose was to disseminate as widely as possible knowledge that would promote public welfare. The subtitle gave an indication of its content: *An Analytical Dictionary of the Sciences, Arts and Trades by a Society of Men of Letters*. Diderot wrote many of the articles himself. It is not surprising that he has received many accolades from subsequent historians and philosophers:

> No-one in the 18th Century promoted that cause (enlightenment) more vigorously than Diderot ... No-one in the Enlightenment achieved greater originality by way of transliteration and commentary, through the re-association of the ideas of other authors.[30]

---

28. Baier, *Pursuits of Philosophy*, 137.
29. Randall, *Career of Philosophy*, 837–44.
30. Mason and Wokler, *Diderot*, x, xi.

Besides the work he put into the encyclopedia, Diderot was a prolific writer of books and articles on philosophy, art, drama, and the natural sciences, and also novels and correspondence. Much of his natural, moral, and political philosophy was written as comments or annotations on the thought of others. Nevertheless, he has never been considered a great writer. He was, however, regarded by his contemporaries as an eloquent conversationalist and debater.

Diderot also deserves his prominent place in the history of philosophy for his ability to review, test, and evaluate some of the most crucial enigmas of human existence:

> Diderot spent much of his adult life wrestling with conundrums posed by fatalism and free-will, materialism and living beings, and the mind and its place in nature.[31]

As we shall see, he was much better at outlining the problems than resolving them. He was not a systematic thinker. Indeed, his fundamental intellectual assumptions did not allow an orderly, structured arrangement of his thinking:

> His thought is hostile to systems for their inability to apprehend the multi-faceted nature of an ever-changing reality and man's constantly evolving perception of that reality.[32]

He was often caught in dilemmas of his own making. As we trace the most characteristic aspects of his thinking, it should become clear why this was so.

His Early Writings

Diderot was brought up in an orthodox Catholic family. His parents would have liked him to have studied for the priesthood. However, after a period of education in the Jesuit college in his home town in Langres, he moved to Paris and began to study law. After a short time, he gave this up as a possible career and decided that he would become a writer. He wrote his first original work in 1746, *Pensees philosophiques* (*Philosophical Thoughts*). Although critical of the Christian faith, at this time he espoused a deistic account of God.

---

31. Makari, *Soul Machine*, 229.
32. Strugnell, *Diderot's Politics*, viii.

Between this book and his brief incarceration in the Vincennes fortress (July 1749) for criticizing the government, Diderot wrote two more significant works, *Promenade du sceptique* (*The Skeptics Walk*) and *Lettre sur les aveugles* (*Letter on the Blind*). Whereas in *Philosophical Thoughts* he defends deism against a comprehensive atheism on the basis of the argument from design, in the latter two books he inclines increasingly toward atheism. The first was written as a kind of allegory, which criticized three main approaches to life: firstly, the religious (Catholicism), which was marked by its fanaticism, credulity, and connivance at the immorality of its clergy; secondly, the hedonist, which was characterized by a self-promoting vanity and escapism; and the third, the philosophical, which was distinguished by its obscurity and its confusion. In the latter case, whereas one might have suspected that Diderot would have approved of the philosophical life, in fact he is caustic in his judgment of the impractical nature of much of its reflection. Diderot shows, at a formative moment of his life, his distaste for mere theorizing. As was the intention in the case of the *Encyclopedie*, thought and knowledge were ill-considered unless they had some practical outcomes for normal daily living.

In his *Letter on the Blind*, Diderot comes to the conclusion that the argument from the design of nature to a nature's designer is inadequate. What is the point of affirming a being who may be inferred from the finished product, but is not otherwise available to human sense perception? Moreover, the argument from design is hardly likely to convince those born blind. For those who cannot see directly the intricacies of the natural world, the introduction of a prime mover to account for the complexity of nature is not obvious. An alternative is available which gains coherence from its simplicity and is supported by the experimental sciences. It is matter in a state of ferment, matter to which motion is not an arbitrary addition,[33] but an intrinsic necessity. The introduction of a god hypothesis is simply an attempt to avoid admitting ignorance; a self-contained science gives a perfectly adequate explanation:

> Motion continues and will continue to combine masses of matter, until they have found some arrangement in which they may finally persevere ... What is the world ... but a complex, subject to cycles of change, all of which show a tendency to destruction: a rapid succession of beings that appear one by one, flourish and

---

33. As in Isaac Newton's cosmology.

disappear; a merely transitory symmetry and a momentary appearance of order.³⁴

Through the device of an argument between a deist clergyman and a dying, blind philosopher and mathematician, Nicholas Saunderson, Diderot espouses the notion of "thinking matter" and its natural evolution through spontaneous self-generation as an adequate, simple account of the origin and subsequent progression of all matter, inanimate and animate; or, at least, he does for the time being:

> If we grant that motion is inherent in matter, and if we are given an infinity of time, then it is possible for an organized universe, such as the one we know, to have developed without guidance from a creative intelligence.³⁵

The creative intelligence might be within nature itself, not outside it. At a later stage in his thinking, he realizes that such a theory, which seems to solve one problem, actually raises others which it cannot solve.

Materialism

By the time that Diderot wrote his *Pensees sur l'interpretation de la nature* (*Thoughts Concerning the Interpretation of Nature*) (1753),³⁶ and in his *Lettre a Landois* (Letter to Landois) of the same year, he had come to a settled view that there was absolutely no existence inside or outside the universe except matter. In this vein, he contributed a number of the most stringent passages to d'Holbach's *Systeme de la nature* (*The System of Nature*) (1770), which has been given the title of "the Bible of atheism."³⁷

> The world is enclosed, with matter becoming the self-causing and self-sustaining principle of itself.³⁸

It is interesting to note that reasoning such as that used by Diderot, and backed up by the evolutionary theory of Charles Darwin, became the standard "scientific" explanation of the existence of the universe and life within it; that is, until the Big Bang Theory of the universe's origin

---

34. Diderot, in Strugnell, *Diderot's Politics*, 18.
35. Quoted in Brumfitt, *French Enlightenment*, 124.
36. One of only a few books actually published during his lifetime.
37. Introduction to *Denis Diderot: Works*.
38. Kirk, *Future of Reason*, 44.

produced a wholly new perspective on an initial cause, and reopened the question of intelligent design.

Diderot, however, made a strange assumption. In order for the physical, psychic, and moral nature of the human being to be properly open to scientific investigation, he supposed that atheistic materialism was a necessary starting point. This radical departure from the traditional view of the universe and the place of humans within it appeared to him to be indispensable in order to study, free of theological dogma, the origins of human knowledge. However, this line of reasoning fails to take into account the fact that atheistic materialism is just as much a matter of faith or dogma as a theistic account of the universe, since the nonexistence of a nonmaterial supreme being is the presupposition of an argument, not its demonstrated conclusion. Moreover, the belief that a true understanding of human nature can be achieved only through the biological sciences is also a presupposition, not one based on a full examination of all the evidence. Finally, it is unwarranted to hold that only atheistic materialism allows an unbiased investigation of human reality. The monotheistic belief in divine creation permits an untrammeled examination of nature in all its aspects, as many early modern scientists of the seventeenth century claimed.[39]

However, it was characteristic of Diderot's approach to knowledge that, although in a number of writings he held to a dogmatic materialism, in others he was a reluctant materialist. He saw reasonably clearly that human experience raised serious questions for an all-embracing materialist view of the world. First, there is the continuing difficulty of explaining how inanimate matter gave rise to organic life; how is it possible to account for something (life) arising from nothing (lack of life)? Secondly, there is the question of making sense of the obvious qualitative differences between humans and animals.[40] Thirdly, a monist, mechanist materialism appears to cut off any possibility of human free will:

> Diderot, in his *Lettre a Landois*, rejects the concept of human freedom, arguing that man like all other natural phenomena acts always and only out of necessity. Free-will is an illusion, for every action is determined by causes external to the individual.[41]

---

39. See ch. 2 of Kirk, *Future of Reason*: "An Enquiry into the Origins of Modern Science."

40. These I have outlined in ch. 1 of this study.

41. Strugnell, *Diderot's Politics*, 4.

Finally, a closed-order material system in nature does not give any plausible explanation for the moral consciousness of human beings. If a wholly enclosed scientific account of the human is the only knowledge that we can acquire, we have only description. We can analyze how humans act and react, how their body functions, how their brain operates. However, none of this will help us to explain why we make distinctions between good and evil, right and wrong. The prescriptive cannot logically be derived from the descriptive; or, in simpler terms "ought" cannot be deduced from "is."

We will now consider these two particular aspects of Diderot's thought.

Determinism

If every event in the world is the result of an inexorable, blind, impersonal cause, the whole language of virtue and vice, praise and blame, becomes empty of meaning. The dreamer in *Le Reve de d'Alembert*, under the influence of a character called "Diderot," voices the opinion that the universe manifests a constant, aimless flux which produced humanity as one of an endless series of episodic phenomena, that possesses no intrinsic purpose.[42] Yet, at the same time, Diderot clings to universal notions such as justice, rights, and progress. Apparently, Diderot inhabited the contradictory world of a deterministic reformer, disbelieving in free will, but campaigning for greater freedom (of thought and expression) from indoctrination and oppression. As he himself expresses it, he was permanently disturbed by the conflict between his abstract deterministic philosophy and the real world of his own experience:

> Oh what a fine system for ingrates! It makes me wild to be entangled in a devil of a philosophy that forces the assent of the mind, but which my heart cannot help denying.[43]

Moral Philosophy

Although it is difficult to see where Diderot would derive a coherent set of ethical principles from, because of his mechanistic theory of human

---

42. Fowler, *New Essays on Diderot*, 2.
43. Quoted in Fowler, *New Essays on Diderot*, 2.

nature and his rejection of any reality beyond the material, nevertheless he was obliged by reflecting on his own humanity, and that of others, to discriminate between virtue and vice. He might have followed the lead of the Marquis de Sade who, embracing the logical implications of the nonexistence of God and monist materialism, would have concluded that the only virtue is the survival of the fittest, and this justifies the strongest in the use of physical or psychological force to pursue their selfish, hedonistic ends. The very existence of violence and cruelty in human nature indicates that it is legitimate to pursue these ends for one's own pleasure. De Sade carried this reasoning to an extreme and was hounded by the authorities for exercising and promoting his view of human nature. However, given his assumptions about the reality of nature, was he wrong to advocate an abandonment to his cravings? There is a certain logic in de Sade's version of what guides the "good" life:

> There is no God. Nature sufficeth unto herself.
>
> All, all is theft, all is unceasing and rigorous competition in nature; the desire to make off with the substance of others is the foremost, the most legitimate passion nature has bred into us and, without doubt, the most agreeable one.
>
> Lust is to the other passions what the nervous fluids is to life; it supports them all, ambition, cruelty, avarice, revenge, are all founded on lust.
>
> All universal moral principles are idle fancies.[44]

Diderot, however, did not follow de Sade's reasoning. We may discuss, however, whether or not he was more or less consistent with his basic worldview, much of which he shared with de Sade. For whatever reason, he drew back from the edge of the precipice of complete moral anarchy. He hovered between committing himself to a *morale universelle* (a universal ethic), which could speak meaningfully of a certain objective justice being implemented for the common good, and the right and duty of individuals to allow their own personal creative impulse to flourish.[45]

---

44. All the quotes are taken from www.brainyquote.com/quotes/authors/m/marquis_de_sade.html.

45. Strugnell, *Diderot's Politics*, 22–24.

From an observational point of view, he would have noticed that individuals do not thrive unless they live in a society regulated by codes of conduct that implement justice, rights, and equality. At the same time, he also noted that in each of these cases there were conflicting notions of their qualities that had to be decided upon to avoid social chaos and that the vast majority of individuals followed patterns of behavior that contradicted such universal values. From the perspective of the legacy that nature's evolution has bequeathed to human life, there is an enormous dilemma. On the one hand, nature has apparently determined a certain course of events, which humans are powerless to change; the only choice is to submit to its *diktat*:

> *Tout ce qui est ne peut ni contre nature ni hors de nature*" ("everything that is cannot be either against nature or outside nature).[46]

On the other hand, he believed that human beings could recognize truth and error and overcome the latter in favor of the former. In other words, they were not confined to a fatalistic attitude to their own tendency toward self-seeking, but could be transformed into beings who cared for the well-being of others. However it came about through nature alone, humans exhibit a refined moral conscience that acknowledges an obligation to care for and serve others. Throughout his life, he appeared to drift between an extreme collectivism, seen for example in his praise of Tahitian society, where

> the individual is reduced to total subservience to the collectivity. He is no more than a utility, his acceptance and cultivation by the community being strictly proportionate to the services he is able to render,[47]

and an individualism born out of the unique value of every specific person.

---

46. Quoted in Strugnell, *Diderot's Politics*, 28.

47. Strugnell, *Diderot's Politics*, 42. He expounds the doctrine of utility through the dialogue between the Tahitian chief, Orou, and the Almoner of the French ship *Bougainville* that had landed on the island of Tahiti; see, "Supplement to the Voyage of the Bougainville" in Kramnick, *Portable Enlightenment Reader*, 267–74.

The Natural State of Human Life

The moral principles of the Tahitians, then, according to Diderot, spring from, and are in harmony with, their nature. Unencumbered by the rules and regulations of a culture shaped by Christian morality, inclinations are the same as duties: men are free to impregnate any woman they fancy, and women are brought up to consider child-bearing as their supreme responsibility to the community:

> In no other text are the elements of Diderot's irreverent, sensuous, liberal, anti-colonial, utilitarian philosophy drawn together more closely.[48]

As we have noted above, Diderot found a strict materialist atheism inadequate as a solid basis for objective moral values. He found his emphasis on the inexorable regulatory function of nature, from which no one could escape, hard to reconcile with any notion of responsibility or obligation—apart from satisfying one's own disposition. He somewhat modified his interpretation of materialism in his *Refutation d'Helvetius*, by allowing that the mind is more than reflexes set off by the impulses of sensation stemming from the physical processes of the brain. In fact, he appears to offer a version of vitalism[49] by allowing that there is at work within the body's machinery an active natural force, not entirely identifiable with a person's physical makeup, that enables volition and reflection and thus ultimately gives a basis for human responsibility for action.[50]

One commentator on Diderot believes that a concept of universal sensibility dominated Diderot's thinking about the universe and the place of the person within it. A theory of its presence in matter is one he needed to believe, as it gives an account both of humans' awareness of being separate from the world and of consciousness. Thus, it is a force that enables humans to control their environment.[51]

Diderot was vague about the nature of sensibility. He conceded that its workings were mysterious, an obscure property of organized matter (that which, for example, caused an egg to turn into a chick). The theory

---

48. Mason and Wokler, *Diderot*, xxi.

49. The theory or doctrine that life forces arise from or contain a nonmaterial living force and cannot, therefore, be entirely explained as physical and chemical phenomena. They are, to some extent, self-determining.

50. Makari, *Soul Machine*, 257.

51. Bremner, *Order and Chance*, 30.

was a concession to the tension he felt between a wholly consistent materialism and his own experience of himself and others. Nevertheless, he rejected the mind-body dualism proposed by Descartes. Active matter was sufficient, he believed, to account for mental functions. He advocated a model of the mind in which the subject is also an object to itself. So, nervous sensibility organized in the brain allowed for the emergence of memory, thought, a notion of self and consciousness.[52] Diderot believed that he had solved the conundrum of the relationship between a person's physical reality and their capacity to reflect on their physical nature, without having to resort to some extraneous "spiritual" entity that completes their being.

Assessment

If the foregoing discussion of his views seems to be abstruse and confusing, it is because it is hard to pin down his thought. He never pretended to be a systematic thinker. He allowed change and revision in his own mind. At one and the same time, he was someone who grappled with complex philosophical issues, and also a keen observer of ordinary people, whose lives often appeared to lie outside the abstract concerns of the *philosophes*. He wrote essays that dealt with core questions of human significance from a theoretical viewpoint, and he wrote novels which explored the practical life of ordinary citizens. He found it hard to resolve the discrepancy between abstract and practical thought:

> Diderot is one of the most difficult among philosophers to capture: versatile, volatile, erotic, experimental, profoundly original, he belongs to no single category, and puzzled everyone who knew him. He puzzled even himself.[53]

Some have suggested that the confusion of his thought is due to the fact that he was a much more coherent speaker than writer. Our difficulty in unraveling his enigmatic statements may, then, be due to only having his written thoughts. (Had recordings and YouTube existed in those days, perhaps our task would be easier).

---

52. Makari, *Soul Machine*, 259–60.
53. Gay, *Enlightenment*, 289.

Siofra Pierse believes that Diderot was a natural skeptic in his unsystematic thinking. His skepticism infuses his novels. In commenting on *Jacques le fataliste*, she says:

> Any claims to narrative reliability have been steadily undermined. Any slight claim of either certainty or veracity has been systematically demolished . . . Each assertion undermines certainty and conformity . . . The text has dissolved . . . If this text is a micro-model for the world as we know it, the *modus operandi* has just been exclusively exposed as a fraud and summarily jettisoned.[54]

Clearly Diderot was distrustful of the ability of philosophers to solve the many enigmas of human existence. In the *Promenade du sceptique (The Skeptic's Walk)*, the *allee* of the philosophers—the allegedly educated, rational, and balanced group—are steeped in doubt and end their day with a lack of resolution.[55] In the novel, *Le Neveu de Rameau (Rameau's Nephew)*, considered by many as his most profound work, the narrator (Rameau, the composer's nephew) instead of aspiring to purity, truth, and certainty (the assumed aim of the philosophers), wallows in his imperfection and mediocrity, with little desire to amend his life.[56] At the same time, in the *allee* of the flowers, Diderot exposes the vanity of indulging in the world's pleasures, a possible escape from the intellectual indulgence of metaphysics. This latter is the way of superficiality, facetiousness, and futility.

There is, then, a strong strain of doubt in Diderot's outlook on life. He did not end up as a complete skeptic, maintaining that no knowledge is possible, or even that we cannot know whether knowledge is possible or not. Rather, he believed that the process of doubting is a necessary preliminary to the process of forming the best judgments we can make on the basis of the most convincing evidence available. This method of arriving at an accurate picture of reality leads him seemingly to a selective agnosticism.

It is strange, therefore, that he should, throughout his life, be so dogmatic about a materialist interpretation of the universe. After all, the nonexistence of any reality beyond the material is not supported by the

---

54. Pierse, "Subversive Scepticism," 78–79. Morley called Diderot's thoughts "a short manual of skepticism" (Morley, *Diderot and the Encyclopaedists*, 1:44).

55. Hanrahan and Pierse, *Dark Side of Diderot*, 70.

56. Hanrahan and Pierse, *Dark Side of Diderot*, 68.

observation of the senses. It is a hypothesis that cannot be either confirmed or denied by the methods of scientific evidence and experimentation alone. Rather, it is generally believed on grounds that take as their starting point a critique of the inconsistencies of religious worldviews or the appalling ethical consequences of some religious beliefs, but critiques that frequently do not do justice to a religion's own self-understanding. In other words, the negative assessment of a nonmaterialistic understanding of the whole of reality is adopted *a priori*, and then the facts are made to fit the theory. Unfortunately for the theory, there are realities that do not fit a materialist reading of existence, such as the functioning of the scientific method itself: for example, intelligibility (why our environment is comprehensible and transparent to us); the anthropic principle (why there is existence rather than nonexistence, order rather than chaos, contingency rather than necessity); and a coherent account of the origin of, and foundation for, ethics.[57]

It is surprising that, despite his hesitancy about the ability of reason to comprehend life as we experience it, starting only from what may be observed in the material world, he was so dogmatic about the materialist nature of the whole of reality. It is plausible to argue that his doubts about many fundamental issues of being human and his skepticism that there could be any credible answers spring directly from his initial assumption. Notwithstanding, Diderot also desired to find stability and order for life. To seek order was to look for meaning in life. However, he was caught in the dilemma of denying that order could have been implanted in the universe by an intelligent creator, whilst also wishing to establish that chaos did not reign. According to some, Enlightenment thinkers, if they are to contribute new ideas into Western culture,

> ought to (be able) to reach a point of equilibrium which would preserve the human mind both from the tyranny of theology and from the servitude of chance.[58]

The old, stable, enchanted world was in dissolution. Human beings were now faced with the destiny of regaining control of the world, without recourse to any support from beyond nature and their own intelligence. In the following few chapters, we will see how this perspective played

---

57. See "The Epistemological Predicament of the West, Dialogue and Inference to the Best Explanation" in Kirk, *Christian Mission as Dialogue*, 109–22. This study is available at http://repository.ubn.ru.nl/bitstream/2066/90917/1/90917.pdf.

58. Bremner, *Order and Chance*, 1.

itself out in the thinking of some of the greatest intellectual pioneers of the nineteenth and twentieth centuries.

Questions

1. Hume and Diderot are considered by many as pioneers of a new wave of creative thinking. In what sense might this be true?
2. How could a materialist view of the universe be vindicated, starting only with the assumption of a materialist theory?
3. What difference does materialism as a philosophical thesis make to one's understanding of human nature?
4. Why did Hume and Diderot part company with many other Enlightenment thinkers by adopting a skeptical outlook on the power of reason to produce a progressive blueprint for social change?

CHAPTER 6

Diagnosing the Human in the Thinking of Karl Marx and His Followers

> The criticism of religion ends with the doctrine that man is the highest being for man, hence with the categorical imperative to overthrow all conditions in which man is degraded, enslaved, neglected, contemptible beings that cannot be better described than by the exclamation of a Frenchman on the occasion of a proposed dog tax: Poor dogs! They want to treat you like human beings!
> —Karl Marx, *Contribution to the Critique of Hegel's Philosophy of Right*

Introduction

IN THE PREVIOUS CHAPTER, on the humanist thinking of Hume and Diderot, we were left with considerable uncertainty about the way ahead for a transformation of society through a new understanding of the place of humans within a wholly materialistic order. They, along with other enlightenment thinkers, pronounced the old regimes to be the main obstacle to a natural progress of the human spirit toward a genuine human community of which the hallmarks were justice, equality, and freedoms. Yet, they were also dubious about its attainment, because they were struck by the propensity of humans, whatever their educational achievements and however radical their thinking, to pursue their own interests before considering the common good.

They were not complete skeptics, for they desired to contribute a serious analytical assessment of their age to the practical use of transforming their societies and cultures. For this reason, they held out some hope that humans were, at least to a small extent, altruistic toward others.

Though neither lived to see the French Revolution and its aftermath, they would have been shocked by the arbitrary political innovations that it spawned and the brutality it engendered. The ancient monarchy had been swept away, but only to be replaced eventually by a kind of hereditary emperorship.

The Original Marxism of Marx

Whilst the French nation was going through turmoil, war, and reconstruction, a new interpretation of history was being proposed by a German philosopher, Georg Hegel. His thought was to have a profound impact on a group of young intellectuals, of whom Karl Marx became the most famous and influential.[1]

Marx's analysis of distinct historical periods through the ages owes a great debt to Hegel's concept of history and the place of humans within it. If it is true, as many have proposed, that Marx's thought represents the most consistent humanism developed this side of the Enlightenment and the French Revolution, it is because he placed it within a dialectical approach to the conflict-oriented nature of human societies borrowed from Hegel. Hegel had added a new interpretative tool to help his listeners and readers understand historical realities. Marx used it to give a new dimension to the rank materialism of the radical thinkers of the Enlightenment. Commenting on his own "dialectical" relationship to Hegel, Marx said,

> My relation to Hegel is very simple . . . I recognize that I am his disciple. Nevertheless, I have taken the liberty of adopting toward my teacher a critical attitude, separating off the mystification from his dialectic, and in this way stamping upon it a radical change.[2]

To understand fully Marx's revolutionary thinking about human history, it is necessary to briefly summarize Hegel's own approach.

---

1. Other well-known members of a circle linked to Hegel's philosophy were David Strauss, Ludwig Feuerbach, Bruno Bauer, and Arnold Ruge.

2. Marx, *Selected Works*, 599–600.

Hegel's Theory of History

Fundamentally, Hegel strove to break with a positivist approach to history, especially when this was translated into a crude materialism which pretended to be neutral about the process itself. According to this latter perspective, history was only the product of accident or fate. The task of the historian was simply to describe and catalog its events. Empirical materialism wished to bury forever any notion that history could gain a significance from beyond its own limits. Hegel, on the other hand, looked at history as a process whose fundamental meaning unfolded in successive stages in accord with the exact point that human development had reached at that juncture. In other words, the secret of history's explanation is hidden within its own evolution; humans are able gradually to become aware of this development.

In order to be able to understand the previous stage of development it is necessary to have reached a certain level of enlightenment. This level is not the result of a sudden flash of inspiration that comes from a transhistorical realm, but is achieved through discerning the shape of that very stage of history in which the interpreter lives. Through the manifestation of the incarnate Spirit of that stage, one is able to understand history as it has followed a particular course toward them.

According to the idea that history reveals itself from within its own processes, it is logical to suppose that only at the very end of history will it be possible to arrive at a complete interpretation of the whole movement. Hegel believed that his explanatory system was the final word in the comprehension of the inner movement of the historical process as a whole. His philosophy represented the recapitulation of all other philosophies, their full understanding, and their transcending.

History, according to Hegel, is manifested as a series of conflicts between "abstract principles,"[3] be they derived from religions, philosophies, cultures, or political systems. In every age, there exists a tension between the current ideas and their potential contradictions. This tension is manifested as the power of negation, through which the actual state of things is set aside and its opposite, which is in the process of becoming, is made present. History, in this way, is pulled forward by a play of opposites, each one of which is already included in embryo in the previous stage. In other words, history represents a constant process of death and resurrection;

---

3. See, Forster, "Hegel's Dialectical Method," 130–70.

each new resurrection signifies a transformation of the one before and a progression toward a goal which increasingly becomes clearer.

Hegel claimed that his system marked the final synthesis of all opposites. He believed that he had managed to understand and include all possible contrasts, by finding a way of reconciling the mind with the material, and humans' being with their doing. Just as the systematic steps of thinking are inseparable from their respective historical reference points, so through the development of reason we have now reached the end of the dialectical movement of history. The culmination is definitive knowing; it is the unification of all reality in the ultimate revelation of the absolute "Spirit."

Hegel's concept of history is eschatological. However, his approach, because it has already found its complete realization, leads him to adopt a conservative outlook in identifying what is thought with reality itself:

> Thought is no longer critically opposed to reality, but confronts it as an ideal reconciled with the ideal. Reason, conscious of itself, the philosophy of the State, and reason, understood as reality concretely existing as the real State, are harmonized with one another, they become one and the same thing.[4]

Just as reality is the manifestation of the absolute Spirit, which is, in its essence, the total freedom of man's self-realization (a freedom which is expressed in and through the interaction of the divine in the human), so final reality discovers its pinnacle in the Prussian state:

> The universal spirit of the world is the sun which arises in the East in order to set in the West. The German-Christian world is the mature fulfillment of history.[5]

Hegel, intoxicated with the new European spirit, shows himself to be influenced by the Rousseauian idea of the "pure, free-will."[6] Hegel emphasizes that this freedom means it is not possible to see the individual as determined by their social environment, although he is happy to allow that "if these circumstances, way of thinking, customs in general, the state of the world, had not been, then of course the individual would not

---

4. Lowith, *From Hegel to Nietzsche*.

5. Hegel, *Phenomenology of Spirit*. For an extensive interpretation of Hegel, see Stern, *Hegel and the Phenomenology of Spirit*.

6. Stern, *Hegel and the Phenomenology*, 157–62.

have become what he is."[7] Karl Lowith sums up this article of Hegel's faith in this way:

> Mankind, for the first time, puts himself "at the head" and the world's happening is identified with the thinking process of philosophy. The philosophy of history whose principle is the "progression of the awareness of freedom" is closed with this fact.[8]

Where Marx Follows Hegel

Although Marx was in the habit of emphasizing the discontinuous aspects of his thinking in relation to the Hegelian synthesis, there are also a number of points of contact which form the substance itself of the dialectical-materialist theory. The following are the main points where the two converge. They help to explain to a considerable degree the internal dynamism of Marx's thought, and subsequently that of his followers.

Firstly, history contains its own meaning. This is revealed as history unfolds. It contains an inner, coherent logic which can be discovered by reason alone. History moves according to the interaction of certain laws which are both comprehensible and verifiable.

Secondly, the interpretation of history is the interpretation of its qualitative progress. Just as the development of history is strictly logical and necessary, so also its latest phases show evidence of being the result of qualitative leaps forward. Marx shares with Hegel the idea that history should be separated into prehistory and history proper.

Thirdly, history's progress follows a rhythm which proceeds according to the continual negation and overcoming of antagonistic forces. The philosophy of history can be summed up in terms of a constant flux of triads which come together, conflict with one another, and then become united in a higher synthesis which overcomes the opposition. In this way history cannot advance unless each affirmation encounters its corresponding negation, and this negation its negation.

Fourthly, history uncovers a progressive evolution toward the complete freedom of human beings. History, for Marx, is the stage on which humans slowly create themselves, transforming their environment and

---

7. Stern, *Hegel and the Phenomenology*, 110–11.
8. Lowith, *From Hegel to Nietzsche*.

their human relationships. At the climax of history, the kingdom of necessity is transformed into the kingdom of freedom.

Fifthly, history marches irresistibly toward its consummation. The final point of the final triad is communist society which is born as the synthesis between the unlimited expansion of technology, when humankind has learned to dominate nature in a totally rational way, with a society based on community and solidarity. The consummation marks the end of all contradictions. What for Hegel was the ideal Prussian state, for Marx was the ideal society without a state.[9]

Where Marx Breaks with Hegel's Thought

After a sudden attack of cholera, Hegel died in 1831. He was followed by a group of disciples, known as "The Young Hegelians." In general terms, they dedicated themselves to dismantling a large part of the philosophy of their teacher, namely his religious and speculative idealism. Before Marx, undoubtedly the most radical, consistent, and systematic of the group, Ludwig Feuerbach was the most destructive of Hegel's system. At the heart of his criticism of spiritual idealism was his belief that anthropology needed to be substituted for Hegel's pseudotheology in the guise of philosophy.

Feuerbach's humanism was built on an exceedingly optimistic view of human nature. It represented a complete inversion of metaphysics:

> The question about God's existence, or lack of existence, the opposition between theism and atheism belongs to the 17th. and 18th. centuries, not to the 19th. century. I deny God. However, for me, I deny the negation of man. In place of man's illusory and fantastic heavenly position, which in real life leads, of necessity, to man's degradation, I substitute his tangible and real, and therefore, political and social, position. The question about God's existence, or lack of existence, for me, is nothing more than the question concerning the existence, or not, of man.[10]

Like the French radicals of the Enlightenment, Feuerbach believed that philosophical reflection must begin from historical reality and concrete nature, not from some abstract idea.

---

9. See Avineri, *Social and Political Thought*, 17–38.
10. Feuerbach, in Lichtheim, *Marxism*, 17.

As far as Marx was concerned, Feuerbach's criticism of Hegel did not go far enough. His thought was still playing around with idealist elements, at the mercy of speculation and not at the service of humanity.[11] Marx undertook the gigantic and heroic task of constructing a theory which would be totally materialist (in contrast to idealism) and totally dialectic (in contrast to contemplative positivism):

> In direct contrast to German philosophy, which descends from heaven to earth, here we ascend from earth to heaven. That is to say, we do not set out from what men say, imagine, conceive, nor from men as narrated, thought of, imagined, conceived, in order to arrive at men in the flesh. We set out from real active men, and on the basis of their real-life process we demonstrate the development of the ideological reflexes and echoes of their life process.[12]

> My dialectic method is not only different from the Hegelian, but is its direct opposite. To Hegel, the life process of the human brain, i.e. the process of thinking, which under the name of the "Idea," he even transforms into an independent subject, is the demiurges of the real world, and the real world is only the external phenomenal form of "the Idea." With me, on the contrary, the ideal is nothing else than the material world reflected by the human mind, and translated into forms of thought... The mystification which dialectic suffers in Hegel's hands... is standing on its head... It must be turned right side up again, if you would discover the real kernel within the mystical shell.[13]

The most important elements of Marx's dispute with Hegel can be summed up in three basic propositions. Firstly, he believed that the purpose of philosophy is not an analysis and critique of the historical process, but its transformation. Hegel thought that his philosophical scheme had ended the eternal struggle of opposites, having solved the problem of the tension between knowing and doing. Marx, on the contrary, understands that his own analysis of history has to start out from an antithesis of the Hegelian consummation:

> The aging of the real world coincides, for Hegel, with the final rejuvenation of Philosophy. For Marx, on the other hand, ... the

---

11. See Lefebre, *Dialectical Materialism*.
12. Marx, *German Ideology*, in Tucker, *Marx-Engels Reader*, 118–19.
13. Tucker, *Marx-Engel's Reader*, 197–98.

ending of philosophy coincides with the rejuvenation of the real world, opposed to the ancient philosophy. Philosophy is superseded through the realization of reason in the real world . . . it is converted into . . . a theory which is immediately practical.[14]

For Marx, history does not end in intellectual contemplation, but begins precisely when reason is put at the service of human beings in a process which molds the future in a human way. In short, philosophy has to be the theoretical arm of the proletarian revolution:

> Just as philosophy finds its material weapons in the proletariat, so the proletariat finds its intellectual weapons in philosophy. And once the lightening of thought has penetrated deeply into this virgin soil of the people, the Germans will emancipate themselves and become men.[15]

Secondly, the key to open the true understanding of history does not consist in abstract principles, but in the economic relations of production. In place of the struggle of ideas, Marx proposes the class struggle, which has surfaced as the result of a determined mode of production:

> The history of all hitherto existing society is the history of class struggles . . . a fight that each time ended, either in a revolutionary reconstitution of society at large, or in the common ruin of the contending classes.[16]

Thirdly, the final product of Hegelian philosophy is the reconciliation of logical thought with what is. It was a massive attempt to reconcile the revolutionary French spirit with the ordering of freedom in the Prussian state, a way of bottling up the history of freedom in one all-inclusive political reality. Freedom had to be protected against its champions, who so easily converted it into the irrational terror of libertarianism. In reality, Marx did not so much oppose the fact that Hegel's final synthesis ended up in the Prussian state, as that Hegel managed to separate the essence of the state from the existence of particular states in concrete history. In part as a result of his experience as a journalist, writing articles for the *Rheinische Zeitung* (1842–1843), in part as an expression of his dialectical materialism, Marx considered that the state represented the quintessence

---

14. Hook, *From Hegel to Marx*.

15. Marx, *Contribution to the Criticism of Hegel's Philosophy of Right*, in Tucker, *Marx-Engels' Reader*, 23.

16. Marx, *Manifesto of the Communist Party*, in Tucker, *Marx-Engels Reader*, 335–36.

of human alienation, because it concentrated and administered nothing more than the interests of the dominant classes:

> The executive of the modern state is but a committee for managing the common affairs of the whole bourgeoisie.[17]

I will make an assessment of both Marx's indebtedness to Hegel's philosophical project, and his divergence from it, later in this analysis of his conception of what it means to be human. It is necessary to try to understand first his relation to the Hegelian dialectic method of analysis, for it dominates his schematic interpretation of historical periods and his belief that the contradictions of history can and will be overcome. His understanding of the human predicament is firmly rooted in the notions of conflict and contradiction. His understanding of the future well-being of the human race is based on his belief that history is on course to a resolution of humanity's main impasse. The overcoming of real human alienation will happen through the elimination of the exploitative system of capital accumulation, owned by a bourgeois class and used as a powerful force to protect their interests and to keep a laboring class in permanent subjection.

Marx's main quarrel with the revolutionary idealists of the eighteenth century was their failure to see where humanity's real problem lay. Ultimately, it did not lie in the *ancien regime*, nor in what Marx would have considered religion's inverted attitude to the world, backed by a powerful ecclesial organization, nor in lack of education. In looking chiefly at equality and freedom in terms of individuals' rights, they had missed the main point. All human beings were in a permanent state of alienation through the way that economic relations were conducted. The French (and American) revolutions, as subsequent history eloquently demonstrated, were no more than a transference of power from a ruling elite to a bourgeois class of entrepreneurs, managers, and professional groups:

> Marx appears to think that the intrinsic forces of technological advance, engendered by the new successes in science and by human labor, once reconciled again to their proper object through the negation of the exploitative action of capitalist accumulation, will produce a qualitatively different kind of society.[18]

---

17. Marx, *Manifesto of the Communist Party*, in Tucker, *Marx-Engels Reader*, 337.
18. Kirk, *Future of Reason*, 145.

Marx's Vision of the Human Being: Principal Themes

Marxist anthropology can be tentatively resumed in the following mini thesis: human beings create themselves in their struggle to subdue nature; they humanize nature; they are the thinking product of their practical activity; the myths of their consciences are due solely to their alienation, whose source can be revealed and whose consequences overcome.

Marx's thought can be summarized in four interrelated stages.[19] The most basic stage, the one from which his materialism is derived, is the negation of any supernaturally created essence in man. According to Marx, there does not exist in humans any intrinsically imposed residue (his underlying being) which somehow is impervious to change. From this negation, Marx draws two very important conclusions. Firstly, the human being belongs exclusively to matter. He is to be distinguished from the rest of nature only by being its reflexive part (he is nature turned conscious). The principal distinction between the animal kingdom and *homo sapiens* is the superior development of the latter's brain.

Secondly, man is changeable. Wherever matter exists, mutability reigns. Human beings are a perpetual flowing stream of consciousness. They arise from nature, in the full sense of the word "arise." There are only two possible anthropologies in this basic sense: materialism and idealism.

According to Adam Schaff, Marx's vision of the human being as an individual does not contain any developed theory of personality, except perhaps in the negative sense that it is not the product of any ultrahuman forces. It is not an indelible reality implanted within the human psyche from birth, but is the product of self-creation. The individual's "ontological status" is not a point of departure, but a goal to be reached through the transformation of human communities by the removal of all forms of human alienation. The communist society is the point when humans recover their full humanity.[20]

The second stage is intimately linked to the first. Human beings are the aggregate of their social relationships. Human beings arise from their context in society in the full sense of the word. Their social existence determines their consciousness, not the other way round (praxis antecedes theory). Everyone acts according to his material circumstances, and in particular, his economic relationships.

---

19. The divisions are mine, not those of Marx.
20. Schaff, *Marxism and the Human Individual*, 94–99.

So, Marx's starting point in reflecting on the reality of human life is not the individual as a self-contained island, but a social individual whose nature can only be understood and realized in community. In his work *Grundrisse*,[21] Marx analyzes the process whereby, in his opinion, individuals became isolated from community, particularly through the exploitation of their labor-power. In the earliest human communities, human beings were "species-beings," with no independent existence. In a sense, they were possessions of the human unit as a whole, rather than free agents with self-interests.[22] However, he also believed that once the interpersonal antagonisms created by the exploitation of people's labor as their essential bond with nature were eliminated, "a society, in which the full and free development of every individual forms the ruling principle" would be created.[23]

A third stage that we can encounter in Marx appears as a development of the idea that humans arise from matter: they realize themselves through work. Work is to be understood as the subjecting and forming of matter. Humans create themselves by the creative act of their labor. This concept helps to explain Marx's very precise view of human alienation. A person is alienated from herself by the bad use of her labor through a defective economic system. History demonstrates a continual struggle to achieve a greater superiority in the possession of property. This possession has given people a greater say in the exercise of political power (the economic factor predominates over the political). The whole process began when human societies passed from practicing common possession of goods to ones which encouraged private property.[24] Proletarians are alienated both within themselves and from their fellows because another expropriates the work of their hands for his own benefit. The bourgeois person, on the other hand, is alienated from everyone, because he has converted all human relationships into money transactions. So,

> the conditions under which man's self-creation takes place in present (capitalist) society are self-defeating. Labor is supposed to be man's process of self-becoming because it is man's specific attribute . . . The idea of alienation is thus inseparably bound

21. Archibald, *Marx and the Missing Link*, 13–44.
22. See Archibald, *Marx and the Missing Link*, 15.
23. See Geras, *Marx and Human Nature*, 85.
24. See Marx, "The Secret of Primitive Accumulation," ch. 26 of *Capital*; Engels, "Barbarism and Civilization," ch. 9 of *The Origin of the Family, Private Property and the State*.

up with the activist, constructive and nonreflective character of consciousness which Marx shows to be man's unique attribute.[25]

The fourth and final stage is a development of the idea that humans arise from their social relationships: they realize themselves by making (or changing) history. The identification which Marx presupposes between the nature of man and his social relationships explains the strong emphasis which he places on praxis. Human beings are humans, not when they are meditating, but when they are transforming the objective world freely (they are *homo laborans*). If they lose this possibility they lose their humanity. The only way they can recuperate this possibility is by means of the revolution, the final phase of the class struggle. Marx speaks of a prehistory, which is the conflictive part of human history, and history proper (after the revolution), which he calls the kingdom of freedom, where there will be no more coercion or limitation. History proper, freed from all class antagonisms, is the place of humans' complete humanization:

> From the analysis of alienation emerges the possibility of a radical revolution in man's conditions that will enable man to achieve the full potential of his self-creativity.[26]

In the first two stages, Marx explains the origin of human life: matter and the aggregate of his social relationships. In the third and fourth stages, he defines the human from the point of view of his action: in nature and in history. His twin concepts of alienation (or evil) and revolution (or salvation) are closely linked to his starting point in his idea of what it means to be human.

Marx places himself firmly within a Hebrew cultural background when he speaks about "total man" or "being-in-species" (*Gattungswesen*).[27] He makes of man a "being-in-history." On the other hand, he also follows the basic presuppositions of the Enlightenment when he emphasizes the fact that humans are solely the subject of their own history; it is as if they alone, when they become aware of the causes of their alienation and the objective laws of the historical process, can achieve true selfhood. According to Marx, human beings must become self-activating (*selbsttatig*).

---

25. Avineri, *Social and Political Thought*, 85–86.
26. Avineri, *Social and Political Thought*, 86.
27. See McLellan, *Marx's Grundrisse*, 23.

Marxist Criticism of Theistic Anthropology

Every religion, according to Marx, demonstrates the existence of a falsified conscience. Belief in any kind of personal object superior to human beings and beyond their world reveals the human search for compensation, a substitutionary recompense for the failure to terminate relationships of alienation. Religion is an integral part of the superstructure of any human culture. It arises as a necessary consequence of the culture's economic substructure. As the superstructure responds to an alienating substructure, religion is also a logical extension of this alienation. Inversely, when the alienation ceases, religion will also disappear.

Following the thought of Feuerbach, Marx concludes that human beings are alone in the universe. If they were not alone, they would be dependent upon something or someone external to themselves. But no form of dependence can be squared with that absolute liberty which is necessary if they are going to be the real and not imaginary subjects of their own history. Whatever kind of religion may be imagined, its real force lies in its ability to project human aspirations from this world to a world beyond the grave. This being so, Marx believed, no religion can finally and absolutely dedicate itself to changing this world. Rather, it will tend to support the status quo in this life, so that it can concentrate undisturbed on the next. Confusing Hegel's idea of a transcendent universal Spirit with the Christian God, Marxists have concluded that Christians, as was the case with Hegel, are bound to defend the powers that be, because they are always, automatically, decreed by God.

Marx used the Hegelian dialectic to analyze transhuman relationships from the very earliest times up to the time in which he lived. He divided human history into consecutive ages, each one following the other with complete inevitability. He begins with the primitive communal society. Then follows a society based on slavery. This is transformed into a feudal society, a guild-society, and finally (as the last economic arrangement of prehistory) into a capitalist society. Each of these different stages of economic development arose of necessity out of the preceding historical movements. Religion also arose of necessity. It too has changed according to changing historical circumstances. However, history has now reached its final stage. With the coming of the consciousness that the "working class" is a "class for itself," and with the inevitable breakdown of capitalism, prehistory has finally reached its limit. When real history is initiated, all religion will become totally superfluous.[28]

According to Schaff, the religious solution is unacceptable for everyone who does not want to reject the scientific point of view.[29] Roger Garaudy rejects the notion that the development of human history since Marx now makes the search for transcendence outside of man absolutely imperative. He believes that transcendence is already present in the complete break with the old order and the ushering in of a new one. The transcendence of human beings is not an attribute of their nature, printed on them on the first day of their creation, but rather of their culture, the work of history, creating themselves as they go along. Humans continually transcend themselves as they freely develop their material and spiritual capacities.[30] Marxism, therefore, naturally rejects any idea of a salvation bestowed on human persons from outside as a gift, on the grounds that such a notion empties human efforts to construct a better world of any significance.

Marx, Marxists, and Morality

Finally, Marxism criticizes theistic religion for its belief in an absolute ethic. Marxists, in their search for an ethic which is consistent with their thought systems, set out from two basic premises: firstly, the central human problem is always social and not individual; secondly, history is a project which continues to be realized indefinitely. An absolute ethic shows its bankruptcy when a situation arises in which contradictory precepts are equally applicable. The only way of solving such a problem is by choosing the solution which is closest to a scientific analysis of the human in society. This analysis arises from an evaluation of those social conditions which are most necessary in order to guarantee humans' happiness.

Many commentators have pointed out that Marx's view of morality is paradoxical. On the one hand, he considered morality in bourgeois society to be a form of ideology. Any given formulation of moral means and ends is inevitably tied to a particular stage of the development of society's

---

28. See Koch, *Abolition of God*, 171.
29. Schaff, *Marxism and the Human Individual*, 69.
30. Garaudy, in Dyson and Towers, *Evolution, Marxism and Christianity*, 68–69.

productive forces and class interests. He often uses the epithets, "morality" and "moralizing" against the "utopian socialists" as terms of abuse. He called their advocacy of working-class demands based on standards of right and justice, "outdated verbiage" and "ideological trash." And yet, on the other hand, his writings are full of the language of explicit and implicit moral judgments. Just to take one short passage by way of an illustration of his fiery moral indignation, here is an excerpt from *Capital*:

> We have seen, too, how this antagonism vents its rage in the creation of that monstrosity, an industrial reserve army, kept in misery in order to be always at the disposal of capital; in the incessant human sacrifices from among the working-class, in the most reckless squandering of labor-power and in the devastation caused by social anarchy which turns every economical progress into social calamity . . . Accumulation of wealth . . . is, therefore, at the same time accumulation of misery, agony of toil, slavery, ignorance, brutality, mental degradation.[31]

How does one account for this apparent discrepancy? One way of dealing with it is to draw a distinction between the area of morality covered by rights, obligations, and justice, terms covered by the German word *Recht* and the area concerned with the emancipation of human powers, once the conditions that require the morality of *Recht* are abolished.[32] This, he and Engels believed, would happen when the working class appropriated the means of production for themselves, eliminated private property, and eradicated the division of society into conflicting classes; in other words, when human beings are freed to develop themselves individually as species-being. According to Engels,

> Marx never based his communist demands upon this (moral principle of justice) but upon the inevitable collapse of the capitalist mode of production, which is daily taking place before our eyes to an ever greater degree.[33]

> A really human morality which stands above class antagonisms and above any recollection of them becomes possible only at a stage of society which has not only overcome class antagonisms but has even forgotten them in practical life.[34]

31. Marx, *Capital I*, quoted in McLellan, *Thought of Karl Marx*, 84, 85.
32. See Lukes, "Article Morals," 388.
33. Engels, *Origin of the Family*, 9.
34. Engels, "On Morality," cited in Tucker, *Marx-Engels Reader*, 667–68.

This may have been Marx's and Engels's definitive word on the subject of morality under the conditions of capitalist society. Nevertheless, if it is not a thoroughly moral concept of human nature, we are left with the profound question of what motivates thought and action in the pursuit of turning actual humanity into true humanity. Were it not for the fact that moral categories of wrong, harm, and distress could be applied properly to the machinations of the capitalist system of production, there would be no grounds for seeking its replacement other than the predetermined march of history.

The alienation of human beings from their essential nature as cooperative and creative workers, due to the external circumstances of the organization of their productive forces, is presumably an evil. By contrast, the ending of a situation of alienation, when humans will come to the full flourishing of their individual capacities in harmony with everyone else's aspirations must be considered a supreme good. Now these categorizations refer to something essential about being human; they do not refer to some necessary course of history. What is it that makes them good and evil? Marx, Engels, and Marxists in general, with their rejection of all contemporary morality as bourgeois, and with their thoroughgoing materialist assumptions, have no way of grounding moral language. One has to assume, therefore, that when they do use moral terms, it can only be in a purely rhetorical sense. Logically, as long as history does not produce the collapse of capitalism, the plight of the alienated worker is not unjust.

Eugene Kamenka, in his analysis and partial defense of Marx's approach to morality, concludes nevertheless that his so-called scientific view is inadequate because it does not consider properly the many causes of good and evil, quite apart from the relations of production:

> Marx is wrong in thinking that vitality, freedom, sincerity and the capacities for production and spontaneous co-operation are somehow more truly human than the search for security, than avarice, the demand for protection, the longing for comfort and consolation . . . Men do display internal conflicts; they are torn by the struggle of goods and evils within them; they recognize both as part of their nature. Nor is there anything in that nature

> to show that goods must triumph, that evil will be eradicated. If evils are divisive and unstable, goods can also be destroyed or weakened... There is no ground, then, for Marx's optimism, for his belief in the inevitable coming of a society completely given over to goods.[35]

In other words,

> what accounts for much of the confusion surrounding the materialist interpretation of history is Marx's inadequate view of causality, his consistent tendency to think of causality in general as the production of an effect by a single cause which is by itself both necessary and sufficient for the effect.[36]

This is tantamount to saying that Marx's understanding of the dynamic of human nature, with its mixture of good and evil motives and actions, is defective. For this reason, he did not contemplate the real possibility that the dialectic of historical forces can be regressive as well as progressive.

Developments in the Marxist Concept of the Human

Lenin

If it is true that Marx turned Hegel upside down, Lenin also turned Marx on his head. According to Georgi Plekhanov, Lenin was not so much a theoretician of Marx as of the revolution. As Paul Lehmann has asserted, "It remained, then, for Lenin to transform the Marxian analysis of the power of ideology into an ideology of power."[37] Lenin, appealing to the idea of progress in Marxist thought, changed the basis of Marxist theory from the predominance of economic factors as the substructure which explains the whole of history, to the predominance of political factors which changes it.

Due to the accelerating changes that took place at the end of the nineteenth century in Europe, Lenin came to the conclusion that the Second International no longer served as a revolutionary force. Faced by the power of "financial capitalism" it compromised and became impotent. He began, therefore, to reorganize revolutionary forces for a final assault on

---

35. Kamenka, *Ethical Foundations of Marxism*, 107–8, 114.
36. Kamenka, *Ethical Foundations of Marxism*, 142.
37. Lehmann, "Christian Theology," 107.

western imperialism.[38] In his book *What Is to Be Done?* (1902),[39] he presents the dictatorship of the proletariat in terms of the dictatorship of the Communist party. The development of this idea is the key to understanding the whole subsequent historical development of Marxism-Leninism and its offshoots. According to Nicholas Berdyaev,[40] because the first proletarian revolution had to be brought about in an agrarian society, Lenin placed himself within the current of populist socialism, affirming that in Russia the revolution had to be original. The Leninist ideology erected the revolutionary will, as interpreted by the elite vanguard of the revolution, into absolute truth. From then on it was the party, and largely Lenin within the party, who decided which course history should take.[41]

Marx had placed his confidence in the course of history bringing about the inevitable ruin of capitalism, and the proletariat taking hold of the reins of history (its history) to implement a new society without a party and without classes. Lenin, on the other hand, did not have confidence in the predetermined course of the successive stages of capitalism. Neither did he trust the proletariat in general to be the true generator of all history, subsequent to the revolution.

The drastic change from Marx's theory to Lenin's revolutionary practice produced a profound effect on the latter's "socialist humanism." The implantation first of the party and then, as an extension of this, the whole apparatus of the state as the arbiter of history, involved substantial changes in the way in which a Communist society of the future would be achieved. In effect, the desired "new person" would have to be created by the organization of a centralized state power.[42]

Classically, the function of ethics has been to direct and orientate every human activity in the light of an encompassing worldview. For Marx, the worldview was the unavoidable direction of history as it moved dialectically from a classbound to a classless society. For Lenin, on the other hand, the worldview was the ideology of the "iron will," exercised by an exclusive group which had captured state power.

38. See Stalin, *Foundations of Leninism*, 1–3.
39. Stalin, *What Is to Be Done?*, 89–100.
40. Berdyaev, *Origin of Russian Communism*.
41. Berdyaev, *Origin of Russian Communism*, 135–45.
42. See Buber, *Paths in Utopia*, chs. 8 and 9.

For Marx, history becomes relatively autonomous because it obeys laws which are imminent to its trajectory. For Lenin, history must be subordinated to the demands of a new theory:

> Without a revolutionary theory there cannot be a revolutionary movement.[43]

Thus, in political life, despite all disclaimers, theory still predominates over practice in Lenin's thought. In consequence, human beings have to obey a new interpretation of history which is essentially non-Marxist.

The Revisionists[44]

One of the first was Rosa Luxemburg (d. 1919). She was keenly critical of what she considered the Machiavellianism of the Bolsheviks. She agreed with Marx's principle that "government only hears its own voice, and demands that the people share the same illusion."[45] She stated that

> freedom is always and exclusively freedom for the person who thinks in another way, its efficacy vanishes when "freedom" becomes a special privilege.[46]

One of the most remarkable characteristics of revisionism is the promotion of the right of the individual or group to discuss openly the current teaching of the Communist party's "magisterium," in defense of a socialism that would be more human. The "new left" proposed a new hermeneutic of Marx's writings with the idea of creatively applying his conceptual analysis to new situations. It seeks to be a dynamic type of Marxism *propter semper reformanda*. In the sections which follow, we will note some of its main characteristics regarding the reality of the human being.

Firstly, there is its attitude toward freedom. One of the most serious objections leveled against "maximalist" (State) Marxism is that it has resolutely opposed the Western tradition of independent, nonauthoritarian thinking won only after many prolonged struggles. The revisionists

---

43. Lenin, *Collected Works*, 380.

44. I am using this label in a neutral sense to describe Marxist theorists or activists who disagree with Lenin's voluntarist interpretation of Marx's revolutionary theory, or who disassociate themselves from Lenin's revolutionary orthodoxy.

45. Conquest, *Where Marx went Wrong*, 92–93.

46. Quoted in Conquest, *Where Marx went Wrong*, 92–93.

struggled against an excessive centralization of state power and against the delay in the implementation of a society which is truly collectivist. Ernst Bloch proclaimed that

> the rights of man under socialism are essentially the rights of an objective and practical criticism, in order to advance the construction of Socialism within a structure of solidarity.[47]

In other words, taking seriously Marx's distinction between prehistory and history proper, it proposes a pluralism of nonantagonistic ideas within a society which supposedly has already abolished the class system.

Secondly, there is its attitude toward the importance of the individual. According to Marx, the individual as he actually exists is not a free being, but the object of various social circumstances which impede the full development of his personality. Once these barriers have been destroyed, people have every chance of creating themselves freely. In those societies which passed through a Marxist revolution, sometimes due to the challenge of Western existential philosophy, the fundamental question of the place, purpose, and worth of the individual has insistently arisen. As Adam Schaff recognizes, the idea of the individual is the starting point for any philosophy of the human person. Every type of reflection depends on the question, who is the human individual?

As far as Schaff is concerned, the central problem of the individual rests in the ambiguous nature of an approach to ethics without absolutes and in the real meaning of happiness.[48] It is the concern of these Marxists to recover the individual's initiative in the process of reconstructing society:

> The task of man is not simply to walk in the direction history takes but to move history in a human direction.[49]

Thirdly, there is the issue of the possibility of new alienations. Admission of failures and retrogressions in the process of human socialization has been perhaps the most important characteristic of the new left. It is a sign that the revisionists take history seriously. Human beings can be responsible authors of the historical process only if it is possible for them to be wrong; if a person or a party is incapable of error they can never advance beyond endless justifications of the status quo. To take history

---

47. Bloch, "Man and Citizen," 224.
48. See Schaff, *Marxism and the Human Individual*.
49. Girardi, *Marxism and Christianity*, 186.

seriously is to admit that the aggregate of humans' social relationships changes quite substantially from one generation to another. It is not surprising, therefore, that the revisionists are well known for their withering attack on the self-justification of any socialist system incapable of sustaining its revolutionary impulse. Part of this self-justification manifests itself in the unwarranted assumption that by calling a movement a revolution, the old class society is automatically abolished. Such crude propaganda, very often is a cover-up for a new kind of class privilege.

Under Communism, the fundamental problem was the appearance of a new class which effectively controlled the means of production. So, as Milovan Djilas maintained:

> It is an historical illusion which is sustained by a new alienating ideology that socialism has already been completed as the first stage of Communism.[50]

The proletariat has once again been suppressed by an institution which has become wholly inaccessible to them. Thus, the central problem for the new left has been how to ensure that the proletariat really is, in practice, the last class.

The final characteristic is the emphasis on the decentralization of power. One of the theoretical solutions to this problem of class, most widely held amongst the new left, is that the manual worker should be allowed to participate fully in the duties of government. Lucien Goldmann, for example, maintained that the "self-administration" of the workers would seem to be the only possible foundation for an authentically socialist program in the modern world.[51] In order for this to happen there would have to be a totally new revolution in which the party is deprived of its administrative monopoly. In order for the proletariat to become genuinely the subject of their own history, the state must wither and eventually disappear.

It would, however, take an exceptionally confident person to believe, against all the accumulated evidence of millennia, that the apparatus of the state could ever disappear. Such a prediction, based on the belief in so-called "iron laws of history," is, according to the philosopher Karl Popper, a mirage. Popper argued that such a belief was based

---

50. Djilas, in Buber, *Paths in Utopia*, 116.
51. Vranicki, "Socialism and the Problem of Alienation," 299–313.

on a fundamental confusion between trends and laws. A law is universal in its formulation and application; a trend is a statement about a particular time and place. It is a singular historical affirmation, not a universal account of reality at all times and in all places. Extrapolating from a trend is the weakest form of prediction.[52]

It is important to note in finishing a descriptive account of the human in the thinking of Marx and his followers, that the philosophical substratum which underlines its basic anthropology has not undergone any radical, or even significant, transformation. The problem of fitting a relatively systematized theory to the complex reality of the human person is as much a difficulty for Marxism as it is for any other contemporary philosophy or ideology, particularly when it is set within an inflexible humanist framework. The final part of this study will be dedicated to a critique of Marxian anthropology in its dependence on the radical humanism of the Enlightenment and on the dialectic of Hegel.

Assessment

It is worth reminding ourselves that Marx is not responsible for the posthumous dogmatic development of his thought. He personally did not want to present a completely rounded system, but rather a method of investigation. The term "dialectical materialism" was first used by the Russian theoretician Georgi Plekhanov; Marx preferred to speak of "the materialist concept of history."

In certain controversies amongst the radical left at the end of the nineteenth century, concerning the relation between the development of capitalism and an anti-Tsarist democratic revolution, Marx remained evasive and anti-dogmatic. The later dogmatism of the Bolshevik Party arose, insofar as Lenin (from 1902 onwards) changed Marx's semi-determinism into an historical voluntarism.

However, it is precisely this semi-determinism that lends itself to a dogmatism whose approach to the problems of historical reality will always be severely limited. We will never know how far Marx himself, if he had lived on into an age of even more rapid changes in the heart of the capitalist system, would have maintained a flexible approach to his

---

52. Kirk, *Future of Reason*, 75–76, commenting on Popper, *Poverty of Historicism*, 106–7.

interpretation of the evolution of societies. How, for example, might he have reacted to the power of recuperation which the system demonstrated after the depression of the years 1929 to 1933, and the second imperialist war. What we do know is that the dialectical method was transformed into a creed which was equally applicable to every circumstance and to every field of investigation (even that of the pure sciences).

According to some readings of Marx,[53] he maintained throughout his whole life the same presuppositions concerning historical laws as those with which he began to develop his analysis (at least from the time of the appearance of *The German Ideology* and *The Poverty of Philosophy*). The major problem of Marx's entire thought is precisely his dependence upon the underlying Hegelian assumptions about the movement of history.

Many interpreters of Marx have pointed out that he did not escape from his own condemnation of idealism. Logically, Marx's rejection of idealism would presuppose that all theoretical thought in one way or another must be done *post-factum* (i.e., it should be nothing more than a process of reflection upon the course of history once it has occurred). Such a theoretical method, however, cannot break loose from the confines of a positivist materialism, which cannot, of itself, offer any substantive interpretation of the process nor any motive for being involved in changing it. Positivism as a method leads to a complete indifference toward the movement of history.

Thus, in order to discover a meaning within the evolution of history itself, beginning *a priori* with a particular hermeneutical key is unavoidable. Marx certainly acted in this way. His key, apparently, was the Hegelian concept of negation. This concept molded his whole thought, from his critique of religion to his anticipation of a free, cooperating society in the future. But, it is not a concept which is derived from a rigorous analysis of history. Marx had already assumed it as a critical weapon before writing his historical and economic monographs.

His theoretical assumptions can be seen most clearly as ideas which float above real history in the concept of the class struggle. The origin of classes comes from the conflict of interests which causes a crisis to explode in the midst of a particular society, provoking a qualitative leap in the historical process to a new stage. The proletariat, for example, as a class, is caused by the specifically capitalist mode of production; it could

---

53. For example, that of Maximilien Rubel, *Pages de Karl Marx pour une étude socialiste—1: Sociologie critique*.

not have existed before, nor can it exist when this mode has been superseded historically. Capitalism alone has created this class. Now, the concept of negation requires that this class struggles against and overcomes the class that created it, namely the bourgeoisie:

> A class must be formed which has radical chains . . . a class which is the dissolution of all classes . . . This dissolution of society, as a particular class, is the proletariat.[54]

In this quote the imperative is provided, not by a particular direction which history is taking, which can be discerned with appropriate tools of analysis, but by the internal necessity of the theory itself. In this sense, reality has to mirror a particular conceptualization.

What, then, did capitalism create? Surely it was not any class conscious of itself and its protagonist role in the evolution of history, not even with the help of dialectical philosophy. As Lenin discovered later, it succeeded in creating only a mass of uprooted workers, condemned to misery and exploitation, and only possessing a trade-union mentality. Lenin's life work, in creating his new party, was precisely to take the concept of negation and make it into real history. But this is pure idealism.

The consequences of this confusion at the very heart of the Marxist theory are many, and mainly negative with regard to the possibility of any real openness to a multiple and changing reality. Firstly, the outcome of history is already included in the premises of the analysis of that history: the negation of the negation will continue because it must, until all classes disappear. This will be the historical moment, which Marx anticipated, in which the final antagonism between human beings comes to an end.

The conclusion which Marx drew from his premise that humanity will reach a state in which society will no longer be based on the antagonism of conflicting sectors of the population is not even based on Hegelian dialectic. He never seriously considered the question of why the process of the negation of the negation should cease to continue after the revolution. In fact, it appears to be based not on mythical iron laws of history, but on the Enlightenment confidence in inevitable progress. Karl Popper once remarked with great discernment:

> Marx shared the belief of the progressive industrialists, of the bourgeoisie of his time, in the law of progress. This naive

---

54. Marx, in Tucker, *Marx-Engels Reader*, 22.

historicist optimism is superstitious. Progress is not a law of nature. The ground gained by one generation can be lost by the next.[55]

Dialectical materialism easily becomes a static and formalist ideology, given the fact that Marx completely took over Hegel's optimism that, in his interpretation and projection of future history, the final unity of essence and existence had been eventually achieved. In both cases, they predict an imminent end to history: Hegel in what is and Marx in what will be. Marx substituted a moral positivism of the future for a moral positivism of the present. In this way, among other equivocations, he evaded any possibility of an ethical critique of what would transpire after the collapse of capitalism, the supposed last stage of prehistory.

As in the case of Feuerbach, the tension in his thinking between idealism and historicism was lessened by his intense ethical conscience, stemming from his original humanism. However, this humanism, detached from its Promethean spirit, is no guarantee of a serious, lasting concern for humankind. Marx was, as everyone is to a certain extent, a child of his time. He strongly inherited the humanist tradition which gradually began to replace a theistic interpretation of human existence and human ethical values from the time of the Renaissance and came to full flowering among the *philosophes* of the Enlightenment.

Marx cannot be said to have added much clarity to the dynamics of human behavior in the continuing saga of seeking to build more wholesome societies. Subsequent history has not born out his beliefs in the way history would be shaped. His thinking about human existence was defective, because it was much too narrowly conceived. He did add a significant dimension to humanism in his emphasis on the power of social structures to influence the formation of both human hope and despair. Communism was built on a fanciful view of what human beings, as they are, were able to achieve. Capitalism remains the dominant arrangement for conducting economic affairs throughout the world. Marx was mainly right in his analysis (through his labor theory of value) of its oppressive and destructive power. He was wrong in imagining that some hitherto undetected force in history, would bring about a hitherto hidden transformation of human social relations. It is so much easier to criticize the capitalist system than to propose a genuine alternative that, given what

---

55. Popper, *Open Society and its Enemies*, 416.

history declares about the dark side of human nature, is likely to function any better.

Questions

1. To what extent, in your opinion, was Marx's interpretation of history influenced by Hegel's dialectic philosophy?
2. In the light of subsequent history, to what extent was Marx's belief in an assured law of progress a reality of the movement of history?
3. What does Marx's underlying concept of morality tell us about his notion of the reality of human life?
4. To what extent, if at all, did the Marxist revisionists bring a more realistic perception of human nature into the long development of socialist thought?

Chapter 7

The Human Species According to Charles Darwin

When I view all beings not as special creations, but as the lineal descendants of some few beings which lived long before the first bed of the Cambrian system was deposited, they seem to me to become ennobled . . . From the war of nature, from famine and death, the most exalted object which we are capable of conceiving, namely, the production of the higher animals, directly follows.

—CHARLES DARWIN, THE ORIGIN OF SPECIES BY MEANS OF NATURAL SELECTION (SIXTH EDITION)

That it (evolution by natural selection) is possible is clear; that it happened is doubtful; that it is certain, however, is ridiculous.

—ALVIN PLANTINGA, "WHEN FAITH AND REASON CLASH," IN INTELLIGENT DESIGN CREATIONISM AND ITS CRITICS

Preface

As the two statements quoted above indicate, "controversy has accompanied evolutionary thought from the very beginning."[1] Leading naturalists during Darwin's lifetime were dubious that his theory of an exceedingly gradual universal descent from one or a few original living organisms by chance mutations and the adaptations caused by natural selection could possibly account for the quite extraordinary variety and ascending

---

1. Shanahan, *Evolution of Darwinism*, 22.

complexity of all living matter. The theory, nevertheless, has gained widespread acceptance within certain branches of the natural sciences, to such an extent that many now declare the debate more or less closed. Renowned biologists declare that the theory has been conclusively demonstrated by the evidence adduced. Those that are doubtful are considered disingenuous, ignorant, prejudiced, unscientific, fallacious, even deceptive. Their arguments are dismissed contemptuously as erroneous and delusory.

Nevertheless, well-researched, cogently argued, evidence-based data continues to be produced that seriously calls into question the likelihood, even the possibility, that Darwin's conclusions are able to explain the origin of species in the general form he proposed. This chapter is not designed to delve deeply into this dispute yet again. It is focused almost entirely on Darwin's own view of the nature and characteristics of the human species and its alleged descent from some lower form.

However, before looking at Darwin's observations on what distinguishes *homo sapiens* from every other living creature, and in particular from the most sophisticated primates, I would like to attempt the task of clarifying certain issues that I believe constantly muddy the waters of the debate about origins and the development of life on this planet. The purpose is to set Darwin's ideas in their own historical context[2] and to avoid turning the debate into an exchange of personal abuse.

Firstly, the main reason for such dissension over what purports to be a serious scientific thesis is that "it bears directly on the origin, nature and destiny of the human species."[3] In a unique way, the human subject of the enquiry (the observer) is also the object of the investigation (the observed). If the Darwinian theory could be established beyond all reasonable doubt, the consequences for understanding the human person

2. By great good fortune, a major new biography of Darwin by an eminent historian of the Victorian era has recently appeared: see Wilson, *Charles Darwin*. He approaches Darwin's theories, not from the perspective of a specialist biologist, but from that of a historian who has explored the intricate cultural background in which Darwin elaborated his famous proposals about the evolution of species. He sheds new light on how and why these suppositions may have arisen. Another book that incorporates an account of a key part of Darwin's exploration of the flora and fauna of specific zones of South America was published some dozen years ago: Thompson, *This Thing of Darkness*. As a well-researched historical novel, it details the voyages of the renowned ship, HMS Beagle, captained by Robert FitzRoy, and comments on subsequent events that arose from it as the result of the taxonomic research findings, published by Charles Darwin, its most eminent passenger.

3. Shanahan, *Evolution of Darwinism*, 4.

would be immense. Likewise, if another theory of the cause of changes in the development of life came to be generally accepted, that also would have enormous implications.

Darwinian theory is based on random but beneficial mutations in living organisms fortuitously selected for survival, meaning for successful reproduction. It is implacably opposed to any notion that some cause, external to the material substance of nature, exists as a designing and directing process. There is no divine being, however conceived, nor external natural law that somehow enters the process from outside to create, superintend, and guide life toward a predetermined end. Teleology (a planned-end product) was effectively left behind with the presumed refutation of William Paley's divine Watchmaker.[4] Evolution (or emergence) was substituted for creation.

So secondly, Darwin himself was explicit in his belief that all change has taken place by causes that are purely imminent to the material world itself. On this supposition, clearly any notion of special creations could not be credited. Whether or not he acknowledged the possible existence of a divine spirit of some kind or was wholly agnostic is a separate issue. He is adamant that there could not be any interference from beyond material existence, although at the end of the *Origin* he enigmatically mentions the "grandeur in this view of life, with its several powers, having been originally breathed by the Creator into a few forms or into one."[5]

Thirdly, following on from a materialist presupposition, it is fairly logical to conclude that the evolutionary grand theory springs from the then-current naturalistic philosophy, which has already been set out in chapters four and five on Enlightenment thinking. If naturalism is a standard metaphysical starting point for investigating the world, it follows that a theory like Darwinian evolution has to be the only kind that can make sense of biological history. Richard Dawkins, the most celebrated contemporary champion of Darwinism, indicated this necessity when he famously said, "Darwin made it possible to be an intellectually fulfilled atheist."[6] It is quite possible, however, that the atheism preceded the theory.

Fourthly, metaphysical (or ontological) naturalism is said to be confused often with methodological naturalism. The latter is the assumption

---

4. Paley, *Natural Theology*.
5. Darwin, *Origin of Species*, 432; emphasis added.
6. Dawkins, *Blind Watchmaker*, 6.

that the whole scientific enterprise can only proceed on the assumption that causes and effects spring from natural (i.e. observable, reproducible and predictable) processes. Any hint of a supernatural agency involved in natural causation would be to infer an instrumental mechanism not susceptible to the normal methods of scientific research. Methodological naturalism has, therefore, to be accepted as an essential premise for the basic standards of empirical research through the testing of evidence.

Fifthly, therefore, the debate about evolution raises at a deep level the nature and definition of what science is. This is a big subject, which cannot be tackled in all its dimensions at this point. I can only present a few, noncontroversial generalizations.[7]

> Science is an enterprise about the real world of sensations. It seeks to understand this world by searching for order or regularities, showing by experimental processes that certain features are the way they are, independently of human desire. Science is a cumulative discipline that builds on past theory-building and experimentation by confirming or falsifying tentative conclusions and predictions.

At one level,

> Science relies in part on the inductive method. In its simplest form (the context of discovery), scientific enquiry moves from data gathering to data processing through observation to experimentation to preliminary general conclusions (theories) about the constitution of mechanisms. In a second stage (the context of justification), the theory (or law) is confirmed or rejected by a further set of tests.

At another level,

> Science also proceeds by means of a hypothetico-deductive method. In this case, the most important initial procedure (context of discovery) is not the raw gathering of facts but the postulation of a conjecture concerning what might be the case. The theory is not inferred inductively from observations and experiments but is a surmise, which may have a number of causes ... produced theoretically in the scientist's mind. Subsequently (in the context of justification), the conjecture is defended by deriving states of affairs capable of being established as true or

---

7. I have explored the assumptions, tasks, and methods of the sciences elsewhere. This brief summary is based on the conclusions I reached in my book *Future of Reason*, 127–32, 204–5.

false by observation. If the observational conclusions turn out to be accurate, the theory is said to be confirmed (or in the case of Popper's falsification thesis,[8] corroborated), in that it is empirically endorsed.[9]

When it comes to explaining the emergence and development of life, both of these methods come into play. The inductive method asks questions like: What is the evidence? Is it adequate to establish soundly the conclusions that are drawn from it? How can these be tested, when much of the crucial data comes largely from the past? The hypothetico-deductive method asks questions about the possible or probable causes of events. It follows a method known as abduction (or inference to the best explanation [IBE]). In the controversy over evolution, it is at least clear that we are dealing with three main cases of what scientists refer to as singularities: the Big Bang (the origin of the universe); the emergence of biological life; and the existence of the human species. These are all unique events; they cannot be repeated or observed. How, then, is it possible to account for them? IBE seems to be the only possible method available.

IBE works by comparing alternative explanations of the data of experience. Inherently it incorporates into its method of working any evidence that seems to be germane to the case. Nothing is ruled out of court *a priori*. The "best" explanation is, at one and the same time, the explanation most warranted by all relevant evidence and one that would, if true, provide the best understanding. It is a probabilistic explanation, one that can arrive at the greatest possible explanation of the truth and that can overcome subjective partialities. IBE is a thoroughly rational consideration of all claims to know the ultimate reality that lies behind the entire experience of being human. No claim is excluded *ab initio*. All may be tested against one another. It is a method that amply satisfies the criteria for solving a crime in a court of law by producing an explanation that best fits the evidence and produces a conviction "beyond all reasonable doubt."

The importance of clarifying the nature and competence of the sciences in the debate over evolution cannot be overestimated. The two currently competing theories—evolution through chance mutation and natural selection, and evolution through preprogrammed information

---

8. See, Popper, *Logic of Scientific Discovery*, and Popper, *Conjectures and Refutations*.
9. Kirk, *Future of Reason*, 128.

existing in and working through the genetic codes of living organisms—are both explanations that purport to elucidate mechanisms that drive an evolutionary history from the first sign of life. They both start out by being hypothetico-deductive; they are both intent on explaining observable and testable experience. One is driven by a naturalistic metaphysics (no being or entity beyond material life, as an agent external to the universe, acting as a necessary and sufficient cause, exists), the other allows for the possibility that such an agent, external to the universe, works within it. Both are equally challenged to account for singularities and for highly complex biochemical processes. Neither can be excluded on the basis of scientific criteria alone. The only basis for exclusion would be that of a prior metaphysical belief, dogmatically applied.

Sixthly, in the discussions around the subject, precise definitions of evolution should be offered. Perhaps at its most basic, evolution is simply a way of giving a name to biological change. There is in the use of the word more than a hint of development. Evolution is a way of explaining the history of a movement from less complex to ever increasingly complex biological units. On the basis of successful artificial selection in plant and animal breeding and cases of temporary morphological adaptations to changing environments within the same species (Darwin's famous Galapagos finches and the story of the peppered moth), there is no dispute over what is generally called microevolution. This is evolution as change within species. A species is defined as a group of natural populations that can successfully interbreed and that are reproductively isolated from other such groups.[10]

The contention arises because the uncontroversial nature of intraspecies evolution has been turned into a theory that is deemed to explain the origin and diversification of all species from one common source. This is interspecies macroevolution: the grand theory that Darwin proposed and that together with Mendel's theory of inheritance now constitutes the neo-Darwinian synthesis. The basic teaching of Darwin's theory has the following main components. Firstly, the earth originated in a remote past (some 4,600 million years ago). The time scale is necessary if evolution happened exceedingly slowly, as Darwin's theory has to presuppose.[11] If it were possible to demonstrate that the earth is actually

---

10. See Mayr, *Toward a New Philosophy*, 318.

11. Darwin affirms that "we see nothing of the slow changes in progress, until the hand of time has marked the long lapses of ages, and then so imperfect is our view into long past geological ages, that we only see that the forms of life are now different

much younger, the theory would break down irrevocably. Secondly, life emerged spontaneously from nonlife, by some kind of chemical synthesis, probably in the unique environment of ancient seas. Thirdly, all species descended from one or a few primitive organisms by a process of random genetic mutations, genetic transmission of traits, and natural selection. By natural selection, Darwin meant "the preservation of favorable variations and the rejection of injurious variations."[12]

As we unfold Darwin's view of the human species, we will see how he interprets the data to conclude that human beings are the latest (not necessarily the culmination) of the one entire seamless mechanism of small changes from minimally complex to incredibly complex organisms. Those who accept the macroevolutionary thesis, within a naturalistic worldview, acknowledge that time, chance mutations, inheritance, and natural selection are the only causes that have driven the whole evolutionary operation forward. Theistic evolutionists, whilst adhering to the standard, current neo-Darwinian synthesis, also add that a supreme spiritual being somehow has guided the whole process from the beginning. This addition seems to be presented in a rather vague manner.

Seventhly, those who maintain a strong, sophisticated skepticism toward the neo-Darwinian synthesis do not do so purely on the basis of religious belief, but on that of scientific method and evidence. Contrary to the accusations of virulent atheists, the tentative support for a possible alternative explanation for the existence and development of life does not emerge from theological dogma, so-called creationism, but from the application of reason to the complexity of biological forms. Likewise, these scientists and philosophers approach the Darwinian theory on its own terms and find the evidence on which it is based unconvincing in most cases.

Now, there has arisen within the domain of the sciences two further questions: Is it part of the scientific endeavor to hold to a coherent theory, despite the evidence, until a more persuasive one is elaborated and comes to be accepted? On which side of the argument does the burden of proof rest? The theory in question is not the reality of evolution as such, but the Darwinian version. The incredible amount of accumulated data (for example, that which has fairly recently emerged as the result

---

from what they formerly were" (*On Natural Selection*, 24); "nothing can be effected, unless favorable conditions occur, and variation itself is apparently always a very slow process" (*On Natural Selection*, 45).

12. Darwin, *On Natural Selection*, 20.

of the completion of the genome project and the information supplied by scanning techniques for the functioning of the brain and the mind) that appears to make the thesis highly improbable[13] would, in normal scientific programs, cause scientists to think again and look elsewhere for explanations. As increasingly in so many ways the theory does not account for what it claims to explain, surely a more comprehensive and compelling proposal should be sought.

Meanwhile, until such a paradigm shift in our understanding of the reality of life, in particular its origin, its diversity, and its complexity, is forthcoming, would it not be truer to reality to remain agnostic about these matters? It is part of human nature to be curious and therefore to try to seek answers to so far unfathomable questions about the biological history of this world. It might well be that the present challenge to the scientific community is to broaden its horizons by looking for clues beyond a merely bottom-up naturalistic causality. By shedding its intransigent attachment to methodological naturalism, by adopting the heuristic approach of inference to the best explanation that allows the inclusion in rational research programs of evidence, from whatever source it may come, as long as it is germane to the project, and by cooperating in multidisciplinary undertakings, real progress in this area could be made.

Although the Darwinian theory of evolution has a long history, since the beginning it has attracted serious misgivings on the part of eminent naturalists and other scientists. Increasing doubts about its explanatory power to demonstrate the claims that it makes appears to many serious researchers to leave it in limbo as a properly accredited scientific inference. There is therefore no logical reason why the skeptics are bound to assume the burden of proof of accepting the theory, until and unless they

---

13. A medical scientist has summed up the situation thus: "There is in the most recent findings of genetics and neuroscience a powerful impression that science has been looking in the wrong place, seeking to resolve questions whose answers lie somehow outside its domain. It is not just a matter of science not yet knowing all the facts; rather there is the sense that something of immense importance is 'missing' that might transform the bare bones of genes into the wondrous diversity of the living world and the monotonous electrical firing of the brain into the vast spectrum of sensations and ideas of the human mind . . . While the similarly genetically unexplained prodigious expansion of the size of the human brain is clearly a prerequisite for the uniquely human attributes of the faculty of language, reason and imagination, the explanatory gap between the physical materiality of the brain and the non-material properties of the mind would seem to defy the simplicity of the evolutionary doctrine that would maintain they are 'nothing but' the consequence of natural selection acting on the random mutation of genes" (Le Fanu, "Doubts about Darwin," paras. 25 and 27).

can produce a more plausible alternative. If, at this moment of history, we simply do not know the answer about how life began, how the cell transmits information, why and how species have diversified, how the human mind works, and the answers to numerous other conundrums about life, would it not be more honest to say so? This might open the way to a properly candid and cooperative exploration of the issues with a view to a better understanding, rather than the present adoption of contentious, mutually antagonistic standpoints.

The Descent of Man

So far, I have attempted to clarify some of the most important issues that continually arise whenever evolution and intelligent design are debated. Darwin's situation was different from ours. He launched the initial idea, and did so having accepted a number of presuppositions, which I have outlined above. His view of human reality, therefore, has to be interpreted within the framework he assumed. His prior beliefs greatly influenced his grand theory.

Statements that confirm his strong antipathy to any notion of special creation are dotted around his two major works: *The Origin of Species* and *The Descent of Man*. He builds his thesis on the supposition that such a possibility must be excluded. He has hitched his carriage exclusively to the conviction that no such action could ever have happened, and that man has developed wholly from below, for there is no above:

> Man in his arrogance thinks himself a great work worthy of the interposition of a deity. More humble and I believe truer to consider him created from animals.[14]

> Thus we can understand how it has come to pass that man and all other vertebrate animals have been constructed on the same general model, why they pass through the same early stages of development, and why they retain certain rudiments in common ... It is only our natural prejudice, and that arrogance which made our forefathers declare that they were descended from demi-gods, which lead us to demur to this conclusion.[15]

---

14. Darwin, *Notebook C*, in Barrett et al., *Charles Darwin's Notebooks*, para. 196.
15. Darwin, *Descent of Man*, 24–25.

> I conclude that the extremely complex and regular construction of many barbarous languages, is no proof that they owe their origin to a special act of creation. Nor, as we have seen, does the faculty of articulate speech in itself offer an insuperable objection to the belief that man has been developed from some lower form.[16]
>
> If I have erred in giving to natural selection great power, which I am far from admitting, or in having exaggerated its power, which is in itself probable, I have at least, as I hope, done good service in aiding to overthrow the dogma of separate creations.[17]
>
> He who is not content to look, like a savage, at the phenomena of nature as disconnected, cannot any longer believe that man is the work of a separate act of creation.[18]

It would seem from these sample quotes (and there are many others of a similar order) that, in part, his research is driven by a visceral need to refute the idea that a personal, infinite God is in any way an active participant in the beginning of life or its development. In particular,

> man with all his noble qualities . . . with his god-like intellect which has penetrated into the movements and constitution of the solar system, with all these exalted powers. Man still bears in his bodily frame the indelible stamp of his lowly origin.[19]

So, if the explanation for the obvious grandeur of the human species with all its distinguishing features in comparison with the highest forms of the animal kingdom cannot be special creation, an alternative (and more plausible) account of its origin has to be demonstrated.

Certainty, Uncertainty, and Probability

The language that Darwin uses as he sets out the arguments he advances for his grand theory of the development of life from its first emergence to its present culmination in civilized human societies is intriguing. The

---

16. Darwin, *Descent of Man*, 48.
17. Darwin, *Descent of Man*, 113.
18. Darwin, *Descent of Man*, 633. This quotation, significantly, comes in the final chapter of the book, "General Summary and Conclusion."
19. Darwin, *Descent of Man*, 647. With these words, Darwin concludes his book.

language expresses various degrees of confidence in the reality of what he is proposing. At one end of the scale he makes highly self-assured claims about the validity of his overall thesis. For example,

> The main conclusion arrived at in this work ... is that man is descended from some less highly organized form. The grounds on which this conclusion rests will never be shaken ... The great principle of evolution stands up clear and firm.[20]

He bases this judgment on a number of general considerations. Firstly, the earth has a very long lifespan (perhaps as much as four and a half billion years). Secondly, life emerged at one or only a few places from inanimate matter by ordinary laws of physics and chemistry. Thirdly, life progressed slowly and steadily from simple to complex forms by means of chance mutations and natural selection in the struggle for existence. Fourthly, all life is related by descent from the original living beings.

The evidence that he adduces for these claims is based on a number of biological factors. Natural selection working extremely gradually on random variations within and between species is nature's version of selective selection carried out by humans in breeding programs on plants and domestic animals:

> If feeble man can do much by his powers of artificial selection, I can see no limit to the amount of change, to the beauty and infinite complexity of the co-adaptations between all organic beings, one with another and with their physical conditions of life, which may be effected in the long course of time by nature's power of selection.[21]

Evolutionary progress happens as a result of advantageous selections being confirmed and deleterious selections being fruitless. The advantageous genetic mutations are transmitted through inheritance causing favorable environmental adaptations. The morphological similarities between species (homology[22]) and the principle of reversion ("by which long-lost dormant structures are called back into existence"[23]) provide strong evidence for an unbroken chain of existence:

20. Darwin, *Descent of Man*, 632.
21. Darwin, *On Natural Selection*, 45.
22. "Identity of relation between parts developed from the same embryonic structures, as the arm of a man, the foreleg of a quadruped, and the wing of a bird" (*Cassel Concise English Dictionary*).
23. Darwin, *Descent of Man*, 97–98.

> It is quite incredible that a man should through mere accident abnormally resemble, in no less than seven of his muscles, certain apes, if there had been no genetic connection between them ... These several reversionary, as well as the strictly rudimentary, structures reveal the descent of man from some lower form in an unmistakeable manner.[24]

Darwin concludes his fundamental conviction that evolution as he presents it,

> being Growth with Reproduction; Inheritance which is almost implied by reproduction; Variability from the indirect and direct action of the external conditions of life and from use and disuse; a Ratio of Increase so as to lead to a Struggle for Life, and as a consequence to Natural Selection, entailing a Divergence of Character and the Extinction of less improved forms[25]

corresponds to the development of all forms of life. Therefore,

> We can feel assured that all individuals of the same species ... have within a not very remote period descended from one parent.[26]

So much for the areas where Darwin was convinced of the absolute certainty of his main thesis. However, he also admitted that many of his arguments were based only on models of probability. Theories that refer to biological probability are quite complex. They arise out of hidden variables in the theories. Whatever the nature of the evidence, "the theory is said to be incomplete."[27] So, perhaps, it is not surprising that throughout Darwin's writings different degrees of probability are assigned to this supposition. Thus, for example, he attributes a high measure of probability to his arguments set out in a chapter on the manner of development of man from some lower form:

> The facts and conclusions to be given in this chapter relate almost exclusively to *the probable means* by which the transformation of man has been effected, as far as his bodily structure is concerned.[28]

---

24. Darwin, *Descent of Man*, 97–98.
25. Darwin, *On Natural Selection*, 117.
26. Darwin, *On Natural Selection*, 117.
27. Sober, "Metaphysical and Epistemological Issues," 307.
28. Darwin, *Descent of Man*, 84; emphasis added.

> It is ... highly probable that with mankind the intellectual faculties have been gradually perfected through natural selection; and this conclusion is sufficient for our purpose.[29]

He is, however, less sure about the distinctions between men and women with regard to intellectual abilities:

> With respect to differences of this nature (the mental powers of the two sexes) between man and woman, it is probable that sexual selection has played a very important part. I am aware that some writers doubt whether there is any inherent difference; but this is at least probable from the analogy of the lower animals which present other secondary sexual characters.[30]

Finally, he is quite candid about those aspects of his grand theory about which there is considerable ignorance or doubt. Toward the end of *The Descent of Man*, Darwin admits that "many of the views which have been advanced are highly speculative, and some no doubt will prove erroneous." However, he contends that "false views, if supported by some evidence, do little harm, as everyone takes a salutary pleasure in proving their falseness; and when this is done, one path toward error is closed and the road to truth is often at the same time opened."[31]

It is helpful to distinguish between facts and opinions, and Darwin makes clear what he believes are the one and what are the other. His grand theory on the development of life was first published well over 150 years ago in 1859. In the meantime, students of his theses have been and still are puzzling over what is incontrovertible fact and what is mere conjecture. It is often when touching upon the alleged evolution of primates into fully-fledged *homo sapiens* that Darwin is at his most speculative.

> In what manner the mental powers were first developed in the lowest organisms, is as hopeless an inquiry as how life first originated. These are problems for the distant future, if they are ever to be solved by man.[32]

We still await the solution. Darwin continues:

> In regard to bodily size or strength, we do not know whether man is descended from some comparatively small species,

---

29. Darwin, *Descent of Man*, 124.
30. Darwin, *Descent of Man*, 584.
31. Darwin, *Descent of Man*, 632.
32. Darwin, *Descent of Man*, 30.

like the chimpanzee, or from one as powerful as the gorilla; and, therefore, we cannot say whether man has become larger and stronger, or smaller and weaker, in comparison with his progenitors.[33]

Undoubtedly, it would have been very interesting to have traced the development of each separate faculty from the state in which it exists in the lower animals to that in which it exists in man; but neither my ability nor knowledge permit the attempt.[34]

In attempting to trace the genealogy of the Mammalia, and therefore of man, lower down in the series, we become involved in greater and greater obscurity.[35]

In a series of forms graduating insensibly from some apelike creature to man as he now exists, it would be impossible to fix any definite point when the term "man" ought to be used.[36]

In analyzing Darwin's own beliefs, it is right to show at what points he made a distinction between firm and assured convictions about facts and provisional probabilities, and where he confessed that his reasoning was either ill-informed or no more than a surmise. Jean Gayon summarizes the epistemological status of Darwin's ideas as "almost always in a zone intermediate between 'general facts' of nature and theoretical 'hypotheses' justifiable through their consequences."[37] I think it shows why many of the hypotheses were challenged during his lifetime and remain disputed a century and a half later. We are dealing with a theory where a good deal of uncertainty is inevitable, given the nature of the subject matter and the scarcity of reliable evidence. In line with the present state of properly assessed and uncontested data, those engaged in the field of evolutionary biology would do well to remain cautious and circumspect about the sure findings of their studies.

33. Darwin, *Descent of Man*, 115.
34. Darwin, *Descent of Man*, 125.
35. Darwin, *Descent of Man*, 156.
36. Darwin, *Descent of Man*, 180.
37. Gayon, "From Darwin to Today," 298.

A Profile of the Human Species in the Thinking of Charles Darwin

In a way, all that has been said so far acts as a kind of prolegomena. Just because the grand theory is being increasingly challenged, mainly on the scarcity of solid, scientifically accessible evidence, I have attempted to set the discussion of Darwin's views within a context which I believe will help to clarify the questions and issues that have been thrown up. In the case of the descent of man from lower-order primates, the study becomes much more personal. We are talking about ourselves!

In his account of the human species, Darwin was faced with a mammoth conundrum: on the one hand, human beings appear to be directly related biologically to what he called their "allies" (meaning old and new world monkeys and apes); on the other hand, they are distinguished by a number of highly significant features, including some related to their physical structure. Darwin's problem, having rejected the notion of special creation and tied himself to a belief in an unbroken chain of speciation, was to make a convincing case for the gradual evolutionary transformation of the higher primates into actual contemporary humans, including credible and verifiable missing links.

The main distinguishing attributes are: an upright stance, a distinct structure of the hand, a much larger skull, the use of language, the development of mental capacity, a moral disposition and aptitude, an advanced form of creativity, an aesthetic sense, and a predisposition to religious beliefs and rituals. Darwin shows his understanding of the nature of the human species in attempting to unravel the likely origin and development of these attributes entirely from within his materialistic framework. I will, therefore, endeavor to trace briefly his thinking on some of these issues.

The Development of Mental Capacity

In a sense, Darwin begins his exploration of the origin or descent of the human species with its conclusion. He quotes one of the most eminent biologists of the nineteenth century and a strong advocate of his views on the origin of species, Professor Thomas Huxley:

> In the opinion of most competent judges, (he) has conclusively shewn that in every single visible character man differs less from

the higher apes than these do from the lower members of the same order of Primates.[38]

Having asserted the physical similarities between humans and the alleged next species down, summarized by Huxley,

> without question, the mode of origin and the early stages of the development of man are identical with those of the animals immediately below him in the scale: without a doubt in these respects, he is far nearer to apes, than the apes are to the dog,[39]

and born out by shared circumstances in life (e.g., certain diseases, same reaction to medicines, an equal liking for tea, coffee, spirits, and tobacco[40]), he moves on to tackle the question of the differences. As far as physical features are concerned, he mentions in particular the nakedness of humans, their upright stance, the structure of their hands, the size of their skulls, and their fairly underdeveloped sense of smell; he also alludes to the fact that humans alone are apparently endowed with certain muscles solely for the sake of expressing emotions.

To survey Darwin's response to the physical discrepancies would take us beyond the main intention of this study. More significant and ostensibly of much more problematical consequence are the distinctions and disparities between human and higher primate mental aptitudes and moral, aesthetic and "spiritual" endowments.

Now, in the case of mental faculties Darwin appears to be equivocal. On the one hand, he affirms that "my object in this chapter[41] is solely to shew that there is no fundamental difference between man and the higher mammals in their mental faculties . . . I will select those facts which have most struck me."[42] He then continues by arguing that humans share with animals the same instincts, intuitions, and coordination of reflex actions. They are excited by the same emotions. They are guided

---

38. Darwin, *Descent of Man*, 4.

39. Darwin, *Descent of Man*, 14.

40. I am not sure that an equal desire for certain foods and drinks can really be taken seriously as evidence of direct descent. At the time of writing, I noticed, for example, a squirrel's craving for strawberries; horses are most willing to eat carrots and are passionate about lumps of sugar!

41. Chapter 2 of Darwin, *Descent of Man*: "Comparison of the Mental Powers of Man and the Lower Animals."

42. Darwin, *Descent of Man*, 30.

by the same principles of imitation, attention, memory, imagination, and reason.[43] He concludes that

> the difference in mind between man and the higher animals, great as it is, is certainly one of degree and not of kind.[44]

On the other hand, Darwin is quite aware that

> there can be no doubt that the difference between the mind of the lowest man and that of the highest animal is immense.[45]

So, how does Darwin account for "a great stride in the development of the intellect?"[46] As was the case for animals in a state of nature, "the intellect must have been all-important to him, even at a very remote period, enabling him to use language, to invent and make weapons, tools, traps, etc.; by which means, in combination with his social habits, he long ago became the most dominant of all living creatures."[47] He summarizes the process, as he sees it, of how the mental powers of humans grew exponentially from small beginnings.

The first step was the discovery of a primitive form of language as a new means of communication. The continual use of language will have reacted on the brain, presumably producing greater complexity. This will have been inherited and passed on to subsequent generations. This will have required a greater brain size in humans in comparison with that of the progenitors, relative to the size of their bodies. Later, the larger brain would have enabled the human to develop his linguistic abilities and "excite trains of thought which would never arise from the mere impression of the senses, and if they did arise could not be followed out."[48] Higher intellectual powers of humans, such as reasoning, abstraction,

---

43. In a recent publication, *Are We Smart Enough To Know How Smart Animals Are?*, Frans de Waal gives evidence that some animals—some great apes, dolphins, the Eurasian magpie, and at least one Indian elephant—possess limited self-awareness; in addition, some apes are alert to the minds of others, and can defer gratification. In other words, more evolved animals are able to think in ways similar to those that humans apply. Darwin himself was struck by the power of reason exhibited in dogs (for example, game dogs during the task of retrieving birds).

44. Darwin, *Descent of Man*, 80.

45. Darwin, *Descent of Man*, 79.

46. Darwin, *Descent of Man*, 636.

47. Darwin, *Descent of Man*, 636.

48. Darwin, *Descent of Man*, 636.

imagination, creativity, self-consciousness, would have arisen in the setting of an increasing social interaction.[49]

The Development of Language

The gradual elaboration of language appears to be, in Darwin's account of the descent of man, the first crucial advancement of the evolutionary process to its highest contemporary instance. Without denying some form of oral communication between animals, Darwin states that articulate language is peculiar to humans. By articulate he means the power to connect definite sounds to explicit ideas. Originally, language came about through the imitation and modification of various natural sounds, such as the voices of other animals and primitive humans' own instinctive exclamations:

> it does not appear altogether incredible, that some unusually wise ape-like animal should have thought of imitating the growl of a beast of prey, so as to indicate to his fellow monkeys the nature of the expected danger. *And this would have been a first step in the formation of a language.*[50]

From there, an increased use of the voice would have had the effect of strengthening the vocal organs through inherited use. However, much more important would have been the more highly developed mental powers in some early progenitors of humans:

> a long and complex train of thought can no more be carried on without the aid of words, whether spoken or silent, than a long calculation without the use of figures or algebra.[51]

Conversely, the fact that the vocal organs in the higher apes were not developed for articulate speech presumably depends, according to this theory, on their intelligence not having been sufficiently advanced.

Darwin, as would be expected from his overall materialistic worldview, signs off his discussion of the origin of language with two creedal observations:

---

49. A summary of the origin and growth of humans' mental capacity can be found in Darwin, *Descent of Man*, 636.
50. Darwin, *Descent of Man*, 45; emphasis added.
51. Darwin, *Descent of Man*, 45.

From these few and imperfect remarks I conclude that the extremely complex and regular construction of many barbarous languages, is no proof that they owe their origin to a special act of creation. Nor, as we have seen, does the faculty of articulate speech in itself offer any insuperable objection to the belief that man has developed from some lower form.[52]

The Experience of Self-Consciousness

Darwin tends to glide swiftly over the reality of self-consciousness and the sense of being an individual, which are two of the marks that distinguish humans from animals. He compares humans' ability to reflect with the thought processes of dogs, and concludes that,

> No one supposes that one of the lower animals reflects whence he comes or whither he goes, what is death or what is life, and so forth.

Nevertheless, he believes that animals (he is still thinking of dogs) retain their mental individuality and, "with an excellent memory and some power of imagination" are able to recall past pleasures in their lives. He does not think that "the hard-worked wife of a degraded Australian savage" is able to "exert her self-consciousness or reflect on the nature of her own existence." In comparing the two (the dog and the Aborigine woman), it might be said that the latter, at least, as has been amply established since the time of Darwin, and has an innate power to reflect on what it means to be human when she has the opportunity to do so. Although it is impossible to enter the mind of a dog, it is highly unlikely that the dog ponders over what it means to be a dog![53]

A Sense of Beauty

Darwin considers that humans are not uniquely capable of enjoying beautiful objects and experiences. Certain birds display their brightly colored plumes and their singing to attract the attention of females. If the females were not able to appreciate the beautiful colors and the songs

---

52. Darwin, *Descent of Man*, 48.
53. The quotes in this section are from Darwin, *Descent of Man*, 48.

of the males, the labor of the latter would have been in vain. Presumably, then, nature would not have devised such splendid aesthetic enticements.

However, these exhibitions of color and music among some birds appear to be related mainly to enticing a mate. One might conclude, therefore, that within the closed circle of the birds themselves, they have one predominant function. On the other hand, humans appreciate both the plumage of birds and their songs for purely aesthetic enjoyment. Moreover,

> obviously no animal would be capable of admiring such scenes as the heavens at night, a beautiful landscape, or refined music; but such high tastes, depending as they do on culture and complex associations, are not enjoyed by barbarians or by uneducated persons.[54]

The first part of this sentence is true, as far as we know; the second part is dubious. Although what constitutes beauty is largely a matter of personal taste, it is not at all obvious that the ability to appreciate what are referred to as the high arts is not equally open to any human being (even the inhabitants of Tierra del Fuego that Darwin met on his travels on the Beagle). The point is that humans are born with an intrinsic capacity to relish the enjoyment of all kinds of beauty; animals are not.

The secular grand narrative of evolution has a hard time explaining how the subtle sense of beauty has developed from nonhumans to humans. Also, with its overall belief that the cause of evolution is change through natural selection to produce the most fitting adaptations for successful reproductive activity, it is severely challenged to explain why aesthetic appreciation, which apparently has no survival value, has arisen to the elevation it has in a completely insignificant state of existence.

A Social Animal

Even a cursory observation tells us that humans thrive when fully part of a sympathetic, caring, supportive community. Conversely, they decline when circumstances force them into solitude:

> solitary confinement is one of the severest punishments that can be inflicted.[55]

---

54. Darwin, *Descent of Man*, 49.
55. Darwin, *Descent of Man*, 65.

Darwin believes that social existence in the human race has been inherited from the higher social animals by the development of special instincts, especially that of mutual sympathy among members of close-knit families and clans:

> the social instincts, which must have been acquired by man in a very rude state, and even probably by his early ape-like progenitors, still give the impulse to many of his best actions.[56]

In addition, the actions of humans "are largely determined by the expressed wishes and judgment of his fellow-men."[57] The love of praise and approbation and the horror of dishonor and scorn would play a huge part in motivating people to keep within the conventions of the social gathering in which they are nurtured. In other words, humans learn through experience and reason to conform to the general sense of what brings honor and avoid what constitutes shame. So Darwin seems to be inferring that behavior is predicated on a utilitarian premise:

> as all men desire their own happiness, praise or blame is bestowed on actions and motives, according as they lead to this end; and as happiness is an essential part of the general good, the greatest happiness principle indirectly serves as a nearly safe standard of right and wrong.[58]

The Moral Sense

Here, the evolutionary story is confronted with its most testing challenge. In attempting to trace a smooth transition from animal to human life, moral consciousness and conscience are the most difficult aspects of human existence to give a cogent account of. Darwin perceives the difficulty:

> I fully subscribe to the judgment of those writers who maintain that of all the differences between man and the lower animals, the moral sense or conscience is by far the most important. This sense ... has a rightful supremacy over every other principle of

---

56. Darwin, *Descent of Man*, 66.
57. Darwin, *Descent of Man*, 66.
58. Darwin, *Descent of Man*, 638.

human action; it is summed up in that short but imperious word ought, so full of high significance.[59]

The problem is in finding a convincing, natural path from the highest form of animal existence to that of humans, as far as discovering the origin, role, and justification for moral convictions and actions is concerned. As we shall see, utilitarianism (the greatest happiness principle) is insufficient (as Darwin himself seemed to intuit), because it begs the question about what is the good in the formula of the greatest good for the greatest number.

However, before we reach that discussion, it is necessary to summarize Darwin's account of the origin of the moral tenets of virtue and vice. According to Darwin, a moral being is a person who can compare his or her past and future actions and motives, and knows how and why some are to be approved of and others condemned. Human beings show regret when they consider that they have taken a wrong decision or followed a false and blameworthy path. They experience guilt, are ashamed, and express repentance. Darwin affirms that there is no reason to suppose that any of the lower animals are able to show these emotions. Given that humans are descended from the same common ancestors as their "cousins," the apes, how was it that moral sentiments arose in the one species, but not in the other?

Here, Darwin is equivocal. On the one hand, he emphasizes the instincts as the source of moral intuitions. He names the impulses of love and sympathy as the foundation of genuine moral motivation. Initially, they are exercised instantaneously, not as the result of a long period of moral reflection. We use the imprecise term "gut reaction" to describe an immediate reflex response to a situation that calls out for compassionate assistance. This kind of response is shared in part by animals. Darwin mentions the case of the heroic little monkey that attacked a much larger and more powerful baboon to save its keeper's life.[60] In a derivative and weakened sense, such an instinct may be called moral in the case of animals.

On the other hand, morality depends on the strength of the power of reasoning which, according to the theory of evolution, took a very long period of time to develop. Through reason, human beings can, independently of any pleasure or pain felt at the moment, weigh up the

---

59. Darwin, *Descent of Man*, 56.
60. See, Darwin, *Descent of Man*, 67.

justification or otherwise of certain lines of conduct. They have risen to the stature of making their own personal, independent decisions about their conduct. In the words of the philosopher Kant, they have "dared to be free."[61] Hence, ultimately following a true moral code is independent of being motivated either by reward and punishment, submitting to a social consensus, or gaining pleasure and avoiding pain:

> the social instincts, the prime principle of man's moral constitution, with the aid of active intellectual powers and the effects of habit, naturally lead to the golden rule, "As ye would that men should do to you, do ye to them likewise;" and this lies at the foundation of morality.[62]

Is this a satisfactory account of the origin and nature of the moral sense in humans? If the notion of "ought" is going to play the pivotal role in the intrinsic understanding of moral motivation and action, it has to have an explanation that removes it from the world of self-interest, however disguised in terms like "empathy" and "altruism." Even the "golden rule," first enunciated in its positive form by the founder of the Christian faith, could be said to reflect a moderate form of mutual self-regard and reciprocal advantage. It is based on the principle of consistency: there is no justification for treating others in ways other than you would desire to be treated yourself; to think and act otherwise is to introduce a double standard of behavior. To break the "golden rule" implies that I am owed a greater status and freedom than other human beings.

Darwin's account of morality, and that of all who have followed him in his philosophical naturalism, is culpable of committing "the deontic fallacy":

> to deduce moral principles from statements of fact, (is) an illegitimate procedure, since premises of one logical type (descriptive judgments) cannot give rise to premises of another type (namely, prescriptions).[63]

Put another way, "of any property that a person can exemplify, an emotion such as love, say or a virtue such as heroism, or a generalized feeling of pleasure, it may sensibly be asked whether that virtue or emotion

---

61. Kant, *Answer to the Question*, 1–11.
62. Darwin, *Descent of Man*, 80.
63. Kirk, *Future of Reason*, 171.

or feeling is good."[64] None of these properties can be identified without remainder as good, for then a negative answer could not be given. There may be occasions when what is designated as love is not good. So, love can never be categorized as good, unless the content of love measures up to the norm of supreme goodness.

If moral claims could be based on facts open to scientific investigation, based on naturalistic premises, it would be necessary for the statement "we ought to do good" to be supplied with a prior understanding of what, naturally, constitutes the good. The answer that Darwin and his followers suggest is that the survival of the species and the well-being of social groups (measured, for example, by the implementation of equality across the whole spectrum of a population) is the norm. However, this commits the fallacy mentioned above: the argument presupposes what has already been determined as the understanding of what is the good; it does not answer the question, "Why do the survival of the species and the well-being of social groups constitute a definition of the good?" As Jonathan Hodge and Gregory Radick have pointed out:

> There is no reason to think that the survival of any particular social group, individual or Homo sapiens in general for that matter, is intrinsically good or morally required.[65]

The only way around this dilemma is to claim that the total reality of what it means to be human cannot be determined by facts, accessible only to a naturalistically conceived method of investigation. If the normativity of moral judgments were to reflect some factual condition in the world, the only option would have to be the nature of the human being, according to data, which does not arise from within the purview of naturalistic science.

In principle, it can be shown (through inference to the best explanation) that humans may best flourish by adhering to precepts for living laid down by the one who created them for a purpose. It is perplexing to imagine how human beings can know how they can fulfill their potential as humans if their existence is a matter of evolution by chance. If there is no all-embracing, intrinsic meaning to being human, an impossible supposition from a secular humanist belief, how would one know what best fits human nature? On one interpretation of Darwin, he substitutes Nature for God:

---

64. Hodge and Radick, *Cambridge Companion to Darwin*, 347.
65. Hodge and Radick, *Cambridge Companion to Darwin*, 349.

> Darwin yet portrayed nature in the Origin of Species in the manner that he had absorbed from his Humboldtian experiences during his youthful voyage of adventure, namely, nature as having a moral and aesthetic intelligence.[66]

> The productions of nature... plainly manifest, in Darwin's resonant phrase, "the stamp of far higher workmanship"... The being that Darwin here imagines has those qualities characteristic of the recently departed Deity.[67]

Belief in God

Finally, this discussion brings us to explore Darwin's explanation of the almost universal practice of some form of religion by humans of all races and all levels of civilization. Why is humankind inclined toward being a *homo religioso*? Given the incredible diversity of religious beliefs and the intrinsic problem of being able to define satisfactorily what constitutes religion, Darwin does not dedicate much thought to what is a highly complex subject.[68]

Darwin tends to rely on a fairly conventional, anthropological account of the origin and development of beliefs in the reality and influence of an unseen world. He ascribes the emergence of religion to the expanding capacity of the human mind to reflect self-consciously on human existence:

> As soon as the important faculties of the imagination, wonder, and curiosity, together with some power of reasoning, had become partially developed, man would naturally have craved to understand what was passing around him, and have vaguely speculated on his own existence.[69]

He agrees with the hypothesis that humans originally believed that natural phenomena are permeated by countless calculating spirits, which drive the forces of nature in ways similar to human action on the environment. He also considers probable the thesis that dreams may have, in

---

66. Richards, "Darwin on Mind," 105.
67. Richards, "Darwin on Mind," 104–5. The quotation from Darwin is taken from *Origin of Species*, 84.
68. I deal with these questions in Kirk, *Church and the World*, 261–69.
69. Darwin, *Descent of Man*, 50.

addition, given rise to the notion of spirits, just because primitive peoples do not distinguish easily the difference between subjective and objective impressions. Thus, figures that appear in dreams are thought to have some kind of tangible, spiritual existence in the everyday world. They are able to appear and disappear at will, and to influence, if not wholly control, the destiny of human lives. Naturally, these early, unsophisticated humans ascribed to the spirits characteristics similar to their own, such as rudimentary forms of retributive justice. It is, perhaps, not surprising that belief in unpredictable and vengeful spirits has been far more common among primitive peoples than the recognition of friendly ones.

The advancement of religious devotion has been dependent, Darwin believes, on the development of humankind's intellectual, emotional, and moral faculties to at least a moderately mature level. These have led to a more sophisticated understanding of a deity to whom complete submission and a sense of dependence is due. Darwin is prepared to draw a parallel between religious devotion to "an exalted and mysterious superior" and "the deep love of a dog for his master, associated with complete submission, some fear, and perhaps other feelings."[70]

Finally, Darwin is agnostic, perhaps skeptical, about the existence of an immortal soul somehow incorporated into the human person at some indeterminate point in their gestation and early growth. As the religions that originated in the Semitic world generally do not subscribe to a belief in the immortality of the soul, but in the unity of the human person, such agnosticism, even disbelief, is not of much consequence. Perhaps, therefore, the first sentence of the conclusion of a review of *The Origin of Species*, in *The Times* newspaper, is somewhat exaggerated:

> It is hard to see how, on Mr. Darwin's hypothesis, it is possible to ascribe to Man any other immortality or any other spiritual existence, than that possessed by the Brutes . . . To put (these views) forward on such incomplete evidence, such cursory investigation, such hypothetical arguments, as we have exposed, is more than unscientific—it is reckless.[71]

The second sentence may be a more faithful reflection of the often highly conjectural nature of Darwin's unstated presuppositions, which have led to decidedly speculative conclusions. In the case of religion, Darwin mentions, but never develops, his thinking on what he calls "the

---

70. Darwin, *Descent of Man*, 52–53.
71. Quoted in Browne, "Introduction," xxv.

ennobling belief in the existence of an Omnipotent God . . . a universal and beneficent Creator of the Universe."[72] Nor does he engage with the evidence that such a monotheistic being has revealed himself unequivocally to humanity as a deity completely at odds with the images of spirits and gods encountered in primal religions.

Assessment

I have attempted to give an account of Darwin's understanding of the origin and nature of the human species. I have purposely emphasized that his views have to be seen from within the constraints of his overriding worldview, which he has tacitly endorsed as the background to his scientific endeavors. Darwin, as has been copiously documented, was a polymath who engaged in a number of intellectual disciplines, concurring with or dismissing the opinions of experts in those subjects as they supported or contradicted his own.

I have done my best to present, in his own words, his interpretations of the reality of what makes a human being human. On the basis of the discussion carried out in this chapter, I believe that his grand theory, even with the modifications subsequently introduced by those who follow its general arguments and conclusions, remains unsettled, because it is uncertain. There are too many lacunae in the evidence adduced to be at all confident that the theory holds water. It should not be asserted that the Darwinian synthesis should be accepted on the basis that there is, apparently, no other theory of the origin and development of life that accounts for its history and diversity.

Personally, I believe that the controversy between Darwinists and so-called creationists is sterile, because it is based on irreconcilable assumptions about the origin of the universe and life, about the limits of scientific methodology, and about the nature and significance of the evidence put forward to confirm or deny the evolutionary thesis. Of course, all of these disputes weigh heavily on what is to be thought about the human species within the immensity of the universe. It would be better, within the confines of the present knowledge we can be sure about, to be more circumspect. Humans are typically characterized by their drive to discover what is true and false about themselves; this is a quality that should be pursued. However, humans need to recognize their fallibility

---

72. Darwin, *Descent of Man*, 50.

and their tendency to make claims that exceed the evidence adduced to support them. Darwinism, unfortunately, steps beyond the bounds of sound scientific procedures, in order to uphold a philosophical doctrine held on quite other grounds.

I would advocate further exploration of all the evidence available, not just that which is said to be open to a narrow interpretation of scientific research. It is not true to real human experience to assert that the sciences alone are implicitly able to fathom the whole dimension of human life. This is clearly a nonscientific, dogmatic claim. Many Darwinists give the impression that this is what they believe. It is to be hoped, therefore, that science will continue to do its vital and impressive work, but within the confines of what it is genuinely able to achieve.

Many of the conclusions that Darwin has drawn from his theory and which have been presented in this chapter have gone way beyond the scope of what it is legitimate, scientifically, to infer from the evidence. That is the main objection to the theory, not because it contradicts cherished religious or philosophical ideas. Nevertheless, acceptance or skepticism with regard to the evolutionary theory has considerable bearing on who we think we are. That is why the debate is so crucial and will no doubt continue well into the future.

Questions

1. What reasons can you give for why Darwin's theory on the evolution of species, and its subsequent modifications, has commanded such general assent in modern societies?

2. For Darwin's thesis to be justified as convincing, what standards of demonstration have to be admissible?

3. What are the crucial differences of opinion between those who accept and those who reject the main arguments for affirming the "grand theory" of evolution?

4. What differences does it make to one's understanding of being human if one either believes in or is unconvinced by the theory?

Chapter 8

Friedrich Nietzsche and the Human Predicament

What does man actually know about himself? Is he, indeed, ever able to perceive himself completely, as if laid out in a lighted display case?

—ON TRUTH AND LIES IN A NON-MORAL SENSE (1873)[1]

God is dead; but given the way of men, there may still be caves for thousands of years in which his shadow will be shown. And we still have to vanquish his shadow too.

—THE GAY SCIENCE (1882)

Anyone who fights with monsters should take care that he does not in the process become a monster. And, if you gaze for long into an abyss, the abyss gazes back into you.

—BEYOND GOOD AND EVIL: PRELUDE TO A PHILOSOPHY OF THE FUTURE (1886)

Introduction

THE AIM OF THIS chapter—to uncover, as far as possible, Nietzsche's beliefs about what it means to be human—puts a necessary constraint on

---

1. The direct quotes from Nietzsche's writings will be taken from Pearson and Large, *Nietzsche Reader*.

FRIEDRICH NIETZSCHE AND THE HUMAN PREDICAMENT   195

how his extensive and diverse material is to be handled. How is it possible to extract from his philosophical and psychological musings concrete conclusions about his views on the characteristics of the human being?

Not only have Nietzsche's writings provoked much controversy amongst those who have undertaken to evaluate his thought, but they have proved perplexing to understand. One commentator, Jacob Golomb, writing on Nietzsche's concept of the will to power, has said that

> the ambiguities and contradictions in his work, as well as his elusive, aphoristic style lend themselves to a wide range of meanings and a multiplicity of interpretations.[2]

I will note throughout this chapter why many students of his writings have felt uncertainties about the meaning of his texts, as they have perused them.

There are a variety of reasons why Nietzsche is not easy to fathom. His style of writing, for example, is not conducive to a straightforward understanding:

> Nietzsche's fragmentary and often aphoristic style makes his thought notoriously difficult to synthesize or summarize.[3]

The editors of *Nietzsche* (*Oxford Readings in Philosophy*), John Richardson and Brian Leiter, confess that it is difficult to distinguish between the tone of his writings and their content, for Nietzsche writes using a stylistic pluralism. It is hard, they say, to discern to what extent his thinking relates, if at all, to the traditional concern of philosophers to convey rational truths (i.e. to saying how things actually are).[4] Perhaps his writing style, its obscurity, and lack of coherence, are a reflection of his own philosophical views: without precise foundations, the task of finding coherence among seeming chaos is almost impossible to achieve.

Nietzsche himself does not help to clarify the way that he seeks to communicate. In the preface to *On the Genealogy of Morality: A Polemic* (written in July 1887), he affirms that

> if anyone finds this work incomprehensible and hard on the ears, I do not think that the fault necessarily lies with me. It is clear enough, assuming as I do, that people have first read my

---

2. Gemes and Richardson, *Oxford Handbook of Nietzsche*, 542.
3. Solomon, "Nietzshe ad Hominem," 184.
4. Richardson and Leiter, *Nietzsche*, 13–14.

earlier works without sparing themselves some effort: because *they really are not easy to approach.*[5]

Writing at the end of his intelligible life, before the descent into mental derangement (January 1889), Nietzsche proclaimed that he was not yet understood.

> It would be a complete contradiction of myself, if I expected ears and hands for my truths already today: that I am not heard today, that no one today knows how to take from me, is not only comprehensible; it even seems to me right. I do not want to be taken for what I am not . . . Whoever believed he had understood something of me had dressed up something out of me after his own image.[6]

A month and a half before the mental collapse, he wrote a letter expressing his conviction about the worth of what he considered his greatest work, *Thus Spoke Zarathustra*:

> There (in EH) my Zarathustra will be shown for the first time in a clear light, the foremost book of the millennia, the bible of the future, the highest expression of human genius which contains the destiny of humankind . . . my Zarathustra will be read like the bible.[7]

Yet, at the same time, he says,

> I am not at all surprised if one does not understand my Zarathustra and see no reproach in this: a book so profound and so strange, that to understand and experience just six sentences of it, is to be elevated into a higher order of mortals.[8]

It is not surprising that, at the beginning of 1888, the year of his greatest literary output, he was known to almost no one. R. J. Hollingdale compares his life to that of Schopenhauer "in hostile independence of the academic world." He goes on to say that "like Schopenhauer he acquired 'disciples' who, heirs of those who had transferred their interest from the

---

5. Nietzsche, *On the Genealogy of Morality*, in Pearson and Large, *Nietzsche Reader*, 394; emphasis added.

6. Nietzsche, "Why I Write Such Good Books," in Pearson and Large, *Nietzsche Reader*, 509.

7. Nietzsche, *Kritische Studienausgabe (KSA)* 15:188, quoted in von Tevenar, "Zarathustra," 273.

8. Nietzsche, *KSA*, in Pearson and Large, *Nietzsche Reader*, 509.

problems of philosophy to the men who produced this philosophy, embraced his legend and ignored his books."[9]

Clearly, it behooves every commentator to apply themselves to Nietzsche's thought, "without sparing themselves some effort." Nevertheless, Nietzsche's approach to philosophical reflection is somewhat unique, in that he appears quite often to turn normal, rational thought upside down. According to Richardson and Leiter, Nietzsche appears to repudiate four so-called philosophical virtues: the search for the meaning of central philosophical concepts and claims; the justification of assertions by acceptable lines of reasoning; the use of scientific methods of discovery and confirmation; and submitting one's thinking to the assessment of one's academic peer group.[10] Thus, for example, in his investigation of the genealogy of morals, he seems to commit the genetic fallacy of making the truth or falsity of a proposition to be dependent upon its origin and the deontic fallacy of seeking to deduce moral principles from statements of fact. He is also renowned for his tendency to resort to *ad hominem* arguments (polemical statements about the character of those whose opinions he wishes to discredit).

Nevertheless, in spite of the difficulties in discerning the tangible meaning of Nietzsche's thought, and the variety of interpretations that have been given it, some important points shine through. I believe it is possible to arrive at sufficient clarity to be able to define some basic ideas and extract from them his views on the human predicament as he understood it. It seems fairly obvious that an appropriate place to begin is by considering the aims he has set himself and the assumptions he has adopted in pursuing them.

Intentions

Overall, one might say that his main objective is to deliver (to those who have ears to hear) a harsh critique of a civilization and culture (particularly of his native Germany), which he believes is in serious decline, in order to prepare the way for the rebirth of excellence. This implies that his version of excellence is possible and desirable. He has come to the conclusion that what Europe in general has inherited from Christianity and Western metaphysics has inflicted a decadent morality on societies,

9. Hollingdale, "Hero as Outsider," 79.
10. Richardson and Leiter, *Nietzsche*, 2–6.

built on a shallow optimism and a herd mentality.[11] In its place, he proposes what the famous Danish literary critic of the time called an "aristocratic radicalism."[12]

Nietzsche did not pretend to be a systematic thinker. He said,

> I mistrust all systematists and avoid them. The will to system is a lack of integrity.[13]

Rather, he attempted to be a problem-thinker, a person who sought provocatively to interpret, evaluate, and above all, challenge other people's interpretations of the character and quality of human life. He calls attention, for example, to ascetic and aesthetic ideals, bad conscience, the will to truth, religion, metaphysics, rationalism, nihilism, freedom of the will, fate, agency, values, life, and above all, morality. According to Richard Schacht,

> Nietzsche's most common strategy ... is to invoke a case to raise a problem, and then to examine it and employ it and other related cases to address the problem ... He typically seeks to make cases against certain ways of thinking. He proceeds by presenting an array of considerations to make us suspicious and aware of just how problematic these methods are, ultimately to deprive them of their credibility.[14]

For him, the role of philosophy was not to answer rational conundrums, but to rise above the merely academic,[15] and to elevate people to greatness, to enhance their will to power and to take hold of the life of the future by creating new values for a renewed civilization.

Crucial Assumptions

What Nietzsche took for granted in the realm of knowledge and understanding was hugely influential in his thought processes. He was not a

---

11. His reinterpretation of morals will be addressed later in the chapter.
12. See Behler, "Nietzsche in the Twentieth Century," 290.
13. Nietzsche, *Twilight of the Idols*, in Pearson and Large, *Nietzsche Reader*, 457.
14. Schacht, "Nietzsche's Kind of Philosophy," 157.
15. Western civilization has tended to look to the academic world of the elite universities to provide the right kind of intellectual insights to guide well-founded social norms and rational thought. Within Germany, in particular, in order to provide a profound alternative to the kind of rationality reflected by Kant, Hegel, Schopenhauer, Herder, and many others, Nietzsche believed that academia had to be deconstructed.

person given to much self-criticism.[16] His fundamental convictions stayed with him throughout his short intellectual life, being developed and reiterated toward the end of his period of mental stability with increasing intensity.

The most fundamental of these opinions was the belief that traditional forms of metaphysics, morality, and religion had proved harmful to the real flourishing of human life in a world that was completely devoid of any transcendent source of knowledge or wisdom. By metaphysics, Nietzsche understands a world of unconditioned principles and values that, outside of all perspectives and temporal conditions, would be absolutely true. He refers often to Kant's quest for the "thing in itself" (i.e., a final, undistorted reality):

> a thing considered as necessarily conforming to our mode of cognition is an appearance (transcendentally ideal), and a thing to which our cognition must conform is a thing in itself (transcendentally real).[17]

Kant proposed that an unbridgeable chasm existed between reality in itself and the human perception of it. This position on the ability to know might seem to support the thesis that all perceptions and the conclusions drawn from them are constrained by the perspectives from which we view them. As our perspectives are relative to the categories that we impose upon the objects we perceive in order that we might be able to experience them as they present themselves to us, we cannot claim to know them as they really are.[18]

However, what Kant seemed to have made impossible in his critique of pure reason he resurrected in his critique of practical reason:

> The notion of God is necessary if Kant's account of morality is going to withstand the criticism that ultimately it is vacuous. He seeks to demonstrate that morality by definition has to be both categorical and *a priori*: i.e. it has to be binding on all rational beings and has to assume within itself its own moral qualities.[19]

Kant recognized three fundamental, and seemingly insuperable, problems with his account of moral action: freedom of the will in an

16. This becomes self-evident in his last major writing, *Ecce Homo*, where his own self-importance is noticeably exaggerated.
17. Gardner, *Kant and the Critique*, 88.
18. See Kirk, *Future of Reason*, 54–55.
19. Kirk, *Future of Reason*, 55–56.

apparently mechanistic universe; the requirement of the moral law for perfection, a demand which the human will is incapable of meeting; and the unity between virtue and happiness. In order to escape from these profound dilemmas, Kant postulated a theory of knowledge which his philosophy denied him, namely that freedom of the will, the immortality of the soul, and the existence of God can be known absolutely.

Nietzsche, to the contrary, dismissed each of these beliefs. He was profoundly skeptical of the belief that humans can arrive at fundamental truths about reality through rational thinking. He was one of the most powerful destroyers of what has been called "foundationalism" in epistemology.[20] In probably the most famous passage that Nietzsche ever penned, he imagined a "madman" rushing into a marketplace, where a group of atheists were standing around, crying incessantly: "I seek God!" The tale proceeds with the madman answering his own question, "whither is God?"

> I will tell you. We have killed him you and I . . . God is dead. And we have killed him. How shall we comfort ourselves, the murderers of all murderers? What was holiest and mightiest of all that the world has yet owned has bled to death under our knives.[21]

In this short tale of the madman, Nietzsche intends a contrast between those standing in the marketplace (perhaps the modern equivalents of the ancient Greek skeptical philosophers, whom the apostle Paul met in Athens[22]) "who did not believe in God," and who suggested that God had lost his way or gone on a voyage, and the madman who realized the enormity of the deed of getting rid of God. The former were meant to represent the humanist atheists of the Enlightenment who just laughed and mocked, for the absence of God was, for them, a trivial matter. But the madman was distraught and, to cleanse his guilt, proclaimed a solemn *requiem aeternam deo*.

Nietzsche understood perfectly that everything in human existence is thrown into the melting pot once one understands that theism is false and that this discernment represents the triumph of the human race over

---

20. The search for a set of foundational beliefs that could not be doubted or refuted, leading to the possession of "an absolute assuredness about certain convictions, of a kind that no amount of incredulity could shake" (Kirk, *Future of Reason*, 150).

21. Nietzsche, *Gay Science*, 3:125.

22. Acts 17:17-18.

the invention of a fictitious supreme being. In *Twilight of the Idols*, Nietzsche affirms that

> the real world, we have done away with it: what world is left? The apparent one, perhaps? . . . But no! With the real world we have also done away with the apparent one.[23]

The death of God implies the metamorphosis of all values and the loss of the center of being. The world, in the complete nonexistence of a divine being who hitherto has held together in human thought the wholeness of human life, has disintegrated.

This is the first and essential presupposition that Nietzsche makes as he seeks to contemplate the real possibility of a transformation of all ideas and judgments. Nietzsche deduced the most extensive consequences of this "fact" in his treatment of morality and values.

Conventional Morality

In his preface to the *Birth of Tragedy*,[24] Nietzsche writes,

> It is apparent that it was a whole cluster of grave questions with which this book broadened itself. Let us add the gravest question of all. What, seen in the perspective of life, is the significance of morality?

Nietzsche seeks to answer this "gravest question of all" in two books, published in succeeding years (1886 and 1887): *Beyond Good and Evil: Prelude to a Philosophy of the Future* and *On the Genealogy of Morality: A Polemic*.

In the former, he proposes for the first time to develop a "Natural History of Morals."[25] In the latter, he unfolds what he calls a genealogy of morals (i.e., a history of the origin and evolution of prevailing moral values). He starts from the premise that the human race has known two types of moral conviction: what he calls "master morality" and "slave morality."[26] He goes back to a period called the prehistory of the human animal, a stage in human evolution when moral judgments were

---

23. Nietzsche, *Twilight of the Idols*, in Pearson and Large, *Nietzsche Reader*, 465.

24. Written in 1886, fourteen years after the original book was published.

25. Nietzsche, *Beyond Good and Evil*, in Pearson and Large, *Nietzsche Reader*, 339–44.

26. Nietzsche, in Pearson and Large, *Nietzsche Reader*, 399–407.

built around customs. This period predates world history, when received moral norms began to be standardized.[27]

Earlier, Nietzsche had argued that,

> to be moral, correct, ethical means to obey an age-old law or tradition ... We call good the man who does the moral thing as if by nature, after a long history of inheritance ... He is called good for he is good for something ... It is primarily the man of goodwill, the helpful man, who is called "good." To be evil is to be "not moral," to practice bad habits, go against tradition ... To harm one's fellow, however, has been felt primarily as injurious in all moral codes of different times ... When men determine between moral and immoral, good and evil, the basic opposition is not "egoism" and "selflessness," but rather adherence to a tradition or law, and release from it ... The origin of the tradition makes no difference; but is rather above all for the purpose of maintaining a community, a people.[28]

> Who is the most moral man? First, he who obeys the law most frequently ... The most moral man is he who sacrifices the most to custom.[29]

Nietzsche's response to the significance of morality might be called pragmatic. He was not interested in a merely conceptual argument about credible reasons for holding to one set of morals or another. His basic case rests on psychological analyses of the motivations and effects that stem from the adoption of what he terms "a slave morality," transposed later into a "Christian morality."[30] Nietzsche asks primarily,

> "What kind of person would be inclined to adopt this perspective?" and "What impact does this perspective have on the way in which its adherent develops and lives?"[31]

---

27. Nietzsche, *Genealogy*, in Pearson and Large, *Nietzsche Reader*, 424–35.
28. Nietzsche, *Human All Too Human*, in Pearson and Large, *Nietzsche Reader*, 176.
29. Nietzsche, *Daybreak*, in Pearson and Large, *Nietzsche Reader*, 192.
30. Magnus and Higgins, "Nietzsche's Works and Their Themes," 34.
31. Magnus and Higgins, "Nietzsche's Works and Their Themes," 34.

Slave Morality

The overwhelming moral tradition of Western Europe, dating back many centuries before the birth of Jesus, Nietzsche characterizes as "slave" (or "herd") morality. He has much to say about what he conceives to be a "life-denying" set of values. It is a morality motivated by those who feel themselves to be inferior. It consists in a devious strategy to replace the strong in their contempt for customary morality and in their claim to have the authority and ability to set their own values:

> Truly, men have given themselves all their good and evil. Truly, they did not take it, they did not find it, it did not descend to them as a voice from heaven. Man first implanted values into things to maintain himself—he created the meaning of things, a human meaning! Therefore he calls himself: "Man," that is: the evaluator.[32]

Nietzsche declared that slave morality is motivated by resentment,[33] and carried out through activities generated by an ascetic mentality.

Resentment[34]

In Nietzsche's eyes, this is the typical response of people who suffer, because of frustration with their lives. The frustration is due to a sense of ineffectiveness, the inability to achieve what one wishes. Its origin coincides with the birth of the slave morality:

> the beginning of the slaves' revolt in morality occurs when *ressentiment* itself turns creative and gives birth to values: the *ressentiment* of those beings who, being denied the proper response of action, compensate for it only with imaginary revenge. Whereas all noble morality grows out of a triumphant saying "yes" to itself, slave morality says "no" on principle to everything "outside," "other," "non-self": and this "no" is its creative deed.[35]

Resentment is revenge against noble (or master) morality. It is a negative reaction that seeks to drag down master morality to its own level

---

32. Nietzsche, *Thus Spoke Zarathustra*, in Pearson and Large, *Nietzsche Reader*, 266.

33. In the literature about Nietzsche, the French form, *ressentiment*, is often used.

34. There is a helpful summary of Nietzsche's thoughts on resentment in Reginster's essay, "Psychology of Christian Morality."

35. Nietzsche, *Genealogy*, in Pearson and Large, *Nietzsche Reader*, 266.

by reevaluating the values of the stronger person. In this way, it seeks to restore the injured feeling of a lack of power.

Nietzsche takes the Christian faith to task for being the paradigmatic example of a belief system that teaches resentment as a fundamental part of its approach to morality. In *The Anti-Christ: Curse on Christianity*, Nietzsche accuses Christianity of having instituted

> the reign of nihilistic values; a religion of decadence, of the weak, it has a depressive effect that drains vitality—the "physiological reality" of Christianity is a degeneration of the instincts.[36]

One of the difficulties in Nietzsche's account of slave morality is how the weak were ever able to persuade the strong to buy into their values, and how the strong, apparently, succumbed, but against their best interests. Nietzsche believes that the key to their "success" was to claim for those values an objective authority as unconditional norms. They had to convince the strong that they suffered from guilt by failing to live up to such norms. In this way, by asserting their own sense of power and control, they turned the tables.

One of the central claims of Nietzsche's *On the Genealogy of Morality* is that conventional morality is not so much lacking in rational foundations, but is dangerous to the psychological well-being of the human individual. Using strong language, Nietzsche asserts that the result of its imposition is to promote a psychopathology or a sickness in people's affections. He believes that traditional Christian morality can be recruited for this type of "narcissistic" pathology, by emphasizing as the center of its message universal human guilt, punishment, the need of repentance, and redemption. In Nietzsche's view, this is a precept that brings humiliation to the whole human race.

One of his most abiding criticisms of Christian morality comes in the notion of pity. Pity is expressed as a response to the inherent weakness of the human spirit in its failure to live up to the standards of justness and purity laid down in the supposed commands of a vengeful God. A bad conscience, which brings shame, self-reproach, and contrition, is pitiful. This morality belongs to the weak, those driven to the margins

---

36. Nietzsche, "Introduction to the Later Writings," 446. In his final work, Nietzsche speaks about how he overcame the temptation of being sucked into resentment himself: it was through activating what he calls "Russian fatalism." See Nietzsche, *Ecce Homo*, 6.

of society, the ones who suffer the most. They alleviate their suffering by inculcating the spirit of pity:

> Assuming that the raped, the oppressed, the suffering, the shackled, the weary, the insecure engage in moralizing, what will their moral value judgments have in common? They will probably express a pessimistic suspicion about the whole human condition, and they might condemn the human being along with his condition . . . Those qualities that serve to relieve the sufferer's existence are brought into relief and bathed in light: this is where pity, a kind, helpful hand, a warm heart, patience, diligence, humility, friendliness are revered—for in this context, these qualities are most useful and practically the only means of enduring an oppressive existence.[37]

The Ascetic Ideal

Conventional slave morality, according to Nietzsche, commends ascetic practices. These are a set of attitudes and actions that spring from "life-denying" values, of which humility is one of the most pathetic and contemptible. Nietzsche sees this virtue, trumpeted by Christianity, as a denial of self-confidence in one's own talents and pride in one's achievements. He aims, in refuting the principles on which it is said to rest, to uncover the real motives that lie behind. According to Robert Solomon, Nietzsche was a "ruthless diagnostician," who sought to cut to the very heart of morality:

> What we call morality, even if it includes (indeed emphasizes) the sanctity of life, displays a palpable disgust and "weariness" with life, an "otherworldly" nostalgia that prefers some other, idealized existence to this one.[38]

In the first essay of his *On the Genealogy of Morals*, Nietzsche proposed that historically the chief purveyors of asceticism were a priestly class who originally categorized good and evil in terms of pure and impure. In other words, goodness was associated with health and badness with sickness. Their essential cure was to recommend abstinence:

---

37. Nietzsche, *Beyond Good and Evil*, 260. Nietzsche mentions the qualities with a strong touch of irony, seeing that he supposes that they typify Christian morality, which he detests.

38. Solomon, "Nietzsche ad hominem," 188.

certain diets (avoidance of meat), of fasting, sexual abstinence, the flight 'into the desert ... the whole metaphysics of the clergy ... is antagonistic to the senses.[39]

In the third essay, Nietzsche elaborates further on what he understands by the ascetic ideal. It is promoted, not only by a priestly caste (in every religion), but also by philosophers, who denied the world, hated life, and doubted the senses. In the ascetic ideal,

> satisfaction is looked for and found in failure, decay, pain, misfortune, ugliness, voluntary deprivation, destruction of selfhood, self-flagellation and self-sacrifice.[40]

He finishes the *Genealogy* by speculating that the ascetic ideal was invented in order to give humans a purpose for their existence:

> Except for the ascetic ideal: man, the animal man, had no meaning up to now. His existence on earth had no purpose; "What is man for, actually?"—was a question without an answer ... behind every human destiny sounded the even louder refrain "in vain!" This is what the ascetic ideal meant: something was missing ... he himself could think of no justification or explanation or affirmation, he suffered, from the problem of what he meant ... The meaningless of suffering, not the suffering, was the curse which has so far blanketed mankind—and the ascetic ideal offered man a meaning! Up to now it was the only meaning, but any meaning at all is better than no meaning at all; the ascetic ideal was, in every respect, the ultimate "*faute de mieux*" ["for lack of anything better"] par excellence. Within it, suffering was given an interpretation; the enormous emptiness seemed filled; the door was shut on all suicidal nihilism.[41]

So the ascetic ideal, by explaining the meaning of suffering, also explains resentment in a profounder psychological sense. Every sufferer cries out for an offender, someone to blame for the suffering:

> The innovation of the ascetic priest is to provide an accessible "culprit," the sufferer himself! ... The sufferer himself is to be the object of his own *ressentiment*, since he is taught that he himself is the cause of his own suffering. As a result, the sufferer now has "a living being upon whom he can release his emotions,"

---

39. Nietzsche, in Pearson and Large, *Nietzsche Reader*, 397.
40. Nietzsche, *Genealogy*, 11.
41. Nietzsche, *Genealogy*, 28.

namely himself. He discharges his emotions against himself . . . by lacerating himself with feelings of guilt . . . Human beings are fundamentally creatures of desire . . . all their basic instincts and inclinations are fundamentally anti-ascetic! The ascetic priest seizes upon this fact in order to provide a meaning for human suffering: . . . one suffers . . . as punishment for failure to live up to the ascetic ideal . . . "The main contrivance" used by the ascetic priest is "the feeling of guilt."[42]

You can now guess what, in my opinion, the healing instinct of life has at least tried to do through the ascetic priest and what purpose was served by a temporary tyranny of such . . . concepts as "guilt," "sin," "sinfulness," "corruption," "damnation": to make the sick harmless to a certain degree . . . to give their *ressentiment* a backwards direction ("one thing is needful") and in this way to exploit the bad instincts of all sufferers for the purpose of self-discipline, self-surveillance and self-overcoming.[43]

Noble Morality

Nietzsche advocates a wholly different approach to the subject of good and evil from that of conventional morality. As we have seen, Nietzsche rejects the culturally dominant distinction between "good" and "evil." In the case of goodness, it is common to identify it supremely with sacrificial acts made on behalf of others. Evil, on the contrary, may be located in acts of hatred leading to exploitation, the suppression of rights, and even the elimination of human beings. Such acts are often symptomatic of authoritarian regimes with a culture of the strong leader and extremely aggressive policies toward weaker groups seen as threats to the power and privileges of the ruling elite.[44]

According to Nietzsche, this common distinction is a reaction to a contrasting differentiation, from which it degenerates:

That earlier "aristocratic" distinction is between the good and the "base" or "bad" . . . a distinction that is virtually the mirror image of the good/evil standard. This dichotomy divides acts

42. Leiter, *Nietzsche on Morality*, 208–9.
43. Nietzsche, *Genealogy*, 16.
44. Many nations in South America, between 1964 and 1988, were prime examples of such regimes.

and characters that are noble, beautiful, or fine ... from the ugly and common; acts done with supreme self-confidence of the agent, with the agent's own sense of worthiness simply to decree how he shall act, and those done in weakness and self-doubt, requiring the reassurance or the consolation of an eternal value or rational criterion or the approval of others.[45]

This aristocratic, noble, or master morality is exercised by those in power. It implies a judgment of oneself as good and others by one's own qualities. It implies the rightness of a society divided by ranks, of which the top order is free to define good and bad according to its own interests. It detests the modern notion of egalitarianism. For Nietzsche, it is a "higher" morality that informs the lives of "higher men."[46]

The higher types tend to be solitary, deal with other people instrumentally, and consider their own understanding of justice as beyond appeal. They are mentally healthy and resilient, even in the face of physical sickness and disappointments. They affirm life and therefore are prepared to will an eternal return to this same life. They possess a "fundamental certainty"[47] about themselves. They determine their own values by giving direction to their own natures.[48]

In Nietzsche's own words:

> The order of castes, the supreme, the dominant law is merely the sanction of a natural order ... Nature ... distinguishes the pre-eminently spiritual ones, those who are pre-eminently strong in muscle and temperament, and those, the third type, who excel neither in one respect nor in the other, the mediocre ones—the last as the great majority, the first as the elite.[49]

Nietzsche explains the purpose of advancing an elevated morality:

> Wherever progress is to ensue, deviating natures are of greatest importance.

These deviating natures belong to those Nietzsche calls "free spirits":

---

45. Pippin, "Nietzsche's Alleged Farewell," 261.
46. See Leiter, *Nietzsche on Morality*, 58.
47. Leiter, *Nietzsche on Morality*, 95–98.
48. See Leiter, *Nietzsche on Morality*, 93–98.
49. Nietzsche, *Antichrist*, 93.

(they are) the exception . . . it is not part of the nature of the free spirit that his views are more correct, but rather that he has released himself from tradition.[50]

Brian Leiter sums up Nietzsche, "as a kind of esoteric moralist, i.e. someone who has views about human flourishing, views he wants to communicate at least to a few."[51]

The Revaluation of All Values

In the preface to *The Twilight of the Idols*, Nietzsche announces his project of working toward the revaluation of all values. The project is to flesh out an alternative morality to that of the herd.

This will be a mammoth task; it will engage many different disciplines:

> All sciences must, from now on, prepare the way for the future work of the philosopher: the work being understood to mean that the philosopher has to solve the problem of values and that he has to decide on the hierarchy of values.[52]

By the end of August of 1888, Nietzsche had abandoned plans to write a book with the title *The Will to Power*. Instead he contemplated a masterwork in four volumes entitled *The Revaluation of All Values*. Whether he would have ever completed such an ambitious task, we shall never know, for a little over four months later, he experienced a complete mental collapse.[53]

He did not underestimate his own abilities. He declared in his autobiography,

> I now have the skill and knowledge to invert perspectives: first reason why a "revaluation of values" is perhaps possible at all to me alone.[54]

---

50. Nietzsche, *Human, All Too Human*, in Pearson and Large, *Nietzsche Reader*, 181–82.

51. Leiter, *Nietzsche on Morality*, 237.

52. Nietzsche, *Genealogy*, 17.

53. His final two publications, following this decision to embark on a new project, *The Twilight of the Idols* and *The Antichrist*, and before "signing off" with his autobiography, *Ecce Homo*, might give an indication of the direction in which he wanted to go.

54. Nietzsche, *Ecce Homo*, 2.

> Revaluation of all values: this is my formula for an act of supreme coming-to-oneself on the part of mankind which in me has become flesh and genius. It is my fate to have become the first decent human being . . . I was the first to discover the truth . . . I am a bringer of good tidings such as there has never been . . . Only after me will there be grand politics on earth.[55]

The context for his revaluation are the signs of a "will to life."[56]

Values

As Nietzsche convinced himself that the uninterrupted hegemony of the reign of God was now at an end, because humankind had eliminated his control over human affairs and was in the process of extinguishing also the shadow of his presence, a new set of values to guide humanity had to be created. Hitherto in the history of Europe, at least for the last two and a half millennia, God and the gods had been the source of the ultimate truth about human life on earth. They had been looked to for answers to meaning, purpose, suffering, prosperity, and life after death. Now, however, the birth of modern science, advances in historical research, and what Nietzsche referred to as the all-around "desire for intellectual purity" provokes the need for "a new spiritual maturity that will enable us to deal adequately with the new situation . . . and not be overcome by disillusionment and despair."[57] As he goes on to say:

> Among some pious people I found a hatred of reason and was well disposed to them for that; for this at least betrayed their bad intellectual conscience. But to stand in the midst . . . of this whole marvelous uncertainty and rich ambiguity of existence without questioning, without trembling with the craving and rapture of questioning . . . that is what I feel to be contemptible.[58]

Nietzsche is actually seeking to create a new atheism. The former atheism of the Enlightenment, according to him, still approved the universality and categorical nature of good and evil, only substituting human reason for divine revelation as the basis for distinguishing the two. Meanwhile, the liberation of the human race from having to trust in God

---

55. Nietzsche, *Ecce Homo*, 1.
56. See Schacht, "Nietzsche's Genealogy," 331.
57. Pearson and Large, *Nietzsche Reader*, xxxvi.
58. Nietzsche, *Gay Science*, in Pearson and Large, *Nietzsche Reader*, 209.

offered an opportunity to create new values that would negate those that had dominated human society for so long past.[59]

Nietzsche knew what values he disdained:

> What is bad? All that proceeds from weakness ... not contentment ... not peace at all ... not virtue ... The weak and ill-constituted shall perish: first principle of our philanthropy ... What is more harmful than any vice?—Active sympathy for the ill-constituted and weak Christianity.[60]

Of all the virtues trumpeted by Christianity, the one he most scorns is pity (*Mitleiden*, literally "suffering with"):

> Pity stands in antithesis to the tonic emotions which enhance the energy of the feeling of life: it has a depressive effect ... If one judges pity by the value of the reactions which it usually brings about, its mortally dangerous character appears in a much clearer light. Pity on the whole thwarts the law of evolution, which is the law of selection. It preserves what is right for destruction; it defends life's disinherited and condemned. Nothing in our unhealthy modernity is more unhealthy than Christian pity. To be physician here, to wield the knife here that pertains to us, that is our kind of philanthropy, with that we are philosophers.[61]

So, God, as portrayed particularly in the Christian faith,[62] is the antithesis of the values that Nietzsche wishes to see implemented in the civilization of the future:

> In God a declaration of hostility toward life, nature, the will to life! ... In God nothingness deified, the will to nothingness sanctified.[63]

---

59. See Janaway, "Gay Science," 252.
60. Nietzsche, *Anti-Christ*, 2.
61. Nietzsche, *Anti-Christ*, 7. The whole book is an excoriating attack on the Christian religion. It is, what we might call, a "rage" against the faith.
62. Nietzsche touches on the multiple defects of other religions, especially Hinduism and Buddhism. However, he deals at length with Christianity, because of its long influence over the cultures of Europe.
63. Nietzsche, *Anti-Christ*, 18.

Life

Promoting the life of the species, advocating faith in life now becomes the reference mark for everything good and beautiful:

> Gradually man has become a fantastic animal that has to fulfill one more condition of existence than any other animal: man has to believe, to know, from time to time, why he exists; his race cannot flourish without a periodic trust in life, without faith in reason in life.[64]

Nietzsche puts forward a number of generalization about what he believes life entails. In the section preceding that on the influence of pity, Nietzsche gives his basic understanding of life:

> I consider life instinct for growth, for continuance, for accumulation of forces, for power.[65]

In accordance with his naturalistic presupposition, life is attached preeminently to the physical and psychological realities of human existence. It is about marshalling the inner desires to overcome the utter banalities of normal being in the world. Living is "the satisfaction of people's most basic instincts."[66]

Life is the very opposite of the ascetic ideal, which is externalized in the world in the form of a denial of sensual pleasures. Nietzsche refers to the ideal in terms of

> an insatiable instinct and power-will that wants to become master not over something in life but over life itself, over its most profound, powerful and basic conditions; here an attempt is made to employ energy to block up the wells of energy.[67]

So life, in Nietzsche's understanding, is expressed in a carefree outpouring of the person's inner wells of energy. These are passed down through the generations by the way of evolution. They form a person's inner constitution:

> We live this personal life, before death, in a body whose biological wills must be given their due.[68]

64. Nietzsche, *Gay Science*, I:1.
65. Nietzsche, *Anti-Christ*, 6.
66. Reginster, "Psychology of Christian Morality," 720.
67. Nietzsche, *Genealogy*, III:11.
68. Richardson, "Nietzsche on Life's Ends," 766.

Morality, then, is encapsulated in this conflict between two wills: the will to life and the will to suppress life. Values are not so much expressions of what makes life valuable; it is life itself that is prized:

> We're to judge values by whether they "say Yes to life," i.e. by whether they are life-affirming.[69]

The Will to Power and the *Ubermensch*

The point to life is growth. Its opposite is stagnation (i.e., to succumb to the reigning culture of the times, by holding back the subterranean drives that wish to manifest themselves in our daily lives). The will to power is the way to overcome all that curtails are bodily passions. It is to say no to the life-defeating values of the herd and to step out into a new world order. Nietzsche seems to think that "for most of us our deepest drives and aims are healthy."[70] Thus, I may trust my passions and follow their promptings, rather than those of the most judicious conclusions of moral thought. In terms of Nietzsche's discussion in *The Birth of Tragedy*, Dionysus, the god of "ecstatic liberation,"[71] has overcome Apollo, associated in Nietzsche's mind with restraint and good order:

> While Apollo is associated with visible form, comprehensible knowledge, and moderation, Dionysus is linked with formless flux, mystical intuition, and excess.[72]

Nietzsche proclaims himself, "the last disciple of the philosopher Dionysus,"[73] who represented

> the most profound instinct of life, the instinct for the future of life, for the eternity of life … felt in a religious way, the very path to life, procreation, is felt to be the holy path.[74]

The will to power is achieved through sublimation:

---

69. Richardson, "Nietzsche on Life's Ends," 775.
70. Richardson, "Nietzsche on Life's Ends," 780.
71. Grant and Hazel, *Who's Who in Classical Mythology*, 112.
72. Pearson and Large, *Nietzsche Reader*, 34.
73. Nietzsche, "What I Owe the Ancients," in Pearson and Large, *Nietzsche Reader*, 485. Not, Apollo! In the light of his characterization of the two gods, it is highly significant that he chooses Dionysus rather than Apollo.
74. Nietzsche, *Daybreak*, in Pearson and Large, *Nietzsche Reader*, 205.

Sublimation, as the mental mechanism that orders and subdues instinctual drives, is responsible for the attainment of one's "self-mastery."[75]

Nietzsche draws an ideal picture of an entire culture driven by powerful individuals generous, independent, unprejudiced, endowed with the ability to perform a creative sublimation of instincts . . . These are the "we free spirits" . . . people who embody intellectual tolerance and existential integrity. They are noble and courageous.[76]

From time to time, Nietzsche gives them the name of *Ubermenschen*.[77] However, his major allusion to these whom he considers to be noble, distinguished, and elevated examples of human beings, comes in Part I of *Thus Spoke Zarathustra*. The first words that Zarathustra spoke to the crowd in the market square were,

I teach you the *Ubermensch*. Man is something that should be overcome.

The crowd (or the herd) just laughed at him, because he spoke in conundrums that they did not understand. So he then spoke to them of the Last Man, those who say,

"we have discovered happiness" . . . and blink.

At the end of his discourse, "the mirth of the crowd interrupted him, 'Give us this Last Man, O Zarathustra . . . make us into this Last Man! You can have the *Ubermensch*!'"[78]

Occasionally Nietzsche mentions the *Ubermensch* in his later works, but the characteristics portrayed are largely veiled. He returns one final time to the theme in his ultimate publication:

The word "*Ubermensch*" to designate a type that has turned out supremely well, in antithesis to "modern man," to "good" men, to Christians and other nihilists . . . has almost everywhere been understood with perfect innocence in the sense of those values

---

75. Golomb, "Will to Power," 526.

76. Golomb, "Will to Power," 539.

77. I keep the German categorization, since every attempt to translate it into English—"the overman," "the higher man," "the superman"—makes it seem rather banal.

78. Nietzsche, *Thus Spoke Zarathustra*, in Pearson and Large, *Nietzsche Reader*, 255–59.

whose antithesis makes its appearance in the figure of Zarathustra: that is to say as an "idealistic" type of higher species, half "saint," half "genius."[79]

Perhaps, the nearest that Nietzsche gets to a living embodiment of the *Ubermensch* is the German writer, Johann Wolfgang von Goethe[80]:

> Goethe conceived of a strong, highly educated man, adept in all things bodily, with a tight rein on himself and a reverence for himself . . . the man to whom there is no longer anything forbidden except weakness, whether it be called vice or virtue . . . Such a liberated spirit stands in the midst of the universe with a joyful and trusting fatalism, with faith in the fact that only what is individual is reprehensible, that everything is redeemed and affirmed in the whole . . . But such a faith is the highest of all possible faiths; I have baptised it with the name Dionysus.[81]

So Nietzsche saw Goethe as a man of the future who would help to redeem humanity from the curse of reigning ideas, an advanced version of the new nobility that would emerge; like Nietzsche, a man born before his time. He lived beyond all current ideas of what constitutes good and evil. He took responsibility for the future, by overcoming obedience to the past.

The Restoration of "Hidden" Instincts

Above all, perhaps, the *Ubermensch* was the person distinguished by his ability to recognize, recover, and manage the healthy physiological and psychological drives with which he was born, but which had been repressed by the culture in which he was nurtured. These drives, referred to also as dispositions, urges, affects, tendencies, desires, instincts, forces, impulses, passions, and functional states, constitute the most fundamental notion in Nietzsche's psychological analysis of human action and morality. They orientate the agent toward certain valuations and interpretations of life.[82]

---

79. Nietzsche, *Ecce Homo*, 1.

80. It is, of course, immaterial whether his characterization of Goethe is accurate or not; this is how he imagined him.

81. Nietzsche, *Twilight of the Idols*, 49.

82. Gemes and Richardson, *Oxford Handbook of Nietzsche*, 16.

People are the product of underlying type facts or traits, which create the people they are. These struggle for supremacy within the person's psyche and will:

> A "person" is an arena in which the struggle of drives (type-facts) is played out; how they play out determines what he believes, what he values, what he becomes.[83]

Nietzsche repeatedly offers the view that individuals are composites or conglomerates of multiple, competing drives, affects, and thoughts. These parts are organized, in his view, in terms of "orders of rank." Several "types" of such orders are discussed at length by Nietzsche, including the types of the "master," "the slave," and the "priest." The "last man" might also be thought of as a type, and the *Ubermensch* could be construed as an as-yet-unachieved type (human, transhuman, or more than human).[84]

According to Knobe and Leiter,

> type-facts play a powerful (but not exclusive role) role in determining one's behavior and values, though a far more powerful role than education or upbringing or conscious choice; indeed, a person's crucial conscious choices and values are themselves explicable in terms of these type-facts.[85]

Freedom, Fatalism, and Self-Creation

Following Freud's claim that the concept of drives is "at once the most important and the most obscure element of psychological research," Paul Katsafanas believes that

> the work of Nietzsche provides ample support for the idea that the drive concept is both tremendously important and terribly obscure.[86]

Not least, the enigmatic nature of the thinking is found in what appears to be an obvious contradiction between what he says about human freedom and about the determining causality of the drives.

---

83. Leiter, *Nietzsche on Morality*, 80.
84. Acampora, "Beholding Nietzsche," 367.
85. Knobe and Leiter, "Case for Nietzschean Moral Psychology," 90.
86. Katsafanas, "Nietzsche's Philosophical Psychology," 727.

For Nietzsche, freedom of the will is an illusion. In *Human, All Too Human*, a book assigned to the middle period of his writing, Nietzsche speaks about the fable of intelligible freedom. By means of a somewhat convoluted argument, he comes to the conclusion that humans do not possess the kind of freedom that makes responsibility for their actions, motives, and nature possible.[87] His understanding of the inner, subconscious human instincts, which propel human thought and action, leads him to infer that "human beings lack free will, and are determined to do what they do, and believe what they believe, by largely natural facts about their physiology and psychological drives."[88]

At an early age, Nietzsche was toying with the idea of the supremacy of a predetermined fate driving human life:

> Fate always prescribes the principle: "Events are determined by events." If this were the only true principle, man would be the plaything of dark effective forces, not responsible for his mistakes, completely free from moral distinctions, a necessary link in a chain.[89]

At this stage, Nietzsche still held to the existence of a limited free will for humans. However, at a later stage, he concluded that freedom of the will was invented:

> Nietzsche argues that the myth of "free will" derives from Christian theology's desire to make people responsible for their actions and thus foster guilt, which in turn derives from the ("slavish") desire to blame and punish (TI VI. 7). Instead, he proposes his own counter-explanation a kind of fatalism: "No one is the result of his own intention, his own will, his own purpose" (TI VI. 8).[90]

Working backwards from his overwhelming desire to rid the world of moral notions such as sin, responsibility, guilt, and punishment, Nietzsche maintains that human agency is already controlled by subliminal forces of which he can only become conversant when they are thrust into awareness:

---

87. Nietzsche, *Human, All Too Human*, 39.
88. Leiter, *Nietzsche on Morality*, 57.
89. Nietzsche, *Fate and History*, in Pearson and Large, *Nietzsche Reader*, 15.
90. Nietzsche, "Introduction to the Later Writings," 444.

> Consciousness is not causally efficacious in its own right. While a person's conscious states may be part of the causal chain leading up to action, they play that role only in virtue of non-conscious facts about the person ... According to Nietzsche ... the will ... is nothing but the effect of type-facts about the person. This means that the real story of the genesis of an action begins with the type-facts, which explain both consciousness and a person's actions.[91]

If Nietzsche's surmise is true, then conscious responsibility for one's thinking, motives, actions, and their consequences seems to be so severely curtailed that, for all intents and purposes, it is nonexistent. The only option available to humans is "to become what one is."[92]

Nevertheless, Nietzsche, in developing his theory of the will to life as the will to power, is bound to consider that people are conscious agents, ultimately in control of their faculties:

> What we call "I" is constituted, takes on a specific character and form, and becomes individual rather than a diffuse mix of competing forces.[93]

Nietzsche frequently refers to "self-creation," "overcoming," "taking responsibility for the future," and other acts determined consciously by a person who has learned how to rank their desires and control their type-facts for "higher" ends. Nietzsche's whole philosophy of the "revaluation of all values" implies that he has moved beyond accepting that we can only become what we already are.

His sustained attack on the notion of morality and Christianity as its principal cause implies that the Christian faith and those who direct it (the "priests") are responsible for the beliefs and actions of the herd. If they are not, then they cannot be judged for their supposed perversity. The failure to take responsibility is, according to Nietzsche, the effect of a weak will:

> The "unfree will" is mythology: in real life it is only a matter of strong and weak wills. Whenever a thinker sniffs out coercion, necessity, obligation, pressure, constraint in any "causal connection" or "psychological necessity," it is almost always a symptom

---

91. Leiter, *Nietzsche on Morality*, 73.
92. Acampora, "Beholding Nietzsche," 382.
93. Acampora, "Beholding Nietzsche," 382.

of where his own inadequacy lies . . . the person is revealing himself.[94]

Human Nature

From the foregoing discussion of the central aspects of Nietzsche's thinking, it is hard to formulate a coherent account of what he surmised about the human animal. There were for Nietzsche at least two fundamental predicaments about the human condition: one was intellectual and the other intensely personal. In the first case, his declamation that human beings could no longer imagine a world in which the monotheistic God, dressed in Christian clothes, remained the centerpiece of moral judgment and rational thought, meant that the meaning of human existence had to be reconsidered from an entirely different standpoint. He saw his task as developing answers to the questions raised by the death of God.[95]

In the second case, also driven by his proclamation of the death of God, he sought to account for the whole reality of human thought and behavior from a naturalistic and historical perspective. What is required is that humans turn inward to discover, and meditate on, what he calls,

> a chemistry of moral, religious, aesthetic ideas and feelings, a chemistry of all those impulses that we ourselves experience in the great and small interactions of culture and society, indeed even in solitude.[96]

So, the reality of human life is to be explained in terms of psycho-physical facts. The beginning of a reformulation of human existence must begin with the de-deification of nature and the naturalization of humanity, in order to discover a new nature.[97]

> Each thinker is driven to construct a quasi-speculative theory of human nature to explain certain features of human belief systems . . . precisely because he finds that these features do not

---

94. Nietzsche, *Beyond Good and Evil*, 21. An illustration of strong and weak wills might be the case of overcoming drug addiction or alcoholism. Some people are able to achieve this, whilst others, tragically, are not. Can we imagine that the positive or negative outcome is due wholly to one's type-facts? Such a conclusion seems, from the evidence, highly implausible.

95. Pearson and Large, *Nietzsche Reader*, xix.

96. Nietzsche, *Human, All Too Human*, 1.

97. Nietzsche, *Gay Science*, III:109.

admit of rational vindication. We must look beyond human reason—to certain natural facts and dispositions about human beings—to explain why they hold these beliefs nonetheless.[98]

In speaking about realism—belief that the world really is the way it appears to the observer (which he denies) Nietzsche posits the importance of physiology in determining what is a human being[99]:

> We no longer trace the origin of man in the "spirit," in the "divinity," we have placed him back among the animals.

However, Nietzsche goes on to designate humans as "relatively speaking, *the most unsuccessful animal,* the sickliest, the one most dangerously strayed from its instincts."[100] Humans imagined themselves as higher than the rest of the animal kingdom, having free will and enjoying a spiritual nature that set them firmly in the context of receiving a gift from "a higher order." This characterization was, however, illusory.

As we have already seen, Nietzsche also denies the central reality of consciousness as a distinguishing mark of human nature. It is not, strictly speaking, a feature of being human, but a coming into awareness of unconscious forces:

> We would also be able to "act" in every sense of that word: and yet none of all this would have to "enter our consciousness."[101]

> Nietzsche often stresses the relative impotence of conscious motives and of our consciousness of ends by itself and surmises that frequently the ends pursued by the organism may not be those which the person is conscious of, our consciousness in these cases resembling an ornamental monarch kept in the dark about policies really determined by scheming nominal subordinates.[102]

Finally, Nietzsche seems to be quite ambiguous about the permanence in individual human beings of a conscious self-identity over their lifetime. His strong assertions that "there is no thing in itself" and that all reality is "becoming" appears to lead him to affirm that in "some

---

98. Leiter, *Nietzsche on Morality,* 8.
99. Nietzsche, *Gay Science,* II:57–59.
100. Nietzsche, *Anti-Christ,* 14; emphasis added.
101. Nietzsche, *Gay Science,* Book IV:354.
102. Poellner, "Nietzsche's Metaphysical Sketches," 690.

places there are no relatively enduring instantiations of fully determinate properties."[103] In other words, there is no discernible, definitive being that a person can say, of their past and present, "that's me."

An Assessment of Nietzsche's Approach to the Human Predicament

Bearing in mind the caveats expressed in the introduction to this chapter about the difficulties in the way of being faithful to Nietzsche's own exposition of his thought, I will attempt an analysis and critique of what he has written. Apart from one biography written by someone who knew him personally,[104] albeit for only a few months, his published works are all that we have to go on.

Perspectivism

As Nietzsche himself would be the first to admit, all evaluations of another's thought are undertaken from a particular perspective:

> Nietzsche's perspectivism figures importantly in his debunking critique of morality . . . Nietzsche denies that morality is anything but perspectival. Contrary to the claims of moralists, morality is not inherent in or determined by reality . . . Instead it is the invention of human beings.[105]

Perspectivism is the

> view that one always knows or perceives or thinks about something from a particular "perspective"—not just a spacial viewpoint, of course, but a particular context of surrounding impressions, influences, and ideas, conceived of through one's language and social upbringing and, ultimately, determined by virtually everything about oneself, one's psychological make-up,

---

103. Poellner, "Nietzsche's Metaphysical Sketches," 693.

104. Salome, *Nietzsche*. His extensive correspondence illuminates his character and style of life. However, generally, they are not considered by Nietzschean scholars to represent his considered thinking, exposed to the general public in written form.

105. Magnus and Higgins, "Nietzsche's Works and Their Themes," 32. It is quite probable that Nietzsche, on account of the role that deep inner drives play in his philosophy, would have endorsed the view that one particular aspect of reality was determinate of how humans deduce moral values.

and one's history. There is no perspective-free, global viewpoint, no "God's eye" view ... There is, therefore, no external comparison or correspondence to be made between what we believe and truth "in itself" but only the comparison, competition, and differences in quality within and between perspectives themselves.[106]

This standpoint could be interpreted as a form of cognitive relativism, for there does not appear to be any kind of intersubjective way of deciding which interpretations of phenomena are superior to others. However, the interpretations can still be compared and there are certain ground rules (such as internal consistency, accuracy in the gathering of data, the justification of what appear to be truth claims, the inadequacy of alternative interpretations) that have to be obeyed in order for a conversation between differences to be possible.

Undoubtedly, there is a limit to Nietzsche's perspectivism. For example, he himself says,

> There is only a perspective seeing, only a perspective "knowing" ... the more eyes, various eyes we are able to use for the same thing, the more complete will be our "concept" of the thing, our "objectivity." But to eliminate the will completely and turn off all the emotions without exception, assuming we could: well? would that not mean to castrate the intellect?[107]

Moreover, Nietzsche certainly gives the impression the he "knows certain truths that others (Christians, most philosophers, moralists) fail to comprehend ... A class of claims can only be epistemically privileged if it is possible for there to be objective truths about them and for us to have objective knowledge of those truths."[108] In a good number of instances, he is almost excessively dogmatic about his opinion: not least, perhaps, in his claim that God is dead. Because he bases his insights on the correct way of interpreting the external world, and his own inner world, he has to make truth claims. In practice, at least, his perspectivism is anti-skeptical. His interest may not be in the abstract intellectualizing of the concept of truth, but he is concerned about uncovering the real-life consequences of people's beliefs and actions and, in particular, their alleged origins.[109]

106. Solomon, "Nietzsche ad hominem," 195.
107. Nietzsche, *Genealogy,* III:12.
108. Leiter, *Nietzsche on Morality,* 11–12.
109. See Richardson and Leiter, *Nietzsche,* 17–18.

A Personal Perspective

It is necessary to consider the question of perspectives, seeing that my analysis and critique of Nietzsche's complex thought is based on fundamental disagreements about assumptions and starting points. Unlike Nietzsche, I hold to the Christian version of theism. That means, at the least, that I hold that the existence of a particular, personal, and infinite nonmaterial Being is the best explanation for the existence and history of the universe, and for the whole of human reality: for the existence of all matter, rather than its nonexistence, for biological life, and for the utter uniqueness of human existence.

I acknowledge that this is an interpretation of all that we can know about ourselves and the universe we live in, from scientific research, philosophy, literature and the arts, anthropological, social, political, and economic studies, and religious claims. I am also a realist in epistemological terms, believing that interpretations can correspond to the facts of the matter and that this can be shown by evidence that is verifiable "beyond reasonable doubt."[110]

My position is, of course, a perspective. If it were irrefutable in an absolute sense, everyone would be bound to come to the same conclusions. It is open to objections. Where beliefs transcend measured, repeatable, confirmatory experimentation, I would appeal to the practice of abduction (or inference to the best explanation) as the most valid method for understanding the real world, including our own experience of ourselves. For me, Christian theism, as rendered in mainstream Christian tradition, provides the best explanation (makes the most sense) of human reality in all its facets. It is inevitable, therefore, that my appreciation of what it means to be human will clash with that of Nietzsche's at fundamental points. Nevertheless, our respective perspectives can enter into an exchange of different readings of life, for both of us are human, mortal, and fallible.

---

110. I have set out my philosophical and religious views in extensive detail in two published works, *The Future of Reason, Science and Faith: Following Modernity and Post-Modernity* and *Christian Mission as Dialogue: Engaging the Current Epistemological Predicament of the West*. Both publications are available electronically: the latter at http://repository.ubn.ru.nl/bitstream/2066/90917/1/90917.pdf.

A Revaluation of Inferences

In what became Nietzsche's farewell discourse, his final self-assessment of his life's work (written when he was only 44), *Ecce Homo*, he asks several times, "have I been understood?" To which one may reply, "I can only hope so, but many questions remain." Those who wish to find in Nietzsche's writings a logical and coherent account of the development of his thinking, easy to detect and reproduce, will probably look in vain. He has been placed subsequently among the philosophers, for undoubtedly he raises issues long dealt with in the field of philosophy, and which continue to be so: concerns about truth, reality, values, the meaning of life, modernity, nihilism, freedom of the will, morality and religion. However, his approach to these matters is atypical, and one might even say elusively idiosyncratic.

Metaphysics

He will have no truck with metaphysics. By metaphysics Nietzsche means a perspective on life that is unconditioned by time and space: "belief in a 'true' world that stands outside time, history and nature . . . the positing of supernatural and imaginary causes, forces, and entities, to a preoccupation with the otherworldly . . . "[111] He proposes a fundamental break with established ways of thinking, for example, about general abstract concepts like truth, goodness, equality, and justice, whose core meaning can be elucidated irrespective of real-life situations and historical inquiry:

> All that has produced metaphysical assumptions and made them valuable, horrible, pleasurable to men thus far is passion, error, and self-deception . . . When one has disclosed these methods to be the foundation of all existing religions and metaphysical systems, one has refuted them.[112]

Unfortunately for Nietzsche, his negative evaluation of metaphysics is itself a metaphysical construction. A dogmatic assertion that something is such and such, because a metaphysical stance has already been assumed that corroborates such a claim, is a faulty way of reasoning; it simply begs the question. Peter Poellner finds three metaphysical inferences already embedded in Nietzsche's writings: reality is fundamentally

---

111. Pearson and Large, *Nietzsche Reader*, xxi.
112. Nietzsche, *Human, All Too Human* I:9.

perspectival, there is no true conception of the world; there is no "thing-in-itself"; and all reality is becoming.[113] Moreover, Nietzsche himself alludes to the fact that science itself requires some kind of metaphysical validation in order for its methods to be warranted. It cannot presume that its practices are self-confirmatory. If all reality is intrinsically perspectival, we could not know the statement's truth, for there could not be any independent source existing against which the claim could be measured, for the claim itself would be perspectival. The other two inferences are, likewise, self-defeating.

Nietzsche's inference to the most comprehensive account of the world is based on the metaphysical claim that all knowledge comes from within the natural world and that nothing that is not amenable to empirical confirmation or rejection is worthy of consideration. This is an *a priori* claim, both unprovable and irrefutable on scientific grounds. Nietzsche comprehensibly starts his philosophizing from a naturalistic perspective: that there is no reality beyond the natural world, open to the exploration of the natural and human sciences, and that all statements about moral principles are statements about the natural world and not about special values that are beyond scientifically deducible knowledge. At the same time, Nietzsche denied that he was a materialist (i.e., that he believed in the reduction of the explanation of all causes to physical forces). He claimed that, in spite of his heavy emphasis on the physiological causes of "psychic suffering,"

> we can, between ourselves, still be the ferocious opponents of all materialism.[114]

Nietzsche's thought here is extremely ambiguous, as Brian Leiter points out:

> The concluding disclaimer about materialism here is clearly motivated by the fact that in every other respect the view endorsed in this passage is naturalistic: psychological claims are, says Nietzsche, explicable in terms of physiological facts. But Nietzsche does not, it appears, want to be understood as making the metaphysical claim that psychological facts are nothing more than physiological facts, the type of Naturalistic view associated with materialism.[115]

113. Poellner, "Nietzsche's Metaphysical Sketches," 692.
114. Nietzsche, *Genealogy*, III:16.
115. Leiter, *Nietzsche on Morality*, 20.

Nevertheless, in view of his antecedent discrediting of metaphysics, it is hard to make a coherent distinction between naturalism and materialism.

Notwithstanding this confusion, his view on metaphysics rules out of court any consideration of any reality that has as its focal point in the affairs of humans the existence and action of a divine being. He is explicitly confined to finding his answers to the realities of all existence from within an atheistic interpretation of the material world of nature. Thus is excluded, in one fell swoop, any possibility that God could exist, that he could have created humans in his own image, that he could have communicated his will and his plans to his creatures, or that good and evil are defined by his nature. Nietzsche does not argue the case, he assumes it.

Christian Morality

Now his principle evidence for this conviction about God lies in what he considers to be the effects of belief in the Christian version of theism.[116] He locates the basic motive for Christian morality in the twin concepts of pity and resentment. He believes that he has uncovered the Christian approach to what is good and evil in applying his genealogical method of investigation to the history of the faith. However, his analysis of early Christianity is highly defective from an historical point of view. Basing himself partly on the theories of extremely rationalistic German theologians of his era, partly on his own naturalistic presupposition and partly on his own personal encounter with the Christianity practiced by his family, he makes sweeping generalizations which bear very little relationship to careful historical investigation. In writing about the apostle Paul, for example, he proclaims that he was

> one of the most ambitious and importunate souls, of a mind as superstitious as it was cunning.[117]

He continues by ascribing to Paul hatred of the Jewish law, epilepsy as the cause of his vision of Jesus on the road to Damascus, his teaching as the desire to destroy the law, having an "intractable lust for power"[118]

---

116. From time to time, Nietzsche appears to be less critical of Hinduism and Buddhism than of Christianity as perspectives on experience.
117. Nietzsche, *Daybreak* I:68.
118. Nietzsche, in Pearson and Large, *Nietzsche Reader*, 194.

and being the inventor of Christianity. At best, this is a serious misunderstanding of the New Testament portrait of Paul; at worst, it is a deliberate travesty of the historical evidence. His rereading of the birth of Christianity gives little or no confidence in his ability to be taken as a serious historian (at least in this instance). It says far more about Nietzsche's prejudices than it does about the real Paul.

The same can be said for his genealogy of morals.[119] For example, his discourse on the so-called "ascetic ideal," that it springs from Christianity's negative assessment of the material world and a longing to be free from the body, is a colossal misunderstanding. Commenting on the alleged perpetrator of this life-denying philosophy, "the ascetic priest," Nietzsche proclaims:

> for an ascetic ideal is a self-contradiction: here an unparalleled *ressentiment* rules, that of an unfulfilled instinct and power-will which wants to be master, not over something in life, but over life itself . . . here, the green eye of spite turns on physiological growth itself, in particular the manifestation of this in beauty and joy; while satisfaction is looked for and found in failure, decay, pain, misfortune, ugliness, voluntary deprivation, destruction of self-hood, self-flagellation and self-sacrifice.[120]

It is historically accurate to affirm that some Christians at certain times have undertaken ascetic practices, in the sense of deliberately depriving themselves of the enjoyment of the good things in life. They have done this as a means of disciplining their senses and regulating their bodily desires. On occasion, these practices have been carried out in excessively rigorous ways. However, it is entirely mistaken, historically, to assert that the Christian faith teaches the ascetic ideal as Nietzsche interprets it. There is plenty of evidence in the life of Jesus to show that material existence is to be enjoyed, particularly eating and drinking; only when, as a result, a person loses control of their decision-making powers, is excess (gluttony and drunkenness) condemned. If forms of legitimate entertainment are done at the expense of vulnerable people, they should be considerably modified.

His view that Christianity was instrumental in deepening a feeling of resentment toward the "master morality" of those who believed in

---

119. Space does not allow a full discussion of the way in which Nietzsche distorts Christian moral ideals. All that is possible here is to state that Nietzsche misconstrues Christian motives, basically for polemical ends.

120. Nietzsche, *Genealogy*, III:11.

throwing off restraints imposed by idealized moral norms is wildly inaccurate. There is plenty of evidence to confirm that Christian convictions have underlain creative achievements in the realms of visual art, music, literature, and the sciences. Nietzsche's account of resentment and pity is based on the theoretical affirmation that evil, as commonly understood, does not exist in the world.

The Christian opposition to Dionysian excesses is founded on the observation that giving rein to bodily passions is, more often than not, destructive to the psyche, to say nothing of the spiritual aspect of human life. It could well be argued that it is not those whom Nietzsche described as "weak" who are the protagonists of resentment because they were unable to fulfill the values of the "strong," but the very reverse: resentment belongs to the "strong," incapable of living up to the values of the so-called "weak."[121]

Nietzsche was confident that

> what defines me, what sets me apart from all the rest of mankind, is that I have unmasked Christian morality.[122]

The death of God has, according to Nietzsche, released European morality from the constraints of what he considers its oppressive and repressive role in guiding thought and behavior. In real life, however, the thought of the nonexistence of God has more often turned the tables back on those who invented the idea that, with one stroke of the pen, one could repudiate the being of God.

Fallacies

His alternative to the morality of the past, where it exists, is full of confusion:

> One problem that seems to haunt the Genealogy is the genetic fallacy, the fallacy of thinking the origin of X demonstrates

---

121. One's appreciation of moral values is often tied in with the use of language. The German word *Mitleid*, usually rendered *pity* in the translations of Nietzsche's works, could just as correctly be translated as *compassion*, as has been done in the case of Schopenhauer's writings in the English language; there is a considerable difference in the connotation implied by the two words in English. It is not self-evident that *Mitleid* (*compassion*) is an example of saying "no" to life (Nietzsche, *Genealogy*, 5); *pity* is a different proposition.

122. Nietzsche, *Ecce Homo*, 7.

something about the value of X ... If Nietzsche is not committing the genetic fallacy, why, then, does he think that the origin of morality in the pejorative sense (MPS) has any bearing on (its) critique ... That ... MPS arose because of hatred might be somewhat embarrassing for the morality of love, but it is hardly a refutation: to think otherwise would ... involve the genetic fallacy.[123]

He also appears to commit the deontic fallacy of deducing moral ideals from statements of fact, which is an illegitimate procedure since premises of one logical type (descriptive judgments) cannot give rise to premises of another type (namely prescriptions). The problem here is that he seems to be expounding a utilitarian or consequential ethic, in that his main critique of "slave morality" is the negative effects it brings in its wake. His remedy is to release what he considers to be the original, creative, life-affirming impulses lodged in the deep unconsciousness of the human psyche, associated with the will to power. These, he asserts, define and increase human prosperity and move human beings in the direction of excellence. As in most accounts of consequential ethics, Nietzsche does not rationally engage with spelling out the criteria by which he defines human well-being. He asks himself the question about moral prejudices:

> what value do they themselves have? Have they up to now obstructed or promoted human flourishing? Are they a sign of distress, poverty, and the degeneration of life? Or, on the contrary, do they reveal, the fullness, vitality and will of life, its courage, its confidence, its future?[124]

He also affirms, alongside this basic question,

> we need a critique of moral values, the value of the values should itself, for once, be examined.

So, he proposes an historical analysis "of the conditions and circumstances under which the values grew up, developed and changed"[125] as the means of providing such a critique. Nowhere, however, quite apart from the historically dubious conclusions he comes to on both scores,

---

123. Leiter, *Nietzsche on Morality*, 140–41.
124. Nietzsche, *Genealogy*, 3.
125. Nietzsche, *Genealogy*, 6 (both quotations).

does he proffer credible reasons for preferring one set of moral values to another.

Rational Discourse

The German philosopher Jurgen Habermas offers an analysis of the conditions necessary for interpersonal communication to be governed by the ideal of rational discourse, such as sincerity, truth-telling, and rational warrant. He refers to this as an ideal speech situation.[126] He hoped that these rules would enable people to conduct the discussion of disagreements in a way most likely to promote understanding of all the issues involved.[127] In the case of Nietzsche, such a hope does not seem to be forthcoming. His critique of the transcendental rationalism of the Enlightenment would not sit easily with the preeminent place given to human reason:

> Nietzsche is proposing an interpretation of the contingent social meaning of modern attempts at rational, or universal binding consensus . . . Nietzsche regards any commitment to an ideal of some sort of inter-subjective acceptability for one's "evaluations" as a "sign" of weakness, and a latent expression of fear of those who need no such support.[128]

His approach to reason appears to make any fruitful engagement with his thought almost impossible. In place of justifiable evidence for his beliefs, Nietzsche tends to use his own historical analysis as a means of debunking religion, morality built on egalitarian principles, politics based on the famous democratic maxim of "governance of the people, by the people, for the people," and the illusions of human progress.[129] Robert Pippin sums up the problem (I think fairly):

> for all the rich complexity of Nietzsche's historical and psychological interpretation, it is this basic, somewhat crude contrast between "self-assertion" and the "weakness" of social dependence that forms the core of all his claims about a great deal

---

126. Habermas, *Theory of Communicative Action*.
127. See Habermas, *Theory of Communicative Action*.
128. Pippin, "Nietzsche's Alleged Farewell," 268.
129. He disdains the assumption of communist theory that the social ownership of the means of production will herald a new era in human living that will overcome the class-inflicted conflicts of the past.

of the deficiencies of modernity, modernity's origins in the premodern, and the new, "postmodern," distinctly self-assertive type for which he hopes.[130]

> Simply to assert the superiority of his own program for the renewal of human existence and to decry as an infirmity the reliance on universally valid rational criteria for human communication will lead to skepticism, and ultimately nihilism. He has no entitlement to claim for himself a privileged perspective.[131]

Nietzsche's contentions about "the fullness, vitality and will of life" is meaningless rhetoric, unless he can supply some credible content to its nature. Moreover, he also has to show why, for example, the Christian claim that Jesus Christ brings "abundant life into the world"[132] through his teaching, life, sacrifice, and resurrection from the dead is objectively not true. He cannot do this by simply advancing a parody of the Christian story (as he does, especially, in *Thus Spoke Zarathustra* and *The Antichrist*). Otherwise, it is fair to claim that the authentic Christian version of "the fullness and vitality of life" makes a much better claim to be real than his own mysterious and perplexing account.

Free Will

One of the most enigmatic and disturbing aspects of his thinking concerns his implacable denial that human beings possess free will. We have already suggested that Nietzsche's repudiation of free will leads him to contradict himself, since a measure of autonomy and self-determination is necessary to achieve the objective of the transvaluation of values. It may be that his thinking here is generally obscure and that he did envisage a measure of personal control over the shadowy drives which, he claims, orientate both mental processes and intended and unintended actions.

What is at stake is his own psychological self-analysis. Nietzsche's own inner, subjective contemplation led him to believe that a person's conscious states, which lead to action, are the end products of nonconscious facts about a person. He also states that these nonconscious facts are unknown until they appear somehow into consciousness. However,

---

130. Pippin, "Nietzsche's Alleged Farewell," 269.
131. See Nietzsche, *Gay Science*, IV:380.
132. John 10:10.

all we know is what is retrievable from conscious reflection. By definition, the nonconscious facts cannot be known as "things in themselves." If his account is accurate, then on the one hand, freedom of the will is put in jeopardy. However, on the other hand, logically we would seem to be free from responsibility for our thoughts and actions.

What is necessary for free will to be real is that our actions could be different, because we make a decision to that end. In other words, it is possible to put our decision-making into suspension and then to change our minds. If we are programed by our type-facts to make only one certain decision, but do not consciously know this, then our decision is free on pain of an infinite regression of a completely hidden, causal chain. To say that concealed first-order desires are caused by our nature is pure speculation, since there is no way of determining this. Nietzsche himself queries accessibility to self-knowledge, since, he asks, do I have to add that

> nothing . . . can be more incomplete than (man's) image of the totality of drives which constitute his being . . . Our moral judgments and evaluations . . . are only images and fantasies based on a physiological process unknown to us, a kind of acquired language for designating certain nervous stimuli? That all our so-called consciousness is a more or less fantastic commentary on an unknown, perhaps unknowable, but felt text?[133]

So, if the type-facts about the person are generally unknown to us, we don't know they exist; they are not empirically available to us. Conjecture on what they might be can lead to error, defamation, false motivation, etc. If values are the result of imagined type-facts, Nietzsche is involved in a circular argument about creating values for ourselves. If a person creates values that contradict those of millennia of tradition, they can only change him if he consciously allows them to do so. Given Nietzsche's assumptions, it is illogical for him to suppose that "he can create those values that (causally) determine which of the possible trajectories is in fact realized."[134]

It would seem, therefore, that if his views are held on the basis of type-facts, they are of little value. Are we not all robots, obeying unknown inner drives? If moral motives are largely unknown, it would make morality either impossible or entirely arbitrary. It is not surprising,

---

133. Nietzsche, *Daybreak*, II:119.
134. Leiter, *Nietzsche on Morality*, 78.

then, that Nietzsche appears to switch categories when speaking about the benefits and losses of certain moral stances—namely, that they either cause health or illness, for the causes of health and illness have little to do with the morality of good and evil. Physiologically people differ; morally they are all held accountable.

How is it possible to defend Nietzsche's view of freedom and causation, springing from his attempt to diagnose his own psychological functionings, when other people can equally claim from their own self-awareness that, although influenced by many internal and external forces and constrained by circumstances, they are ultimately free to decide how they are going to react. Is this not simply arguing on the basis of different experiences, which settle nothing (once again, the deontic fallacy)? Nietzsche's account of the unconscious is highly anti-intuitive, and therefore, for most people, highly implausible. Perhaps, half-conscious of the unconvincing nature of his discourse on free will, Nietzsche in places praises the sovereign, autonomous individual, who possesses an independent will:

> This man who is now free and who really is permitted to make a promise, this master of the free will, this sovereign . . . How could he, with his self-mastery, not realise that he has been given mastery over circumstances, over nature and over all creatures with a less durable and reliable will? The "free" man, the possessor of a durable, unbreakable will, thus has his own standard of value . . . The proud realization of the extraordinary privilege of responsibility, the awareness of this rare freedom and power over himself and his destiny, has penetrated him to the depths and become an instinct, his dominant instinct.[135]

This argument suggests that only the one who has achieved insight into the master morality has also achieved freedom. Such is the tortuous logic of Nietzsche's thought.

Conclusion

Nietzsche's thinking was a bold effort to break the mold, as he saw it, of millennia of false beliefs that set out criteria for a morality that would bring security and a refuge from the trauma and indecision of independent thought and action. Interestingly, in spite of all his prolonged

---

135. Nietzsche, *Genealogy*, 2.

invective against the Christian faith, for Nietzsche this trajectory of conformist behavior encountered its zenith in the promotion of a rationalistic approach to intellectual analysis and moral argument. Nietzsche's alternative proposals, though obscurely set out (his lucid mental activity ceased, after all, when he was only 44), have not attracted much further public reflection on their possible implementation throughout a reinvigorated society, as he had hoped.[136]

Western civilization and cultures now hover uncomfortably and uncertainly between their long Christian heritage, currently under considerable assault, and the residue of the Enlightenment project, with its constricted view of the reality of what it means to be human. Nietzsche's last published words were,

> Dionysus against the Crucified.[137]

The animosity and repugnance that Nietzsche felt (in his bones?) against all that he believed Christianity represented has not been developed by subsequent thinkers influenced by his thought, perhaps for reasons that he himself intuited, namely that Christian moral values, though with increasing exceptions, remain the bedrock of a civilized society. What is left seems to be an increasingly vociferous secular humanism which, like Nietzsche's thought, is founded on an invincible naturalistic worldview that, in its turn, prescribes a confined, contained, and controlled view of the meaning of human nature and existence. Christian faith, as at the beginning of its existence, will once again become a minority system of belief (even a sect) that will probably remain on the sidelines of, because it is antagonistic toward, much consensual morality, but always providing an irritating alternative. The meaning of being human and the interpretation of life will continue to remain a matter of polemical controversy.

---

136. However, his genealogical survey of past history and its influence on present thought and activity has appealed to certain promoters of the "Post-modern Condition." I will explore this in a subsequent chapter.

137. Nietzsche, *Ecce Homo*, 9.

Questions

1. How does one account for Nietzsche's profound switch from being raised in a conventional Protestant home to professing profoundly anti-Christian convictions?

2. What strikes you as being Nietzsche's most penetrating and essential insight?

3. Why do you think Nietzsche considered his work, *Thus Spoke Zarathustra*, his most significant?

4. How would you characterize the human predicament for Nietzsche and his response to it?

CHAPTER 9

Sigmund Freud and Human Pathologies

The theory of repression became the corner-stone of our understanding of the neuroses . . . The (aim of) the task of therapy (was) to uncover repressions and replace them by acts of judgment which might result in the accepting or condemning of what had been formerly repudiated. I showed my recognition of the situation by no longer calling my method of investigation and treatment catharsis but psycho-analysis.

—FREUD, AN AUTOBIOGRAPHICAL STUDY (1925)

It may be asked whether and how far I am myself convinced of the truth of the hypotheses that have been set out in these pages. My answer would be that I am not convinced myself and that I do not seek to persuade other people to believe in them.

—FREUD, BEYOND THE PLEASURE PRINCIPLE (1920)

We still have to struggle for an incalculable time with the difficulties which the untameable character of human nature presents to every kind of social community."

—FREUD, "THE QUESTION OF A WELTANSCHAUUNG" IN NEW INTRODUCTORY LECTURES (1933)

Preface

The choice of persons for this book, whose diversity of views on the meaning of human existence is worthy of study, depends upon the extraordinary influence their ideas have had upon Western thought and action. Sigmund Freud undoubtedly belongs within this category. Even those who are skeptical about the validity and value of many of his theories have little doubt about the impact that his writings and his persona have provided far beyond the circle of those who continue to adhere to his methods of analysis.

Pamela Thurschwell, for example, says about him:

> Sigmund Freud's impact on how we think, and how we think about how we think, has been enormous. The twentieth century has been called the Freudian century ... the twenty-first century ... will be on some level indebted to Freud ... His core of ideas function like myths for our culture; they present transformative ways of looking at the world[1]

Peter Gay has written:

> Sigmund Freud ... is among that small handful of supreme makers of the twentieth-century mind whose works should be our prized possession[2] ... Freud is inescapable ... Freud's terminology and his essential ideas pervade contemporary ways of thinking about human feelings and conduct.[3]

One of Freud's many critics, Richard Webster, nevertheless admitted that:

> The psychoanalytical tradition has every claim to be regarded as richer and more original than any other singular tradition in the twentieth century.[4]

Another critical commentator on Freud, referring to his book *The Interpretation of Dreams* (1900), commends him as

> the man universally recognized as having created the climate of opinion of the twentieth century.[5]

Finally (and the list could be extended greatly) Todd Dufresne, in a book recently published, claims that

> Freud's combination of intelligence, curiosity, creativity and ambition has been nearly unequalled in the history of Western

---

1. Thurschwell, *Sigmund Freud*, 1.
2. He also mentions Karl Marx, Charles Darwin, and Albert Einstein.
3. Gay, *Freud Reader*, xi, xiii.
4. Webster, *Why Freud was Wrong*, 8.
5. Isbister, *Freud*, 45.

thought ... Given Freud's stature as one of the most significant thinkers of the twentieth century, everything he wrote rewards close scrutiny.[6]

At the same time, and in spite of the numerous eulogies that have been handed to him, there have been many, beginning with one of his most famous former pupils and collaborators, Carl Jung, who have been distinctly uncomplimentary about some of the most important findings in the science of the mind that Freud purports to have discovered. These, too, should be evaluated as impartially as possible.

When reviewing[7] Freud's immense amount of writing over some four decades (roughly from 1895 to 1939),[8] which included full-length books, monographs, articles, and voluminous correspondence, there are a number of important issues that are difficult to resolve. The first, perhaps, is how far it is necessary to relate Freud's output to the particular circumstances of his own personal life or that of the major events of his era: for example, the death of his father in 1896; or his daughter Sophie in 1920; or the catastrophic traumas caused by the First World War; or the rise of Nazi ideology in the 1930s, characterized by a vitriolic anti-Semitism.

A second major issue concerns his Jewishness. What part did his own self-conscious reflections on the nature of belonging to the Jewish race, with both the immense richness of its historical heritage but, at the same time, its sufferings from centuries of harassment and discrimination, play?

A third problematical matter were the claims that Freud made throughout his life for the strictly scientific nature of his methods of gathering data and the critical, rational way in which he interpreted them. These claims have been keenly debated and contested both in his lifetime and subsequently. Does psychoanalysis, as practiced and defined by Freud, intrinsically abide by the strict guidelines of scientific investigation of cataloged observations and the creation, testing, and reexamination of

---

6. Dufresne, *Late Sigmund Freud*, ix, 29.

7. In the case of this one chapter, I have dedicated myself to reading the entire text of *The Freud Reader*, comprising extracts from all the major works (amounting to well over eight hundred pages), and a dozen substantial studies of Freud from different perspectives. In this way, I have been able to engage with Freud's thinking firsthand, and also learn from experts in Freud's biography and theories.

8. From Freud and Bruer, *Studies on Hysteria* (1895) to *Moses and Monotheism* (1938 German Edition; 1939 English Edition).

hypotheses to determine their explanatory powers in the interpretation of the data uncovered and in their practical effectiveness? Or, do his theories lack sufficient empirical support to be counted as genuine science, as his critics have claimed?[9] Freud himself was transparent enough about some of his own theories to recognize their highly speculative nature. In one case, he himself admits that

> in the present discussion, I am only putting forward a hypothesis, I have no proof to offer.[10]

A fourth difficulty arises from the nature of this particular study. The purpose is to discover, in broad terms, Freud's perceptions on human nature, as they may be derived from a multiplicity of sources—clinical, historical, and philosophical. He himself believed that he was contributing something specifically new to the enormous reservoir of centuries of discourse on what it means to be human. The problem is to be able to hit on reasonably clear notions from the vast bulk of literature that he has left behind. In my investigation, I have discovered at least twenty-four main themes on which he dwelt at various stages in his own thinking,[11] as well as the variety of assumptions that he made in coming to his conclusions.

Due to the limit of space, it is quite impossible to enter into the complex discussions that surround all the themes he touched upon. So, what I will attempt to do is make a deductive analysis from his major works, wherever they make inferences about his judgment on what it means to be human. It may be helpful to undertake the task by referring to the writings chronologically, dividing his life's work into some four separate parts[12]: a) 1886 to 1897, from the time he returned from Paris to Vienna, after working with Charcot, until he abandoned his seduction theory; b)

9. See, for example, Tauber, *Freud*, xii–xv.

10. He was discussing (in his work *The Ego and the Id*) the hypothesis that "there existed in the mind—whether in the ego or the id—a displaceable energy, which neutral in itself, can be added to a qualitatively differentiated erotic or destructive impulse" (see Gay, *Freud Reader*, 648).

11. In no particular order, they are: the Oedipus complex; dreams; the unconscious; inheritance; repression; transference; the id, ego, and superego; the pleasure principle; libido; the instincts; neuroses; guilt and shame; religion; civilization; seduction theory; sexuality in general, infantile and female sexuality in particular; melancholia; inversion; defense-mechanisms; anxiety; worldview (*Weltanschauung*); and psychoanalysis. This is not an exhaustive list.

12. It is quite possible to divide his life and career into other chronological sequences—for example, as is done by Isbister in *Freud*, 166–91. The schema I am proposing is my own.

1897 to 1920, from the elaboration of the Oedipus complex to the writing of *Beyond the Pleasure Principle*; c) 1920 to 1926, during which time he elaborated his theories about the relationship between the mind and the instincts in the concepts of the Ego and the Id, and published his autobiography; d) and 1926 to 1939, the years in which he amplified, especially in *The Future of an Illusion, Civilization and its Discontents,* and *Moses and Monotheism,* his opinions about the contributions that psychoanalysis could make to the present and future of cultures and civilizations.

The advantage of following his thinking chronologically is that it allows for discernment about how it developed and changed. It is possible to identify those convictions that remained constant throughout each stage and those that were either augmented, altered, or relinquished. At the same time, it is possible to pinpoint and examine the key themes that were occurring during the different phases of his life.

Assumptions

As Freud himself admitted, for all his claims to the objectivity of his own observations and theories,

> people are seldom impartial where ultimate things, the great problems of science and life, are concerned. Each of us is governed in such cases by deep-rooted internal prejudices, into whose hands our speculation unwittingly plays. Since we have such good grounds for being distrustful, our attitude toward the results of our own deliberations cannot well be other than one of cool benevolence.[13]

He is simply reiterating a truism built into human existence: our views on so many subjects, which determine our thoughts, decisions and actions are shaped by such realities as our personalities, the family into which we were born, the way we were brought up by parents, caregivers, or guardians, the education we received, the people who have influenced us, the aspects of culture that have particularly impinged upon us, our particular interests and concerns, and so on. So it was for Freud.

It is a matter of interpretation as to which of the assumptions that Freud came to (before his clinical work was initiated or his theories began to take shape in his mind) may be considered the most fundamental. Undoubtedly, two particular convictions pervaded his mental apparatus

---

13. Gay, *Freud Reader*, 624.

from an early age: the indispensability of scientific endeavor for uncovering the nature of reality, and the origins and nature of religious commitment and discourse.

The Scientific Enterprise

Many commentators on Freud's methodological commitment to what he took to be the objective, impartial, prejudice-free procedures of scientific research have referred to his approach as, in reality, "a philosophy of science founded on positivist principles . . . a particular form of naturalism."[14] His aversion to philosophy is that it "elevates non-scientific forms of knowledge to an epistemological level rightly reserved only for positivist findings." Freud claims to have accepted "the immediacy of experience and the objectivity of scientific observation."[15] On a number of occasions he dismissed the ability of instinct, intuition, mystical experiences, or religions claiming to be based on divine revelation, to render any assured knowledge of the real world. Speaking about notions such as "ego-libido, an energy of the ego-instincts," Freud remarks that there is a

> difference between a speculative theory and a science erected on empirical interpretation. The latter will not envy speculation its privilege of having a smooth, logically unassailable foundation . . . For these ideas are not the foundation of science, upon which everything rests: that foundation is observation alone.[16]

It would appear that Freud's frequent appeal to the indisputably scientific nature of his findings concerning the working of the mind is an attempt "to counter the, by definition, (hysterical) fear that his findings are illusory, by tying psychoanalysis to science, science to proof, and proof to reality."[17] In the *Future of an Illusion* (1927), Freud alludes to the possible criticism of his theories by an imaginary opponent that, in fact, Freud is the one who is "carried away by illusions . . . because they betray clearly enough the influence of your wishes," whilst the contestant argues "for the claims of reason, the rights of skepticism."[18]

14. Tauber, *Freud*, xii.
15. Tauber, *Freud*, 18.
16. Freud, "On Narcissism," quoted in Gay, *Freud Reader*, 548.
17. Dufresne, *Late Sigmund Freud*, 53.
18. Gay, *Freud Reader*, 718.

Religious Commitment

Freud belongs to the strictly atheistic tradition stemming, as we have already outlined, from certain hypotheses put forward by skeptical philosophers of the Enlightenment period. He came to the conclusion, at a fairly early age, that he could not hold to the Jewish monotheistic tradition of his parents and ancestors. Commenting on his paper "Obsessive Actions and Religious Practices," Peter Gay affirms that

> Freud was a consistent, aggressive, dogmatic atheist, a child of the Enlightenment who saw a world at war to the death between science and religion.[19]

The French analyst, Rene Laforgue, recalls a conversation he had with Freud in 1937, when he urged him and his family to leave Vienna, because of the imminent danger of persecution by the Nazis:

> He responded almost with contempt . . . "The Nazis? I am not afraid of them. Help me rather to combat my true enemy." Astonished, I asked him just what enemy was in question, and I heard him reply: "Religion, the Roman Catholic Church."[20]

Freud's dogmatic atheism, as is the case with all who reject belief in a divine being who created and sustains the universe and designed the reality that is the human being, led him to embrace the alternative thesis that all of life has arrived by chance and serves no transcendental purpose.

This was an assumption he carried through the whole of his adult life, as did Marx and Nietzsche, and which affected every aspect of his beliefs, whether about mental processes, psychic health and disorder, morality, or the future of civilization. It would be difficult to ascribe this assumption to the nature of the scientific operation, because, by its very nature, it remains unaligned on the question of the existence of an extra-material living being. However, having taken this stance, Freud was restricted, in his ability to discern the nature of human life, to strict naturalism, the assertion that all true belief arises solely from explanations derived from a study of the natural world and that any other possible source of knowledge about human reality is inadmissible. Post-Darwin, naturalistic evolutionary theory had increasingly become the creedal

---

19. Gay, *Freud Reader*, 429. We will explore further on in the chapter Freud's views on the origin and nature of religion.

20. Quoted in Dufresne, *Late Sigmund Freud*, 142.

norm of intellectual life, designed to replace completely any form of theism as an explanation of how humans have come into being and act as they do. The theory makes three successive claims:

> natural selection is a fact of life; it is sufficient as a mechanism to have produced the diversity of species, both living and extant; the operative force that has pushed the process along has been the struggle to survive and reproduce.[21]

So, Freud is committed, by both his two basic presuppositions, to a reductionist explanation of human meaning. He held tenaciously and pugnaciously to his (metaphysical) principles all his life. However, according to Alfred Tauber, he was unable to provide a necessary and sufficient explanation of human experience from his self-confessed, restricted, intellectual commitments:

> he founded his own philosophy of human nature on both empirically based psychology and a humanistic philosophy of human freedom, coupled to a vision of moral responsibility... He brought together two disparate forms of knowledge: a rigorous empiricism tempered by a broad human appreciation of the complexity of the human soul.[22]

Therapeutic Methods and an Early Theory about Infantile Sexuality

At the beginning of his psychological, analytical career, Freud was intrigued by the power of hypnosis to uncover streams of human experience that had never made their way into consciousness. It was the first method he used seriously as a means of uncovering the origin of traumas (especially that of hysteria).[23] On the use of hypnosis as a means of cure, Freud has the following to say,

> It thus came about ... that in the first years of my activity as a physician my principal instrument of work ... was hypnotic

21. Kirk, *Future of Reason*, 199.

22. Tauber, *Freud*, xiv, xv.

23. He was indebted to two French physicians, Charcot and Bernheim, working respectively in Paris and Nancy. The former suggested that both hypnosis and hysteria have a physiological explanation, whilst the latter believed that they both had a psychological derivation.

suggestion ... With the idea of perfecting my hypnotic technique, I made a journey to Nancy in the summer of 1889 ... I was a spectator of Bernheim's astonishing experiments upon his hospital patients, and I received the profoundest impression of the possibility that there could be powerful mental processes which nevertheless remained hidden from the consciousness of men ... I must supplement what I have just said by explaining that from the very first I made use of hypnosis in another manner, apart from hypnotic suggestion. I used it for questioning the patient upon the origin of his symptom, which in his waking state he could often describe only very imperfectly or not at all.[24]

In these few sentences Freud alludes to two crucial aspects of his early insights into clinical, restorative practice: the existence of a sphere of reality buried deep in the mental phenomenon of human beings, but "hidden from the consciousness of men," (at least in "their waking state") and the use of suggestion in uncovering the origin of the symptoms of a patient's disturbed mental condition. However, he fairly soon abandoned hypnosis as a legitimate means of helping patients to explore the hidden profundity of their mental processes.

In 1889, he began to develop his classical, alternative therapy of free-association. Freud's fundamental rule was to encourage the patients to say whatever came into their mind without inhibition or censorship. The patient was free to choose at what point to begin. They were never to leave out memories because they either seemed irrelevant to the symptoms being discussed or too unpleasant to reveal. The technique of the analyst was to draw out gaps in memory and overcome the resistance to disclosing material that was being repressed.[25]

Freud's early clinical work led him to believe that much in the way of repressed memories that produced the symptoms of neuroses that he was engaged to treat were due to acts of sexual seduction in childhood of which the patient was the object. For a short time, he believed that every neurosis, and especially cases of hysteria, could be traced back to the effects of sexual abuse by those who were supposed to protect the vulnerable child. By and large his patients were unconvinced when confronted

---

24. Freud, *Autobiographical Study*, quoted in Gay, *Freud Reader*, 9–10.

25. Isbister, *Freud*, 3–4. Freud himself later sets out the nature of the treatment that he gives in "*Notes upon a Case of Obsessional Neurosis*" (1907) and a paper entitled "On Beginning the Treatment" (1913). See Gay, *Freud Reader*.

with this interpretation of their psychological illness, although under suggestive pressure they could come to believe it.

By 1897, in a letter to his friend Wilhelm Fliess, Freud abandoned the theory, having decided that the patients may well have been influenced to confuse actual sexual harassment for fantasies about the probability that they would have taken place.[26] He came to the conclusion that it could have occurred in some cases, but could not be generalized to have happened in all of them. He drew a distinction between material reality (had they happened or not) and psychic reality (the patient's conviction, through the uncovering of repressed memories, that that was what they were suffering from later in adult life).[27]

Infantile Sexuality: The Cornerstone of Freudian Psychoanalysis

In 1905, Freud wrote a treatise with the title, *Three Essays on the Theory of Sexuality*, which summarized his views on the centrality of early sexual experiences for the treatment of later psychological pathologies. He began by repudiating the general psychological consensus of his time that the sexual instinct "is absent in childhood and only awakens in the period of life described as puberty." He believed strongly that sexual activity of a kind is manifest in small children, although, as the result of amnesia, it has not been recognized by the person concerned. Lack of memory is not the same as the total abolition of the impressions of childhood; it may occur as a withholding of these impressions from consciousness, by repressing them.

Freud argues that "the sexual wishes, fantasies and (physical) pleasures of children begin almost at birth and continue, except for a brief period,[28] throughout a person's life."[29] These sexual drives pass through oral, anal, and phallic stages—Freud uses the term, sexual, in a wider sense than just referring to genital manifestations. Neuroses or sexual

---

26. See Gay, *Freud Reader*, 112.

27. The seduction theory was resurrected during the latter quarter of the twentieth century, especially in the United States, in the Recovered Memory Movement. It hypothesized that vulnerable women, under treatment for extreme forms of anxiety and guilt, could be freed by recovering their memory of acts of early sexual exploitation. The theory was used for purposes of litigation against the alleged offenders; see "Webster, *Why Freud was Wrong*, 511–28.

28. From the age of roughly five to the onset of puberty.

29. Kahn, *Basic Freud*, 35.

perversions are to be explained by regression in later stages of sexual development to earlier phases that have become fixated in the unconscious, prior to recall and retention.

Pathological aberrations in adult life (post-puberty), whether manifest in hysteria, obsessions, paranoia, or other symptoms, are all caused at some stage before sexual maturity. The cause is a defense-mechanism used against an aversion to unpleasant results stemming from psychic energy. Displeasure is often released by a sense of shame at the sexual acts committed. Disgust at sexual fantasies, acts and, even the organs themselves, is often due to the imposition by parents and society, as a whole, of a censorious morality (often given the name, "Victorian").

It is important to note that psychopathological symptoms are indeed defensive, but not all defense mechanisms are pathological. Take the case of rationalization, for example: a certain subject S rationalizes a certain situation P, so that S can avoid the stress of P. However, although rationalization is defensive, it is not necessarily pathological. Hence, it would not be entirely correct to link defense mechanisms and pathology.[30]

The Oedipus Complex

So Freud, fairly early on in his examination of the origin of psychological disorders, came to the conclusion that forms of repressed (because it was unwanted) sexual stimulation from a premature age should be identified as the main cause. Partly due to his own self-analysis at the time of his father's death, Freud came to the conclusion that being "in love" with one parent and disliking the other was a common trait in early childhood:

> In the first years of infancy, the relation known as the Oedipus complex becomes established: boys concentrate their sexual wishes upon their mother and develop hostile impulses against their father as being a rival.[31]

Having rejected the notion of sexual seduction as a universal explanation for later sexual afflictions, he conjectured that "the possibility

---

30. I owe this observation to Dr. Pablo Lopez-Silva.

31. Freud, "An Autobiographical Study," quoted in Gay, *Freud Reader*, 22. At the time that Freud wrote this (1924), he assumed that "girls adopt an analogous attitude" (22). However, in 1935, he added a footnote to his original text, admitting that a complete parallel between the sexes does not hold: "further investigation and reflections reveal profound differences between the sexual development of men and women" (22).

remained open that sexual fantasy invariably seizes upon the theme of the parents."[32] He then confesses that such an experience was true in his own case:

> I have found . . . falling in love with the mother and jealousy of the father, and I now regard it as a universal event of early childhood.[33]

Although he had long used the term in letters and private papers, the first published mention of the complex comes in the first of his *Contributions to the Psychology of Love* (1910). The assignation to Oedipus recalls the Greek myth that Oedipus had unwittingly murdered his father, whom he met when disguised, and married his mother.

Freud believed passionately that "to an ever-increasing extent the Oedipus complex reveals its importance as the central phenomenon of the sexual period of early childhood."[34] Indeed, later on, he comes to believe that the complex is at the foundations of what "being a human" means.

Later in the child's sexual development, its dissolution takes place and it succumbs to repression. Exclusive love for the parent of the opposite sex gives way to the father's punishment and the mother's divided loyalty to other children, so

> the absence of the satisfaction hoped for . . . must in the end lead the small lover to turn away from his hopeless longing. In this way the Oedipus complex would go to its destruction from its lack of success, from the effects of its internal impossibility.[35]

---

32. Freud, in Gay, *Freud Reader*, 112.

33. Freud, "Letters to Fliess" (October 15, 1897), quoted in Gay, *Freud Reader*, 116. In the same letter, Freud speculates that the Oedipus complex lies at the bottom of Shakespeare's characterization of *Hamlet*: for example, his affirmation that "conscience makes cowards of us all" (116) refers to his extreme hesitation in avenging the murder of his father by his uncle; "the torment he suffers (springs from) the obscure memory that he himself had meditated the same deed against his father from passion for his mother . . . His conscience is the unconscious sense of guilt" (116).

34. Freud, "Dissolution of the Oedipus Complex," quoted in Gay, *Freud Reader*, 661.

35. Freud, "Dissolution of the Oedipus Complex," quoted in Gay, *Freud Reader*, 661–62.

Dream Analysis and the Discovery of the Unconscious

From early in his clinical practice, Freud came to rely heavily on the interpretation of his patients' dreams. Having been persuaded already, through hypnosis, that there existed a storage region in the mind not accessible directly to consciousness, but which nevertheless influenced behavior, Freud, through his therapeutic methods, became convinced that dreams played a highly significant role in uncovering the relationship between the unconscious and later traumatic symptoms. A number of his published works on his psychoanalytical practices involved the transcription of dreams recited by his patients.

Dreams could work as means to discovering hidden depths of the psyche, because the defense mechanisms of the conscious mind had been (literally) put to sleep. According to Freud,

> the dream-work is an excellent example of the processes occurring in the deeper, unconscious layers of the mind, which differ considerably from the familiar normal processes of thought.[36]

In other words, dreams have access to material in childhood that is later forgotten. However, the training and experience of the psychoanalyst can overcome infantile amnesia by recourse to interpretation of the symptoms they are seeking to alleviate.

In the work of explaining the latent meaning of the dream, there often arose a sharp discrepancy between the professional analyst and the patient. Freud put this down to the instinctive work of repression, of which the patient had no inkling. The dream disguised a wish that could not be fulfilled because of the activity of conscience that did not allow the thoughts of sexual desire to surface. Hence, the patient's own interpretation of the dream differed markedly form that of the analyst, because in their waking life the censorship applied by conscience had been switched back on.

In his analysis of the first dream of one of his most celebrated patients (Dora), Freud comments that dreams may be of many sorts: "a fulfilled wish . . . a realized fear . . . a reflection persisting into sleep . . . an intention, or a piece of creative thought during sleep, and so on."[37] For Freud, the meaning of the dream "stands . . . upon two legs, one of which

---

36. Freud, "An Autobiographical Study," quoted in Gay, *Freud Reader*, 28.

37. Freud, "Fragment of an Analysis of a Case of Hysteria ('Dora')," quoted in Gay, *Freud Reader*, 209.

is in contact with the main and current exciting cause, and the other with some momentous event in the years of childhood." Freud elaborates his understanding of the significance of dream interpretation in the same passage that speaks about his understanding of Dora's dream:

> The dream sets up a connection between these two factors—the event during childhood and the event of the present day—and it endeavors to re-shape the present on the model of the remote past. For the wish which creates the dream always springs from the period of childhood; and it is continually trying to summon the childhood back into reality and to correct the present day by the measure of childhood.[38]

At a later stage in his own development of the meaning of dreams, Freud veered away from defining their intention largely in terms of wish-fulfillment. In a rather obscure passage, in which Freud introduces the concept of external stimuli—added to that of internal stimuli, forcing their way through a protective shield and causing various psychic traumas—Freud states that "this would seem to be the place, then, at which to admit for the first time an exception to the proposition that dreams are fulfillments of wishes." He further adds:

> Thus it would seem that the function of dreams, which consists in setting aside any motives that might interrupt sleep, by fulfilling the wishes of the disturbing impulses, is not their original function. It would not be possible for them to perform that function until the whole of mental life had accepted the dominance of the pleasure principle. If there is a "beyond the pleasure principle," it is only consistent to grant that there was also a time before the purpose of dreams was the fulfillment of wishes.[39]

Freud in this passage is affirming the likelihood that dreams may also repeat traumatic experiences of adult life, such as the experiences of war or other forms of violence that have caused syndromes. In other words, sufferers often relive in their dreams the traumas brought about by contemporary, external, violent episodes they have experienced.[40]

Freud's analysis of dreams confirmed his belief in the reality and the power of the unconscious, which he had originally taken on board

---

38. Freud, "Fragment of an Analysis of a Case of Hysteria ('Dora')," quoted in Gay, *Freud Reader*, 211.

39. Freud, "Beyond the Pleasure Principle," quoted in Gay, *Freud Reader*, 609.

40. See Dufresne, *Late Sigmund Freud*, 15.

through the influence of Professor Bernheim's exploration of the nature of hysteria.[41] In an early work, *Studies on Hysteria* (1895), he put forward a theory to throw light on the origins of its symptoms:

> It laid stress upon the significance of the life of the emotions and upon the importance of distinguishing between mental acts which are unconscious and those which are conscious (or capable of being conscious); it introduced a dynamic factor, by supposing that a symptom arises through the damming-up of an affect, and an economic factor, by regarding the same symptom as the product of the transformation of an amount of energy which would otherwise be employed in some other way.[42]

So, many neuroses (such as phobias, paranoia, and obsessions) are said to be derived from one traumatic experience or another, going back into the patient's preconscious past. The method of treatment was to bring it into consciousness, confront it, and remove the predicament.

> Freud appropriated the term unconscious and transformed it into an unusually influential concept and complete theory of the mind.[43]

It became the guiding principle of psychoanalysis, which Freud claims to have created and developed. Psychoanalysis was a particular method of treating nervous disorders and a science dedicated to exploring and charting unconscious mental processes.

Subsequent commentators on Freud's method of making inferences from symptoms of malaise to hidden causes point to the deterministic nature of his views on the unconscious. There is a broad spectrum of human behavior that can only be explained in terms of usually hidden mental processes or states which determine it. So, the behavior of a neurotic had to be explained by searching for the individual's mental states. The mind is not to be identified so much with conscious as unconscious states, which have to be uncovered by the painstaking work of psychoanalysis. Freud used two metaphors to illuminate the pattern of discovery: the iceberg with nearly 90 percent of its volume hidden under the

---

41. Freud, in Gay, *Freud Reader*, 548.

42. Gay, *Freud Reader*, 13. Freud referred elsewhere to "the energy, that would otherwise be employed in some other way" (*Freud Reader*, 13), as *sublimation*.

43. Suprenant, *Freud*, 2

sea, and an archaeological dig, where hidden artifacts and treasures are uncovered through the removal of various layers of strata.[44]

Repression

In his clinical work, Freud often discovered resistance by the patient to his type of analysis in which he suggested the origin of the abnormal symptoms he was hired to cure. When he proposed certain events that had happened in the patient's past, he would be confronted by the latter's rejection of his prognosis. Freud interpreted the resistance as a defense mechanism against the traumatic experience, identified by the analyst, as they passed from the unconscious to the conscious:

> The repressed ideas—so we must believe—are present in and enter without inhibition into the most rational trains of thought; and the memory of them is aroused too by merest allusions. The suspicion that "morality" is put forward as the repressing force only as a pretext is confirmed by the experience that resistance during the therapeutic work avails itself of every possible motive of defense.[45]

The outcome is that during treatment, when the patient speaks his or her mind, they are continually confronted with interruptions of hitherto unrecognized thinking. For example, in the case of guilt feelings, self-conscious reflection may be utilized as a defense against the analyst's deciphering of the repressed causes. This may be due, perversely, to the patient's desire to maintain the guilt-ridden world, just because he or she gains pleasure from feeling that way:

> in this way the activity of thinking takes on its own peculiar pleasure and a life of its own . . . Obsession with guilt loses contact with normal rational discourse. Safety is found in persuading oneself one is always guilty and not in resolving the problem.[46]

---

44. See Thornton, "Sigmund Freud."

45. Freud, "Project for a Scientific Psychology (Draft K)," quoted in Gay, *Freud Reader*, 94.

46. Lear, *Freud*, 10.

The Id, the Ego, and the Superego

Following the end of the carnage caused by the First World War, Freud took a new turn in his psychoanalytical reflections. The same year of the war's beginning, Freud set out his theses concerning the person's most powerful self-identity and driving motivation: the ego. He proposed that, between the infant's stage of auto-eroticism and the child's adherence to a love-object (father, mother, siblings, caregivers), one could find a narcissistic stage. This term was chosen

> to denote the attitude of a person who treats his own body in the same way in which the body of a sexual object is ordinarily treated . . . that is to say, (he) strokes it and fondles it till he obtains complete satisfaction through these activities.[47]

From Freud's contention that there has always existed in the human being an "ego-libido" as well as an "object-libido" (i.e., a desire for someone else), he deduced that repression proceeds from self-respect for the ego. The person sets up an ideal self, by which the actual ego ("I") is measured. When he or she is confronted by undesirable experiences hidden in the unconscious, they will interpret them as contributing to a dismantling of the ego-ideal, and therefore to be resisted:

> The formation of an ego ideal heightens the demand of the ego and is the most powerful factor favoring repression.[48]

In 1923, Freud's book *The Ego and the Id* was published; it encompassed "the 'speculation' which revealed his new model of the mind."[49] In this work, Freud reinterpreted his long-held theory of the relationship between the unconscious and the conscious. He now proposed a threefold division of the psyche. The id was the venue for the unconscious, impulsive, instinctual drives that require immediate satisfaction, functioning on the basis of the pleasure principle. The superego was that part of the psyche that housed a person's conscience. It functioned as a socially imposed, moral control mechanism, producing feelings of guilt when moral guidelines were relaxed. The ego was the conscious, rational self, that attempted to mediate between the conflicting forces of id

---

47. Freud, "On Narcissism," quoted in Gay, *Freud Reader*, 545.
48. Freud, "On Narcissism," quoted in Gay, *Freud Reader*, 558.
49. Isbister, *Freud*, 265.

and superego. All conscious thoughts reside here, whereas what belongs largely to the unconscious is located in the id:

> The super-ego also resides in the unconscious as a screening mechanism, which seeks to limit blind-pleasure by the imposition of restrictive rules.[50]

Psychological well-being is established when a *modus vivendi* is created between the three.

Freud himself defines the ego "as a coherent organization of mental processes ... it is the mental agency which supervises all its own constituent processes."[51] It links the inner world with the outer world of reality:

> It is easy to see that the ego is that part of the id which has been modified by the direct influence of the external world ... The ego seeks to bring the influence of the external world to bear upon the id and its tendencies and endeavors to substitute the reality principle for the pleasure principle which reigns unrestrictedly in the id. For the ego, perception plays the part which in the id falls to instinct. The ego represents what may be called reason and common sense, in contrast to the id, which contains the passions.[52]

Another way of describing the superego is to see it as standing over against the id as the ego-ideal (i.e., the part of the psyche that the individual strives to emulate as its model pattern of thought and behavior). However,

> it must, of course, be admitted from the outset that there are varying degrees of capacity for resistance, which decide the extent to which a person's character fends off or accepts the influences of the history of his erotic object-choices.[53]

The relationship between these three factors is complex. However, it helps to understand the relationship between the unconscious and the conscious, between the external and internal worlds (using different types of perception), the causes of repression, the way the ego can maintain some control over the id by steering it into forms of sublimation: "the power to replace its immediate aim by other aims which may be valued

---

50. Thornton, "Sigmund Freud," para. 5.
51. Freud, "The Ego and the Id," quoted in Gay, *Freud Reader*, 630.
52. Freud, "The Ego and the Id," quoted in Gay, *Freud Reader*, 635–36.
53. Freud, "The Ego and the Id," quoted in Gay, *Freud Reader*, 638.

more highly and which are not sexual."[54] This was, for example, Freud's explanation for the amazing artistic accomplishments and mechanical inventions that compensated for the apparent lack of sexual interest in Leonardo da Vinci's life.

The Pleasure Principle and the Death Wish (*Eros* and *Thanatos*)

In 1920, Freud published what some people consider the most far-reaching development of his psychoanalytical theory:

> He now replaced the pairing of drives—libidinal and egoistic—that had served him for more than a decade of psychoanalytical theorizing and that he had called into question not long before the World War, with a new more dramatic pair of contestants: life against death ... As the first statement of the new "structural" theory of the mind, it is indispensable to an understanding of fundamental shifts in psychoanalytical thinking.[55]

Freud summarizes what he means by the pleasure principle and how it works in relation to the ego, id, and superego in these words:

> There exists in the mind a strong tendency toward the pleasure principle, but ... that tendency is opposed by other forces or circumstances, so that the final outcome cannot always be in harmony with the pleasure principle ... From the point of view of the self-preservation of the organism among the difficulties of the external world, it is from the very outset inefficient and even highly dangerous. Under the influence of the ego's instincts of self-preservation, the pleasure principle is replaced by the reality principle ... The pleasure principle long persists ... as the method of working employed by the sexual instincts ... starting from those instincts ... it often succeeds in overcoming the reality principle, to the detriment of the organism as a whole.[56]

In this book, declares Dufresne, "Freud had discovered the link between individual psychology and the history of society, and so rediscovered his youthful interest in *Kultur*—a German word meaning culture,

---

54. Freud, "Leonardo da Vinci and a Memory of his Childhood," quoted in Gay, *Freud Reader*, 452.
55. Gay, *Freud Reader*, 594.
56. Freud, "Beyond the Pleasure Principle," quoted in Gay, *Freud Reader*, 596.

society, and civilization."⁵⁷ In an interview in 1926, Freud claims that the message of this book is that "Death is the mate of Love. Together they rule the world."⁵⁸ And in an earlier letter to Arthur Schnitzler, a Viennese playwright and novelist, he affirms that the book attempts "to reveal Eros and the death instinct as the motivating powers whose interplay dominates all the riddles of life."⁵⁹ These two instincts, henceforth, were to govern his thinking and writing until his death in 1939. So, Freud now elaborates extensively on how he understands the nature and operation of the most basic instincts in human beings, and gives us insights into how he understands human nature.

Instincts and Drives

Freud himself defines an instinct (provisionally) as

> the psychical representative of... a continuously flowing source of stimulation, as contrasted with a "stimulus," which is set up by single excitations coming from without... The simplest and likeliest assumption as to the nature of instincts would seem to be that in itself an instinct is without quality, and, so far as mental life is concerned, is only to be regarded as a measure of the demand made upon the mind for work... The source of an instinct is a process of excitation occurring in an organ.⁶⁰

As we have already observed, Freud in 1920 began a new phase in his understanding of the theory of the instincts (or drives) with the publication of *Beyond the Pleasure Principle*: "He retained his traditional division of conscious, pre-conscious and unconscious (but) now postulated a no less dramatic confrontation of drives: the drive toward life and that toward death."⁶¹ Prior to that, in 1915, he published the first of a series of five essays with the title, *Instincts and Their Vicissitudes*. Here, he summarized his thinking on the subject up to that point. Amongst other concepts, he writes briefly on the aim and object of an instinct:

---

57. Dufresne, *Late Sigmund Freud*, 1.
58. Dufresne, *Late Sigmund Freud*, 1.
59. Gay, *Freud Reader*, 1–2.
60. Freud, "Three Essays on the Theory of Sexuality," quoted in Gay, *Freud Reader*, 256.
61. Gay, *Freud Reader*, xxviii.

> The aim of an instinct is in every instance satisfaction, which can only be obtained by removing the state of stimulation at the source of the instinct ... The object of an instinct is the thing in regard to which or through which the instinct is able to achieve its aim. It is what is most variable about an instinct and ... becomes assigned to it only in consequence of being peculiarly fitted to make satisfaction possible.[62]

Up to 1920, although with increasing misgivings, Freud stuck to his theory that the psyche operates principally through the tensions produced by the antithesis between ego-instincts and sexual instincts ("ego-libido" and "object-libido").[63] By 1920, however, he had come to the conclusion that "science has so little to tell us about the origin of sexuality that we can liken the problem to a darkness into which not so much as a ray of a hypothesis has penetrated."[64] Having observed that within the "object-libido" there existed in reality, not only a love (or affectionate) instinct, but also a hate (or aggressive) instinct, he asked himself the question as to how the sadistic instinct, whose aim is to injure the object, could be derived from Eros, the preserver of life. The answer seems to be that the former, which leads to the desire to destroy, is a separate instinct, of which sadism is its representative.[65]

Freud postulated that human beings are driven from birth by the desire to acquire and enhance bodily pleasure. Sexual energy (libido), redefined as any form of bodily pleasure, is the single-most important motivating force in adult life. It is expressed as a self-preserving and pleasure principle. At the same time, humans universally demonstrate the trait of an irrational urge to destroy the sources of all forms of sexual energy in the annihilation of the self. From where does this aggressive, self-destructive, and cruel instinct arise? This was a problem that he now had to address.[66]

According to Dufresne, Freud began to advance

> the darkest possible claim about human nature: that we possess a demoniacal impulse that undermines life, love and sociality; and just as disturbingly and indeed paradoxically, that

---

62. Gay, *Freud Reader*, 566, 567. Freud also said that "the study of the sources of instincts lies outside the scope of psychology" (*Freud Reader*, 567).
63. Freud, "On Narcissism," quoted in Gay, *Freud Reader*, 548–49.
64. Freud, "The Pleasure Principle," quoted in Gay, *Freud Reader*, 622.
65. Freud, in Gay, *Freud Reader*, 645–50.
66. See Thornton, "Sigmund Freud."

this impulse is a significant part of biological evolution, human progress, and the claims of civilization.[67]

Civilization

In the last twelve years of his life, Freud sought to extend his psychoanalytical theories from the interpretation and therapeutic healing of the neuroses of individuals into the wide domain of culture and social reality. In 1927, he published *The Future of an Illusion*, his most comprehensive critique of religion. In 1929, his book *Civilization and its Discontents* saw the light of day. In 1933, in order to help out the failing psychoanalytical publishing house in Vienna, a number of papers on different topics were published as *New Introductory Lectures*. The thirty-fifth and final one, "The Question of a *Weltanschauung*," tackled the question of the theoretical nature of psychoanalysis: To what extent, if at all, does it encompass a worldview? Finally, a year before his death, his last book, *Moses and Monotheism*, was published in German; an English edition was produced a few months later. In all these writings, in light of the events of the time, Freud ranged widely over his own philosophical and humanistic beliefs, interjecting into them the findings of his psychoanalytical research of the previous decades.

Civilization and its Discontents, probably the book by Freud that is most often read, contains some of his most significant thoughts on social reality. For Freud, civilization represents "beauty, cleanliness and order," when human beings decide to create together a common life, united against the dominance of any separate individual or small group of people:

> The first requisite of civilization, therefore, is that of justice—that is, the assurance that a law once made will not be broken in favour of an individual.[68]

The parents of civilization, according to Freud, are Eros and Ananke (Love and Necessity):

> The communal life of human beings had, therefore, a two-fold foundation: the compulsion to work, which was created by external necessity, and the power of love . . . The first result of

---

67. Dufresne, *Late Sigmund Freud*, 4–5.
68. Freud, *Civilization and its Discontents*, quoted in Gay, *Freud Reader*, 740.

civilization was that even a fairly large number of people were now able to live together in a community.[69]

Freud strongly links the indispensability of civilization to human beings' innate aggressiveness:

> Men are not gentle creatures who want to be loved, and who at the most can defend themselves if they are attacked; they are, on the contrary, creatures whose instinctual endowments is to be reckoned a powerful share of aggressiveness . . . Homo homini lupus (man is a wolf to man).[70]

> Civilization has to use its utmost efforts in order to set limits to man's aggressive instincts and to hold the manifestations of them in check by psychical reaction-formations . . . hence the restriction upon sexual life, and hence too the ideal's commandment to love one's neighbor as oneself—a commandment which is really justified by the fact that nothing else runs so strongly counter to the original nature of man. In spite of every effort, these endeavors of civilization have not so far achieved very much. It hopes to prevent the crudest excesses of brutal violence by itself assuming the right to use violence against criminals, but the law is not able to lay hold of the more cautious and refined manifestations of human aggressiveness.[71]

Freud alludes to the Marxist thesis about the way in which bourgeois property is the main cause of aggression, in order to refute it:

> Aggressiveness was not created by property. It reigned, almost without limit in primitive times, when property was still very scanty, and it already shows itself in the nursery.[72]

In other words, for Freud, aggression is part of the very being of each and every human being. The way that bourgeois property works is merely part of a superstructure, built on an underlying narcissistic impulse, built into the human psyche from birth.

Freud concludes his exposition on aggression with further devastating comments that finish up with one of his most memorable sayings:

---

69. Gay, *Freud Reader*, 743.

70. The Latin quote is derived from Plautus, *Asinaria* II.iv.88; see Gay, *Freud Reader*, 749.

71. Gay, *Freud Reader*, 750.

72. Gay, *Freud Reader*, 751.

> I can no longer understand how we can have overlooked the ubiquity of non-erotic aggressivity and destructiveness and can have failed to give it its due place in our interpretation of life . . . In all that follows I adopt the standpoint, therefore, that the inclination to aggression is an original, self-subsisting instinctual disposition in man, and I return to my view that it constitutes the greatest impediment to civilization . . . This aggressive instinct is the derivative and the main representative of the death instinct which we have found alongside of Eros and which shares world-dominion with it. *And it is this battle of the giants that our nursemaids try to appease with their lullaby about Heaven.*[73]

In his discussion of communism, Freud dismisses the idea that economic life is the substratum on which the history of civilization is built, everything else being merely a reflection of economic relations. It is based, he believes, on the illusion that, once economic relations are used solely for the common good (i.e., for the equal well-being of all citizens), a society that needs to keep aggression in check by the use of a more potent aggression will fade away. For Freud, psychology (the deep exploration of the workings of the human mind) antedates economics. The latter is postulated on the basis of the former. In the case of communism, its economic theories that are designed to solve permanently the problem of exploitation are, because of its deluded view of human nature, the result of wishful thinking.

Freud's reflections on the state of civilization and what keeps it in place could hardly be more pessimistic. In the "battle of the giants" happiness is pure illusion. It is, he thinks, like egoism, "reserved for Death and nonexistence, while unhappiness, like altruism, is left for Life and existence."[74] The cost of civilization is a serious disruption of the pleasure principle (i.e., the release of erotic libido to tread unimpeded the paths of its desire). Though he does not use the language, he appears to be saying that civilization is the antithesis to anarchism. It is, therefore, highly significant that, although in a different format, he signs off his life (Eros) in the same way as Nietzsche, by a telling reference to the god Dionysus. In Freud's case, three days after his death his ashes were buried in an ancient Greek urn, decorated by two figures in red: Dionysus and a Maenad, one of the god's fanatical female followers. It was, as it were, the final submis-

---

73. Gay, *Freud Reader*, 754, 755, 756; emphasis added.
74. See Dufresne, *Late Sigmund Freud*, 120.

sion to *Thanatos* in the hope that, through death, true happiness would be kindled again.

Guilt

According to Freud then, whilst in this life, humankind is assailed by a permanent sense of guilt. Guilt is the most important problem in the development of civilization, because the price we pay for ever-more-sophisticated advances in civilization is the loss of happiness through a heightening of the guilt-feeling:

> If civilization is a necessary course of development from the family to humanity as a whole, then as a result of the inborn struggle between the trends of love and death there is inextricably bound up with it an increase of the sense of guilt.[75]

Feeling guilty has two principal causes. In the case of the individual it arises out of the internalization of the anxiety caused by the conflict between the pleasure-loving ego and the controlling effect of conscience, which resides in the superego. Its cause, in the psychic development of the individual in its early stages, springs from the disciplining authority of the father and the fear of the mother's loss of love. These two forces create in the child a sense of uncertainty. This may develop later into an obsession with guilt and the perverse sense of security provided by admitting that one is always guilty.[76] The superego expresses itself through conscience as the punishing agent. Individuals turn this consciousness of deserving punishment inward, because of the shame they feel for their hatred of their father as a rival for their love of the mother, or vice versa; in other words, through the repercussions of the Oedipus complex.[77]

The second principal cause of guilt lies in the demands of civilization:

> This "sense of guilt" does not stem from the infringement of any objective, eternal moral code . . . but from the unsuccessful resolution of natural, psychological mechanisms which have internalized social conventions and prohibitions.[78]

---

75. Freud, *Civilization and its Discontents*, quoted in Gay, *Freud Reader*, 763.
76. See Lear, *Freud*, 10.
77. See Freud, in Gay, *Freud Reader*, 651–58.
78. Quinodoz, *Sigmund Freud*, 222.

Freud says that the deployment of guilt is civilization's most important tool in the struggle against the "primary mutual hostility" of individuals; a hostility that is biologically given.[79]

Religion[80]

It is not in any way surprising that Freud dedicated himself to expounding his views on religion, seeing that he grew up educated in the principles of the Jewish faith. He attempted to interpret religion from within his own psychoanalytical theories, although he also borrowed material from outside his own discipline. The result, as we shall see, was somewhat of a hodgepodge of speculations on the origin of religion, the historicity of its founding documents, its practice, doctrinal beliefs, and moral criteria. Naturally, his overall dismissal of theistic belief as illusory has extensive consequences for his views on what it means to be human.

Freud closely linked the origin of the religious impulse in human beings to the supposed discovery of the Oedipus complex. As he says,

> in a study of the beginnings of human religion and morality which I published in 1913 under the title *Totem and Taboo* I put forward a suggestion that mankind as a whole may have acquired its sense of guilt, the ultimate sources of religion and morality, at the beginning of its history, in connection with the Oedipus complex.[81]

Freud came to believe that all religious sentiments were manifestations of guilt and neurosis. God is a human creation whose function is to assuage the sense of suppressed outrage which the child directs against itself when it realizes the enormity of its sexual fantasies. The need to believe in God represents a regression to an immature state of human development: the ultimate basis of a human's need for religion is infantile helplessness. It is a childish hangover which must be abandoned if a person is to become a psychologically integrated person.

---

79. Dufresne, *Late Sigmund Freud*, 113.

80. Freud derived much of his understanding of religion from his own interpretation of the Bible (Old and New Testaments), based on some of the most historically skeptical conclusions that emanated from radical German scholars of the nineteenth century. Therefore, his views almost entirely excluded nontheistic religions.

81. Freud, *Introductory Lectures on Psychoanalysis*, 375.

Religion is the result of a terribly obsessive illusion, whose driving force is wish-fulfillment. As such, for Freud, it is destructive of emotionally normal behavior:

> The common man cannot imagine this Providence otherwise than in the figure of an enormously exalted father. Only such a being can understand the needs of the children of men and be softened by their prayers and placated by their signs of remorse. The whole thing is so patently infantile, so foreign to reality, that to anyone with a friendly attitude to humanity it is painful to think that the great majority of mortals will never be able to rise above this view of life.[82]

So, religion can be seen as the projection of a set of deep-seated, conflicting desires, an inadequate response to the basic need to resolve conflict. Its effect is to compound the problem. Freud believed that he had uncovered the secret of the origin of religion as a universal phenomenon among all people. He thought that there is a close parallel between what is early historically in the life of the species and what is early psychologically in the life of the individual:

> the events of human history, interactions between human nature, cultural development and the precipitates of primeval experiences (the most prominent example of which is religion) are no more than a reflection of the dynamic conflicts between the ego, the id and the super-ego . . . (they) are the very same processes repeated upon a wider stage.[83]

Freud believed that he had discovered in his clinical work, particularly in his analysis and explanation of dreams, an overarching theory to account for the highly persistent and, in his view, deeply irrational place of religion in most people's lives. Like Marx and Nietzsche, he viewed religion as the major obstacle to humanity discovering the real cause of its distress and embarking upon the conquest of a new and more glorious stage of human development.

Freud's view of religious belief and practice was primarily functional (i.e., that it has arisen in order to meet substantial human needs). In his following understanding of the role of religion, he compares and contrasts it with his view of the nature of science:

---

82. Freud, *Civilization and its Discontents*, in Strachey, *Standard Edition*, XXI:74–75.
83. Freud, *Postscript to an Autobiographical Study*, in Strachey, *Standard Edition* XX:72).

> If we are to give an account of the grandiose nature of religion, we must bear in mind what it undertakes to do for human beings ... It fulfills three functions ... It satisfies the human thirst for knowledge; it does the same thing that science attempts to do with its means, and that point enters into rivalry with it ... To its second function ... it no doubt owes the greatest part of its influence. Science can be no match for it when it soothes the fear that men feel of the dangers and vicissitudes of life ... In its third function, in which it issues precepts and lays down prohibitions and restrictions, religion is furthest away from science.[84]

Many of Freud's opinions about religion, at least in the case of Christian faith, are wholly erroneous (as we shall point out below), nevertheless he supplies a good (and fairly objective) definition of what it is about:

> Religious ideas are teachings and assertions about facts and conditions of external (or internal) reality which tell one something one has not discovered for oneself and which lay claim to one's belief.[85]

He seems to subscribe to a view, one that bears out his definition that religion offers a true description of human life, that is unavailable to human thought bereft of its epistemic sources:

> The question of the purpose of human life has been raised countless times; it has never received a satisfactory answer and perhaps does not admit of one ... Only religion can answer the question of the purpose of life. One can hardly be wrong in concluding that the idea of life having a purpose stands and falls with the religious system.[86]

It is worth pointing out, in view of Freud's consistent hostility to everything he believes religions represent, that in this passage there does not appear to be any irony or cynicism.

---

84. Freud, "Question of a Weltanschauung," quoted in Gay, *Freud Reader*, 786.

85. Freud, "Future of an Illusion," quoted in Gay, *Freud Reader*, 700; emphasis added.

86. Freud, *Civilization and its Discontents,* quoted in Gay, *Freud Reader*, 729. In a letter he wrote to Marie Bonaparte in 1937, in the face of his impending death, he confessed that "the moment one inquires about the sense or value of life one is sick, since objectively neither of them has any existence ... The explanations of mine are certainly not on a grand scale, perhaps because I am too pessimistic. There is going through my head an advertisement which I think is the boldest and most successful American one I know of. 'Why live, when you can be buried for ten dollars?'" (Storr, *Freud*, 228).

Worldview

In contrast to religion, ideologies (like Marxism or fascism) and various philosophies and ethical systems (that use an intuitive approach to knowledge that goes beyond the observation of empirical data), Freud was adamant that his own definition of psychoanalysis was not a worldview or a belief system, and was never intended to supply one. He defines a worldview (*Weltanschauung*) as

> an intellectual construction which solves all the problems of our existence uniformly on the basis of one overriding hypothesis, which, accordingly leaves no question unanswered and in which everything that interests us finds its fixed place ... It is among the ideal wishes of human beings.[87]

His reason for rejecting psychoanalysis as a *Weltanschauung* is that it is

> a specialist science, a branch of psychology—a depth psychology or psychology of the unconscious—it is quite unfit to construct a *Weltanschauung* of its own: it must accept the scientific one ... It asserts that there are no sources of knowledge of the universe other than the intellectual working-over of carefully scrutinized observations—in other words, what we call research—and alongside it no knowledge derived from revelation, intuition or divination.[88]

As has been pointed out, numerous times, Freud's assertion that his own version of psychoanalysis is a science is naive. It is ingenuous both about the nature of the scientific enterprise and about psychoanalysis conforming to the criteria of scientific research. His claims about science amounted to a positivist portrayal of its aims, objectives, and methods. It actually turns science into a philosophy by according to its ideal a reductionist account of human knowledge, virtually a dogma that any statements that could not be verified by empirical means were devoid of meaning. It could be said that his own claims about his findings being the result only of scientifically approved research methods amounted to a kind of defense mechanism: he attached the highly esteemed methods of science to his theories, in order to avoid the accusation that many of

---

87. Gay, *Freud Reader*, 783.
88. Gay, *Freud Reader*, 784.

them were no more than speculative ideas that he had derived from various sources, including religion, metaphysics, and moral philosophy.

Alfred Tauber sums up Freud's real sources of inspiration in the following way:

> He founded his own philosophy of human nature on both empirically based psychology and a humanistic philosophy of human freedom, coupled to a vision of moral self-responsibility. This mixture of objective empiricism and subjective interpretation challenges the scientific basis of psycho-analysis and points to its ultimate ethical mission. (His use of) active extrapolations of psycho-analysis to (construct) hypotheses about human history, culture and religion reveals persistent efforts to produce a social philosophy . . . Freud brought together two disparate forms of knowledge: a rigorous empiricism tempered by a broad humane appreciation of the complexity of the human soul.[89]

It might be said that Freud, as a matter of fact, separated the conclusions he drew from his clinical practice concerning the origin and treatment of neuroses, from his deliberations on religion, morality, civilization, war, and other more abstract concerns. However, he rarely admitted that his views on issues that went far beyond the analysis of individual psychological pathologies were not also part of his scientific endeavors. It is obvious, however, that, time and again, his writings, particularly in his later years, arose from the general metaphysical assumptions that he carried throughout his adult life. If this observation is true, it might be fair to say that his exposition of psychoanalysis in a narrow (strictly empirical) sense did not pretend to offer a worldview that encompassed all the problems of human existence.

Nevertheless, his excursions into anthropology, sociology, moral philosophy, theology, and other disciplines were justified on the basis of what he considered a new scientific exercise could offer the world. Perhaps intuitively, Freud recognized that his psychoanalytical probes into the deep workings of the human psyche were not sufficient as an explanation of the complex, multifaceted nature of human life.

So, his claim that he did not make an attempt to shape a *weltanschauung* from his own history and imaginings falls short of reality. Carl Jung, a former colleague of Freud's and, then later, a bitter opponent, was right in his assessment of the need of a worldview that would somehow give meaning and hope to a culture that was in the process of abandoning

89. Tauber, *Freud*, xiii–xv.

the one that had shaped European history and thought for nineteen hundred years:

> Religion can be replaced only by religion . . . 2000 years of Christianity can only be replaced by something equivalent.[90]

Freud disassociated himself from such notions. However, it is likely that in his later writings he was attempting to forge something that looked markedly like "something equivalent."

According to Dufresne,

> the late Freud theorized the internal world of the psyche, measured it against the external world of material reality, grounded it in the truth of archaic prehistory and myth . . . and presented the totality . . . as a bridge between our animal past and our human future. Psychoanalysis was thereupon revealed as the most important science among all sciences.[91] These are the essential premises and conclusions . . . upon which Freud psychoanalyzed modern Western society.[92]

Concluding Observations

Whatever else we may want to say about Freud's prodigious intellectual productivity, it has both remained influential and divided opinion. To say that it is complex is to state a truism, for Freud himself as a human being, alive for eighty-three years, was a complex person with respect to his inherited background, personality, and thought processes. Now, at the end of this short survey, my task is to attempt to distill, from the most significant material that he left, his musings on what it means to be human.

Before beginning, it is necessary to enter one or two caveats into the process. Firstly, the process is personal. Whilst endeavoring to be as impartial as possible, the task is a matter of one individual's assessment of what are the most crucial aspects of his theories. Secondly, my

---

90. Freud and Jung, *Freud/Jung Letters*, 294, cited in Dufresne, *Late Sigmund Freud*, 226. Jung's own attempt at supplying "something equivalent" through combinations of mystic writings, the Hermetic traditions, and Greek mythology was quite banal.

91. Equivalent, perhaps, to theology, designated historically as "the queen of the sciences."

92. Dufresne, *Late Sigmund Freud*, 257.

survey does not claim to be based on an exhaustive reading of all Freud's writings. I have considered a condensed eight-hundred-page selection of what another commentator regards are his most significant compositions, and some secondary literature written by Freudian scholars. Thirdly, it is hard to weigh up the evident points of dispute between those who continue to favor Freud's psychoanalytical insights and those who differ, often profoundly.

How is it possible to take a line that recognizes fairly both the strengths and weaknesses of his theoretical observations? What weight does one give to both aspects? Where might the tipping points be located? Nevertheless, these predicaments face anyone who wishes to attempt to penetrate his mindset. If they were insurmountable, there would be no point in writing anything about his thought and its potential legacy for future generations. If they were easily fathomable, further thought on his contributions to the science of the mind would hardly be required. So, what follows amounts to my assessment, in line with what I have attempted in previous chapters.

Assumptions

These are the beliefs and opinions that Freud brought to his intellectual work. He was undoubtedly a child of the Enlightenment, which had, one hundred years before his birth and the gradual formation of his ideas, adopted the steady conviction that nothing existed beyond the universe that could bring information to bear on the origin and purpose of life, especially human life. Humans were entirely on their own to make of the world whatever they were able to discover by their own unaided investigation. Thus, for Freud, at least in theory, the inductive method of the empirical sciences was the only path to reliable knowledge about any matter connected to either the external or internal worlds of the human species.

The Approach to Science

The corollary to this principle was that, for him, any claim to truth that could not be fitted into a worldview that only encompassed material reality was automatically bogus: an illusory wish-fulfillment. Although he spoke against what he considered to be the false claims of ideologies such as Marxism and anarchism, he reserved his greatest invective for all kinds of religion, and especially for the Christian faith. The consequence of this assumption, quite beyond the range of knowledge that science was competent to pronounce judgment on, was the inevitability of his belief that the beginnings of human life arose quite by chance. Out of an incredibly long process of evolution, through mutations and natural selection, more complex species gradually arose from less complex ones

Although doubtful about some aspects of the Darwinian synthesis, he really had no option but to accept the theory in broad outline. Human beings are not created in the likeness of God (as his Jewish faith asserted). They do not, therefore, owe their unique features—rationality, intellect, moral convictions, conscience, consciousness, ability to show compassion, sense of justice, family, and community life—to the way they have been crafted by an infinite, morally perfect, spiritual being who existed before anything material came into being. They have to be entirely self-sufficient, accountable only to themselves, the only source of understanding, and the originator of all that distinguishes virtues from vices.

Nevertheless, in spite of his twin foundational beliefs in the entire efficacy of scientific methods of discovery and the destructive illusion of religious faith and practices, Freud returned again and again to both these subjects, right up to the year of his death. One might have thought that, once he had, in his own mind, convincingly dismissed the claims of religion, as a kind of fantasizing that has close parallels with both the social development of human societies and the beginnings of the unfolding of the human ego in early childhood, he would have dismissed any further concern with religion. This, clearly, was not the case.

The reason for his almost obsessive interest in both these subjects may have had many motives. His treatment of both of them leaves a lot to be desired. He was forced to fit his view of scientific method around his claims for psychoanalytical procedures. However, on at least two significant counts, they do not measure up. Firstly, they do not pass the falsifiable test of authentic scientific practices: claims that particular theories have been demonstrated in clinically-impartial and disinterested observation must be capable of being falsified (declared unproven) under rigorous testing procedures. A number of Freud's theories do not meet these particular criteria: for example, the conservation of psychic energy, repression, the Oedipus Complex, and the existence of the unconscious.

Secondly, they do not pass the coherence test. Freud based his conclusions on entities, said to be the unobservable causes of certain types of behavior; yet, they arise in the unconscious to which we have no direct access.

However, in the case of the analysis of neuroses, the alleged cause cannot be identified except by reference to the effect it is said to occasion. The unconscious agent is only identifiable by the behavior it is said to produce, not as an independent entity. In other words, Freud's theories, based on the workings of the unconscious, have not been properly tested, because a) the unconscious is not directly accessible for critical examination, and b) the proven value of the treatment prescribed on the basis of the theory has not been verified by a control group, undergoing another form of treatment, or no treatment at all.

So Freud's claims (on which he based so much of his understanding of human nature) that his theories were scientifically rooted were based on an inadequate appreciation of the nature of the scientific enterprise. The problem for Freud was that he had nowhere else to go but to a strict, limited, scientific rationality. In the process, he made claims for science that it is unable to bear. He unwittingly succumbed to the uncritical acceptance of a positivist philosophy, unable to capture the real in a definitive sense. In his writings, therefore, because he far exceeded the potential of science to solve all the riddles of life, he was obliged to borrow from a number of other sources to fill the gaps.[93]

The Approach to Religion

Freud's entry into the field of religion is peppered with misunderstandings, false assumptions, dogmatic assertions, *ad hominem* arguments, and his own type of wish-fulfillment. Let us begin with his reconstruction of the origin of religion. In his first major excursion on religion in *Totem and Taboo*, he puts forward the weird thesis that religion originally was a derivative of the Oedipus complex: the guilt associated with murderous feelings toward the father by the boy child which, when subsequent human communities raised into the desire to rid the earth of a supreme Father (an exalted father figure), had to be atoned for. The relationship

---

93. See Tauber, *Freud*, 3-4, 17-22. Freud was ambiguous about his approach to the scientific nature of the findings of his analytical work. He defended the scientific method of his studies in his early works. Later, however, he separated himself from that attempt. On the general question of both the real possibilities and limits of science, as a means of gaining knowledge, see Stenmark, *How to Relate Science and Religion*.

with the Father had to be restored by appeasing him through compliance with his commands:

> Religion was based on the sense of guilt and the remorse attaching to it; while morality was based partly on the exigencies of . . . society and partly on the penance demanded by the sense of guilt.[94]

The way that Freud attempts to connect the biblical understanding of original sin with murder of the father that needs to be atoned for by the murder of the son and then commemorated by a (totem-like) meal, in which the flesh and blood of the son is consumed, is utterly bizarre. It is an interpretation of the Christian faith that has no support from either its foundation document—the writings of the New Testament—or the doctrine of the church. Freud, in his general treatise on religion, relied on historical speculations attributed to academics like Sir James Frazer,[95] a cultural anthropologist, and Robertson Smith,[96] an orientalist and biblical scholar.

In the case of his rendering of Christianity, he seemed to rely on his own imaginative reconstruction, rather than employing an objective account of its own interpretation of the reality of God, sacrifice, sin, and guilt. Nevertheless, to be fair to his own account, he did demonstrate a certain degree of misgiving about his theories:

> Though my arguments have led to a high degree of convergence upon a single nexus of ideas, this fact cannot blind us to the uncertainties of my premises or the difficulties involved in my conclusions.[97]

In the faith portrayed in the Bible, original sin (as Eric Fromm pointed out)[98] "arose directly from the original misuse of freedom. By going beyond the limit (to the extensive freedom authorized by the Creator), the first pair broke the harmony of the created order and the result was the tragic disruption of the harmony of relationships . . . and so, it has been ever since."[99] Guilt, in Christian theology, has nothing to do with

---

94. Freud, "Totem and Taboo," quoted in Gay, *Freud Reader*, 503.
95. Frazer, *Totemism and Exogamy*.
96. Smith, *First Series*; Smith, *Second and Third Series*.
97. Freud, "Totem and Taboo," quoted in Gay, *Freud Reader*, 511.
98. See Fromm, *Fear of Freedom*, 27.
99. Kirk, *Meaning of Freedom*, 203.

the shame induced by having "murdered God" or had murderous intentions about him as a vindictive Father. It is the result of having broken the only relationship able to secure the full flourishing of human life in conformity to the intention of the Creator, who made all things good. Atonement recreates the original relationship, by God himself (not by humans) bearing the guilt of its rupture. By this means he restores the harmony disrupted between creature and Creator, other creatures, the natural order, and within the psyche. Freud was right to note "the difficulties involved in my conclusions," but wrong in his diagnosis of the most fundamental problem.

Freud was right to insist on the reality of the observed world as a counterweight to the fallacies created by wishful thinking. He was wrong, however, to associate the Christian awareness of reality with illusion. His own understanding of reality was tied irrevocably to an alternative worldview, whatever he may affirm about the relationship between psychoanalytical theory and worldview. His assumptions, numerous times, commit the mistake of *petitio principii*. He presumes, for example, that religious faith is based on claims that are not open to question (i.e., to being critically examined). On the contrary, however, Christian faith rests on well-founded evidence: that which rests on the findings of well-founded historical investigation, for example, or the kind of evidence that gives the best explanation for the complexity of human existence, including some of the evidence that Freud himself infers. It is entirely open to genuine scientific research in the exact and human sciences, and possesses a predictive faculty that can foresee the precise consequences of patterns of human behavior. Moreover, the biblical doctrine of creation gives a firm rational foundation for holding that scientific investigation touches reality and can be processed accurately by the human mind.[100]

---

100. I have presented numerous arguments to confirm the true nature of faith in *The Future of Reason* and *Christian Mission as Dialogue*. It is a shame that Freud never entered into dialogue with people who hold to a rational (not rationalistic) approach to the real character of faith, but chose to base his assertions on misconceived errors of judgment. He might, for example, have studied Archbishop William Temple's Gifford Lectures, *Nature, Man and God* (which I explore in chapter 11), published four years before Freud's death.

Anthropology

We come finally to Freud's more comprehensive conceptions about what it means to be human. Freud's creation of a new form of therapy for people with physical or psychic symptoms that seemed to betray deep inner disturbances, began with the uncovering of a realm-of-being hidden from rational, reflective consciousness. Mental processes can often only be explained by presupposing other modes of operation, of which consciousness affords no evidence (for example, ideas that appear in the mind without any prior thought). Freud believed that, through careful analysis, this hidden sphere could be exposed to consciousness. This belief seems to have some validity. It might be true that in some instances humans think and act wholly instinctively, without having reflected on what has driven them to make decisions, or fail to make decisions, which others have deemed quite irrational.

At first, Freud believed that all that is stored in the unconscious springs originally from early childhood experiences, long repressed and forgotten. As these experiences are no longer accessible for investigation, the so-called unconscious tends to fade from view. Analytical therapy as a means of retrogressive discovery operates by means of suggestion, since, if the people being analyzed cannot make any connection between the alleged experiences and their later manifestations, they have to be cajoled into a process of retrieval. Later, Freud came to the conclusion that by no means could all psychic disturbances be traced back to influences present in a person's early years. Many, perhaps most, have arisen as the result of relationships and events that happened later in life.

Freud desired to explain human reality in terms that could be universalized for the whole human race, racial and cultural differences notwithstanding. It was important, therefore, for him to be able to identify the forces (or nervous energy) that drive humans to commit themselves in particular ways. He located these as instincts that propel people to take certain actions in later life. In his earlier analytical work, he identified these as life forces deriving from biological impulses that sustain the will to live, with hunger and thirst being the most obvious. These he called the ego-libido, the urge to live and to be satisfied emotionally and intellectually in all the happenings of one's life. Human beings are predetermined by their drives to act in ways that fulfill their physical and emotional necessities.[101]

101. See Surprenant, *Freud*, 5.

From the 1920s onwards, Freud in a somewhat dramatic change of direction added to the life-affirming stimuli of Eros the impulses toward death and destruction, which he referred to as Thanatos. The latter occupied his thought for the remaining years of his life and could be summed up in one word: aggression. Aggression can be self-imposed by forms of masochism or enforced from outside through acts of sadism. It is as powerful, if not more so, than Eros. It arises in part through the fact that all of human life is lived, consciously, within the inevitable horizon that death consummates existence. It manifests itself in guilt toward oneself, the result of the constant failures to live up to one's own ego-ideal, and in the destructive critique of others, whom one blames for one's own unhappiness.

The discovery of Thanatos as a major influence on the human psyche led to a profound increase in Freud's pessimistic outlook on the world:

> The death drive theory countenanced a disturbing form of therapeutic nihilism. For if life really is set asunder by the forces of death, and these forces are the genetic inheritance of our phylogenetic past, then there is, in the final analysis, very little that therapy can do to assuage the roots of human suffering ... Nature trumps nurture—a troubling conclusion for anyone seeking to ameliorate human suffering.[102]

For Freud, the death drive is "a second form of traumatic energy that originates from inside the brain."[103] One of its most disturbing features is a fatalistic outlook on life.

Dufresne summarizes, in the following way, Freud's ultimately tragic response to what he derived from his meditations on both psychoanalysis and the development of civilization as he conceived them:

> Here is the idea, quickly put: every organism seeks constancy, ultimately the constancy of non-existence, death; but life ... demands otherwise. The organism's existence is henceforth determined by a reactive or defensive response to an external world that demands growth and life. The individual's ultimate defense, the expression of its biologically-determined individuality, is to find its "own way to death" amidst all the possible choices available in the external world. Existence is therefore the consequence of a battle between life and death drives ... the end

---

102. Dufresne, *Late Sigmund Freud*, 9.
103. Dufresne, *Late Sigmund Freud*, 15.

of which is the termination of this seemingly interminable battle of drives.[104]

This summary of the late Freud's final thoughts about the human plight seems to be where he concluded his reflections on being human.

Questions

1. To what extent, in your opinion, was Freud guided by his early understanding of the human unconscious in building a solid foundation for interpreting the human constitution?
2. What were the main causes of Freud's dismissal of religion as an illusion? How far were they based on sound rational and historical foundations?
3. To what degree was Freud's analysis of scientific methodology compatible with his own psychoanalytical procedures?
4. How would you react to Freud's conviction that the impulses of Eros and Thanatos encapsulated his view of the working of the human psyche?

---

104. Dufresne, *Late Sigmund Freud*, 130.

CHAPTER 10

Human Existence in the Thought of Secular Humanism

Humanism is a democratic and ethical life stance, which affirms that human beings have the right and responsibility to give meaning and shape to their own lives. It stands for the building of a more humane society through an ethic based on human and other natural values in the spirit of reason and free inquiry through human capabilities. It is not theistic and it does not accept supernatural views of reality.

—*BYLAW 5.1 OF THE INTERNATIONAL HUMANIST AND ETHICAL UNION.*

Humanism is dead, and has been so since the nineteenth century . . . Let us bury it with appropriate rites, which means honoring what was good, and understanding what went wrong and why . . . Its rallying illusion is bred deeply into us by now that knowledge will make us better and happier, and that we are free, free to improve ourselves.

—*JOHN CARROLL, THE WRECK OF WESTERN CULTURE: HUMANISM REVISITED.*

Introduction

Humanism, as an overarching world view, has a long history. In the process of our enquiry, we have encountered it, in one form or another, in every chapter. The distinguished thinkers of the eighteenth and nineteenth centuries, whose views on the reality of being human we have described, all advocated their own version of humanistic principles.

Until roughly the middle of the eighteenth century, humanism still aligned itself with a view of the universe that was theocentric in its core conviction. "All that is seen and unseen," to use the words of the Christian creed, is made "by one God, the Father, the almighty." God alone is uncreated, infinite, eternal, and personal, and exists in a nonmaterial manner. This God is the origin of all life on planet Earth, which he has endowed with its myriad of distinct characteristics. The species *homo sapiens* has been set apart, dissimilar from all other species in being formed in the image and likeness of this one God. Humans have been assigned the task of developing and caring for the rest of creation for their own use, sharing its resources equitably.

John Locke still held to this fundamental belief in a personally composed and orderly existence that includes ourselves and everything that surrounds us. Fairly swiftly, during the eighteenth century, the so-called "sacred canopy" of God's overall governance of the universe was dissolved. In its place arose an increasing confidence in the power of the new sciences and independent human reason to explain the whole of reality and to overcome inherent human problems without recourse to an alleged divine communication, shut up in a professed holy book. The primacy of the secular was conceived, gestated, and born.

The first serious step away from a theistic worldview was a significantly modified version of the reality of God:

> The history of secularization can be described in part as a radical, intellectual and cultural shift: from a God who, being an ever-present reality in human affairs . . . to a God that has created an intricate and balanced natural order, from which he has stepped back and told his creatures they are in charge and can find the route map to their providential destiny within the imminent order itself. It is not surprising that the final destination of this train of thought is the disposal of God altogether; God is an unnecessary hypothesis, as he himself has allegedly authorised his creatures to work out their own salvation.[1]

God became replaced by Nature (capitalized). The highest living organism in the universe (yet encountered) is the human being. "There is, therefore, no possibility of transcending ordinary human experience

---

1. Kirk, *Church and the World*, 305. This brief summary of the move from theism through deism to nontheism owes much to the extensive study, Taylor, *Secular Age*.

... There is nothing beyond the powers of human reason, self-love, the moral will and rightly guided education"[2]:

> Conditions have arisen in the modern world in which it is no longer possible honestly, rationally, without confusions, or fudging, or mental reservation, to believe in God. These conditions leave us nothing we can believe in beyond—human happiness, or potentialities, or heroism.[3]

Charles Taylor calls this intellectual and emotional stance "exclusive humanism." Contemporary humanists use the term "secular humanism." It is this form of humanism, the direct heir of the main emphases of Enlightenment thought, that I will unfold in this chapter in order to discover what alternatives to a theistically guided understanding of being human have been proposed. Although the wider use of the term "humanism" (including "Christian humanism") will be included, the focus will be on contemporary interpretations of secular (i.e., nontheistic or anti-theistic) humanism.

Recognizing Secular Humanism

It is logical to expect that no one definition of secular humanism (SH) is sufficient to do justice to all the nuances embedded within its modern use. As we shall see, different people who adhere basically to a humanist creed, not only express themselves in varied ways, but also support contradictory beliefs. I will attempt to articulate a variety of beliefs, many of which are superimposed on top of a generally agreed substructure. First, I will present the foundational belief. Secondly, I will elaborate on the assumptions. Thirdly, I will suggest the most common characteristics of SH.

Foundational Belief

Secular humanism states in the strongest terms that there is no reality of any kind that exists beyond the natural world. As far as can be determined, human beings know themselves to be alone. There may be other creatures somewhere within the bounds of the vast universe that share

---

2. Taylor, *Secular Age*, 306.
3. Taylor, *Secular Age*, 560.

characteristics similar to those of earthlings, but no such beings have yet been detected by instruments developed on this planet. Therefore, for all intents and purposes, earthly humanity is the highest form of life that we are aware of.

The consequence of this belief is that no other dimension beyond the physical exists.[4] All talk of a supernatural or transcendental realm inhabited by a deity (or deities), angels, demons, and spiritual beings that live on after their material life ends, is make-believe. It arises out of the fictitious imagination of human inventiveness, driven by immature longings for a greater existence beyond the merely human, and for life after death. Such beliefs demonstrate an infantile failure to break free from some kind of celestial parent, who becomes a permanent counselor, comforter, and controller, available mainly in times of adversity or sorrow.

Naturally, such a conviction leads to human beings having to set their own agendas, and carry them out, without any external support, except from other human beings. Humanism designates

> a doctrine that grants the human being a particular role . . . It consists . . . of initiating one's own acts (or some portion of them), of being free to accomplish them or not, therefore of being able to act at one's will . . . It implies that the ultimate end of these acts is a human being not supra-human entities (God, goodness, justice) or infra-human ones (pleasures, money, power).[5]

In accordance with the thinking of the vast majority of authors who believe in the tenets of secular humanism, this is the foundational belief that marks it out from all other kinds of humanism.[6] It is the type of humanism that I shall be exploring in this chapter.

---

4. It is important to clarify that, although, according to SH belief, all is dependent on physical reality, not everything can be reduced to the physical. There is a version, known as 'non-reductive physicalism' that states that mental processes arise from physical entities, but once they have emerged they function according to their own particular rules.

5. Todorov, *Imperfect Garden*, 30.

6. SHs will acknowledge the complexity of human self-consciousness, which for some may open up the possibility of appreciating a realm of inner-human reality which can be referred to as 'spirituality'. This realm, somewhat like that of thought, cannot be reduced to material existence alone. On the other hand, it is a vague concept: explaining what it means, or how it may be discovered, has proved almost impossible. On secular humanist terms, a spiritual realm of being does not extend beyond all that can be encompassed within strictly limited human data.

Assumptions

Clearly, if there is no divine being, the universe has not been created by any entity that possesses eternal existence, intelligence, creativity, will, purpose, and unrestricted power.[7] If there is no creator of all that exists, the universe must be self-generating and self-sufficient. Life on planet Earth has not arisen as the act of an unrestrained, self-determining being, but rather has evolved out of the most primitive of living cells through a long process of the coming into being of emergent phenomena at successive levels of complexity. The process has been called "evolution" and is empowered by an intrinsic will to survive. This is the only force that can be conceived as enabling the progress of living matter from lower to higher forms of ever-more-intricate attributes.

With regard to human existence, evolution is the one alternative theory of causation to theistic creation that has been suggested. Humans are here by chance, and there is no transcendent motivating reason why they should exist, rather than not exist. There is, according to the theory, an underlying mechanism of adaptation, mutation, and variation by which all species have arrived at their present destination. It is self-evident that everything that exists today has survived; everything that has not survived has, for various reasons, become extinct. We know this because the former have outlived all other erstwhile living forms.

Human life has no personal origin. Personality has evolved somehow through the fortuitous but random development of the human brain.[8] Once a theistic account of origins is rejected, there is no other viable anthropology to lay hold of. Humans are bound, by this assumption, to make sense of their world by dint of using reason and their own experience; there is a vacuum to be filled. As one writer has characterized the

---

7. It would be possible for a SH to deny the existence of any divine personality and yet to speak about the totality of nature in terms of divinity. When nature is referred to with a capital N and used as a subject, it appears to take on the function of a creative power, acting independently of human action. It takes on some of the functions, ascribed in a theistic world-view to a personal divine being, but cannot be equated with that which is declared to be non-existent.

8. One advocate of secular humanism suggests that its system of beliefs "might, and to some extent actually does, arise from contemporary sociobiology or evolutionary psychology" (Brecher, "Politics of Humanism," 114). Adaptation to the environment for the sake of survival, as a cause of the emergence of the human primate, is hardly an adequate explanation for its remarkable differentiation from all other living beings. It would presuppose that survival is itself a conscious end in itself, somehow injected into the evolutionary process. Such a hypothesis begs more questions than it answers.

dilemma, the mere denial of religion leaves human needs unaddressed. A fully secular life cries out for orientation. It urgently needs to respond to a sense of loss.[9]

A significant body of reliable knowledge that humans need to understand themselves and the world around them can be "arrived at by scientific inquiry, and thoughtful applications of science and technology can enhance the human condition."[10] In place of an understanding of reality that, it is alleged, comes from a source supplementary to scientific investigation (namely extraterrestrial revelation), the whole developing apparatus of the natural and human sciences are sufficient to give us all the information we need to live a well-considered, well-rounded, meaningful, and satisfying existence.

Scientific exploration and discovery has filled the gap that has been left by the uncritical, credulous nature of religious faith. As Kurtz states, "humanism is unwilling to declare any belief as validated by private intuitive, mystical or subjective appeals."[11] We may have confidence in the sciences, because the research they undertake and the discoveries they make are, in principle, verifiable by methods universally approved. Science engages in open-ended inquiry, experimentation, and analysis, which anyone having mastered the tools of a particular discipline may join. Their racial, national, religious, or gender background is deemed irrelevant to their ability to be proficient in the testing and interpretation of natural phenomena. Scientists may disagree about certain findings that are published in the public domain. Yet, these are always open to critical examination by other experts in the field; so a candid debate can ensue based on the range of evidence presented in each case.

Such a procedure, it is maintained, is not available either to confirm or discredit the claims of religious belief. When religions disagree about aspects of their articles of faith, there is no method in existence that can settle the disputes. No individual nor body can claim to have the final word on what is or is not the true opinion. Moreover, religious belief is not ultimately open to being falsified:

> Science can generate and defend conclusions that can be tested independently for reliability and put to work in a host of successful predictions and interventions (e.g. molecular genetics)

---

9. Kitcher, *Life after Faith*, 1–2.
10. Kurtz, *What is Secular Humanism?*, 24.
11. Kurtz, *What is Secular Humanism?*, 25.

> ... One cannot compare access to transcendental claims to truth with those open to confirmation or falsification in the natural world ... Specific religious doctrines are not held as items of knowledge that require reliable ways of generating and sustaining belief.[12]

In light of what appears obviously to be the case, secular humanists often believe they have ended the debate about the generation of secure knowledge by quoting the famous *bon mot* of W. K. Clifford, "it is wrong, always, everywhere and for everyone to believe anything upon insufficient evidence."[13] The saying presupposes that the only possible sufficient evidence is that provided by experimental data that is open to being conclusively falsified. It is, therefore, totally valid to conclude that

> none of the canons of good explanation ... sanction the idea of a transcendent creative mind as an explanatory hypothesis.[14]

At a later stage in our inquiry, we will investigate the claim that, as a matter of fact, there is sufficient evidence to ground claims to truth that are not premised on empirical data alone: for example, scientifically confirmed results depend on basic convictions that are not verifiable by scientific means, and yet we are right to take them as true.

Characteristics

Helpfully, some authors who espouse SH have indicated their understanding of its basic, distinguishing qualities. Stephen Law, for example, posits the following traits: a) no beliefs may be protected from rational scrutiny; b) skepticism about the existence of a deity or any other supernatural being leads either to atheism or agnosticism; c) this life is the only life—neither reincarnation, heaven nor hell exist; d) moral values do not depend on the existence of a deity who commands the nature of good and evil—the good life springs from the penetrating study of human needs and what promotes human flourishing; e) individuals are responsible for making their own moral judgments, rather than handing

---

12. Kitcher, *Life after Faith*, 10, 16.
13. Clifford, *Lectures and Essays*, 185.
14. Kitcher, *Life after Faith*, 21.

them over to some external authority; and f) human lives have meaning without any reference to what an alleged deity may have intended.[15]

A little more briefly, Paul Kurtz presents SH as a new paradigm with the following characteristics: a) it is a method of inquiry; b) it provides a naturalistic cosmic outlook; c) it is nontheistic; d) it is committed to humanistic ethics; e) it offers a perspective that is democratic; and f) it is planetary in scope.[16]

Sometimes the distinguishing marks of SH do not center so much on its human-oriented goals, but on the means to achieve them. One would imagine, for example, that few would disagree that it accords with the good life to focus on deep questions like: What is ultimately real? What makes life worth living? What is morally right and wrong and why? And how should society be ordered? They might well disagree, however, on the answers to some or all of these questions, because of the different foundational beliefs and assumptions that control the responses.

The SH belief that the capacity of humans to use their intelligence and to be responsible for making their own choices and for owning them without indulging in excuses when they don't go to plan, are two reasons for confirming human dignity. Others emphasize that there are even more basic reasons—that do not depend on human qualities alone—for asserting the intrinsic worth of human life. Their dignity is predicated on their nature as humans, irrespective of their situation in life—their nationality, race, sex, age, educational achievements, physical/mental health, or moral qualities. So even people who commit terrible atrocities remain human. All humans are open to the possibility of having their lives changed toward righteous living, although for some their depravity makes transformation highly unlikely.

A person born with severely limited physical or mental capabilities is no less human than another person gifted with a healthy physique and a penetrating mind. People who have succumbed to any form of dementia toward the end of their lives are no less human than others with an intellect that has achieved a first-class honors degree, followed by a doctorate in some aspect of their chosen specialty. It is not certain, however, that all secular humanists really believe that people with severe disabilities can be counted as fully human, otherwise why would some countenance the

---

15. Law, *Humanism*, 1–2.

16. Kurtz, *What is Secular Humanism?*, 21–22. In this case, it is perhaps significant that religious believers could easily endorse three of the six attributes, namely a), e) and f) in the first list, and a) and e) in the second.

abortion of preborn children when diagnosed with Down's Syndrome or the assisted suicide of people with intense and distressing mental impairments or physical incapacities?

One of the core characteristics of SH is its conviction that all we need to know about being human can be derived from careful, sustained and tested observation of the human condition:

> In the contemporary sense the term "humanism" denotes the view that whatever ethical outlook we adopt, it has to be based on our best understanding of *human nature and the human condition.*[17]

This injunction may sound well-founded; however, it clearly begs the question about human nature and the human condition. Supposing SH, with its polemical rejection of the validity of any knowledge claimed to come from outside human reasoning powers, was too limited in its understanding, then it has intentionally confined its thought within an unduly narrow range of possibilities. It is quite probable that its best understanding is inadequate, and therefore not the best understanding possible.

Tzvetan Todorov, in describing the dilemma of what he calls the "revolution . . . which led to the establishment of the modern world," states:

> to grasp it in its most general sense, we can describe it as the passage from a world whose structure and laws were preexisting and immutable givens for every member of society, to a world that could discover its own nature and define its norms itself . . . Before this revolution, an act was declared just and praiseworthy because it conformed either to nature . . . or to divine will . . . Both require that human beings should submit to an authority external to them . . . a tradition accepted and transmitted by society *without one's consent* . . . It was revolutionary to claim that the best justification of an act, one that makes it most legitimate, issues from man himself: from his will, from his reason, from his feelings.[18]

Most of this historical description is correct. The one significant exception are the words in italics: human beings have always had a propensity to rebel against imposed authority, backed up by severe punishment

---

17. Grayling, "Humanism, Religion and Ethics," 47; emphasis added.
18. Todorov, *Imperfect Garden*, 9; emphasis added.

for those who disobey. From the time of the Reformation in Europe onward, people were gradually winning the right against the state and established religion to make up their own minds about ultimate truth. The main impetus for this change came from the nonconformist conscience, arising out of Christian belief that religious allegiance, if coerced, was false. So Todorov's account of the revolution leaves a major part of its cause unstated.

Nevertheless, SH is convinced that (nearly) everything that religion (Christianity in the context of Europe) represents is detrimental to the self-authenticating well-being that purely human-induced wisdom provides. It appears to take the stance that its view of the world comes naturally to civilized, rational people; it simply pursues what common sense dictates. It has become the basic creed of the West, justifiable ethically (although many would deny its origin) on the twin moral absolutes of Kant's ethical theory: treat all people as an end in themselves, not as a means to another end, and treat others as you would wish to be treated yourself.

So, SH is supremely confident that reason, using the scientific methods of induction and deduction, is quite capable of discerning right and wrong belief and action, understanding all the intricacies of experienced reality (including the hold that diverse religions exercise over millions of people), and suggesting the conditions necessary for a fulfilled life.[19] It strongly supports the three key passions of the modern age: liberty, equality, and well-being. [20] It believes that humans possess the power to solve their own problems. Therefore it is opposed to all fatalist theories that suppose that human life is predetermined. It is assured that humans are endowed with sufficient freedom to be able to make creative choices and take independent action.[21]

Most secular humanists are averse to considering their beliefs to be part of an established worldview. They advocate for every human being's freedom to think critically for themselves and express their convictions independently of any authoritarian or dogmatic articles of belief imposed by some external institution. Human beings are capable of deciding for themselves what is the best for their own lives. They alone are responsible

---

19. See Cave, *Humanism*, xii.

20. Todorov, *Imperfect Garden*, 16 (derived from Alexis de Tocqueville, *Democracy in America* and *The Old Regime and the Revolution*).

21. See Lamont, *Philosophy of Humanism*, quoted by Geisler, *Is Man the Measure?*, 84.

for exploring and correcting their core beliefs and the actions which should be derived from them. This approach to life has to be an open process. Life should not be contained by intrinsically unchanging opinions and attitudes. Rather, it should be guided by honest doubts that a number of complex issues will ever be finally resolved.

So, SH is not an unchanging, inflexible creed; rather, it is "a developing philosophy, ever open to experimental testing, newly discovered facts, and more rigorous reasoning."[22] The logical outcome is that societies should promote free expression by artists, writers, and commentators of a variety of views about current affairs, moral issues, and answers to the basic questions of existence. If culture is to progress, it is essential that all censorship must be excluded. Grayling sums up the humanist approach to intellectual integrity in the following way.

> Humanism is a philosophical outlook, but in itself is a minimalist one, deliberately so because a key requirement of it is that individuals should think for themselves about what they are and how they should live . . . All the great philosophies have a metaphysics that underwrites the ethics they urge. But humanism requires no commitment to teachings beyond its two fundamental premises, and it imposes no obligations on people other than they think for themselves. Because it does not consist in a body of doctrines and prescriptions, backed by sanctions for not believing in the former and not obeying the latter, it's as far from being a religion as anything could be.[23]

The Anthropology of SH

There is some debate between secular humanists about whether human beings possess an immutable essence, with which they are born and which is universal among all races and classes of people. According to Jean-Paul Sartre, the atheists of the Enlightenment believed that humans possess a human nature in which all universally participate, "meaning that they all possess the same basic qualities;" "the essence of man precedes his historically primitive existence in nature."[24] Sartre strongly disagrees:

22. Lamont, *Philosophy of Humanism*, 14.

23. Grayling, *God Argument*, 149.

24. Sartre, *Existentialism is a Humanism*, 22. The original publication in French was *L'Existentialisme est un humanisme* (Paris: Editions Gallimard, 1947).

> What do we mean here by "existence precedes essence"? We mean that man first exists: he materializes in the world, encounters himself, and only afterwards defines himself. If man as existentialists conceive of him cannot be defined, it is because to begin with he is nothing. He will not be anything until later, and then he will be what he makes of himself. Thus, there is no human nature since there is no God to conceive of it . . . man is nothing than what he makes of himself. This is the first principle of existentialism.[25]

Other humanists beg to differ. They point out that it is naïve to believe that all human beings are nothing, when born into the world. They are born into a specific context and, long before they are mature enough to decide what they will be, they have been influenced by their parents, their education, their culture, their economic circumstances, their peer group, and so on:

> Intellectual culture has traditionally been central to our concept of what it is to be human.[26]

> Every Human being is born an heir to an inheritance and to enter this common inheritance of human achievements through education is the only way of becoming a human being, and to inhabit it is to be a human being.[27]

In other words, according to this view, humans already exist as humans when they first see the light of day. They may, of course, choose to adapt themselves to their environment in a whole variety of ways. So, in some senses they do make themselves into who they wish to be:

> The human being is not the plaything of forces from which he cannot hope to escape . . . Our species is characterized by its plasticity, its capacity to adapt itself to all circumstances, to

---

25. Sartre, *Existentialism is a Humanism*, 22.
26. Hayes, "Re-Humanising Education," 84.
27. Michael Oakshott, quoted in Hayes, "Re-humanising Education," 84. The influence of a culture which we inherit, simply because we are immersed in it, may cause us to determine our nature as a human up to a point. However, is there any way of being sure that we have interpreted it correctly, unless there is a given ontological reality about being human that allows an accurate perspective from which to assess our belief? It is here that SH flounders: it is not rooted in anything substantial; only vague surmises. One might be influenced by X, and X might give rise to the belief I'm Y. However, that belief is still compatible with the view that Y is just an illusion, as no real Y exists. The problem is, I would not know.

> change . . . (Humanists) value voluntary action, yet without the need to believe in men's unlimited malleability or in their omnipotence: the place of the given is also irreducible. Humanists do not think, as Sartre does, that man alone makes his own laws: first because man is multiple and this multiplicity can be problematic; then because men today are made also from the past, and this past is in turn shaped by men over whom one has no power; finally and above all, because men must take into account the constraints over which they have no control . . . imposed by their bodies, the physical characteristics of the country they inhabit, Earth's place in the universe.[28]

Todorov admits that

> the humanist doctrine's anthropology . . . is relatively weak. Apart from the biological identity of the species, it is reduced to a single feature, sociability; but its consequences are numerous. The most important in our view, is the existence of consciousness of self, which animals never achieve . . . Such is the basis of human liberty . . . Sociability and liberty are intrinsically bound together, and they make up part of the very definition of the species.[29]

Whether the term "weak" is an adequate characterization of SH or not, in its own terms it is limited. According to the standard theory of biological evolution, human beings have been transformed by a mysterious process from primates, developing into separate species, to human beings, with features far more advanced than any other living class of beings. Darwin calls it "the Descent of Man." The best guess as to how this may have come about is that the mind has acquired new properties that enable the existence of consciousness, conscience, personality, and advanced reasoning powers.

If the evolution of species, of which the most advanced is *homo sapiens*, is due entirely to significant changes in the brain, then mind is the product of matter alone. If it is true that all living matter has emerged by pure chance, with no external directing process, then intelligence has arisen out of nonintelligence. Adherents to SH, if consistent in their beliefs, are materialists (i.e., they allege that whatever exists just is and depends wholly on matter). To understand the reality of human life, it is necessary to return to the origin of life and trace the chain of being

---

28. Todorov, *Imperfect Garden*, 34–35.
29. Todorov, *Imperfect Garden*, 32.

through its inferred multiple mutations from less complex to more complex organisms.

According to Ayn Rand,

> man's consciousness shares with animals the first two stages of its development: sensations and perceptions; but it is the third state, *conceptions*, that makes him man. Sensations are integrated into perceptions automatically, by the brain of a man or an animal. But to integrate perceptions into conceptions by a process of abstraction, is a feat that man alone has the power to perform—and he has to perform it by choice.[30]

Strangely, Rand rejects a strict materialism, presumably on the grounds that the power of rational reflection is a reality that somehow transcends matter. However, if mind is dependent on brainpower and brains consist entirely of physical elements, it is hard to envisage how thought processes have been engendered. It would seem that the mind cannot be reduced to potentially locatable operations in the cranium. On the grounds of rational conception (her phrase), one might depict the origin of the mind and rational thought that flows from it like a kind of conjuring trick. Rand is a confirmed atheist, and so denies any ultimate mind in existence before the foundation of the universe. Nevertheless, she speaks of the laws of thought as though they were intrinsic; human beings may discover them, but did not create them. Out of apparently nowhere, the rabbit is pulled from the hat!

It follows logically that, if the mind is inseparably joined to the brain's functioning, to create an indivisible unity of body and personality, there can be no conscious survival of the individual after death, when the brain's cells have ceased altogether to function. There appears to be an obvious inconsistency in the view that mind is dependent on matter. If it were so, it would not be able

> to make statements . . . from a standpoint independent of matter . . . for one must step beyond something to see it all . . . Thus mind cannot legitimately make the statement "mind is dependent on matter," for what appears to be transcendent knowledge actually rests on an imminent basis of operation.[31]

This inconsistency does not seem to perturb secular humanists like Abhijit Naskar. He states that

30. Rand, *Virtue of Selfishness*, 14.
31. Geisler, *Is Man the Measure?*, 178.

the Absolute Principle of Humanism, is—*Self is All* . . . The Self is the measure of everything.[32]

The Self, he believes, creates its own self-made reality through:

> the beliefs . . . the ambitions, intuitions, sentiments and everything that makes you who you are. At a molecular level, it all arises from the electrochemical impulses passing through billions of neurons in your head . . . The Self is a part of the Consciousness and Consciousness is a part of the Mind. And this entire system that involves your exclusive mental universe, is the majestic creation of the protoplasmic realm of your brain . . . One intricate reality of the human life to be aware of is that the Mind and the Body are not distinct systems after all . . . You live in a world where we Neuroscientists are peeking through the Brain to look into the Soul. The Soul . . . is basically what we today call the Mind. Mind is the creation of the Brain.[33]

Finally, in what seems to be a straight contradiction of his very physicalist outlook, he states that

> the basic biological faculties of life arose out of the need for survival. In time the need for survival got intertwined with a uniquely human need for understanding and progress. Hence empowered by the natural process of selective pressure, *the human Self transcended beyond its physical limits*, unlike any other creature on earth.[34]

Ethical Theories and SH

As an overall principle of judgment, one might propose that the adequacy of different views on human nature stands or falls on the proficiency of their perspectives on moral values. Moral judgments pose three main questions that require satisfactory answers: On what basis can we humans justify our convictions about good and evil, right and wrong? From what source(s) have ethical judgments flowed? And in response to the answers to the first two questions, we must then ask how then should we live, and what in real life constitutes good deeds and bad ones? We will look at each of these in turn.

32. Naskar, *Principia Humanitas*, 11.
33. Naskar, *Principia Humanitas*, 12, 13, 14.
34. Naskar, *Principia Humanitas*, 13; emphasis added.

The Basis for Ethical Reasoning

Secular humanists are probably more certain about what they do not believe in than in their case for a convincing theoretical grounding for their ethical precepts. Dylan Evans (a secular humanist) argues thus:

> Since they do not believe in God, atheists and humanists cannot appeal to any objective or absolute basis to legitimize their own sacred values.[35]

Nevertheless, sacred values such as racial and sexual equality, democracy, justice, and free speech are treated as though they possess a moral status that cannot be contravened. To be consistent, a secular humanist should have to admit that, because "there is no ultimate authority, no divine lawgiver, to which humanists can appeal to sanction their moral principles . . . [they] must accept some form of moral relativism." Paradoxically, however, "their ethical relativism is subject to a selective blindness, according to which everyone's moral beliefs are relative except their own . . . Many humanists react with moral outrage when someone dares to analyze, let alone dispute, one or more of their sacred values."[36]

There is clearly some debate among humanists about the ultimate truth of their ethical stances. Another contributor to the collection of essays on humanism flatly denies that SH stands for a relativistic approach to moral decision-making:

> Humanists . . . must stand against relativism and for universal values in an open society, modeled in our schools.[37]

Clearly there is a dilemma here for SH. On the one hand, the affirmation of universal values does seem to imply a moral judge entirely independent of human interests, who is able to deliver universally valid rulings on the content of ethical uprightness. On the other hand, if no such being exists, humans are left to their own devices to create for themselves moral values that might have some hope of being acceptable to

---

35. Evans, "Secular Fundamentalism," 16.

36. Evans, "Secular Fundamentalism," 19, 18.

37. Copson, "Humanism and Faith Schools," 76. Some humanists might object to the notion of universal values (some post-modern thinkers, who reject all-inclusive explanatory narratives, for example). Nevertheless, what they reject as a theory, they will show they accept in practice, by drawing their own 'red-lines' in the sand, beyond which they will not allow anyone to pass.

a majority. One extreme form of this quandary is Sartre's exposition of existentialism:

> If I have eliminated God the Father, there has to be someone to invent values... To say that we invent values means neither more nor less than this: life has no meaning *a priori*... Value is nothing more than the meaning we give to it... Man makes himself... he makes himself by choosing his own morality... We can define man only in relation to his commitments. It is, therefore, ludicrous to blame us for the gratuitousness of our choices.[38]

Sartre appears to be advocating an uncompromising form of subjectivism. This has given rise to a kind of "emotivism," which Alasdair MacIntyre defines as "claims one might make in argument (that) can be subjected to no court of appeal, in the absence of a common standard of truth, other than the subjective beliefs of the isolated individual."[39] Emotivism is exemplified in the current trend among some students to "de-platform" certain speakers invited to the university at which they are studying because they abhor their views. It is manifest in small groups of students disrupting a speaker by continuously shouting adverse slogans. Such behavior, it has to be said, contradicts SH's commitment to the human right of free thought and speech.[40] Nevertheless, it may be judged as a logical outcome of secular individualism. Elisabeth Lasch-Quinn suggests that,

> one of the most promising ways to address the crisis in secularism—but one that is rarely attempted—would be to refuse to fall prey to the simplistic dichotomy between secular and religious visions of humanity. A creative fusion of religious and secular humanism that searches for points of commonality and affinity, common intellectual sources and traditions, and shared moral premises, but at the same time acknowledges the inherent tensions between competing visions, is not just desirable but

---

38. Sartre, *Existentialism is a Humanism*, 51, 46.

39. The quote comes from Elisabeth Lasch-Quinn, "Morality and the Crisis of Secularization," 33. It is a brief summary of MacIntyre's critique of contemporary Western culture as devoid of a coherent moral framework, in his book *After Virtue*.

40. No doubt secular humanists would rightly deny that such behavior exhibits the stance of secular humanism.

perhaps also necessary, if any form of humanism is to survive, given today's culture wars.[41]

Given the current state of moral confusion in the West, brought on, religious believers might contend, by the untrustworthy understanding of Christian belief and ethical teaching put forward by some humanists,[42] such an aspiration is unlikely. It is true that secular humanists and Christians do share a number of values. Many of the media-based petitions, for example, asking people to sign causes that uphold worthy moral concerns, such as saving the bee population through the legal exclusion of lethal insecticides, or saving African elephants through the prohibition of trophy hunting, will be signed by both secular humanists and Christians. Nevertheless, there is still a huge divergence on other issues, such as the reality of sexual identity. If anything, the gap is widening, rather than narrowing. The main reason for the continuing culture wars between the two sectors is precisely the issue of an objective moral standard and its foundation.

SH strives to fill the void created by the refusal to consider a morality based on the best of contemporary Christian thinking. It is difficult to see how many ethical issues could be reconciled when definitive truth claims about ultimate reality spring from incompatible premises. SH is constrained to rely on three lines of thought: it will attempt to reconstruct a genealogy of the beginnings of moral reflection in the distant past; it will then trace the development of moral consciousness from ancient civilizations to the present; and it will choose the moral judgment it finds most appropriate to its sentiments.

Philip Kitcher, for example, believes that agreements, conducive to creating harmony, were gradually constructed by preliterate, hunter-gatherer communities for conducting their social life. The main guiding principle would have been a rough equality between families. It would have been risky, he thinks, not to allow all voices to be heard and not to seek resolutions of conflicts that all could accept. So, these ancient ancestors formulated codes that could govern social interaction.

The vital directives combined the need to share resources and avoid unprovoked violence. Codes were tried out by different groups in

---

41. Lasch-Quinn, "Morality and the Crisis," 33–34.

42. In the next section of this chapter, we will consider such ill-considered understandings put forward by one of the foremost campaigners against the Christian faith, Anthony Grayling, in his book *The God Argument*.

different epochs. Those that seemed to work well became built into human conscience, as a way of "internalizing preferred patterns of conduct." Motivation for keeping to the rules was supplied negatively by fear of punishment and positively by respect for the group(s) and their traditions. An ethos of shame took hold of these primitive societies when customs and conventions were broken.[43]

Such an attempt to reconstruct periods of prehistory is bound to be based on conjecture. In the absence of recorded excerpts indicating some of the processes whereby moral constraints were introduced into interhuman relations, there is little alternative but to speculate about the ways in which normal everyday life may have been regulated to its best advantage. Other attempts at formulating satisfactory principles of ethical conduct have been derived from the study of nature and the power of rational imagination in defining ideal situations. In the first instance, secular humanists, limited by their naturalistic worldview, are bound to attempt to build their case for moral principles from within the acceptance of a neo-Darwinian version of the development of species:

> If the universe is the result of impersonal forces that just happened to have produced the universe as we know it, then there are no guiding principles, intrinsic ends or rational processes that have at any stage shaped the stages of life . . . (So), the existence of ethical intuitions has to be explained on the basis of an absolutely consistent evolutionary materialism.[44]

Following on from this premise, the basic empirical data adduced from purely natural causes is the altruism needed for cooperation in the interests of survival:

> On this view, somehow the evolutionary process (nature) has programmed us to believe that co-operation is an obligation . . . The justification for moral action is reduced to the necessity to survive.[45]

This is the overriding intent of the evolutionary process. The means to achieve it is to act altruistically.

Another alternative grounding for a belief in moral facts is given in what has been called "the Ideal Observer Theory." This view attempts to

43. Kitcher, *Life after Faith*, 31–35.

44. Kirk, *Christian Mission as Dialogue*, 115.

45. Kirk, *Christian Mission as Dialogue*, 115–16.

give a coherent rationale for a metaethics (i.e., a fundamental principle by which ethical judgments could be rightly considered true or false).[46] It is based on the supposition that an independent observer (IO), a hypothetical being whose two main characteristics would be the possession of full information concerning any situation that demanded moral choice and complete impartiality between divergent opinions about the matter, can be appealed to as an objective standard for making moral judgments:

> In order to be rationally justified in one's ethical judgments about some action or event one must base these judgments on one's estimate of the reaction of an Ideal Observer.[47]

The criterion by which one knows whether an action is morally right or wrong is the feeling of approval or disapproval with which the IO would react to the action in question.[48] At this juncture, we cannot fully discuss reasons for accepting or rejecting this hypothetical proposal for grounding an objective, but nontheistic, rationale for a universally valid moral theory. We will leave the debate until the final chapter. Suffice it to say that this thought process is put forward as what Philip Kitcher describes as an "idealized process of practical reason."[49]

Secular humanists appear to accept as empirically verifiable the notion that human beings are born into the world with an inclination to be guided by ethical ideals.[50] Thus, for example, in the course of human history, often by means of trial and error, societies have come to realize that equality is an absolute moral good. Thus, as a result, slavery or any form of coerced servitude of one group by another is morally illegitimate. Yet equality is not an empirical fact; quite the reverse. The high-sounding phrase that "all men and women are born equal" is not true to real life.

---

46. The theory is set out comprehensibly in Martin, *Atheism, Morality and Meaning*, 85–110.

47. Martin, *Atheism, Morality and Meaning*, 51.

48. John Stuart Mill, at the end of his life, advocated the necessity to visualize a morally perfect Being as a standard to regulate our lives, even if such a being was merely imaginary; see Hobson, *God Created Humanism*, 92.

49. Kitcher, *Life after Faith*, 29.

50. Naskar states that "goodness and evil both are biological traits of the mind" (*Principia Humanitas*, 42). However, if that is their origin, they are neither good nor evil, they just are. If that was the case, one imagines that they would never be disputed. However, as they are disputed, the distinction between them cannot be innate. If we have to choose between them, traits of the mind are wholly insufficient as the origin of guiding principles.

Equality may be projected as a moral ideal, even though its implementation in practice often begs more detailed moral questions; it is certainly not based on the observation of nature, nor on rational abstractions from idealistic fantasies. According to Anthony Grayling, quoting George Bernard Shaw, we cannot even apply the "Golden Rule" of "do to others as you would have them do to you" (the most likely, nontheistic, universally warranted principle of ethical behavior), "because others might not share one's own interests and tastes, and one might not understand theirs . . . How can one make what conduces to one's own good the benchmark and standard for the good of others?"[51]

Secular Humanism and a Religious Worldview

Throughout this discussion of the convictions of secular humanism, religion has thrown its shadow over the inquiry. This antipathy between the two systems of belief is the ground that secular humanists have chosen as a starting point to explain their outlook. It does not have to be that way. In the Western world, the dominant religion for the last seventeen centuries has been Christianity. Although within the last forty years or so Islam has become increasingly prominent, the Christian faith is the religious faith that has molded, for good or ill, the consciousness of Western nations. Christianity possesses within its core convictions its own version of humanism. Some secular humanists have acknowledged this, but the majority, judging by what has been written in books and articles explaining their beliefs, have chosen to denounce this variant of religion among the others.

Some will argue that belief in a personal God who has created and shaped the universe and designed human beings to be like him is redundant. Peter Cave, for example, says that

> understanding the world without God, giving sense to the world without God, is the heart of today's humanism. The humanist stance can and should flourish . . . without God.[52]

In the famous words, attributed to Pierre-Simon Laplace, in a conversation with Napoleon, "*je n'ai pas eu besoin de cette hypothese*" ("I had

---

51. Grayling, *God Argument*, 192.
52. Cave, *Humanism*, 1.

no need of that hypothesis"). Humanists can be morally upright and lead meaningful lives without any recourse to an alleged supernatural reality.

Others will promote more stringent reasons for rejecting Christian faith. Building on the critique of religion advanced by some of the exponents we have already studied in previous chapters, they will explain religion by explaining it away. Of necessity, within a naturalistic worldview, they are bound to consider all religious persuasions to be the creation of the human imagination. Humanists will argue that the so-called "proofs" for the existence of a God are unconvincing. They will further claim that religious beliefs, of their very nature, do not pass the rational test of sufficient evidence. So, they will contrast the methods of scientific verification to those of faith. They assume that faith cannot be based on proof that is open to demonstrable evidence, nor can it be falsified. In other words, faith places itself beyond rational criticism. Religions are distinguished by their invocation of something beyond the mundane, physical world and offer claims about a "transcendent" world, not accessible via methods people use to investigate other aspects of reality.[53]

Yet others, in an even more polemical mood, start from the premise that all religious belief is both illusory and destructive. It is invented by particular human cohorts in order to maintain their superior position of power in society, while claiming to be the purveyors of ultimate truth. This stance against religion is then supported by some of the most rudimentary misunderstandings of the nature of religion that are possible to contrive. One of the worst offenders is Grayling. In his short article on "Humanism, Religion and Ethics,"[54] elaborated at greater length in a more recent writing on the subject,[55] he asserts one kind of fallacy after another. Here are some examples:

- "religions of the book . . . are modeled on monarchy, the system in which authority resides in a paramount ruler to whom all must submit *in hope of reward and for fear of punishment.*"[56] (The emphasis is added, in order to accentuate the falsehood of this interpretation of Christian motivation);

---

53. See Kitcher, *Life after Faith*, 4.
54. Cummings, *Debating Humanism*, 47–54.
55. Grayling, *God Argument*.
56. Grayling, "Humanism, Religion and Ethics," 48.

- "the religious concept of sin means disobedience to the punitive authority of an invisible dictator."[57] (This definition of sin is simply a blinkered, distorted view of the nature of God, phrased this way to provoke maximum aggravation);
- "those who embrace the humanist outlook as meant here agree in nominating individual liberty, the pursuit of knowledge, the promotion of culture, and the fellowship of man, as guiding generalities when thinking about the good for humankind."[58] (The implication of this claim, within the context in which it is set, is that the Christian faith suppresses all of these values);
- "the quest for knowledge is a dangerous sin: the first man and woman were forbidden to eat the fruit of the tree of knowledge, and all religions since have censored, burned books (and all their authors), and promoted ignorance as a route to salvation."[59] (If this were true—and it is neither a correct quotation from Genesis 2 nor a summary of a genuine Christian strategy—it is strange that Christians throughout their history have founded universities, promoted education, especially amongst the dispossessed, and championed the endeavors of the first modern scientists, many of whom professed Christian belief);
- "the appeal of religion is . . . not intellectual but emotional, and therefore non-rational, so that arguments concerning the irrationality of religious belief avail little."[60] (This remark is made as a sweeping, doctrinaire generalization, devoid of any evidence to support its claim).

Were Grayling, as an academic, to follow proper intellectual lines of reasoning, namely to engage with the most cogent expositors of the Christian faith, citing his rational evidence for such categorical claims as the ones exposed above, one might take him more seriously. As it is, they can only be dismissed as being frivolous. Perhaps one of the most absurd pieces of false assertion that can be found among secular humanist writers is that made by Simon Blackburn in the same volume:

57. Grayling, "Humanism, Religion and Ethics," 48.
58. Grayling, "Humanism, Religion and Ethics," 48.
59. Grayling, "Humanism, Religion and Ethics," 49.
60. Grayling, "Humanism, Religion and Ethics," 50.

> In the eighteenth century the Christian God endorsed slavery and the death penalty for poaching; now he does neither.[61]

The reality is that he never did either. Some misguided, self-confessing believers might have done, but nowhere in the Christian foundation documents will you find either alluded to as emanating from Jesus Christ. The historical records show that Christians were in the forefront of the struggle to abolish slavery and reform the penal code in many of its most inhumane punishments. It is easy to put up straw men and knock them down. It is not fitting that this should be done by professed professors.

A much more reliable account of historical processes would draw the conclusion that humanism ultimately is dependent on the core convictions of Christian doctrine. There is space here to give just one example. It is not often recognized that the origin of the acknowledgment of basic human rights came in the sixteenth century from two quite separate and contrasting Christian sources:

> The prolonged efforts of Fray Anton de Montesino, Fray Bartolome de las Casas, Bishop Antonio de Valdivieso and other missionaries in the Americas in the sixteenth century to protect the indigenous populations, in respect of God-given freedoms, against their merciless exploitation by Spanish settlers is, for the time, a remarkable example of the exercise of justice. With the support of theologians and jurists at the University of Salamanca, they began to carve out the first systematic articulation of basic human rights.
>
> For the following two centuries (after the Reformation) the Anabaptists and other nonconforming groups were harassed by the establishment (church and state). Eventually, their determination not to be subjugated to what they considered to be merely human-made laws and their willingness to suffer abuse for their convictions was probably the single most important contributory factor in the gradual implementation of rights and freedoms in modern societies.[62]

---

61. Blackburn, "Humanism and the Transcendental," in Cummings, *Debating Humanism*, 102.

62. Kirk, *Church and the World*, 325–26, 326–27. For a summary of both the benefits and the problems of human rights discourse, see Kirk, *Future of Reason*, 191–95. A much fuller treatment of the reliance of humanistic beliefs and values on authentic Christian presuppositions is given in Hobson, *God Created Humanism*.

These are but two historical instances of the championing of human rights, on the basis of the God-given, sacrosanct nature of human beings. The fact that human nature is God-endowed removes human rights from the authority of sovereign states either to award or withhold. It is somewhat insincere of secular humanists to ignore plain facts of history, in the interests of pretending that all Christians at all times have thwarted attempts to recognize basic freedoms, or to suggest that humanists have been the main instigators of the drive for their recognition. Bernard-Henri Levy, a French philosopher (and not known to be a professing Christian), confirms the thesis that human rights are the result of a "progressive universalism" that is, in itself, a religiously rooted phenomenon:

> I'm certain that there would be no human rights without the highly audacious Christian hypothesis of man as a creature in God's likeness and therefore inviolable.[63]

Concluding Comments, Positive Gains

Whenever humanism lays aside its intense, and often intellectually flawed, anti-Christian polemic and asserts positive values, rather than negative stereotypes, it has much to offer society in terms of valuable values. In spite of his dismantling of secular humanists' rational and moral pretensions, John Carroll acknowledges that some of its core beliefs uphold and promote virtues that genuinely contribute to human flourishing:

> Humanism's greatest achievement was a liberal-democratic kingdom of ends, a society based on universal human rights governed by Kant's absolute moral laws and guided by civic common sense, practical reason operating in its fitting place.[64]

Likewise, Theo Hobson appreciates the constructive contribution of some elements of SH to the future well-being of society. He talks about its core conviction being

> the belief that all human lives matter and should flourish, and that part of such flourishing is the freedom to express one's core beliefs; it of course entails "human rights."[65]

63. Levy and Houellebecq, *Public Enemies*, 159–60.
64. Carroll, *Humanism*, 263.
65. Hobson, *God Created Humanism*, 1.

It takes for granted

> that all human lives are valuable and of equal worth, and that all suffering is a matter of urgent concern. This assumption is our form of the sacred.[66]

He goes on to say that SH "is a moral aspiration," and "that it is closely associated with . . . a belief in rational progress."[67] Later in his book, Hobson, citing John Stuart Mill, suggests that SH assumes that secular ethics takes for granted that human flourishing is an obvious goal for the whole of humanity. In order to achieve this, people must put the general good of the human community before their own good. They will do this naturally, because moral idealism is built into their nature. In other words, a universal morality that promotes the good is axiomatic to civilization. At its best, it has been strongly influential in helping to initiate liberal democracy, with its main achievement being the defense of the rights of the individual in the face of the state's overweening desire to control all aspects of life.[68]

Having commended SH on the best of its ideals and practices, he puts its achievements into historical perspective by arguing that much of its moral benchmark is parasitic on the moral perfectionism taught by the Christian faith:

> To claim that Christianity is the primary source of secular humanism might sound excessive. But where else did secular humanism get its optimistic moral vision, its idea that human beings ought to seek the well-being *of all other* human beings? Is this just the morality that comes naturally to all human societies, the evolved instinct for altruism perhaps? No, that sort of instinctive morality certainly exists, but is frail, ambiguous . . . It does not come naturally to us to believe that we can move toward a world of ever-greater justice for all, that all lives are of equal worth, that oppression and discrimination must end. It comes far more naturally to us to see drastic inequality as inevitable,[69] and distant others as inferior.[70]

---

66. Hobson, *God Created Humanism*, 2.
67. Hobson, *God Created Humanism*, 88–92.
68. Hobson, *God Created Humanism*, 88–92.
69. As did Mr. Wilcock in Forster's novel, *Howard's End*.
70. Hobson, *God Created Humanism*, 4; emphasis added to reflect Christianity's impartiality in considering all to be worthy of their needs being met.

Internal Critiques

It is worth bearing in mind that not all secular humanists condemn the Christian faith so forcefully and ignorantly that they fail to see that actually its moral code champions the highest good for humanity that has ever been put forward. Moreover, some are honest enough to admit that SH as a worldview has serious inadequacies. Kitcher, for example, recognizes that SH is open to the criticism that it allows only an impoverished form of human existence, and that its worldview is inadequate for grounding claims that some things are valuable and morally required of us and others are worthless and to be prohibited.[71]

He recognizes the strength of the negative judgment that SH does not possess an adequate account of ethical life, because it cannot appeal to an external standard arising from its own system of beliefs. In other words, it lacks an external standard that can be universalized. Morality, then, devolves to local ethical codes. However, there is no way of assessing the rival codes of different societies. This dilemma accounts for the timidity with which Western cultures confront some of the abuses perpetrated in the name of multiculturalism (e.g., the way of slaughtering animals, and the use of shari'a law in validating marriage between two Muslims).

Blackburn identifies two perennial doubts about SH. It becomes

> allied ... with "materialism" and with the denial or downgrading of any spiritual dimension to human life, ethics and politics; ... (it is) associated with "relativism," or with a drifting, unprincipled way of life, incapable of sustaining real standards, values and commitments. The first charge is that humanism is crass, and the second is that it is soggy.[72]

Naturally, as one who identifies with SH, he does not accept the doubts, but he does recognize that they genuinely exist.

Perhaps it is Todorov who most openly confronts the numerous critical evaluations of SH. He puts them in the form of a pact that the devil offers to humanity about what will be lost if they accept the temptation to yield to the seduction of attaining individual autonomy. If God is rejected, the individual may attain autonomy, but will become alienated, an inauthentic being, and no longer deserving of being called

---

71. Kitcher, *Life after Faith*, 2.
72. Cummings, *Debating Humanism*, 101.

a subject. Modern man will be condemned to be nothing but a materialist who cherishes no value beyond personal interest. Pursuing one's own self-interest, however, may well result in degrading oneself. The result of individualism is the disappearance of the individual. At the end of his book, Todorov puts forward what he calls the "humanist wager." It makes sober reading for anyone who believes that SH is the best hope for the future of the human race:

> The humanist enterprise . . . rejects the dream of a paradise on earth, which would establish a definitive order. It imagines men in their current imperfection and does not imagine that this state of things can change . . . Rather than a science or a dogma, humanist thought proposes a practical choice: a wager. Better to wager that they are capable of acting wilfully, loving purely and treating one another as equals than the contrary . . . The humanists of the French tradition do not necessarily believe in final causes, but they judge it useful to act as if this way were really open to men. It is true that, unlike Pascal, they do not promise those who wager "an eternity of life and happiness," but only a fragile and fleeting felicity.[73]

Questionable Assumptions

Contrary to its own opinions of itself, SH is predicated on a fundamental act of faith. It claims that nothing should be believed, unless it is based on sufficient evidence. However, its core conviction that nothing outside the material universe exists (a negative conjecture) is turned into a positive statement that "we currently have no evidence for the existence of the transcendent."[74] In other words, it completely sidesteps the need to support its negative supposition with enough evidence to demonstrate that God could not possibly exist. This it does not do. In its place, it pronounces a dogmatic judgment:

> Soft atheists are as firm as their harder cousins; there are excellent grounds for supposing all such doctrines (about the reality of the transcendent) to be thoroughly false.[75]

---

73. Todorov, *Imperfect Garden*, 236–37.

74. Todorov, *Imperfect Garden*, 236–37.

75. Kitcher, *Life after Faith*, 23, 24. The problem, not addressed, is what counts as evidence. Empirical evidence sanctioned by experimental testing is by no means the only kind of evidence that could be true; the practice of justice, delivered in a law

What the argument amounts to is that, for a radical secularist, *a priori*, there could be no satisfactory (i.e., acceptable to a skeptic) grounds for upholding the existence of a nonmaterial realm parallel to the universe, and yet nevertheless able to interact with it. The position is not defended by an empirical demonstration, but is based on an anti-religious prejudice and the *a priori* acceptance of an atheistic worldview. It is as if the atheist parodied the first sentence of the Bible: "in the beginning, there was no God." Consequently, insofar as they lack scientifically verifiable knowledge to prove or disprove their presupposition, secular humanists put themselves in the same position as Christian believers.

Everything that secular humanists believe or do not believe is colored by this initial act of faith. It has enormous consequences for their version of humanism. The result is that they are bereft of any notion of creative acts introduced within material existence by a Being who contains the characteristics of being artistic, imaginative, ingenious, resourceful, and productive. In such a Being's place, they speculate that the universe is somehow self-generated out of nothing and has expanded and evolved in a random fashion. There is no plan, no objective, no purpose already built into the existence of living creatures, except perhaps that of survival; but even survival is an arbitrary operation, inferring a limited intention already given within the structures of life.

Making a plausible guess at the original cause of biological life, given that there could not be, for an atheist, any prior external agency, is highly speculative. So far, no evidence has ever been produced that life arose from nonlife; in other words, that biology sprang from a mixture of chemistry and physics alone. It would be amazing (almost magical) if the laws of physics and chemistry could account for the beginning of life. The standard theory of evolution has not explained how laws governing lower organisms are adequate to produce higher organisms by completely chance operations. Transferring genetic information from one form of life to another by random selection is contrary to all observation. Natural selection does not account for the arrival of entirely new forms of life, but only the survival of old ones. In other words, selection is a conserving, rather than a productive force. It appears that each living thing always generates another like itself. Now, if scientists were able to produce an entirely new form of life by genetic manipulation, it would only demonstrate that an intelligent being was able to produce a higher

---

court, demonstrates this.

form of life, exactly what theists claim for the intelligent, creative powers of a supreme Being.[76]

The same is true for the existence of *homo sapiens*. If it is true that humans evolved over an immense period of time from the highest primates, how does one account for the fact that not all primates generated the next class of elevated being? Presumably some did and subsequently died out, since there is no record of an intermediate species—except in Darwin's imagination—whilst for others, evolution came to a halt. Where is even the remotest piece of evidence to suggest that this is what happened? How does an organism attain a higher level of development by a sudden leap? It is like suggesting that, on its own, a ball can spontaneously bounce upstairs without some outside force directing it.

Nevertheless, in spite of the fact that the standard evolutionary theory is not a testable scientific hypothesis, but as Karl Popper once declared "a metaphysical research program,"[77] many scientists declare that its thesis is proven. There can only be one convincing reason why they take this stance. Standard evolutionary theory is the only alternative to a thesis that states that the world as we know it can only exist due to the creative acts of an externally existing Being acting from outside time and space. As secular humanists have dismissed such a possibility, *ab initio*, they have to invent an alternative. In a new biography of Charles Darwin, the author, an expert in the social mores of Victorian England, suggests that this was precisely a major motivation for Darwin's grand theory.[78] It was to offer what appeared to be a perfectly simple, common-sense, demonstrable thesis to account for the rise and development of living matter, without any need to rely on extramaterial intervention.

However, once the evidence is shown to be intrinsically unverifiable, scientifically, it lacks an adequate explanatory force for deciding the likely origin of human beings. Consequently, those who put all their eggs in the evolutionary basket are bereft of their most cherished alternative description (to the creative design account) of the origin of humanity. It is hard for them to accept that science *qua* science is limited in its ability to explain the whole complexity of human existence.

---

76. Some of the arguments given here against the possibility of life being conceived and developed by purely random, nonintelligent causes are based on the discussion in Geisler, *Is Man the Measure?*, 139–47.

77. Popper, *Unended Quest*, 168.

78. Wilson, *Charles Darwin*.

Ethics and the Naturalist Fallacy

SH undoubtedly advances high social, moral ideals. It is based on the premise that all human beings have an equal dignity, irrespective of the circumstances of their birth, and that all have a right to have access to the opportunities and goods that will enable them to flourish. In other words, human beings are ends in themselves and their exploitation by others, who have accumulated more power, to further their own interests, is the antithesis of authentic humanism. Secular humanists tend to favor a view of justice that advocates the creation of an increasingly egalitarian society into the forefront of its agenda.

In spite of its strong moral impulse, SH lacks an underlying intellectual framework to connect its moral convictions with its insubstantial sentiments about what makes a human actually human. It has arbitrarily reduced the scope of its survey by limiting knowledge to what can be deduced from methods of observation on the material world, and is scientifically verifiable. Over and over again, proponents of SH assert that all we need to know about human existence can be gathered from scientifically controlled scrutiny.

One of the latest examples of this trend is to attempt to deduce all the workings of the mind by exploring the functionings of the brain. This approach, which is determined by its adherence to a naturalistic worldview, commits the error of scientism—the belief that "every genuine question can in principle be answered by science."[79] There are a number of questions that science as an observational and inferentially based method cannot explain:

> Questions about the nature of reality, of why the world is as it is, how is it that human beings are able to understand its mechanisms and why we should be interested to know the answer to these questions.[80]

To be forced to take for granted such realities as intelligibility, existence rather than nonexistence, or an ordered rather than a chaotic natural pattern of existence and contingency, without possessing any plausible explanation, is surely an inferior intellectual standpoint to one that has a perfectly credible explanation for all these things.

---

79. Law, *Humanism*, 5. Law is one of few humanists who believe that humanism does not have to embrace a worldview that predicates a science-based reductionism.

80. Kirk, *Christian Mission as Dialogue*, 110.

SH, because of its naturalistic bias, is also required to commit the naturalist fallacy with regard to ethical theorizing (i.e., that moral obligation can be derived from description alone):

> John Mackie, for example, a professed atheist, recognizes that, if the God hypothesis were true, objective moral norms would have a substantive basis, and that without belief in God objective moral principles would be inexplicable. Mackie ... did not have recourse to a theistic foundation for ethical practice. He was left with the dilemma of how it is possible to derive an intrinsically prescriptive quality from a naturalistic view of the world.[81]

Even if an evolutionary account of the origin of ethical values, that the necessity of survival has programed humans to adopt an altruistic response to the absolute requirement to cooperate, was a correct historical deduction from the way things have happened, it would not amount to more than a narration of the past. It would not explain the universal perception that humans are driven by a sense of duty and responsibility, and that a lack of these is morally reprehensible. Theo Hobson makes the discerning consideration that evolution could not have created a moral instinct:

> To say that evolution has given us the ability to understand this "cruel process" (that of evolution) claims too much, for in reality evolution has no discernible role in our tendency to judge this process as cruel ... In reality it sheds no light on why we should oppose the processes it reveals. To talk about this *why*, a totally different discourse is needed.[82]

The truth is that evolution is not a subject. It teaches nothing. It is simply a theory concocted by humans, who are subjects, on the basis of inconclusive bits of evidence. Nor is it legitimate to pretend that nature is a subject by the recourse of writing it with a capital N.

Some secular humanists have recognized that the bridge between "is" and "ought" cannot be built by any form of empirical study, however accurate it may be. Such study may help to inform the context in which ethical decisions have to be made, but it cannot decide on the principles that make them properly grounded and cogent. For example, the pursuit of happiness may be observed to be an almost universal human desire; the observation, however, cannot inform us as to why this is a good end

---

81. Kirk, *Christian Mission as Dialogue*, 117.
82. Hobson, *God Created Humanism*, 18.

to aspire to, or why the pursuit of someone else's well-being should come before my own, or vice versa.

So, collective human experience does not afford the data necessary to determine the ideals of the good and the right and to condemn the bad and the wrong. This is partly the reason why human rights discourse is so ambiguous. On the one hand, rights may be demanded because they fulfill a self-validated entitlement, and yet, on close scrutiny, they are judged as no more than a personal desire. On the other hand, rights terminology has no justifiable, principled basis for deciding between conflicting rights. This is the reason for the intense conflict in the case of abortion between those who promote the right of choice and those who support the right to life. Choice is determined by personal preference, which can hardly be termed a right. Life, however, is determined by a fundamental ethical precept; it is acknowledged as a universal right.[83]

Ethical decision-making requires an objective standard of what is truly good that can only be found in a realm of reality that transcends either individual or collective self-introspection:

> As the naturalist fallacy of trying to derive moral obligation from observation of the facts of a case, for natural facts do not constitute moral facts, (SH) lacks a proper moral ontology, namely that it has no basis for warranting a metaphysics of personhood and its intrinsic dignity or value—this, on the basis of a consistent naturalism, can hardly be a natural property.[84]

It is plainly self-evident that knowledge (justified, true beliefs) of moral facts, such as the wickedness of trafficking children to be exploited for sexual gratification, has no kinship with evidence based on knowledge deduced from scientific experimentation. The latter is highly commendable, not as an end in itself, but as a means to other ends, beyond the scope of science to determine. It possesses no mechanisms to establish either moral virtue or moral vice. These have to find their source in an existence beyond the observable world of the natural, though not necessarily beyond the world of human experience.

---

83. "Everyone has the right to life, liberty and security of person" (Article 3 of *The Universal Declaration of Human Rights*). In the UDHR, individual choice is protected in a number of cases, in order to enhance freedoms. However, individual choice is not regarded as an open invitation to choose anything that a person may desire. The subsequent extension of rights beyond those manifested in the foundation document has led to conflicts of rights, not originally envisaged, with abortion being one of them.

84. Kirk, *Christian Mission as Dialogue*, 119.

Historical investigation shows repeatedly that secular humanists do in fact borrow their ethical principles from beyond all that rational thought on its own can ascertain:

> The conventional story of modernity . . . goes something like this: secular humanism emerged when people gradually dared to question religion and to see that morality could exist without it, on both an individual and a cultural level—they thus discovered the true universal morality, compatible with rationality. What's wrong with this story? It implies that this nonreligious moral vision is natural, is just there, waiting to blossom forth once religion is replaced by rationalism. In reality, this universal humanism was *shaped* by the Christian centuries. Humanitarian ideals are not natural, nor are they rationally deducible; they are complex cultural traditions, brewed over centuries. And the main ingredient in this brewing was the story of God taking the side, even taking the form, of the powerless victim; and the promise that the humble shall be exalted, and the higher sort knocked from their glamorous perches. Only after centuries of this myth having a dominant cultural place did the idea of the equal worth of all human beings begin to seem axiomatic.[85]

Conclusion

It is simply amazing to think that some human beings, with highly developed intellectual powers, can imagine that unplanned, purposeless, natural processes can produce the utter complexity of the human mind, with its sophisticated ability to plumb the depths of moral thought. It is much more rational to conclude that this outcome must have been directed from somewhere else. It is logical, therefore, to conclude that SH falls far short of being able to give a comprehensive and lucid explanation of what causes humans to be able to understand their own experience and the reality that surrounds them. Likewise, it is astonishing to find that secular humanists can believe that theists substitute irrational, delusional faith for sound, sane judgments that alone can pass the test of enlightened rationality. Dylan Evans, a self-confessed atheist, derides this stance as "a torrent of religious bigotry."[86]

---

85. Hobson, *God Created Humanism*, 6–7; emphasis his.
86. Cummings, *Debating Humanism*, 13.

The main problem with SH, in spite of its high-sounding advancement of humane ideals in place of other belief systems which, in its opinion, denigrate them, is its far-too-limited basis for being able to explain the full manifestation of human experience. It fails at a number of levels to supply inferences to the best explanation of the full range of human existence. Sadly, except in a few cases, secular humanists seem to be satisfied with their restricted vision of what it means to be human. We will continue to explore this defect in the final chapter, not to have an intellectual debate for its own sake, but because in real life SH is impoverishing human nature.

Questions

1. To what extent have secular humanists taken over from Christians the task of setting the moral agenda for current Western cultures?
2. On what coherent basis do secular humanists derive their grounding of moral obligations to practice the good and reject the evil?
3. From what credible sources do secular humanists seek to derive their explanation of the widest possible breadth of human experience?
4. What is your personal opinion about the essential differences between secular humanists and Christians concerning the human predicament?

Chapter 11

The Nature and Destiny of Humanity and the Messianic Hope

We serve truth as a whole most effectively, not when we seek to impose religious ideas upon science, nor when we seek to impose scientific ideas on religion, but when studying both religion and the physical world with open and unprejudiced minds we seek to read their lesson."

—WILLIAM TEMPLE, *NATURE MAN AND GOD.*

"It is easy," said Marx, "to be a saint, if you have no wish to be human." But did Marx think it easy to be human without being a saint?

—JACQUES MARITAIN, *TRUE HUMANISM.*

It is not unfair to affirm that modern culture, that is our culture since the Renaissance, is to be credited with the greatest advances in the understanding of nature and with the greatest confusion in the understanding of man . . . Not the least pathetic (of modern assumptions) is the certainty of a naturalistic age that its philosophy is a final philosophy because it rests upon science, a science which betrays ignorance of its own prejudices and failure to recognize the limits of scientific knowledge.

—REINHOLD NIEBUHR, *THE NATURE AND DESTINY OF MAN: VOL. I.*

A supernatural viewpoint does not draw us away from our daily task nor deprive it of importance. On the contrary it offers us a new interpretation of man and his destiny as God's gratuitous gift in Christ. Salvation is not some history different from human history; it is history as interpreted by the message which enables us to comprehend its profundity and destiny.

—JUAN LUIS SEGUNDO, GRACE AND THE HUMAN CONDITION.

Man becomes more human if he is put in the position of being able to abandon his self-deification and his idolatry with all its gains and achievements. It is the critical task of theology to take away from anthropology the absolute and totalitarian element and the legalistic view of salvation.

—JURGEN MOLTMANN, ON BEING HUMAN: CHRISTIAN ANTHROPOLOGY IN THE CONFLICTS OF THE PRESENT.

Preface

SO FAR IN THIS inquiry, I have explored the ideas mainly of prominent Western thinkers from the past five hundred years who have renounced the long-established Christian teaching on the subject of being human. Now is the moment to return to a more contemporary exposition of Christian theory, as it seeks to respond to the often-concerted assault on the Christian faith from the early eighteenth century onward. Times have changed considerably since the eruption of the period known as the Renaissance, even though the seeds of later controversies were being planted in that age. It is only fair, therefore, that a few eminent Christian theologians, who have engaged specifically with modern beliefs on the nature of being human, should be allowed to enter the debate at the end of the five-hundred-year dispute.

The controversy will undoubtedly continue into the future. However, the end of half a millennium is a suitable time to stop the clock momentarily to record, as it were, the state of play in the long-running, often combative, dissent between viewpoints. I have chosen, therefore, in this chapter to consider briefly five theologians' reflections on what it means to be human. Each one, from within a mainstream Christian position, has engaged specifically with contemporary secular thought on the issue in direct conversation with thinking that strongly confronts their own. It is not surprising that the approach occasionally demonstrates a certain polemic; one, however, that is concerned primarily with setting the record straight since secular humanist thought, according to them, is often wide of the mark in its description of Christian belief. Anyone would find that frustrating, for no one likes to be attacked for serious misconceptions about their convictions.

By and large, on the main points in question, the five are in agreement, although they represent different Christian ecclesial traditions: two are Roman Catholics, two are from a Reformed tradition, and one is Anglican. Of course, the choice is personal, but it is not arbitrary. They are all known as being some of the most far-ranging, creative, and arresting theological thinkers of their generation, and all are extremely well-versed in the matter at hand. Needless to say, given the limited space, my exposition of their thoughts will be little more than a thumbnail sketch. In each case it will center on one book that gives sufficient evidence of where they stand. I believe the reader will gain enough understanding to appreciate core Christian thinking about human life, bearing in mind that the enquiry has not, and cannot, ever be terminated. The order follows that of the publication of the works being treated.

William Temple (1881–1944)[1]

The former Archbishop of Canterbury undertook, in the series of lectures he gave, to show why Christians hold that their core beliefs offer the best explanation for the meaning, significance, and value of human life. He engaged critically, with a wealth of erudition, with the most popular belief system of his time (and our time), that which he refers to as "the world-process." He wrote:

> our course hitherto has led us to the conception of a World-Process in which are found, as episodes of the process, minds which apprehend the process.[2]

At other times this system of opinions has been known as a worldview or spirit-of-the-world (*weltgeist*).

---

1. Temple, *Nature, Man and God* (the Gifford Lectures that were delivered in the University of Glasgow in the academic years, 1932–1933 and 1933–1934.
2. Temple, *Nature, Man and God*, 135.

Assumptions

His aim was to open a dialogue across an intellectual divide, which increasingly was splitting thoughtful people into two rather hostile camps: those who believed that the best explanation for human existence resided in the living presence of an eternal Spirit endowed with absolute free will and intelligence, and those who thought that such a hypothesis was, at best, highly conjectural and unprovable and, at worst, irrelevant for making sense of human experience:

> Theology, which is the science of Religion, starts from the supreme Spirit and explains the world by reference to Him. Philosophy starts from the detailed experience of men, and seeks to build up its understanding of that experience by reference to the experience alone. Its inevitable and wholesome kinship to Science inclines it to account for everything by the "lowest" category that will in fact account for it; Theology begins with the "highest" category of all and fits the "lower" categories in the most orderly hierarchy that it can devise in subordination to that "highest" principle.[3]

This distinction is a succinct summary of much of the descriptive analysis presented in all the previous chapters of this book.

Temple believes that the dialogue is a worthwhile undertaking, because all human beings are endowed with a reasoning mind that is, given a willingness to listen to others, able to commune sanely with other minds, accept their interpretation of their views, and respect them. Such a dialogical disposition does not exclude sharp disagreements, for

> let it . . . be frankly and fully recognised that there neither is, nor can be, any element in human experience which may claim exemption from examination at the bar of reason.[4]

The nature of reason and how it functions may be part of the dispute in the conversations. Nevertheless,

> criticism must be sympathetic, or it will completely miss the mark; but it must also be dispassionate and relentless, and nothing whatever must be allowed to escape its universal inquisition.[5]

---

3. Temple, *Nature, Man and God*, 45.
4. Temple, *Nature, Man and God*, 17.
5. Temple, *Nature, Man and God*, 27.

With these short principles of engagement, Temple invites those with fundamentally different presuppositions to enter into a dialogue about the nature and destiny of human beings.

Temple begins with the assumption that

> so far as there is a tension between Religion and either Science or Philosophy, this cannot be due to any of the actual conclusions reached by several sciences within their own spheres ... The main type of that tension ... is not caused by particular doctrines either of Religion or Philosophy, but consists in a sharp difference in mental habit and outlook with reference to the same objects of attention.[6]

If there is to be any meaningful dialogue between divergent world-processes, such an inference is necessary; otherwise the conversation will occur between two totally deaf participants.

Characteristics of Christian Belief

Temple instigates the discussion by expressing his view that divergences are specially evident in relation to three central convictions of religion: that Spirit is a true source of the initiation of processes; that all existence finds its source in a supreme Reality whose nature is Spirit; between that Spirit and ourselves there can be true fellowship.[7] These claims are enough to deny the doctrine of materialism (that the natural order is entirely closed and the only source for verifiable knowledge), and to affirm the notion of creation by the will of a personal God as the reason for the universe's existence. A Christian, moreover, would argue that only such a perception can confirm the reality of the material world.

This core belief in a supreme, independent creator may be false, as many people are convinced that it is, but it is not unreasonable. For people of flesh and blood, immersed in a reality which they perceive and experience through their physical senses, such a concept may be hard to grasp. However, alternative beliefs about the origin and unfolding of the universe—and particularly of a world that has been born and produced life out of inanimate matter and a unique species, *homo sapiens*—are unsatisfactory.

---

6. Temple, *Nature, Man and God*, 34.

7. Temple, *Nature, Man and God*, 35.

THE NATURE AND DESTINY OF HUMANITY

Temple argues that the occurrence of the amazing minds that humans develop, with their incredibly intricate workings, is surely impossible without a cause adequate to bring them into being:

> it has been argued that this occurrence of minds within the process itself is grounded in Mind.[8]

Temple undertakes to test this hypothesis in the context of other suppositions about how they have come to exist.

He proposes that "mind recognises in Truth . . . a proper object of reverence quite other than is appropriate as a part of mind's apprehension of bare fact."[9] He goes on to say that "the sense of moral obligation toward Truth is of that quality which is only appropriate in connexion with personal claims."[10] He concludes this argument by presupposing that

> this quality of reverence for Truth is specially evident among those who have felt bound, out of loyalty to Truth itself . . . to abandon the belief which alone could justify it. It would seem as if there were some potent force compelling in them an attitude of mind which their own convictions have rendered obsolete. All this is intelligible on a basis of avowed Theism, but highly paradoxical on any other.[11]

The Reality of Being Human

As one might expect, Temple engages with actual human experience through observation, both personal and that which emerges from careful research. In this way, he concurs with many perceptions about the way humans generally think about themselves and behave, whatever their fundamental values and principles may be. At the same time, due to his basic theistic convictions, he perceives a wider vision of human actuality (such as the fact that all humans are constituted in the image of a personal, spiritual, supreme Being) through the lens of theistically grounded core beliefs.

---

8. Temple, *Nature, Man and God*, 135.
9. Temple, *Nature, Man and God*, 249.
10. Temple, *Nature, Man and God*, 250.
11. Temple, *Nature, Man and God*, 251.

To begin with, then, "human beings act differently (from any other living creature) because they are conscious and self-conscious."[12] As they move from actual observation of their surroundings to reflection upon them, they fall behind the facts they are accumulating. A child, for example, develops its own self-consciousness by becoming aware of the distinction between a subject and object in its experience. Consciousness first arises in a form centered on the emotions, not so much as knowledge or as purpose, but as a reaction to its significance in terms of pleasure and pain.

From the beginning of intellectual life, the mind has its being in an actual apprehension of a world first realized in consciousness through its emotions. Through the medium of social contacts, expressed in language, the child begins to unify its many experiences. The key to learning is that all that is perceived, whether through scientific disciplines or artistic imagination, is there from the outset. That is why consciousness presupposes experience, rather than the reverse. Nonhuman living creatures take their surroundings for granted. For the most part, they do not mull over the nature of the existence into which they were born. Humans, however, constantly inquire; the why questions come naturally to children as young as two—"Why is it thus and not otherwise?"[13]

The concrete person can be characterized as

> a self-organizing system of impulses, instincts, sentiments, emotions, ideas, and all the rest that psychological analysis may set out . . . Consciousness is itself psychological . . . in other words cannot be accounted for without remainder in terms of pure physiology, for this does not allow for causation operating on the present from the anticipated future.[14]

Growth into maturity requires a process in which order is imposed upon the free exercise of a riot of disorder. This is supplied by the human will, which appears first as exercising constraint on impulses and desires, through the making of resolutions and keeping them. The will is that part of a person's nature that chooses, decides, and carries out certain courses of action, rather than others. One of the main functions of education is

---

12. Temple, *Nature, Man and God*, 37.

13. These reflections on consciousness and self-consciousness are found in Temple's thoughts on the world as it is apprehended by the human mind (*Nature, Man and God*, 121–31).

14. Temple, *Nature, Man and God*, 231.

to fashion it. This requires discipline in the processes of parental care and teaching methods and self-discipline in acquiring the ability to change thought processes and behavior:

> If (the will) is set on selfish ambitions or carnal pleasures . . . (this) fact precludes it from changing direction; it cannot change because it does not will to change; if it did will to change, that itself would be the change.[15]

The will constitutes the person's moral agent. Humans find in themselves the reality of good and evil. Sometimes this distinction is confused, particularly when a young person is trying to make sense of responsibility. Why, for example, do children often blame themselves for the breakup of their parents' marriage, when actually they are the victims, not the perpetrators? The human mind does not act purposively only in tracing out logical correlations and observing sequences (as in scientific investigations), but also in making value judgments.[16] Scientific procedures are achieved by following routine methods, honed in the course of cumulative research; moral discernment depends upon the unique human capacity to transcend personal acts and requires an intellectual basis that goes beyond the collection of pure data. Hence the well-known maxim that what ought to be done cannot be deduced directly from what is:

> Personality in a grown man shows its special quality neither in mechanical constancy of reaction, such as that of those who always, or never, fall in with suggestions made to them, nor in caprice, so that they are unreliable, but in a discriminating control of action in the light of accepted principles.[17]

Morality

Moral thought and activity have to do with arriving at the most satisfactory accepted principles of virtuous action as possible, and the avoidance of all forms of vice. To a large extent, the discernment of good and evil depends on the commitment of a person, community, or nation to a particular way of seeing the meaning of life. Where core beliefs conflict, controversies are bound to break out. One key area is that of the origin

---

15. Temple, *Nature, Man and God*, 234.
16. Temple, *Nature, Man and God*, 277, 280, 284.
17. Temple, *Nature, Man and God*, 289.

and nature of evil. It is a problem, not only for theists as is sometimes imagined, but also for secularists.

Temple takes a bleak attitude toward the problem of evil. It assumes, he believes, an overwhelming dilemma for the human race. However hard people may strive to eliminate evil thoughts from their minds and evil actions from their daily lives, they fail. How is it that evil is part of human existence? Why are not all our thoughts and actions benevolent and benign, not just occasionally, but at all times and in all circumstances? It appears that the mind is naturally warped and the will is too weak to save it from committing malicious acts that the mind then finds reason to justify, thus adding to the sum total of dishonesty.

For Temple, the cause of evil in specific cases is the product of exaggerated or misdirected desire. Even cruel acts are committed because they appear to be good as the means of gratifying the lust for self-assertion or to allay panic or fear. A person's character determines the apparent good at any moment, and the apparent good determines conduct. However, the apparent good is often not the real good[18] (as dependence on alcohol or recreational drugs or sexual promiscuity illustrates).

The reality of evil, as the acceptance of a seeming good in place of a real good, demonstrates a bias toward evil rooted in human nature:

> theologians have called this Original Sin; and if those words mean that every human being has in one respect or another such a . . . tendency to evil, they do not stand for a mysterious doctrine but for an evident . . . fact.[19]

We are reminded that, in the Hebrew Scriptures, the prophets trace this to "an evil imagination." In modern parlance, we might speak of a self-centeredness that manifests itself as self-assertion when people choose for their own good what satisfies them, even though it may have damaging consequences for others.

What remedies has the human race conceived to try to eliminate or curtail this evil imagination? Educational systems are designed not only to impart knowledge, but more importantly to inculcate civility (i.e., a kind, caring, and compassionate attitude toward all other humans). The law and the punishments for breaking it may make people aware of the limits to self-regarding motives and action by demonstrating the need to be protected by the law from the selfishness of others. But systems of

---

18. Temple, *Nature, Man and God*, 361–62.
19. Temple, *Nature, Man and God*, 363, 364.

justice are often quite defective in defining what is a right or wrong action, what it is permissible to say, or how the law is administered. Is it, for example, conducted with total impartiality, and as an ideal before whom everyone is equal?

Education and the law may be able to curtail to some extent external manifestations of malign behavior. Nevertheless, Temple contends that

> we totally misconceive alike the philosophic and the practical problem of evil if we picture it as the winning of control over lawless and therefore evil passions by a righteous but insufficiently powerful reason or spirit. It is the spirit which is evil; it is reason which is perverted; it is aspiration itself which is corrupt.[20]

> The devices of education aim at keeping passion in check while the development of reason is hastened. At last it may be hoped that reason will take complete control, and then all will be well. Of course that picture is not wholly false. But it is more false than true, because it misses the vital point. That point is that reason itself as it exists in us is vitiated. We wrongly estimate the ends of life, and give preference to those which should be subordinate, because they have a stronger appeal to our actual, empirical selves.[21]

There can be, as a consequence, no perfection in life, nor salvation, without the total elimination of self-centeredness through disinterested love. Corruption and perversion is not so far gone that human nature is totally insensitive to all forms of goodness, otherwise redemption would be impossible and self-forgetful love nonexistent.

The Christian faith refuses to dilute the strength of evil or excuse its corruption. That is one main reason why it is so vilified by people who have no convincing way of contending with evil's perversity. Their denigration, however, merely confirms the reality of a deceitful hypocrisy that is rightly directed against all of us. People will invent all kinds of devious ways of diminishing its seriousness, at least in their own lives, particularly by self-righteous self-justification. The attitude is summed up brilliantly by Jesus in his story of the religious practitioner and the transgressor:

---

20. Temple, *Nature, Man and God*, 368.
21. Temple, *Nature, Man and God*, 368.

> God, I thank you that I am not like other people: thieves, rogues, adulterers... I fast twice a week; I give a tenth of all my income.[22]

One may comfort oneself to a certain extent by the practice of comparing one's life favorably with that of others, thus betraying the very self-deception one is attempting to avoid:

> Self-cure is impossible. The man is free, for the origin of his actions is himself; yet he is bound hand and foot, for from himself there is no escape.[23]

The Resolution of Evil

It is an almost universal truth that the greatest argument against the existence of God, if one exists, is that such a supreme Being should be endowed with the greatest possible compassion for the creation he is supposed to have generated, and possess all the power necessary to direct the world in accordance with this compassion, and yet he has created it in such a way that evil and innocent suffering is possible. Such a reality would seem to show that such a God could not exist, for he would lack perfection. If someone, not knowing anything of God, came from outer space to earth, he or she might conclude that whoever created the world made a mess of it. The experiment seems to have gone hopelessly wrong. Either God is not in control, or he is not morally virtuous. If he could have built a world without evil and suffering, but has not done so, does that not prove that evil originated in his will?

Temple takes up this challenge that the actual world—every day, every hour—denies the evidence that the creator of all is free to design a world of living creatures free from suffering, misery, and distress:

> Religious people are driven to ask why God permits the occurrence of events that involve apparently useless waste and sorrow.[24]

The principal response to this powerful objection to a theist's highly problematical claim about the God he believes in begins with a hypothesis and centers on the nature of God. The hypothesis is that the God who

---

22. Luke 18:11–12.
23. Temple, *Nature, Man and God*, 241.
24. Temple, *Nature, Man and God*, 291.

creates, sustains, and recreates living matter is actually perfectly good. This being so, the accusation that the evidence contradicts this has to be answered. The best explanation that can be given is that God has built free action into the working of nature, for that is his nature:

> If in any sense man has freedom to choose and to act on his choice, this of itself involves a breach in the rigid uniformity of nature. I am free to choose whether I shall stand still or walk across the room. If I choose the latter, I effect a redistribution of the mass of the world and shift its centre of gravity. That I only do so to an extent negligible in the most precise astronomical calculation possible to man, does not affect the principle. And if I can do this to any extent at all, then God, if he exists, can do it to any extent that He pleases.[25]

In other words, the world is not created mechanistically, without any variability, and human beings are not made to function as though they were robots. Such a world would, actually, deny its appropriateness for the existence of real humans, turning them into automatons and zombies. There would be nothing to admire, nothing to achieve. There would be nothing good and, by logical implication, nothing evil, for no belief or act would carry any responsibility with it.

Were it not for the existence of evil, goodness would not be able to flourish. It is often said by ethicists that evil is the absence of the good. The reverse is also true: goodness is understood in contrast to wrongdoing; evil highlights its opposite. In the absence of evil, goodness is shorn of its sharpness and outstanding nature. We should not conclude, however, that evil is thereby justified, because it may promote a greater good.

Finally, God has shown historically and conclusively that he is not indifferent to the pain and suffering caused by evil. In Jesus Christ, God has freely exposed himself and experienced the full horror of evil. He has born it in his own person, and thus created a means of escaping its tragic consequences:

> The presence of evil can enhance the excellence of what on the whole is good, and the event or act which in isolation is evil can be itself an integral and contributing part of a whole which, as a whole is good.[26]

---

25. Temple, *Nature, Man and God*, 295.
26. Temple, *Nature, Man and God*, 358.

Even those who do not accept what Christians proclaim to be the truth about Jesus, are likely to judge, if they have a coherent understanding of justice, that his trial, condemnation, and crucifixion were by normal standards of virtue, highly malevolent acts,

> supremely bad when taken in isolation, but when taken as part of the whole scheme of things of which it is the pivot, it is supremely good.[27]

Some may not agree with the last sentiment; very few, however, will consider the Jesus portrayed in the only substantial historical accounts we have of him to be anything but a supremely good person, whose influence, if taken seriously, would be morally exemplary.

So, unless humans experience evil as well as good, there would be no way of being able to distinguish one from the other, nor say why one is to be commended and the other condemned. If evil was imaginary, only a thought experiment, but never a reality, morality would effectively collapse.

Evil, then, is a trial to be overcome. The Christian answer is clear and precise. The innate, self-centered imagination that rules personality has to be changed from the inside out. Only submission to the active, unconditional, and wholly just love of God, consequent upon Jesus' offering of himself in death to atone for sin, is sufficient to conquer the ingrained, self-seeking nature of human beings. Within the world as it is, a new world is also evident, where true righteousness is paramount.

"To thine own self be true"[28] is a piece of high-class ethical futility which Shakespeare appropriately puts into the mouth of his own most priceless old dotard.[29]

> Your being is personal; live as a person in fellow-membership with all others who, being personal, are your fellow-members in the community of persons. Strive to grow in the fullness of personality, in width and depth of fellowship; and seek to draw the energy for this from that to which you and all things owe their origin, the Personal Love which is creator and Sustainer of the world.[30]

---

27. Temple, *Nature, Man and God*, 358.
28. Shakespeare, *Hamlet*, Act I, scene 3, line 9 (the words are those of Polonius).
29. Temple, *Nature, Man and God*, 26.
30. Temple, *Nature, Man and God*, 196.

The final sentence from this quote distinguishes two separate humanities who inhabit two potentially different domains: those who believe and act on the reality of this personal love who has dealt finally with the reality of evil and is working for their good, and those who do not care for his involvement in their lives. This might suffice as a summary of Temple's treatise on Nature, Man (and Woman), and God.

Jacques Maritain (1882-1973)[31]

Our second exponent of the Christian faith's view of human significance was a French Roman Catholic philosopher. His academic studies incorporated the natural sciences, aesthetics, political theory, philosophy of science, metaphysics, and moral philosophy, as well as aspects of church teaching. He is best known both within and outside Christian circles for his major contribution to the drafting of the *Universal Declaration of Human Rights*.

Humanism

Whilst studying at the Sorbonne, Maritain met and eventually married (in 1904) a Russian Jewish emigre called Raissa Oumancoff. They became disillusioned with the limitations of scientism (science, as a method of investigation, is presumed to offer a complete account of the whole of reality) to explain the full meaning of human life. As a result, they made a pact to commit suicide together after one year if they could not find a deeper meaning to life more convincing than that offered by the unreserved confidence of some scientists in the ability of science alone to give a wholly adequate account of all life's experiences. They were released from their pact by listening to the lectures first of the philosopher Henri Bergson, and later by their encounter with the Roman Catholic faith.

Thirty years later, Jacques Maritain confronted the secular humanist worldview, which he interpreted as the philosophical rendering of what he considered to be the myth of scientism. He began his thesis by assuming that there are two main intellectual reflections on being human that have been in contention since the Renaissance. The consciousness of one's humanity differs enormously if one confines it entirely to the

---

31. Maritain, *True Humanism*. The book has also been published under the title of *Integral Humanism*.

natural world or if one holds that its fullest expression requires a sense of a reality beyond space and time. It is impossible to encompass entirely the experience of being human unless one bows before an authentic personal Being, existing from all eternity. Genuine personhood cannot be discovered fully unless it is encountered in an existence beyond its physical embodiment alone.

Whereas secular humanism by definition has to be anti-religious, for Maritain, Western humanism springs from religious and transcendental sources. By transcendental he means "all those forms of thought, however otherwise diverse which find the true principle of the world in a Spirit greater than man."[32] He interpreted the Renaissance as being the beginning of the modern anthropocentric rehabilitation of the creature. It transformed the previous worldview from centering on God as the finally significant implication of all things, to revolving round what can be learned about human nature by human reason alone.

As Maritain summarized the magnitude of the change, the new humanism sought to save human freedom at the expense of divine causality on the grounds that submission to the divine would inescapably mean the loss of humanity's own control of its destiny, and therefore of its humanity. From then on, two kinds of humanism struggled for supremacy: theocentric and anthropocentric. However, the problem is not in claiming a true humanism for one's own view, but in discerning its authentic source.

Autonomous humanism sets up an image of the human person which is inviolable, jealous of its own imminence, and good in its essence. In name of absolute rights and self-determination, rationalism condemns any intervention from outside its own self-appointed sphere of mortal being. Writing in the 1930s, Maritain found the most representative expression of this type of humanism in contemporary Soviet atheism: shallow and bourgeois. In its liberal form (as represented by Marxist thinkers in Western democratic societies) it makes the opinions of each individual the only source of all right and truth. It has shown itself to be capable of creating an almost religious devotion, whilst in actual practice it lives by anything other than that which could be characterized by religion.

---

32. Maritain, *True Humanism*, xv.

The Human Condition

Following the thinking of Nietzsche and Freud, Maritain interprets contemporary secular humanism in terms of the world of instinct and desire. The human person lives in the intersection of the conflict between a primary sexual libido and the desire for death. They struggle to free themselves from the pain of earthly existence, in order to attain a state of bliss in this life, for there is no other. This kind of humanism, says Maritain, "ends in despair and the decomposition of human personality; carries atheism, anthropocentrism and immanentism to an extreme point of exasperation."[33]

Fundamentally, those who have rejected a transcendent reality as the supreme explanation of being human have been deceived. If humanity lived entirely within its own limited boundaries, having dismissed all reference to knowledge coming from beyond its own self-induced reach, it would end up in self-destructive chaos and dissolution. Humanity carries the burden of original sin, wounded in its nature, ignorant of the role of God as the true source of everyone's humanity and of creative liberty. It lives by a twisted appreciation of God as creator and genuine liberator.

Because of the weakness of our species, evil occurs more frequently than good; it is the statistical law of human behavior. In Christian civilization, there have been more bad than good Christians. By means of a sociological naturalization of religion, Christianity has been transformed into a utility for wholly secular ends, such as gaining secular power, wealth, property, and privileges for itself.[34] Only sporadically have Christians recaptured their ministry to live for the well-being of the disadvantaged poor.

Christian Integral Humanism

Maritain boldly outlines an alternative humanism to that which has gained a controlling perspective on social and moral integrity in the modern world. He seeks to determine, from the standpoint of modern history, the concrete and practical position and destiny of the human person as a creature before God. He is confident that, were humanism to revert to its proper Christian roots, living in the light of the teaching and

---

33. Maritain, *True Humanism*, 73.
34. Maritain, *True Humanism*, 104, 110.

action of Jesus, to serve others in a generous and self-sacrificing spirit, a new humanism could be born that would challenge and change the influence of liberal, bourgeois ends and means.

Ambitiously, Maritain proposes a new Christendom[35] which will be secular in the sense of according no special privilege to the Christian church, and communal in the sense of always searching for programs and projects that promote the common good and are superior to individual interests. His desire is to promote the rebirth of civilization as a social reality in which the human person, whatever his or her position in the world, is treated as equally precious in the sight of a God whose image they bear. It is, however, impossible that such a rebirth could happen without the destruction of the evil within the human being. If humans continue to deceive themselves, denying the destructive and irrational elements of their nature, pretending, rather, that it is possible to sidestep the corrupt aspects of their characters, there is no hope of escaping from the vicious circle of illusion and deception.

Sin is a natural occurrence within the human consciousness. It is at its peak when the individual refuses to recognize that it exists in his or her case. It comprises a forlorn effort to pretend that our conscience may be commendable and we may rest content with ourselves. Maritain characterizes this state as most clearly seen in petit-bourgeois liberalism.

He has a number of running skirmishes with the ideals of communist ideology, mainly because it is clear that it badly misconceives the way out of the contemporary predicament of human alienation. He says:

> communism hopes to change the old regime mechanically from without, by technical and social means, by pedagogy and propaganda.[36]

Whereas the Christian, following the teaching of Jesus, knows that the deep impediment facing honest change lies within human nature:

---

35. To use the term "Christendom" in the light of a post-Constantinian social and political order is to demonstrate naivety. Secular people would dismiss the idea as a recapitulation of the false attempts by Christian institutions to control the whole of life: personal, private, and public. However, a careful reading of Maritain will show that such an ambition is far from his purpose. He places his Christian humanistic aspirations firmly within a democratic, pluralistic social order that does not seek to impose its own values, but persuade citizens that they are the most productive for the most thriving community possible, within the limitations of a wayward human essence.

36. Maritain, *True Humanism*, 72.

> Listen to me, all of you, and understand: there is nothing outside a person that by going in can defile, but the things that come out are what defile . . . for it is from within . . . that evil intentions come: fornication, theft, murder, adultery, avarice, wickedness, deceit, licentiousness, envy, slander, pride, folly. All these things come from within, and they defile a person.[37]

And the profound dilemma does not lie only in the willingness to admit one's own guilt for one's own unrighteousness in thought and deed, but to know what to do about it. How can the wound be healed without a remedy from outside the human person, whose source is absolutely pure?

So, Maritain's version of humanism implies that human beings have to be changed from within by the grace of God, for there is no other power capable of effecting the change. However, they have to wish to be changed. Change is not intended only for individual moral conversion, but for interpersonal relationships and, insofar as is possible, structural relationships. Although it sounds utopian, Maritain hails the challenge as that of installing the sociotemporal realization of the Christian message.[38]

Maritain makes it absolutely clear that his vision of the future is not intended to Christianize Marx's historical dialectic, in which the end product of a socialist revolution turns out to be a society in which those who expend their human power in their employed labor own the means of production and rule society. He does not either wish to defend a modified, softer version of bourgeois capital in which the investors in industry share with the workforce by far the largest percentage of the wealth created by industry.

He criticizes Marxism for continually failing to see that the material conditions, causing the misery of bourgeois society, are not the prime causality of human estrangement. Marx speaks of the infrastructure of capitalist economic organization being planted firmly in the soil of the organization of the means of production. However, even using his language and concepts, this organization was merely the superstructure. The real infrastructure, the one true impulse, that drives capitalism to wreak the economic and social havoc that it does among sections of the population of an industrialized society, has a spiritual and moral basis.[39]

---

37. Mark 7:14–15, 20–23.
38. Maritain, *True Humanism*, 86.
39. Maritain, *True Humanism*, 37–42.

Marx recognized this in his own "spiritual" indignation at the oppressive conditions which humans had to suffer in the work of their hands. Nevertheless, Marx was sure that "the cessation of inhuman conditions of the proletariat did not happen in the name of personality (spiritual dignity rooted in transcendental rights and interests), but in the name of collective man." [40] So, both capitalism and Marxism, for different reasons, in attempting to solve the problem of class enmity, have placed the cart before the horse:

> Marxist humanism is reduced to a mere emotional connotation, a certain messianic claim, and his idea of revolution a secular transposition of the last judgment and the kingdom of God.[41]

> Bourgeois humanism rejects asceticism and claims to replace it by a technical or technological one, which aims at peace without conflict, at an indefinite progress in a perpetual harmony and satisfaction, made in the image of the non-existent man of rationalism.[42]

The New Christendom describes a certain secular Christian concept of a temporal order. It is opposed to the liberalism and humanism of an anthropocentric age. Rather, it reflects the fruits of a theocentric humanism. One of its visions is to restore a family type of economy and ownership under modern forms, in which the primary relationship will be between ownership of the means of production and those exercising their labor-power within the manufacturing process. The purpose of the accumulation of capital is not to increase wealth and redistribute it to the few who extend their economic power at the expense of others, but to enable all in the workplace to possess a full share in the company, in a just allocation of the company's profits, in its ownership, and in its governance. The purpose of production is not to maximize profits, whatever the cost to the well-being of the workers (long work hours, low wages, poor conditions), but to promote their well-being by incorporating them in decision making and recompensing their work with an acceptable income.

Small- and moderate-sized experiments in worker partnership have been successfully undertaken, which have steered between

---

40. Maritain, *True Humanism*, 39.
41. Maritain, *True Humanism*, 50.
42. Maritain, *True Humanism*, 51.

state-controlled industries, companies split between owners and trade unions, and those controlled by a small group of proprietors keen to maintain a strict line between employers and employees. The purposes of the state are to defend its citizens against external aggression, monitor the health of the economy, preserve and enforce humane and just laws, offer a universal health service at the point of need, provide an education system of high quality, and to collect and utilize taxes to fulfill these objectives.

A vision of this nature appears idealistic. In view of all that has been said about the evil spawned by self-interest, reality would seem to demonstrate its unworkable nature. Maritain puts forward a social and economic model that, if operated, would create a society in which everyone thought the best of their neighbors and colleagues:

> There would be a social guarantee to bring into action what is functionally and inalienably the property of the worker: his personal powers, intelligence the skill of his hands . . . Such form of possession rouses in us primordial feelings, which are at the base of natural law: the desire to see work well done and the dignity of work. It represents an effective economic defense for the activity and liberty of the person, not to be at the mercy of the moment. It is implied in the worker's intellect in the management. It presupposes "associative" ownership of the means of production . . . personal democracy, suffrage and personal participation of all interests . . . [It is] founded on the notion of a moral personality at once autonomous and subordinate.[43]

To come anywhere near such a dream, the implementation of a unique Christian humanism among the whole population would be required:

> When we adopt a Christian philosophy of man, of work, of the ownership of material goods, the whole aspect of these important economic problems changes its meaning.[44]

Such a humanism is utterly remote from the self-interested, pleasure-seeking individualism that has grown exponentially over the last half century in Western nations. The idea of working for a New Christendom, inspired first and foremost by a God-centered generosity and kindness, is far from most people's minds and agendas:

---

43. Maritain, *True Humanism*, 183, 184.
44. Maritain, *True Humanism*, 189.

There is no more anti-political frame of mind than a profound distaste for the idea of a fraternal amity entertained by enemies of the Gospel.[45]

Maritain himself was a major contributor to the founding of the Christian Democrat political tradition, seeking to stimulate, at least in part, the implementation of a New Christendom in modern dress. Nevertheless, he remained substantially pessimistic about the considerable changes that would be necessary to achieve some of the ends:

> Modern civilization is a worn-out vesture: it is not a question of sewing on patches here and there, but of a total and substantial reformation, a trans-valuation of its cultural principles... What is needed is a change from primacy of quality over quantity, of work over money, of human over technical means, of wisdom over science in the common service of human beings.[46]

Reinhold Niebuhr (1892-1971)

For a person who taught theology for over 30 years at Union Theological College in New York (1928-1960), Niebuhr had an unusual influence on social ethics and political philosophy. His own thought and commitments changed quite remarkably over his lifetime, mainly from a liberal idealism that held that human beings were in essence perfectible, to a radical Christian realism. In the latter case, he expounded the depths of human depravity and its negative consequences for community well-being (as, for example, in the deeply ingrained racism of the Southern U.S.A. in the 1950s and 1960s) and for international relations.

Toward the beginning of the Second World War, Niebuhr rejected his consistent pacifism and advocated the U.S. joining the coalition of nations fighting to defeat Germany and Japan. After the war, he disengaged himself from the utopianism of socialist doctrine, taking a strong stance against the ideology and policies of Soviet communism. His changed thinking on the most fundamental aspects of human nature had a profound influence on his social, political, and economic theories; these he translated into practical policies. He strongly influenced some of the political and cultural leaders of the Western world during the latter thirty

---

45. Maritain, *True Humanism*, 200.
46. Maritain, *True Humanism*, 201.

years of his life, such as Arthur Schlesinger Jr., Dean Acheson, Martin Luther King Jr., Jimmy Carter, Madeleine Albright, and Barack Obama. He also made a positive impact on Dietrich Bonhoeffer, one of the principal Christian leaders in the resistance to Hitler and Nazism.

His most celebrated writing was probably *Moral Man and Immoral Society: A Study of Ethics and Politics*.[47] However, his most penetrating publication on the subject of human character was undoubtedly the two-volume Gifford Lectures of 1939, *The Nature and Destiny of Man: A Christian Interpretation*.[48]

General Comments on Being Human

Niebuhr begins with a basic question: "What is the character of the ultimate subject, the quintessential 'I,' which passes such devastating judgments on itself as object?"[49] As *homo faber*, a tool-making animal, humans stand outside nature in a way no other living being does. Also humans' rational capacity involves a further ability to stand outside themselves, and the capacity for transcendence (i.e., to make themselves their own object).

Niebuhr makes a general historical observation that modern culture has taken the form of a battleground between two opposing views: one stemming from the Renaissance, and the other, the Reformation. He then uses the book to explain what he means by this broad observation. From a Christian perspective

> human nature is involved in the paradox of claiming a higher stature for man and of taking a more serious view of his evil than any other anthropology.[50]

Neither Nietzsche nor Freud, whom he influenced, had a good opinion about human nature. They were pessimistic. Yet they, and many others, considered egotism and the will to power, in view of bourgeois liberalism, normal and normative.

---

47. Niebuhr, *Moral Man and Immoral Society*.

48. Niebuhr, *Nature and Destiny of Man*. The quotes in this book are taken from the earliest edition. This study of Niebuhr's anthropology will be selected from the first volume: *The Nature of Man (NOM)*.

49. Niebuhr, *Nature and Destiny of Man*, 2.

50. Niebuhr, *Nature and Destiny of Man*, 18.

The human being enters the natural world as a starkly different creature from all others. Nonhuman nature only experiences an endless repetition of events, propelled by instinct. Human animals, however, are free to transcend natural forms, within certain limits, and direct their vitalities. They are able to create new forms and new realms of coherence and order.[51] To the essential nature of humans belong all their natural endowments, physical and social impulses, sexual and racial differentiations, their entire characters. It also includes the freedom of their spirit and their self-transcendence. It ceases to be an object, serviceable to self; it is itself a subject, a unique center of life and purpose—there is an I and a Thou. Humans, nevertheless, are caught in the tension of creative reason and destructive reflexes. The natural impulse of sex exemplifies this strain: it is both the condition for all higher forms of family organization and also leads to the destructive forces of sexual deviations and exploitations.

The Reality of Evil in the Human Inner Being and Its Causes

Within modern Western cultures it is not congenial to reflect on and speak about the dark side of life, unless perhaps it happens a long way away from our normal experience of life and we can gain some pleasure by exercising a self-righteous condemnation of others' misdeeds. However, the reality and nature of evil cannot be evaded. It is as much part of our encounter with the world as any other aspect of life.

For Niebuhr, evil is the result of human freedom. It would be wholly misplaced to accuse any nonhuman animal of being evil. They may be violent and, from a human point of view, cruel. They are not, however, morally culpable for the suffering and injury they cause to other sentient beings. Evil is serious in human beings alone, because it is placed at the center of the human psyche: the will. It is not the consequence of finiteness, flowing from the contingencies and necessities of nature. If the essence of the human being is its freedom, and evil is committed within that freedom, it cannot be attributable to his essence.

> It can only be understood as a contradiction, made possible by the fact of his freedom but not following necessarily from it.[52]

---

51. Niebuhr, *Nature and Destiny of Man*, 27–28.
52. Niebuhr, *Nature and Destiny of Man*, 18.

One of the deepest problems for modern humanists is how they can give an account of the origin and nature of evil. The problem arises mainly because Western culture can no longer make sense of the language of sin. To speak meaningfully about sin it is necessary to believe in the eternal existence of a perfectly good and just God, for sin refers to the breaking of a relationship with this God:

> The whole burden of the prophetic message is that there is only one God . . . and that the sin of man consists in the vanity and pride by which he imagines himself, his nations, his cultures, his civilizations to be divine . . . The catastrophes of history by which God punishes this pride . . . are the natural and inevitable consequences of men's effort to transcend their mortal and insecure existence and to establish a security to which man has no right.[53]

In other words, according to Niebuhr, since the time of the Renaissance, sin is not recognized in these terms by culture in general. Modern anthropology is optimistic about evil. It inculcates an easy conscience:

> Nothing gives the diverse and discordant notes of modern culture so much harmony as the unanimous opposition of modern man to Christian conceptions of the sinfulness of man. The idea that man is sinful at the very centre of his personality, that is in his will, is universally rejected.[54]

Nevertheless, sin is laid bare in everyday life by the negative consequences that it inevitably brings. God's existence may be refuted. Nevertheless, in everyday life, God's judgments are delivered by creating the circumstances in which humans reap the grave effects of what they shamefully sow.[55] Sin and evil are sure signs of the permanent reality of a moral universe in which the standards of right and wrong are set by the God who brought everything into being. Christian faith provokes an uneasy conscience, for it both understands the reality of evil within oneself, and also escapes from the error of attributing it to anyone but oneself.[56]

Thus, since the Renaissance, the Western world has been divided into two camps. First, there are those whose outlook on human life is

---

53. Niebuhr, *Nature and Destiny of Man*, 148, 149.

54. Niebuhr, *Nature and Destiny of Man*, 24.

55. Rom 1:24, 26, 28; Gal 6:7-8.

56. A brilliant literary example of this unsettled conscience is given in Thomas Hardy's characters, Jude Fawley and Sue Bridehead, in his novel *Jude the Obscure*.

basically optimistic. Humans are essentially good and sufficient within themselves:

> The sense of sin is, in the phrase of a particularly vapid modern social scientist, "a psychopathic aspect of adolescent mentality."[57]

They are, moreover, the judge of all things. God has become redundant; there is no higher being in the universe than *homo sapiens*.[58] There are others who believe that such a superficial view of the reality of sin and the nature of evil exemplifies an inherited moral blindness:

> Contemporary history is filled with manifestations of man's hysterias and furies, with evidence of his daemonic capacity and inclination to break the harmonies of nature and defy the prudent canons of rational restraint. Yet no cumulation of contradictory evidence seems to disturb modern man's good opinion of himself.[59]

Niebuhr painted a dismal and depressing picture of "man's inhumanity to man." He listed three key pictures of sin. Firstly, *self-glorification* (i.e., the sin of pride, the lust for power and intellectual pride, all fueled by insecurity) the besetting sin of bourgeois society. Humans are tempted to deny the finiteness of knowledge in order to escape the skepticism it threatens. Secondly, *the pride of virtue*, or moral self-righteousness. Humans are tempted to dismiss God in order that they may boost their self-esteem and reign supreme. An unbridled human assertion needs to eliminate religion. Thirdly, *sensuality*. It leads to the destruction of an inner harmony by the self's undue identification with, and devotion to, particular impulses and desires. It is expressed in inordinate love for all creaturely and mutable values, resulting primarily from self-love, lack of moderation, and lack of discipline in sexual adventures and in

---

57. Niebuhr, *Nature and Destiny of Man*, 100.

58. One of the results of this view of reality has come to the fore in the last fifty years or so. Given that humans alone decide what is right or wrong, if something is declared *legal* by an act of Parliament, it must be good and legitimate.

59. Niebuhr, *Nature and Destiny of Man*, 100. Niebuhr was giving the lectures in April, May, and October of 1939, when the persecution of the Jews by the Nazi regime was increasing. Hitler had invaded Poland and Czechoslovakia just when the oppression and subjugation of all supposed enemies of the Soviet Communist regime were being exposed in the Gulag Archipelago.

accumulating possessions. It is the aberration of sex that creates shame, not sex as such. Sensuality is used as an attempt to escape from shame and guilt.[60]

The Christian Understanding of Human Existence

As would be expected, the characteristics of being human are perceived, first and foremost, from God's perspective, not from that of either nature or reason. The most fundamental ontological claim made by the Bible is that human beings are created in the image of God. God is Spirit who possesses will and personality. God is the ultimate reality in whose presence all of life is possible and explicable. God's being, as revealed through the history and message of the people of Israel, Jesus the Messiah, and the early church, is the lens through which all that is obscure in human experience becomes clear.

Coming into the world in God's image means that every human being is predisposed to know and love God and communicate with him. It also means that humans are set up to think and act in particular ways. It is only as they conform to this image that they are able to be completely fulfilled as humans. God's original creation was exceedingly good, but the world became corrupt when humans decided to use their God-given freedom to turn against his perfect plan for them. Sin springs from humans' determination not to submit to God's will. This means that

> the world is not evil because it is temporal ... the body is not the source of sin in man ... individuality as a separate and particular existence is not evil by reason of being distinguished from undifferentiated totality, and that death is no evil though it is an occasion for evil, namely the fear of death.[61]

It also means that humans, who refuse God's call to seek intimacy with him, are not made free to do as they wish, but are deprived of their freedom. They are consigned to self-centeredness, ignorance, and complacency. They lack the one compass that can guide them surely to the truth about existence. Knowledge of the good is what fits perfectly with all that is best for fulfilling the way they have been designed to flourish:

---

60. Niebuhr, *Nature and Destiny of Man*, 190–255 (chs. 7 and 8, "Man as Sinner").
61. Niebuhr, *Nature and Destiny of Man*, 179.

> The freedom of man creates the possibility of actions which are contrary to, and in defiance of, the requirements of his essential nature.[62]

This is the supreme tragedy that has invaded humans in the depths of their being. They refuse to be governed by absolute goodness and, as a consequence, exchange their own ideas and ideals for the perfection they could achieve if they lived in God's light. The problem is that they have turned to nature as the only verifiable source of wisdom and their own reason as its interpreter. However, nature is devoid of knowledge; it only yields data. Reason is corrupted and cannot be relied on to make true sense of perception.

Niebuhr claims that real human individuality can only be maintained within the parameters of a prophetic religion. It interprets history from beyond history. The individual has a place within a world of meaning, even when particular historical moments disintegrate:

> The unique individual finds the contingent and arbitrary aspect of his existence tolerable because it is . . . judged and redeemed by the eternal God, who transcends both the rational structure and the arbitrary facts of existence in the universe.

In the words of the psalmist, two of the most fundamental truths about human life come together:

> For with you (O God) is the fountain of life; in your light we see light.[63]

The human being is created and sustained by the one and only God ("the fountain of life") and is the source of all true understanding ("in your light we see light").

An Analysis of Modern Understandings of Being Human

Niebuhr, as already mentioned, believed that the modern view arrived with the bourgeois individual of the Renaissance. He[64] was characterized by a feeling that he was himself master of his own destiny. Along with this conviction, he developed a high opinion of his own virtue and a weak

---

62. Niebuhr, *Nature and Destiny of Man*, 286.

63. Ps 36:9.

64. It is appropriate to use the masculine pronoun for this period, seeing that women were largely disregarded at the time.

sense of his failings. He did not deny the reality of evil, but tended to derive most cases of it from specific historical resources (for example, bad priests, evil rulers, the ruling classes). The problem with this explanation was to account for the fact that evils that did not occur in nature could have arisen in human history. From where did the inclination of some particular people to commit evil acts come?

According to Niebuhr, there is a contradiction within contemporary social philosophy in assuming a distinction between humans in nature and in history, although the distinction is denied in psychology. In other words, there is a voluntarism built into modern social theory, but a determinism into its psychology. This way of perceiving human nature is forced to be positive about the probability that reason will favor social rather than egoistic impulses. Belief in natural human virtue is guaranteed by a rational preference for a benevolent lifestyle as against egoistic impulses; it is a definite strand of modern thought. Modern humans hope to free themselves from an evil involvement in natural impulses by increasing their rational faculties through advancing their educational attainments. They also believe that social, economic, and political conditions can be so changed that progress toward a much healthier society can be achieved by imminent forces in history or the extension of rationality or the elimination of external forces of evil, such as class divisions.

The mistake of the Renaissance was to overestimate the freedom and power of humans in history. Beginning with Hobbes, there has been a consistent denial of the significance of the self (i.e., of the transcendental individual) running through the empirical and naturalistic traditions. Naturalistic philosophy interprets human history as being due to pure human decisions, as no one possesses sufficient transcendence over social processes to make significant decisions.

Idealism, on the other hand, discovered the human spirit in transcendence over natural processes, but lost it again because the uniqueness of individuality does not conform to its pattern of rationality, its sole principle of interpreting reality:

> In naturalism humans face either the submergence of individuality and spirit in natural causality, or of his individuality and deification of his spirit in the universality of reason (rationalism).[65]

Confronted with annihilation through either the abasement of naturalism or the deification of rationalism, some humans sought another

---

65. Niebuhr, *Nature and Destiny of Man*, 86.

escape through romanticism. The romantic tradition, says Niebuhr, exalts the individual in a more unqualified fashion than any other philosophical stance, but also loses him or her more quickly and completely:

> Sooner or later the romantic thinker must . . . recoil from the pretension of this purely individual self-deification; and all but Nietzsche do recoil.[66]

From Rousseau, romanticism derives its emphasis on the nonrational forces in human personality, on emotion, imagination, and will. From pietism, it takes the sense of individuals' unmediated relation to God, which it secularizes, so that the individual is not only not directly related to God as source and center of meaning, but becomes a self-justifying and autonomous being. Romantic doctrine led to relativism in morals, religion, and politics. It foreshadowed Nietzsche's doctrine of the autonomous and self-justifying *ubermensch* (superman) with his contempt for the morality of the herd.

The Relevance of the Christian View of Being Human

There are, thinks Niebuhr, three major errors in the modern estimate of human nature. Firstly, there is a perennial debate between rationalists and romanticists, one deprecating and the other glorifying the power and virtue of subrational vitalities. Secondly, it fails to find a secure foundation for the individuality which it ostensibly cherishes so highly. Thirdly, its estimates of human virtue are too generous and optimistic to accord with the known facts of human history.[67] There is one single and common source of these errors:

> Man is not measured in a dimension sufficiently high or deep to do full justice to either his stature or his capacity for both good and evil or to understand the total environment in which such a stature can understand, express and find itself . . . this total environment . . . includes both time and eternity.[68]

In other words, the human race, entirely on its own, without any additional information from beyond itself, is deficient in its self-understanding. In the last analysis, human self-consciousness is limited by the

---

66. Niebuhr, *Nature and Destiny of Man*, 89.
67. Niebuhr, *Nature and Destiny of Man*, 132.
68. Niebuhr, *Nature and Destiny of Man*, 133.

boundaries of its own self-exploration. Only with the aid of divine revelation is it possible to move beyond the article of faith that "the final depth of human consciousness (is) in some sense identical with the eternal order, and . . . men may know God if they penetrate deeply enough into the mystery of their own being."[69]

To have a full understanding of who they are, according to Christian faith, it is necessary for humans to have access to, and to accept the truth of, God's specifically recorded acts of revelation. Without this special revelation, the general revelation recorded in conscience becomes falsified, "because it is explained merely as man facing the court of social approval or disapproval or as facing his own best self . . . Man does not know himself truly except as he knows himself confronted by God."[70] Unless a perfectly just and merciful God exists, who is involved, personally and collectively, in human lives, judging and forgiving, humans have no transcendent vantage point from which they can call themselves and others to account. Without an objective moral order built into the warp and woof of social life, there is no possibility of making moral judgments which are not arbitrary.

In Niebuhr's final word, he sums up both the deep dilemma of human life in a fallen world and the means that are available for humans to extricate themselves from it and to live as they were always intended to:

> The issue . . . is not primarily the problem of how finite man can know God, but how sinful man is to be reconciled to God and how history is to overcome the tragic consequences of its "false eternals," its proud and premature efforts to escape finiteness.[71]

Juan Luis Segundo (1925–1996)

By birth, Segundo was an Uruguayan citizen. At the age of sixteen, he joined the Jesuit order and studied in Argentina and the Faculty of Theology in Louvain. He received a doctorate from the Sorbonne with a thesis on the Russian Christian philosopher, Nikolai Berdiaev. On returning to Uruguay, between 1961 and 1964 he dedicated himself to teaching an extended course for Catholic laypeople. The whole program was published

---

69. Niebuhr, *Nature and Destiny of Man*, 135.
70. Niebuhr, *Nature and Destiny of Man*, 140.
71. Niebuhr, *Nature and Destiny of Man*, 158.

in five volumes, and was later translated from Spanish with the title, *A Theology for Artisans of a New Humanity*.[72] In this short review of his thinking about the reality of human life, I have selected two volumes from this collection: *Grace and the Human Condition* and *Evolution and Guilt* (volumes 2 and 5). Segundo was known globally as one of the foremost early "theologians of liberation,"[73] along with Gustavo Gutierrez, Hugo Assmann, Jose Miranda, and Severino Croatto.

An Overview of Christian Belief: The Apprehension of Grace

"Grace" is a key word in the language of the New Testament. It is a personal gift of God, not a reward for a virtuous life. Nature cannot acquire it, demand it, or even prepare for it. In the angel's announcement to Mary of the birth of the Messiah, he declared that she was "filled with grace," not "full of grace."[74] It is a word, used to specify a unique reality—a gratuitous benefit. It is not the result of an obligation or a social mechanism, but an aid granted out of pure mercy, nothing that a human being can lay claim to.

It is synonymous with a new creation, the liberation of the inner person. It is a supernatural gift, given in conversion, when one ceases to be just an ordinary human being and takes on new characteristics that reflect the life of Jesus. It is, therefore, a transforming agent, opening up a new depth of human existence ("life in its fullness"). Its end product is complete hominization (i.e., the full flowering of a humanity which has been restored to its original intention). It is not an addition to nature but a transforming of its deterioration.

The Human Condition

In trying to make sense of the human state, Segundo grapples with the thinking of some of the profoundest humanist philosophers of the past century and a half. To begin with, he engages with the maxim of the

---

72. Segundo, *Theology for Artisans*. The Spanish Edition had the title, *Teología abierta para el laico adulto* (Buenos Aires: Carlos Lohlé, 1968).

73. Kirk, *Liberation Theology*.

74. Luke 1:30. The usual translation is "you have found favor" or "you have been favored."

French philosopher, Jean-Paul Sartre, that "existence precedes essence." By this, Sartre means that "man does not carry the being that he will be at the end of his life as something already inscribed in the essence with which he was born . . . It is not that man *wills* in accordance with what he is; he *is* what he wills."[75] What Sartre is opposing is the notion that a fixed reality exists within my nature which limits my freedom, which has been imposed on me and which I cannot recognize as my deepest and most authentic ego.

Sartre sees these two factors as being in conflict. He emphasizes the belief that we are most authentically ourselves when we exercise a liberty to be whom we choose to be, not what our nature dictates our personality must become. Segundo agrees that these two factors play a huge part in who we become as individuals. Nevertheless, he criticizes Sartre for his naivety if he thinks that there is a clear temporal disjunction between existence and essence. Existence does not begin when a baby is born, but when it is conceived. A baby is not a living being that comes into the world as a kind of clean slate, free from then on to write its own script. It has inherited characteristics from both parents and it will respond to the kind of upbringing both parents inculcate. In other words, its existence is already predetermined to a considerable degree. It may, toward the end of its secondary education, opt to pursue a career in medicine. However, it finds that its given abilities (its essence) have not equipped it with skills in the biological sciences that are proficient enough to have a chance of qualifying as a doctor. This may be modified to a certain extent by an excellent education and hard study, but unfortunately not to the standard required:

> The unhappy fact is that every project we envision must be carried out with "borrowed" instruments that have a life of their own, that have dynamisms which ignore our pretended claims to utilize them.[76]

These instruments belong to my nature and *shape my existence*. Segundo does not think that such a reality means that liberty is illusory; but nor is it a faculty (like memory or the senses) which can, with the use of careful, reflective reason, produce free acts rather than those determined by first impulses. Liberty is a possibility that is given to a certain degree

---

75. Segundo, *Grace and the Human Condition*, 30.
76. Segundo, *Grace and the Human Condition*, 31.

and is won by handling determinisms with the greatest amount of wisdom: "(it is) a liberation that is freely realized."[77]

In discussing authentic human egos, Segundo touches on Freud's consideration of Marx's analysis of alienation, Nietzsche's problem of human weakness, and the apostle Paul's dilemma over the conflict in the inner person between the will and a principle of conduct more powerful than the ego. Freud frames his understanding of the id and the superego in terms of domination and alienation, both of which deprive the ego of the ownership of its own personality:

> We could say that they represent the two elements which unite against liberty: (1) the primary nature that suffuses man by virtue of his biological and instinctive life; (2) the secondary nature introduced into man through cultural imperatives, an ethical code that is regarded as natural, and a religion conceived as a magical illusion.[78]

Segundo agrees with the conclusion Ricoeur draws from his study of Freud that his practice of

> psychoanalysis seeks to replace an instinctive, deceitful conscience dominated by an inner darkness with a reflecting consciousness that is guided by the reality principle.[79]

Confronting this profound disjunction within the core inner being of the human personality with the language of the Christian faith, Segundo shows that we are dealing with a natural human facility to adhere to a reality which can only be overcome by divine grace. He cites, as his ground for coming to this conclusion, Paul's discourse on the daily experience of the division we experience between what we desire to do and our ability to do it.[80] He follows, at the end of the passage, by asking the deeply existential question:

> Wretched man that I am! Who is there to rescue me from this body doomed to death?

He responds with a cry of triumph:

---

77. Segundo, *Grace and the Human Condition*, 34.
78. Segundo, *Grace and the Human Condition*, 36.
79. Ricoeur, *Freud and Philosophy*, 43.
80. Laid out in Rom 7:14–24.

Thanks be to God through Jesus Christ our Lord![81]

So, Segundo concludes,

> the New Testament gives us a picture of the human condition as the departure point for grace. It is a picture of a being who is divided within. There is a profound tension between what he desires and decides within himself and that which he decides within himself and that which he ends up doing externally.[82]

Evil

As this chapter has already emphasized several times, it is not surprising that the Christian faith's diagnosis of the most profound human frailty, inherited corruption, is so despised and repudiated. Human beings, to a greater or lesser degree, when they are prepared to be absolutely honest with themselves, have to admit that they do not and cannot achieve their highest ideals. In a sense, the Christian message rubs salt into the many wounds caused by the deficiencies of our personalities. Segundo emphasized that people cannot hear the good news from God unless and until they have heard the bad news of their inherent perversion:

> According to our faith, man in the concrete without God's grace would not be a human being fully capable of carrying out his life. He would be an infirm, divided, tragic being. He would be dominated or enslaved by a force or tendency that is labeled *concupiscence* by theology.[83]

According to Segundo, evil in interhuman relations is most clearly seen in the exercise of an inauthentic love, which actually flows not from a genuine self-sacrificial commitment to caring for others, but from egotism. Perhaps this unreliable face of love is seen most clearly in marriage or cohabiting. Two people come together, sworn to increase their love for one another, whatever the circumstances, for the rest of their lives. They will never betray one another; they will always be faithful. They will encourage each other to be the best person they can be within their

---

81. Rom 7:24, 25.
82. Segundo, *Grace and the Human Condition*, 15.
83. Segundo, *Grace and the Human Condition*, 21; emphasis his. Concupiscence is derived from the Latin *concupiscere*, "to covet ardently," and is usually understood to mean a strong, immoral desire.

range of talents, skills, qualifications, and capabilities. But, over a period of time, the first flush of enthusiasm wears off. Subtly and gradually the other becomes increasingly a means to my ends. Eventually, one or the other, or both, decide they are no longer in love. In many cases, the union breaks apart; the original flush of love does not have the strength to hold the relationship together:

> What is . . . important to realize here is that while love may penetrate our being forcefully, egotism by contrast quietly takes control of our love . . . It is expressed obscurely in *bad faith*, whereby we maintain the forms and expressions and gestures of love even though we have already said no to its spirit and its demands.[84]

The non-Christian reaction to this Christian tail of woe may be manifold. One common ploy is to accuse Christians of overstating the problem of evil and its consequences, so that they can entice them to join their flock and avail themselves of their remedy. Another tactic will be to compare their character and practices favorably with others. It is not too difficult to find someone we can measure ourselves against beneficially, right up to those we wish would burn in hell! Yet a further stratagem might be to excuse ourselves by referring to adverse circumstances as the cause of our troubles and tribulations. We fail simply because we have had a run of bad luck; we are victims of evil rather than its agents.

All along, however, if we are courageous enough to be truthful with ourselves, these maneuvers are put up as smokescreens. We may be ashamed when things go wrong, we may be remorseful when we have not acted as we intended, or vice versa, but we rarely experience a sincere conviction of guilt:

> If we speak about "guilt" in connection with another human being, we do so because we have posited something of importance, something of the absolute in him; we see in him some trace of the primordial features of the deity. If this were not the case, we would use some other term besides guilt. We would talk about inconvenience, harmfulness, self-interest, opportunism, or some other term of that sort.[85]

Turning to the writing of Paul in the first century, Segundo makes the significant point, which is not only written on a piece of parchment or

---

84. Segundo, *Grace and the Human Condition*, 26.
85. Segundo, *Evolution and Guilt*, 7.

codex, but is burnt into our everyday experience. If we do not recognize it in our own experience, we will in judging other people:

> Once moral conscience awakes in man and he allows himself to act against its dictates, then he is caught in the sway of death ... Human existence can be maintained as such only by exerting a certain amount of violence against the instinctive, innate tendency to follow the easy way.[86]

Segundo is convinced that human beings, left to themselves, will continue to remain morally imperfect. Morally speaking, they are constituted in a particular way once for all. To sin or not to sin is something history will never change. No evolution will ever displace one of these two alternatives:

> Whether we are rich or poor, educated or illiterate, affluent or underdeveloped, we are all confronted with the same option between good and evil that faced our predecessors and will face our descendants.[87]

He might have added that is one of the main reasons why we can fully enter into the reflections on human attributes penned by people like Shakespeare, Victor Hugo, Fyodor Dostoevsky, Albert Camus, and countless others, from ages vastly different from our own.

Conclusion

It is a truism that every human being, however short or long his life span, will change:

> His psychic structure and his social relationships will continue to evolve and become more complex. His store of knowledge will increase, thus bolstering his capacity to dominate nature.[88]

Nevertheless, as far as the reality of a human's flawed disposition is concerned, nothing will have changed. This Christian outlook on the possibilities that humans can (and will), even if only gradually, improve their moral achievements, sounds depressing. Surely, non-Christians will assert, progress is happening all the time. Christianity cannot be a guide

---

86. Segundo, *Evolution and Guilt*, 43.
87. Segundo, *Evolution and Guilt*, 9.
88. Segundo, *Evolution and Guilt*, 8.

to the future, they will argue, because it is so pessimistic. It is as if it almost revels in dismissing the idealistic confidence in the future that is promoted by all with an optimistic temperament, for whom their cup is always half-full (or more than half-full), rather than half-empty. Above all, Christians are wrong to proclaim, in the second half of the *Gloria*, which they recite, that "as it was in the beginning, is now and ever shall be, world without end. Amen."

This latter affirmation appears to endorse a wholly static worldview, a circular view of history, a denial of the possibility of progress. In other words, whatever technological inventions may be achieved, whatever medical remedies may be discovered, no profound changes about human nature will ever be secured.

The Christian response may be twofold. Firstly, there are plenty of non-Christians who are just as distressed and dispirited about the likelihood that a new period of enlightened, moral intelligence and action will ever grip a whole population. Some of them have been mentioned in preceding chapters. It may be that advanced age brings on increasing discouragement. If this is partly true, it is because in their lifetimes there seems to be no evidence of an average increase in moral goodness from the days of their youth. They are convinced by Freud's reality principle that humans are more driven by antipathy toward one another than by altruism. In other words, Christians are far more realistic in their appreciation of the prospect of a gradual betterment of human kindness, gentleness, and compassion compared to former generations. "Whistling in the wind" is an arbitrary and irrational way of facing the future.

Secondly, Christians live by a solid hope, expressed famously by the medieval Christian writer, Julian of Norwich:

> Here I was taught by the grace of God that I should steadfastly keep me in the faith . . . and that at the same time I should take my stand on and earnestly believe in what our Lord shewed in this time—that "all manner [of] thing shall be well."[89]

And, if we ask how "shall all manner of thing be well?" we return to Segundo's emphasis on divine grace. History and personal experience have shown countless times that humans are incapable of freeing themselves from their enslavement to sin. Hope rests in the liberation that God has accomplished by releasing enslaved people into freedom and paying

---

89. Julian of Norwich, *Revelations of Divine Love*, 54–55.

the price to achieve it. Grace allows humans to take hold properly of their God-designed destiny to be recreated in the image of God's perfect love.[90]

The final reality of this universe is the creation of a new heaven and a new earth in which sin and evil will be eliminated and righteousness will dwell complete and unceasing. There are already signs of it present within the existing world, because God is already in process of creating it in cooperation with those who are laying hold of his grace. It will, however, never be achieved by human effort alone. If there is no God in whom to put one's trust, there is no hope of a new world; all is sound and fury. It is both surprising and depressing that the vast majority of humankind prefers to trust their own self-reliance rather than be open to God's offer of new life.

Jurgen Moltmann (1926–present)

The last of the five distinguished, twentieth-century theologians chosen to represent a cross section of Christian views on what it means to be human is one of the most prolific theological writers of the second half of the century. The scope of his reflections is wide. They are usually set off in response to historical circumstances that challenge the claims of the Christian faith, particularly the suffering of humanity (in war, poverty and exploitation) and the affliction of the natural order through lack of care for its wise, sustainable use.

Moltmann was brought up in a secular family, devoid of any noteworthy Christian influence. Drafted into the German army in the last year of the European war at the age of eighteen, he had a near-death experience in the firebombing of Hamburg when an army colleague standing next to him was annihilated by a direct hit. His reading matter, during his participation in the German war effort, was the poems of Goethe and the writings of Nietzsche. Eventually he surrendered to a British soldier and was interned in various prisoner-of-war camps in Belgium, Scotland, and Northern England. It was whilst a prisoner that he came to Christian faith, through meeting Christians and reading the Bible.

Whilst before his experience of the war he was planning to study mathematics at university, after the traumatic years of 1944 to 1948, his whole life shifted and he became engrossed in the academic investigation of Christian faith and preparation for the ordained ministry of the

---

90. Segundo, *Evolution and Guilt*, 80.

Reformed church. In 1967, he was appointed Professor of Systematic Theology at the University of Tübingen and remained there until his retirement in 1994 (now Professor Emeritus). At the time of writing (2018), he is still alive at the age of ninety-two.

The main source for this brief exploration of his anthropology is the concise monograph, first published in 1971 under the title, *Mensch: Christliche Anthropologie in den Konflikten der Gegenwart*.[91] In the second edition, Moltmann appends a new preface, in which he explains the reason for the change of the title and adds that it was the only book he published explicitly on human being. However, he also emphasizes that it was not his only writing that brings up the question of human meaning at the end of the twentieth and beginning of the twenty-first century. He also specifically mentions *God in Creation* (1985) and *The Coming of God* (1995). He finishes this new preface with these provocative words:

> In contemplating the beauty of God "face to face," the passion of human life will find its fulfillment, for "our hearts are restless, until they find their rest in thee," wrote Augustine, the Father of Western anthropology, in his *Confessions*. For me, this divine unrest is the secret of human existence. This book is meant to be a step along this restless path, and is intended as a stimulus to further thought of one's own—no more than that, but no less either.[92]

Anthropology

In the simplest terms, human beings can be identified as "all who have a human countenance."[93] And yet it remains an open question what the humanity of the human being consists of. It remains a case in open court, in which several arguments are put forward on various sides of a legal action, with a view to achieving a verdict that is probable, but not yet beyond all reasonable doubt.

There are many places one can begin the discussion. It could be by unfolding the bodily nature of humans and, therefore, their ties with the earth, which is undoubtedly important in the context of the current

---

91. Translated into English: Moltmann, *Man*. The title was changed in a second edition, published in 2009, to *On Being Human*.

92. Moltmann, *On Human Being*, xii.

93. Moltmann, *On Human Being*, xiii.

ecological concerns for the planet. Or, it could be by comparing *homo sapiens* with the sentient animal kingdom. In the latter case, we can readily notice a number of crucial differences because humans, unlike animals, are not social automata. Their instinctual nature is not free-ranging, but rather is regulated through education. The malleability of their instincts is the reverse side of their capacity for conscious action. Another possible starting point would be humans' capacity to create culture or to think imaginatively by virtue of the innate ideas of reason that are common to us all. Within the tradition of the theistic religions, all humans share a common destiny: judgment of how we have used our lives by the one who has made us like himself.

No account of human beings is satisfactory that does not have a plausible way of measuring the difference between justice and injustice, the question of the existence of natural rights and social responsibilities, the profile of a life worth living. None of these profound queries can be answered without possessing even more far-reaching conclusions about the core reality of human existence. When looking at human life from the perspective of purely social contexts and functions, personal lives fulfilled in specific neighborhoods and work environments, we find pluralistic beings discharging different claims, standards and expectations.

It has been calculated that the inhabitant of a country has at least 9 distinct characteristics:

> a professional, national, a civic, a class, a geographical, a sex, a conscious, an unconscious and perhaps even too a private one; he combines them all in himself.[94]

Undoubtedly, all of these realities help to shape a person's self-identity. However, how does a person combine these harmoniously? Is the person's social self-image really sufficiently comprehensive to do justice to the fullness of human being? How can people free themselves from the social compulsion of their roles? They may give him some security in the world, but how do they become released from the powers and laws of the world, from potential or real totalitarian claims of society, where an elite group of "experts" may be those who decide who we are and how we should live (the Communist or Nazi parties, for example, or a legal profession who decides what constitutes human rights and who benefits from them)?

---

94. Moltmann, *On Human Being*, 92.

The Christian View of Human Being

Christian anthropology is set within a broad confessional framework that begins with the creation of human beings by a supreme, singular, and exclusive spiritual being, in order to be like himself, to follow his perfect pattern for living, and to experience his continual presence. Humans, however, have chosen their own ways to live, refusing the exemplary paths offered them by their creator. The result has been catastrophic, for humans have adopted lifestyles that are destructive of their very best well-being. This is what Christian anthropology calls "the fall" (i.e., the personal decision to create one's own world, rather than live in the one created for them). The prophet Jeremiah has used a penetrating metaphor to describe the process:

> My people have committed two evils: they have forsaken me, the fountain of living water, and dug out cisterns for themselves, cracked cisterns that can hold no water.

The result is that

> my people have changed their glory for something that does not profit.[95]

Original sin springs from the arrogance that doubts that God's will for humankind is perfect and, in its place, devises one's own program for life. Significantly, Jurgen Moltmann interprets this arrogance in terms of the way in which modern humanism is obliged to lay hold of a distorted theology in order to give an account of the necessity of exchanging the self-deification of human beings for the deity of God:

> The basis of the modern anthropocentric understanding of the world, according to which, man is the criterion of God. With the Renaissance and the Enlightenment . . . the anthropocentric age began. Anthropology in the modern emphatic sense . . . presupposed a theology which has been given up, and understands itself as the heir of that theology . . . It is not men that are in the image of God. The gods are the image of man . . . The gods are the creation of man's anxieties and longings.
>
> Ludwig Feuerbach gave a lasting expression to this suspicion held by modern man in his criticism of religion. He exchanged subject and predicate, and so reduced all predicates about God to a human subject . . . God is a wish-projection of

---

95. Jer 2:13, 11.

man, who has fallen out with himself . . . Feuerbach believed in all the predicates of God, and only transferred them to man and to mankind . . . If the heir puts himself in his place, he is not man any more, but is himself God . . . As total man, as ideal man . . . man must accomplish things which he cannot accomplish.

The modern age has made "man" an iconoclastic word against God: out of human self-awareness an iconoclastic attack has gone out against the religious images of God. But this remains meaningful only so long as, conversely, the real God is an iconoclastic against man . . . an iconoclastic attack . . . against the images of man in which man reflects himself, justifies and divinizes himself . . . Man becomes more human (only) if he is put in the position of being able to abandon his self-deifications and his idolatry.[96]

Salvation

The modern anthropological rebellion against the real and living God is not the end of God. That God has died, killed by present civilization, as Nietzsche so famously claimed, proclaims the birth of tragedy in its most extreme form.[97] The one remaining hope for humankind is that God is eternally living and, in both judgment and salvation, active in his creation:

> There is no comfort to be had by a belief in a supposed progressive unfolding of a rational spirit in the achievements of human endeavor.[98]

It is because God is the final and pure criterion of absolute righteousness and love, not because he is the dispenser of an arbitrary set of moral laws, that we can live according to the unchanging nature of the one who created us. However, before that can happen, fallen human nature needs to be restored to what it has always been intended to be. This is the point at which salvation is essential. Even those who reject entirely the Christian notion of salvation have their own versions of it.

---

96. Moltmann, *On Human Being*, 105, 106, 107.
97. See Kirk, *Future of Reason*, 155–57.
98. Kirk, *Future of Reason*, 157.

Moltmann, writing at the beginning of the 1970s, paints a picture of romantic ideals as the hoped-for remedy for the ills of a meaningless existence:

> Romanticism and underground cultures have been the constant accompaniments of industrial society from the very beginning ... What is the industrial system other than "work, production, and consumption," and again "work, production, and consumption"; a meaningless cycle of what is eternally the same? ... The romantic dream of the "simple life" ... becomes the model ... (a) flight backwards into a rustic idyll or forwards into a revolutionary future ... or in that other world which one can reach through transcendental meditation or in intoxication through marijuana ... The "closed society" knows nothing new under the sun of its neon-lights, but it is exhausted in the incessant reproduction of itself in the constant variation of what already exists.[99]

Moltmann picks out three trends in contemporary Western culture that express the revolt against meaninglessness: social romanticism; "inward emigration," and Utopian consciousness.

> It is in these that what may be termed human rights in an industrial society live today.[100]

> This social romanticism wishes to lead men who must live their lives in the conditioned and the derivative, in the rational and the complicated, back to the area of their origins, to give back to their lives the purity and security which it is assumed they cannot find in the modern world.[101]

> By inward emigration we understand a retreat of the educated intellect from circumstances which are deplored as being mindless ... An attitude of irony often then enters in. With the help of ironic reflection and ironic observations on the situation, one obtains a standpoint outside the misery and creates a distance over against everyday life.[102]

---

99. Moltmann, *On Human Being*, 33, 36.
100. Moltmann, *On Human Being*, 37.
101. Moltmann, *On Human Being*, 38.
102. Moltmann, *On Human Being*, 40, 41.

He goes on to say, "Utopias are sketches of a desired future situation which, in comparison with the present situation, is more worthy of man, more worth living and freer."[103] Moltmann believes that neither abstract nor concrete utopias have any chance of being implemented, seeing that they are always imaginations of vague future possibilities. However,

> human hopes for the most part go beyond the real prospects of success, *and indeed have to do this*, for "man" is as things are a fairly Utopian being.[104]

Moltmann's reference to romanticism is an indication of the predicament faced by those who are confined in a mechanistic, rationalized, production-creating world which offers nothing that can entirely satisfy the deepest longings of the human psyche. Some forty years after he painted this kind of picture of anguish and despair, with its accompanying daydreams of revolutionary new worlds, contemporary humankind has turned either to a hedonistic culture (if wealthy enough to enjoy one) or to a daily struggle to keep existing (if living on the breadline).

For contemporary human history in the so-called advanced and progressive societies, the most momentous problem is its lack of understanding of what is its inherent problem. Human beings and the kind of societies they produce on the basis of the misconception of their real selves need liberating. At the same time, they have massively spurned the one and only source of their deliverance. The source is external, not internal. It is offered in one single matchless historical fact, which can be appropriated in another historical act, that of an individual's commitment to the meaning of the fact. The fact is the atoning sacrifice of the Son of God (the anointed Messiah sent into the world to deal once for all with the crisis of sin).

The real meaning of the death of Jesus seems a complete paradox:

> Man is revealed as the being accepted and loved by God in the manner of Jesus, and God is revealed through him as this human God . . . Faith says of the crucified Jesus, "*Ecce homo*," "behold the man," in the reality of his total rejection. But it also says, "*Ecce Deus*"—"behold God," in the reality of his infinite love, in which he rejects himself in order to be the God of the rejected, and the father of those who despair, and the acquitter

---

103. Moltmann, *On Human Being*, 42.
104. Moltmann, *On Human Being*, 43; emphasis added.

of those who accuse themselves, but also the judge of those who boast in themselves.[105]

Throughout history and until the end of time, human beings from all nations, peoples, cultures, and faiths are confronted with the dilemma of choosing to decide between two human-shaping alternatives: either to maintain their illusions about themselves, that their sin does not need to be atoned for, forgiven, and conquered by a power not their own, or to confess their guilt and to trust their creator and redeemer to make them into new creatures.

Martin Luther, the German Reformer, put it this way:

> God became man in order out of proud and unfortunate gods to make real men.

Moltmann, the German theologian, says:

> The memory of the crucified Jesus is a dangerous one, both for the established Church itself, and for a society which erects its idols and taboos in order to make itself safe. For from this memory emerges again and again an iconoclasm of liberation against the images of the beautiful and pious pretense in which men live, and with which they deceive themselves and others about the truth.[106]

In the writings of Moltmann, we return to the German philosopher Friedrich Nietzsche's option, in the starkest possible form:

> Dionysus against the Crucified.[107]

Only in the Crucified (and Resurrected) one, however, is there hope for the world. Accepting the Crucified means rejecting Dionysus.

Questions

1. Each of the five theologians engaged critically with the secular humanist tradition. What, in your opinion, were their strongest and weakest arguments?
2. On what assumptions did the theologians base their reasoning?

---

105. Moltmann, *On Human Being*, 19.
106. Moltmann, *On Human Being*, 20–21.
107. Nietzsche, *Ecce Homo*, 9.

3. Two major systems of belief have generated conflicting worldviews in the West over the last half millennium; those springing from the Renaissance and the Reformation. How would you characterize their essential elements?

4. To what extent do you think it is fair to portray Christianity as being pessimistic about human nature and secular humanism as being optimistic? Are there good grounds for hope in either belief that the inner constitution of humans can be significantly transformed for the better?

Chapter 12

The Gaining of Wisdom?

What are human beings that you are mindful of them, mortals that you care for them?

Yet you have made them a little lower than God, and crowned them with glory and honor.

You have given them dominion over the works of your hands; you have put all things under their feet. (Ps 8:4–6)

We have made you a creature neither of heaven nor of earth, neither mortal nor immortal, in order that you may, as the free and proud shaper of your own being, fashion yourself in the form you may prefer. It will be in your power to descend to the lower, brutish forms of life; you will be able, through your own decision, to rise again to the superior orders whose life is divine.

—*GIOVANNI PICO DELLA MIRANDOLA*

Rather than a science or a dogma, humanist thought proposes a practical choice: a wager. Better to wager that they are capable of acting willfully, loving purely and treating one another as equals than the contrary . . . The humanists of the French tradition do not necessarily believe in final causes, but they judge it useful to act as if this way were really open to men. It is true that, unlike Pascal, they do not promise those who wager "an eternity of life and happiness," but only a fragile and fleeting felicity.

—*TZVETAN TODOROV*

Prelude

These three quotations, from vastly different epochs in my historical inquiry over the past half millennium about what it means to be human, have come to substantially different conclusions. The response of many inhabitants of present-day Western culture might well be, "So what?" "Does it matter?" "Is not one of the glories of our modern secular, humanly-oriented societies in the West that they promote free thought?" Sartre forcefully portrays an existential reality that we have at last grasped for ourselves after several centuries:

> Man will be what he makes of himself. Thus, there is no human nature since there is no God to conceive of it . . . man is nothing other than what he makes of himself.[1]

We are at liberty to choose the wager of which Todorov speaks: to believe that humans are, generally speaking, "more capable of acting willfully, loving purely and treating one another as equals than the contrary." And, even though life may appear at times spiritually, mentally, and physically painful and incomprehensible, it does afford some "fragile and fleeting felicity." Trying to wrestle with the empirical and philosophical complexities of being human may be of interest to a small minority of intellectually inclined people, but frankly it does not fascinate the majority of humankind.

This conclusion to an inquiry like this one may seem relatively commonsensical to most people, and yet, in reality (as most politicians, in giving responses to hard questions, love to repeat), the notion that we owe ourselves the duty of discovering our own identity as a member of the human species is not entirely absent. One author has made the point that:

> in the contemporary sense the term "humanism" denotes the view that whatever ethical outlook we adopt, it has to be based on our best understanding of *human nature and the human condition*.[2]

It is not too difficult to cite countless examples of "in reality," where convictions about what is authentically human greatly influence our laws, our institutions, our own self-assessment, and the way we treat people.

---

1. Sartre, *Existentialism is a Humanism*, 22.
2. Grayling, "Humanism, Religion and Ethics," 47; emphasis his.

What sort of creatures we are in relation to the teeming myriads of other creatures that inhabit the same planet becomes a key question in ecological matters to do with environmental care. Human rights spring from, and depend in their interpretation and application, on society's consensus about the significance, purpose, and value of the human person. So, in actual fact, societies and cultures do not easily dismiss the fundamental importance of searching for the truth about being human.

Assumptions

Unlike Sartre's type of existentialist belief, we are not born as though we were clean slates, on which we can write our own versions of what we want to call ourselves. Along the way, through parental nurture, education, the media, our peer group or people we respect, or what we pick up to read, we acquire assumptions that guide what we believe. We have perceived in every chapter of this inquiry that such a process is inevitable. Assumptions are opinions we adopt as foundational beliefs or principles that allow us to organize our thoughts into more or less coherent convictions that then direct our actions.

In the course of this study, we have encountered two fundamental assumptions, from which flow numerous lesser ones, that give rise to criteria to which we adhere. The first assumption, prevalent and predominant in the Western world from approximately the second quarter of the fourth century—when the Christian faith became the officially recognized religion of the Roman Empire—until the late eighteenth century—when the *Ancien Regime* was overthrown in France and select divine rights were contested elsewhere—was that of *theism*. A supreme spiritual being who "inhabits eternity,"[3] known in the Hebrew Scriptures as *Yahweh* and in the Christian Scriptures as *Pater hemon* ("our Father"), was acknowledged as the creator of the universe, the solar system, and within it a small planet known as Earth. Everything that exists, and ever existed, was due to the creative act of this Being. Not only did this God set the universe in motion, as though God was a kind of preeminent watchmaker that wound the whole machinery up and, thereafter, allowed it to continue perpetually under its own mechanism, but he maintained a moment-by-moment creative involvement in its life and development.

---

3. Isa 57:15.

According to this assumption, this same, sole divine Being created another being like himself, with whom he communicated through specially chosen messengers known as prophets and apostles. What they heard in the conversations are recorded, in their own words, in a variety of publications and collected together in one single volume known as the Bible. The central thesis of God's action has been his own short residency in the world, in the person of his beloved Son (or Messiah), to bring a message that God's rule over all peoples had now arrived. The meaning of this event is summarized in two short statements from the prophet Isaiah:

> How beautiful upon the mountains are the feet of the messenger who announces peace (*shalom*), who brings good news, who announces salvation, who says to Zion, "Your God reigns."[4]

> I will give you (my people) as a light to the nations, that my salvation may reach to the ends of the earth.[5]

So, the principal assumption, which totally shapes the way Christians perceive the reality of human life on this small planet, is that all this truly happened in space and time, and this is the right framework within which the role of human living is to be played out. In the course of its lengthy history, many accretions have been added to the essential, core statement of belief, some faithful to the original communication, and many erroneous. The latter have, undoubtedly, damaged the purity of faith and caused the watching world to walk away in disgust.

The second major assumption carries the name of *materialism*.[6] It has appeared under a number of different names and in a variety of assorted forms. They are all linked together with one overriding core conviction: all that humans can possibly know about themselves and the entire environment in which they live is limited to what can be assessed by the senses or derived, by deduction, from what they are capable of perceiving and conceiving. Anything knowable, beyond the world of

---

4. Isa 52:7.

5. Isa 49:6.

6. Some might have expected the alternative assumption to have come with the name of humanism. This, however, would be incorrect for two reasons. Firstly, humanism has its own distinct Christian interpretation, as Jacques Maritain showed, and therefore cannot be expropriated as a definition by one particular philosophy. Secondly, materialism denotes the specific alternative to theism, in that it proposes a radically different, restricted ontology.

the material, belongs to a world of make-believe, for it is not open to observation or investigation. It cannot, therefore, be a source of factual knowledge and understanding. Freud, for example, mirrored the belief of many that the only knowledge that can be justified as true is that which can be demonstrated by the means of empirically proven evidence. It is important, then, to note that, within this framework, when it comes to tracing the origin of the human species and the rise of its moral sentiments, it is obliged to adopt a genealogical approach (i.e., to resort to an historical, or even prehistorical search of evidence that might be counted as sufficiently credit-worthy to be classified within the bounds of the natural sciences).

Materialism, by its very nature, is compelled to dismiss the entire notion of an extramaterial reality—usually referred to as a spiritual or transcendental realm—that can also be a reliable cause of knowledge and understanding of human existence. Perhaps the easiest and quickest way of accomplishing this end is by ridding the human imagination and fancy of the conviction that a deity, deities, or lesser spirits exist in a parallel domain from that which humans inhabit, but which are undetectable by them. The most famous example of this deicide is Nietzsche's madman, whom he portrays as answering his own question in the public square: "Where is God?" "We have killed him, you and I . . . God is dead. And we have killed him."[7] For Nietzsche and all atheists, of course, God was never alive. He never was, except in the mythological world of a false vision.

Strict materialists, as a consequence, are convinced that they live in a purely natural order, totally devoid of any extraterrestrial explanation. In Nietzsche's fable, God's alleged assassins are those who are now prepared, firstly to rejoice at being relieved of God, and secondly to take up the task of creating a different world order from that handed down by religions. Nietzsche called it the revaluation of all values:

> All sciences must, from now on, prepare the way for the future work of the philosopher: the work being understood to mean that the philosopher has to solve the problem of values and that he has to decide on the hierarchy of values.[8]

Nietzsche was the most consistently dedicated to this task. There was nothing of Christian morality that he wished to keep. It was, he believed,

---

7. Nietzsche, *Gay Science*, in Pearson and Large, *Nietzsche Reader*, 224.
8. Nietzsche, *Genealogy*, 17.

the morality of the herd, kept in moral bondage by a dominant body (the priests of the church) who wished to impose their illusory beliefs on the population and, thus, keep themselves in power.

If there is no God, there is no creator. Faith in an eternally existing supreme Being, who is the source of all being and meaning, is a myth in the sense of a fantastical daydream. All the deeply human questions that the Christian faith thinks it has solved have to be reopened: such as, the origin of life on earth; the origin of the first members of a fully human species; a convincing and dependable foundation for human behavior; the creation of a worthwhile meaning for one's existence; a plausible explanation of the human belief in evil; the intuition that personal life does not cease at death. Secular materialistic humanism has no right to build its beliefs and values on foundations which it has disowned. Or, as Tolstoy intimated, to go on picking chosen flowers once the roots had been destroyed.

If there is no creator of all that exists, it follows that the universe must be self-generating and self-sufficient. It has no personal cause: life on planet earth has not arisen as the act of an unrestrained, self-determining being, but rather has evolved out of the most primitive of living cells through a long process of phenomena emerging at successive levels of complexity. This is what a materialist has come to accept as a proven and coherent theory. If this is the logical conclusion from the materialist assumption, and the assumption is now taken for granted, the materialist should be prepared to live consistently with all the rational consequences of the belief, as should Christian theists with their beliefs. Both sets of assumptions are founded on hypothetical-deductive theories, warranted by different types of evidence, but ultimately guaranteed by extrascientific presuppositions. To a certain extent, both a theist and a materialist confirms as a belief what he or she has already assumed. Freud acknowledged this reality:

> People are seldom impartial where ultimate things, the great problems of science and life, are concerned. Each of us is governed in such cases by deep-rooted internal prejudices, into whose hands our speculation unwittingly plays.

Is there any possibility that these great debates about ultimate things can ever be settled? As I shall argue later, the matter can only be potentially resolved by means of wielding properly the epistemological principle of "inference to the best explanation" (abduction). Before we reach that point, there is more to explore from our findings.

The Origin of Species

We saw that when first announced, Darwin's epoch-making theory aroused a considerable amount of skepticism inside and outside the scientific community. That lasted for several decades, in spite of the sophisticated defense of the thesis made by Thomas Huxley and others. Gradually, however, what came to be known as the General Theory of Evolution, with revisions incorporated into Darwin's first draft in the *Origin of Species* (some by Darwin himself), gained general acceptance by people working in the field of evolutionary biology and other allied sciences. From those considered experts in the field, the theory spread to the general public in, at least, the self-affirmed developed countries. By the time that Thomas Huxley's grandson, Julian, published his classic exposition of the theory, *Evolution: The Modern Synthesis*, in 1942,[9] most people took for granted that the "tree of life theory" represented a correct account of how all species evolved from primitive beginnings to their highest point in the coming of *homo sapiens*.

The modern synthesis is now taught to children of a fairly young age as if it depicted the conclusive fact of the matter. Any other theory is now rejected as incompatible with the best scientific conclusions. Indeed, their failure is due to the fact that they cannot, in the nature of the case, be submitted to empirically verifiable tests.[10] The notion of an extramaterial agent intervening in a causal process is simply not open to investigation by verifiable means. Any other such theory, therefore, is ruled out of court as, at most, an interesting, but ultimately make-believe, hypothesis that should not be taught as though it possessed any kind of scientific credentials.

This is not the place to enter once again into the often highly polemical debates about the grand theory. However, it is necessary to point out

---

9. A third edition was published in 1974, and a definitive edition in 2010.
10. See, for example, the lengthy debate undertaken in the symposium: Pennock, *Intelligent Design Creationism*.

the recent arrival of a new account of how and why Darwin's own growing conviction about his evolutionary proposition took such a hold. In a recent biography,[11] A. N. Wilson, an eminent historian whose main field of expertise is Victorian England, has come to the conclusion, against his initial supposition and following his close research into Darwin's background and life's work, that Darwin's ideas were incorrect. Having cited the philosopher Thomas Nagel (not a religious believer) to the effect that Darwin's "explanations" of complex phenomena—above all, *consciousness*—are reductionist and simplistic,[12] said that "it was not possible to tell the story from a simple belief in *The Origin of Species*." He continued, and this is the nub of his findings:

> The more I thought about it, the more I saw that Darwin's errors sprang from the mindset of his particular age and milieu. They were programmed to have a particular view of the world by the economic and social world in which they lived . . . In time I came to see Darwin as two men. One was the observant naturalist, who spent nearly a decade writing a book about barnacles. The other was the theorist. The theorist is the one whose name is invoked in our day to justify the theories of those who espouse them. Often these theories have nothing to do with science. I therefore find myself writing the biography not merely of a man, but of his idea; and not merely of his idea, but of his age.[13]

The point, from the perspective of this inquiry into being human, is that evolutionary theory as set out in the neo-Darwinian synthesis is not in the least plausible, because it does not explain how human beings arrived on earth. They are far too complex for a general genetic theory, based on materialistic assumptions, to be able to elucidate. However many millions (nay, billions) of years one wishes to interpose between the most cultured primate and a human being, the latter could not have arisen from the former by the naturalistic mechanisms of evolution. Evolution is not an inference to the best explanation of what we already know about ourselves. The whole reality of moral awareness and intelligent capacities with which humans alone are endowed demand another explanation, even though it may not be confirmable by deduction from observable evidence. The means of its inference has to be different. Science, as it is contemplated and evaluated today, does not possess the tools

---

11. Wilson, *Charles Darwin*.
12. Nagel, *Mind and Cosmos*.
13. Wilson, *Charles Darwin*, 6.

to explain human nature in full. In this respect, human self-consciousness and scientific assertions, dependent on philosophical materialism as their presupposition, do not match.

So, in summarizing what can be known for certain about the origin of human being on earth, we should, as a human race, still be circumspect. There is a time and place for agnosticism about the origin, diversity, and complexity of human existence. If we are to understand more fully the nature of human experience, we will need to widen our horizons as to the sources of knowledge, jettisoning a merely naturalistic causality as the complete explanation needed. If we wish to do justice to all possibilities, it is necessary to adopt a rational research program that is willing to consider seriously all germane evidence. The prevailing secular humanist procedure is guided by the perceived requirement to prove a negative, namely that there is no God and, therefore, humans cannot be the end product of his creative genius, however it was brought about.

Neo-Darwinism is undoubtedly in limbo as an accredited scientific inference. Skeptics of the theory are not obliged to assume a burden of proof. It is more honest to admit that we do not know conclusively detailed answers to all the basic questions about life generally, and human life in particular. It is more impartial to ponder objectively all claims to possess credible information about human meaning, rather than dismiss certain evidence because it contradicts *a priori* presumptions. Theists have no difficulties at all in fully accepting conclusions based on persuasive scientific data. Why should they? They see nature as a God-given reality to be explored in all its immense variety and employed for the benefit of humans' well-being. They are, however, highly suspicious of research programs designed to come to conclusions which are favorable to predetermined ends. This, they and many nontheists conclude, was and is the main reason for the highly speculative evolutionary project, set out within a Darwinian structure.

Humanism

The use of the designation is nobody's monopoly. No group can claim an entitlement to possess it for their exclusive use. Historically speaking it comes in different forms. Until roughly the mid-eighteenth century, humanism was aligned with a theocentric view of the universe. John Locke, for example, still held to this view of a personally and orderly composed universe. During this century, however, belief in the sacred canopy of God's overall governance of the universe was dissolved. In its place arose confidence in new scientific endeavors and independent human reason to explain the whole of reality and overcome inherent problems without needing recourse to a divine communication in a holy book. The primacy of secular reality was conceived, gestated, and born. The Age of Enlightenment had arrived. Charles Taylor called this exclusive humanism.

Historians also speak of the humanism of the Renaissance period. This may be summed up by a number of significant new turns: to the *past*, a rediscovery of the classical golden age of the high culture of Greece and Rome; from previous stylized religious paintings (icons) to recognizable human figures of the everyday; to the *individual*, typified in Pico della Mirandola's *Oration on the Dignity of Man*, and Erasmus as an independent thinker; to *cultures and civilizations beyond Europe*, with which trade and intercultural exchange was enacted; to *migration* from rural to urban life, partly due to the effects of the Black Death.

From the perspective of our discussion, Renaissance humanism has been interpreted in opposing ways: either as the rejection of Christian faith, or as its purification. Certainly, pagan cultures from the past were allowed much more prominence in the world of visual art, architecture, and sculpture: Donatello's statue of David is probably a depiction of Lorenzo de Medici, the archetypical aristocrat of the new urban elite. It was possibly depicted to represent the dawning of a new civilization confident in its ability to overcome oppression, threats, and fears.

Nevertheless, there is little evidence that the artists, courtiers, and business entrepreneurs were about to turn their backs on Christian belief. Marsilio Ficino, for example, defended the immortality of the soul against a materialistic philosophy. He emphasized that humans were created in the image of God, with an intelligence whose source was the mind of God, and born for the contemplation of the one who inhabits eternity. Pico della Mirandola declared that the final reality of all reality is the Trinitarian God. Erasmus developed his own form of spirituality, influenced by the Brethren of the Common Life. It is true that these writers were advancing some beliefs that the Roman Catholic Church at the time would have considered revisionist, if not heretical. However, none of them were schismatics. Erasmus, in his famous treatise, *In Praise of Folly*, wrote a satire on the offensive and absurd operations of the official church, but never abandoned the core beliefs of Christianity. He remained a member of the Catholic church until his life's end.

Renaissance humanism was a reality, and though it was considerably skeptical about many of the beliefs and practices of the church, it was far from being rationalist or secular. Nevertheless, the mood of the age was one that tended toward the autonomy of the individual and resistance to autocratic authority, whether exercised by the state or the church. Such an authority survived within different institutions for another two hundred years, but was gradually challenged by those who defied the imposition of beliefs and practices by an external authority without the consent of the people.

The Reformation in Europe marked the end of the hegemony of one single interpretation of the Christian faith, more profound than the split between the Western and Eastern traditions of Christendom in 1453. From then on, an opposition was created to unquestioned power, whatever its source. A pluralistic society began to emerge and minority groups began to gain democratic rights as full citizens. Secular humanists are historically incorrect in thinking that all this happened as the result of an Enlightenment-inspired rejection of traditions based, in its view, purely on dogma. This rejection was first exercised by religious nonconformists in the 1520s, most notably the Anabaptists, who suffered enormous persecution as a result of their refusal to conform to state-controlled religious institutions.[14]

Contemporary secular humanists cannot disassociate themselves from the Christian humanism of the past. One of its most powerful core convictions—that human dignity is predicated on being human—is derived from an intuition, seeing that being human is a matter of conviction based on a reality beyond the consensus of a majority. History demonstrates, time and again, that the irreducible humanity of the individual cannot be founded on what a community agrees to be the case. The fundamental nature of being human is not decided by any human authority, even that of the majority of a population. That is why racism, sexism, xenophobia, and the disputed status of the preborn child and the psychologically restricted are all inadmissible. As beliefs and practices, they depend on the purely human opinion of some theorists. Conversely, their eradication is not based on the consensus of the majority, who may or may not reject the theories. The status of being human can only be defended against all attempts to downgrade and violate certain distinguishing groups by a power completely independent of human decision-making.

---

14. See Kirk, *Church and the World*, ch. 6: "The 'Old' World: Church and Mission in the Radical Reformation."

Humans tend to define the standing of other humans according to their own interests, as witnessed to, most severely, by the several holocausts that have happened in the last one hundred years or so. As Jacques Maritain observes from a careful reading of historical sources,

> genuine personhood cannot be discovered fully, unless it is encountered in an existence beyond its physical embodiment alone . . . Western humanism springs from religious and transcendental sources. By transcendental he means "all those forms of thought, however otherwise diverse, which find the true principle of the world in a Spirit greater than man."[15]

> The new humanism sought to save human freedom at the expense of divine causality, on the grounds that submission to the divine will inescapably meant the loss of humanity's own control of its destiny, and therefore of its humanity. . . . From then on two kinds of humanism struggled for supremacy, theocentric and anthropocentric. However, the problem is not in claiming for one's own view a true humanism, but in discerning its authentic source.[16]

Modern humanists, claims Niebuhr, rely entirely on their own reason and insight to gain knowledge, by observing events going on around them. However, nature is devoid of knowledge; it only yields data. Reason has become corrupted. The evidence for making this claim is the necessity of having, on many occasions, to distinguish between truth and falsity. Christian humanism is convinced, in the light of its observation of the distinction between the ways that Christians and secularists behave and its listening to God's self-revelation, that submission to God does not diminish human eminence, but on the contrary, expands its grandeur. Only in the latter case can human beings fulfill all that they are intended to be; otherwise they are, as it were, like a chicken scratching about in the dirt for a scrap with which to nourish its life.

Morality

Although the origin, nature, foundation, and content of moral consciousness is widely disputed, the fact that humans are deeply moral in their daily lives is indisputable. Someone once used the illustration of

15. Maritain, *True Humanism*, xv.
16 Maritain, *True Humanism*, 13, 19.

a recording machine. Supposing humans at birth had a machine hung around their neck, which only recorded the moral judgments they made about others, and at the end of their lives they had the entire recording played back to them, they could not escape the conclusion that, whether or not the pronouncements were soundly based, they were certainly moral. Moreover, it would become clear that none of them were moral relativists, all of them abided by some form of absolute moral principles. Whatever their moral theories might amount to, in practice they had wielded a set of coherent, or perhaps not so coherent, moral ideals.

The reality of our moral consciousness and conscience are two of the most penetrating facets of our humanity. As a part answer to the question of who we are, it is indisputable that we are people who are primed to make and pursue moral precepts. Thus a large part of the inquiry into who we are has to follow the discussion about moral truth.

There are many places we could begin. I will start with a brief critique of the weakest theories that have been advanced and, hopefully, be able to move on to stronger schemes. Helvetius, in his *A Treatise on Man*, comes close to expounding a cynical view of moral values. He considers that moral sensibilities are based on the self-interests of individuals. This leads him to claim that the faculty of judgment emerges wholly out of the faculty of sensation. The interest in making judgments is founded on the love of happiness and the avoidance of pain. The principles of pleasure and pain materialize in feelings of remorse, friendships, the love of power, sociability, and moral attitudes of sympathy and compassion. This view of morality is little more than a self-directed concern for one's own contentment. What is right is what affords personal happiness. In the last resort, "the love of others is never anything else in man than an effect of the love of himself."[17] If it is true that the natural world is entirely devoid of moral indicators, where else do humans go to define their moral principles than their own selves?

David Hume's understanding of moral convictions also rests on a kind of solipsism: the basis for moral beliefs and behavior rest on our sentiments and feelings, whatever causes pleasantness and unpleasantness in our psyche. It is a form of moral subjectivism—all moral facts can be reduced to personal desires and feelings. The only basis for obligation and duty could be found in what I owe myself. Diderot could have pushed this self-serving notion of morality even further: Why would one not

---

17. Helvetius, *Treatise on Man*, 296.

follow the leaning of the Marquis de Sade and abandon oneself to one's own cravings? Embracing the logical implications of the nonexistence of God and a monist materialism, it would be right to conclude that the only virtue is the survival of the fittest, and this justifies the strongest in the use of physical or psychological force to pursue their selfish, hedonist ends. The very existence of violence and cruelty in human nature indicates that it is thought to be legitimate to pursue these ends for one's own pleasure: "There is no God. Nature sufficeth unto herself."[18] In fact, Diderot did not follow de Sade, but in moral persuasion drifted between an intense individualism and a broad collectivism. He hovered between committing himself to a *morale universelle* (a universal ethic), which could speak meaningfully of a certain objective justice being implemented for the common good, and the right and duty of individuals to allow their own personal creative impulses to flourish.

Marxist morality is based on a kind of utilitarianism in which the promotion of the greatest happiness is a collectivist notion that takes its roots in the overriding necessity to see the end of the alienation of the proletariat caused by the capitalist mode of production. The good is defined by a dialectical process of human history, which ends in the abolition of economic slavery. Although Marx, Engels, and the later generation of Marxist leaders disdained the whole notion of an an ideal vision of society based on universal principles of justice, freedom, and equality, their writings are shot full precisely of moral judgments based on universal moral prescriptions. However, apart from a deterministic and progressive reading of history, there is no credible reasoning within their ideology for considering a Communist society to be a rightly preferred alternative to that of a capitalist one.

Darwin agreed that it is difficult to explain a moral sense in human beings on a secular evolutionary basis:

> I fully subscribe to the judgment of those writers who maintain that of all the differences between man and the lower animals, the moral sense or conscience is by far the most important. This sense . . . is summed up in that short but imperious word ought, so full of high significance.[19]

Although he tended to accept a utilitarian basis for moral values, he was hesitant in ascribing to it the ability to bear the whole weight of

---

18. www.brainyquote.com/quotes/authors/m/marquis_de_sade.html.
19. Darwin, *Descent of Man*, 56.

moral virtue. The greatest good of the greatest number begs a number of fundamental questions, not least the question about what is good. There has to be an independent, objective way of deciding whether what the majority of a population of citizens consider is good really is good. William Temple talks about apparent good and real good. How is the latter to be discovered and who is able to disclose it?

Nietzsche's revaluation of all values does not need to be taken seriously, since it is based on a series of misinterpretations of what he considered to be the prevailing morality of the age. His notion that the reigning conventional morality (by which he means Christian-based morality) is founded on resentment, the ascetic ideal and pity and brings humiliation to humankind, is so far from an accurate account of what he is referring to that it can be justifiably cast aside. His alternative is a vision of the good that promotes his understanding of life, namely to satisfy the basic instincts of human experience; to promote "the inner wells of energy." It is a view of morality with close affinities to that of Hume, Diderot and de Sade, only with a stronger touch of narcissism.

It was Kant who, having like all rationalists abandoned the Christian framework as an adequately grounded foundation for moral belief, made a gallant effort to come up with a convincing set of universal moral principles, ones that could be applied to all people in all circumstances. The twin dictums of Kant's ethical theory—"to treat all people as an end in themselves, never as a means to another end," and "treat others as you would wish to be treated yourself"[20]—have probably come to represent the default moral absolutes of Western-inspired human rights objectives.

These are some of the most important conclusions about the reality of moral consciousness that have been encountered in the course of this inquiry. As already indicated, they have many defects from a rational and experiential perspective. The lack of a coherent and comprehensive view has led to a good deal of moral confusion and deception in current ethical theory and practice. This has already been highlighted by the eminent twentieth-century theologians, whose perceptions of human nature were discussed in the last chapter. At this juncture, I will summarize the underlying points they have made, in order to propose a Christian moral code that (a) takes seriously the best of Christian moral consciousness, and (b) also acknowledges the genuine critiques that have been made of

---

20. Kramnick, *Portable Enlightenment Reader*, 304.

Christian-based morality, where it has drifted away from its own moorings in its early history.

In debate with secular humanism, authentically established Christian faith shows how and why it alone provides an unmatched approach to moral reasoning. It is hard to justify the truth of moral righteousness and goodness that can claim universal credibility without the existence of a moral judge entirely independent of human prudence and intelligence. Without the existence of such a judge, able to make known with certainty the content of good and evil, humans have to invent values with only nature—created by a random evolutionary process—to guide them.

An attempt has been made, through an imaginative device (or thought experiment), to provide humankind with a nontheist version of such an arbiter: the ideal observer (IO). The IO does not exist in any living form. It is a purely hypothetical being, supposedly possessing full information of all the facts surrounding a moral case and complete impartiality between divergent opinions about the matter. The criterion by which one knows whether an action is morally right or wrong, according to this theory, is the feeling of approval or disapproval with which the IO would react to the action in question. It is hard to envisage anyone taking such a theory seriously:

> As the IO does not exist, the ordinary human being (not being ideal in the sense described) still has to decide what the IO would approve or disapprove of, for the latter cannot communicate its feelings. This being so, how does this theory escape the accusation that it merely projects the subjective feelings of the ordinary human on to a hypothetical figure. In the last analysis, the IO is a fiction; the one who decides is not the ideal Observer, but the ordinary observer who decides what is to be approved or disapproved. The whole theory confuses means and ends. It simply does not answer the question about how we know that the feelings of the IO are rightly expressed. In other words, omniscience and impartiality do not constitute the source of ethical values; they merely tell us something about optimum conditions for exercising good moral judgments. For moral approval or disapproval to have any purchase, moral rightness and

wrongness must be assumed. However, the IO is not the source of this knowledge.[21]

The theory demonstrates that a consistent naturalism comprehensively lacks a basis for warranting a metaphysics of personhood and its intrinsic dignity and value, for these cannot be natural properties. All the qualities that the IO is fancifully imagined to possess already are possessed by the Christian vision of God: God exists; is personal, and is the complete expression and fount of all moral virtues, the very definition of goodness, compassion, justice, and so on.

Perhaps the greatest moral dilemma for a secular humanist is the inability to deduce a moral obligation from an existential or material fact. As William Temple rightly says, moral discernment requires different thought processes, based on contrasting thought processes, from those necessary to arrive at scientific conclusions.[22] By committing deicide (not only by declaring God dead, but also by exercising complete indifference to the possible existence of God), the opinion-formers of modern Western culture have stolen the emperor's clothes. For example, the magnificent declaration of the French National Assembly in 1789 that "men are born and remain free and equal in rights"[23] is a false statement, if taken as one of fact. Two hundred years after the abolition of slavery, it remains widespread in the modern world. With regard to equality, it would be much more accurate to declare that "humans across the globe are in reality, for a number of reasons, born unequal." It is only a true statement if taken as a matter of how humans are constituted in essence by their creation, only if their humanity is interpreted in a particular way. If that interpretation is denied, their intrinsic equality is lost, not only in practice, but also as a well-grounded theory.

Locke, at the beginning of the century that introduced the so-called Age of Reason, saw clearly the implication of atheism. He believed that, if tolerated, atheism would create a moral vacuum:

---

21. Kirk, *Christian Mission as Dialogue*, 118–19. I use torture as a moral illustration in my discussion of the absurdity of this proposition as a means of establishing an intelligible approach to an objective moral philosophy.

22. Temple, *Nature, Man and God*, 34, 53.

23. *Declaration of the Rights of Man and the Citizen*. See, Kramnick, *Portable Enlightenment Reader*, 467.

The taking away of God, though but even in thought, dissolves all.[24]

His reasoning may be correct. However, his conclusion that moral sentiments would fade away did not coincide with his series of arguments on behalf of tolerance. As a matter of historical fact, by and large, atheists have tended to adhere to basic Christian moral principles, in order to be able to give their own some kind of intellectual rationale.

Evil: Origin, Reality, and Overcoming

As we have already discovered, secular humanist thought tends to be optimistic about the future of humans' being. Does it, however, have adequate justification for confidence in the improvement of human well-being? Evil is a reality no one would dispute, unless they had a serious personality disorder or a woefully misguided religious or ideological conviction which causes them to delight in callous acts of violence. In countries where media outlets are not politically controlled, reporting calamitous and corrupt events appears to dominate the news that is disseminated, or if not evil as such, then unfortunate, distressing, and adverse circumstances. Do the purveyors of news assume that those who receive it prefer to read, listen to, or view news about current affairs that transmit dismal and menacing tidings of disasters, tragedies, and failures? It might seem that from the amount of negative thoughts communicated on social media each hour of each day that this would be the case. However, accounts of bravery, sacrificial service, generosity, understanding, and gentleness—all of which lift the human spirit—might appear to be much more acceptable as the core of media output than those stories that bring doom and gloom.

Most human beings, whether believers or nonbelievers in God, have a reliable idea of what is good and evil. But in either case, where the existence of a morally perfect divine creator is dismissed as an illusion, can they justify their beliefs? Their worldview is constructed on the basis that humans are the result of an evolutionary process without any overall given purpose or meaning. By an amazing set of circumstances and coincidences, it is presumed to exist by self-generation. The only built-in motivating power is survival, with the major impulse being that of reproduction. On the basis of this fundamental conviction, where does

24. Locke, in Sigmund, *Selected Political Writings*, 158.

the notion of evil come from? Logically speaking, one might conclude that the only evil we can talk about meaningfully, from this perspective, is whatever hinders reproduction by the fittest.

As far as we know, animals have no sense of right and wrong, for they do not possess a conscience. Thus, if a dog kills a small child, we do not have it put down as an act of punishment because it has knowingly transgressed the law "you shall not kill," but in order to stop another tragedy from happening. Dogs are not responsible for their actions; we do not put them on trial. Rather, we hold their owners to account for their behavior. On the naturalistic evolutionary hypothesis, however, human beings are merely animals that walk upright, have more complex brains, and more dexterity in their hands. How, one might ask, do these distinguishing marks give them a capacity for making moral judgments between good and evil? How does one build a bridge between the most advanced primate, lacking a highly developed moral consciousness, and human sentiments of responsibility, blame, guilt, a stricken conscience, and penitence?

Paul Bloom, in his study, *Just Babies: The Origins of Good and Evil*,[25] acknowledges that a naturalist, by means of evolutionary biology or social psychology, has to attempt to explain how a moral sense in humans might have arisen and developed. No other option, he believes, is an open possibility. Neuroscientists, he affirms, can look at parts of the brain involved in moral reasoning; sociologists may explore how features of the environment encourage kindness or cruelty.

His own research into how very young children (even those of less than one year) react to examples of moral goodness and badness, incline him to believe that moral discernment is innate from the beginning of a child's existence. Humans are simply endowed with a capacity to distinguish between kind and cruel actions, have compassion, and have a sense of fairness and justice. However, this innate goodness is limited by self-interest, indifference to the needs and plight of others, hostility toward strangers, bigotry, and disgust. He quotes a statement of Thomas Jefferson:

> Man was destined for society. His morality therefore was to be formed to this object. He was endowed with a sense of right and wrong merely relative to this. This sense is as much part of

---

25. Bloom, *Just Babies*.

his nature as the sense of hearing, seeing, feeling; it is the true foundation of morality.[26]

He seems to be talking about conscience. However, this does not solve the conundrum, for how can a moral foundation be a product of evolution? How is it possible for the wholly amoral force of natural selection to produce a sense of moral thought and action? That, surely, is a dilemma for all those who believe that human beings are the product of blind evolutionary forces, directed by natural causes alone.

According to the Christian worldview, the existence of evil presupposes a moral order put in place by God to reflect his character. Just as the physical world functions according to physical laws that are not invented by humans, but are a given in nature, so humans function best when they adhere to God's moral laws that also are part of the warp and woof of existence. Evil, then, is the result of human beings choosing to abandon God's directions for a full human life and deciding to create their own kind of world.

In a remarkable passage, Paul calls it *exchange*.[27] People have exchanged the truth about God, creation, and God's way to live rightly for their own invented handiwork. Evil, therefore, is life based on a fundamental lie; people trying to live on the basis of unreality. According to the narrative which recounts the origin of evil,[28] evil entered the world as the abuse of freedom. We now call it humans' desire to be autonomous.

The serpent's question, "Has God said . . . ?"[29] is the most fundamental temptation that humankind faces. The response can be, "Yes, he has; it is for our maximum well-being." Or, it could be, "no he hasn't." Or, again, it might be, "I don't care whether he has or has not, I will choose my own path." Finally, and more likely in a secular environment, it is likely to be, "as God does not exist (nor the devil disguised as a serpent), nor any established moral order, we will invent the latter as we go along."

A blind, random, impersonal evolutionary process knows nothing of good and evil. In the eternal struggle for survival, morality has no place. At the same time, it occurs to humans that living in a "condition of perpetual war of every person against every person,"[30] a "life (which is)

---

26. https://founders.archives.gov/documents/Jefferson/01-12-02-0021.
27. Rom 1:22, 25, 26.
28. Gen 2—3.
29. Gen 3:1.
30. Hobbes, *Leviathan*, I.13.9.

solitary, poor, nasty, brutish, and short"[31] is not very satisfactory. So, they create an order of their own to limit and attempt to reverse their natural aggression.

Juan Luis Segundo agrees with the conclusion Ricoeur draws from his study of Freud that his practice of

> psychoanalysis seeks to replace an instinctive, deceitful conscience dominated by an inner darkness with a reflecting consciousness that is guided by the reality principle.[32]

Confronting this profound disjunction within the core inner being of the human personality with the language of the Christian faith, Segundo shows that we are dealing with a natural human facility—he calls it concupiscence—to adhere to a reality which can only be overcome by divine grace. He cites, as his ground for coming to this conclusion, Paul's discourse on the daily experience of the division we experience between what we desire to do and our ability to do it.[33]

In our inquiry, the two protagonists who most profoundly analyzed the inner human psyche—Nietzsche and Freud—came to the conclusion that humans are constitutionally under the domination of two powerful basic instincts. In Nietzsche's case, they are represented by two of the gods of Greek Mythology: Apollo and Dionysus. Apollo represented order in human life, the curtailing of uninhibited instincts by a life-denying set of values, the purveyor of the banalities of normal being in the world. Dionysus represented the "will to power" or the conquest of all that curtails bodily passions. To take on the stature of the *Ubermensch*, the person who recognizes, recovers, and manages the healthy drives with which all are born, but which are repressed by culture, is the main goal of human existence. Nietzsche identified himself with the latter.

Freud affirms that his most startlingly contentious book, *Beyond the Pleasure Principle*, attempts "to reveal Eros and the death instinct as the motivating powers whose interplay dominates all the riddles of life."[34] He came to the conclusion that within the human libido existed not only the love instinct (*Eros*—affection[35]) but also the hate instinct (*Thanatos*—

---

31. Hobbes, *Leviathan*, I.21.97.
32. Ricoeur, *Freud and Philosophy*, 43.
33. Laid out in Romans 7:14–24.
34. See Dufresne, *Late Sigmund Freud*, 1–2.
35. In terms of the use of social media, "liking" might be a more appropriate designation.

the desire to destroy). He began to advance a theory that, built into our nature, we possess a demonic impulse that undermines life, love, and sociability. Freud postulated that human beings are driven from birth by the desire to acquire and enhance bodily pleasure. Sexual energy (libido), redefined as any form of bodily pleasure, is the single most important motivating force in adult life. It is expressed as a self-preserving and pleasure principle. At the same time, humans universally demonstrate the trait of an irrational urge to destroy the sources of all forms of sexual energy in the annihilation of the self. From where does this aggressive, self-destructive, and cruel instinct arise? This was a problem that he had to address from then on.[36]

In both cases, these two profound thinkers, whilst hoping to navigate a way through the immense tensions set up by opposing instincts, came to pessimistic conclusions about natural human dispositions. They coincide, to some extent, with those discovered by Paul within his own being nineteen centuries previously. They are profoundly significant for casting light on the reality and nature of evil. Of the three, only Paul has a message that has, when acted on, proved itself able to overcome the psychic stress caused by the inherited tension: the free, unmerited grace of God.

Human Identity

We have now arrived at the end of our journey, or as some might say, "the end of the beginning." The inquiry has thrown up an amazing variety of beliefs, theories, conjectures, ideas, opinions, proposals, and propositions about the nature of being human. Anyone who underestimates the deep complexity of human experience will never gain wisdom about this fundamental question: Who, then, are we? Anyone who easily dismisses ways of thinking they do not immediately share or misinterprets other people's convictions, in order to escape having to respond honestly to intellectual challenges, displays an unhealthy rational superficiality.

Those confronted with such a divergence of perspectives that they avoid coming to conclusions by resorting to a skeptical attitude toward all viewpoints deceive themselves for, as Hume discovered, it is not possible to live on such a basis; one would have to, logically, be skeptical about one's skepticism. Such a position would, one imagines, end up in a

---

36. See Thornton, "Sigmund Freud."

reductio ad absurdum of complete mental paralysis. Strong doubt about all responses to human meaning should, if consistent, produce cynicism and pessimism. Cynicism evades honesty, for it presupposes that those inclined to practice it have a superior attitude to all the statements of belief they criticize whilst ignoring the weaknesses of their own beliefs. Pessimism may embrace honesty, up to a point. It can also, however, if there is no realistic source for hopeful anticipations, lead to depression or even suicide.

Others, confused by the conflicting judgments about their own human reality, may console themselves by handing over the disentangling of the matter to those they consider experts: "I am prepared to believe what the scientists, such as physiologists, psychiatrists, anthropologists, and sociologists, have demonstrated as beyond doubt." There are, unfortunately for those who believe this may grant them some comfort, several difficulties. What can be demonstrated about the human being that is beyond doubt? Beyond the functioning of the physical body there is very little. Some optimists have put their hope in the fact that exploration of the functioning of the brain, that can be detected through sophisticated brain scans, may uncover links between physical changes within the cerebral cortex and human experience. Such a procedure, however, is unlikely to be able to build convincing bridges from analysis of the brain to the mind and its ways of thinking, as though we were somehow born in the image of a robot.

Yet others are persuaded to wait until there is a consensus in society about some potentially significant belief that is worth holding on to. In recent years in Western cultures, there has been huge compulsion by well-organized pressure groups to change traditional beliefs about human sexuality. These small minorities have managed to achieve significant changes in the laws about what has been promoted as homosexual, bisexual and transsexual rights. It is, however, not certain at all that the arguments put forward accord with indisputable facts. Nevertheless, from a particular perspective, the campaigns have been highly successful. The promotion of homosexuality, for example, has been achieved largely on the basis of two pieces of propaganda: the misuse of language in the definition of the notion of homophobia, and support for the belief that anti-homosexuality must be treated in the same category as racism, sexism, ageism and disabilityism, since homosexual attraction is dogmatically alleged to be an innate characteristic with which one is born. Meanwhile, transgenderism is based on a mental fiction, seeing that the personal opinion that a person can change their biological sex by merely asserting they now wish to be recognized as a person of the opposite sex has no effect on the sex with which they were born. Even sophisticated surgical procedures that alter certain gender-relevant bodily phenomena do not make a man into a woman or a woman into a man. This is to reduce the human to the physical, to deny a holistic understanding of the whole person and to create even greater confusion. Being born homosexual is likewise simply asserted, and not because there is any convincing evidence to support it as an established fact. [37]

Any Way Forward? Dialogue in the Context of Truth[38]

After this lengthy discourse about what eminent people have considered to be the main characteristics of being human, what main conclusion can we draw? It could be that we will simply have to beg to differ. In the face of growing intolerance about other people's views, proliferating divisions between groups with strong convictions around issues such as human rights and identity politics, often based on divergent interpretations of who we are, that would be a tragic conclusion to arrive at. The result could have serious consequences for the future of the well-being of Western societies, heralding a serious loss of cohesion. I will end, then, with a proposal (already hinted at) for a method of serious dialogue that, if carried out, might help to heal the wounds.

In the experimental sciences, one of the main methods of assessing the outcomes of research work is called "Inference to the Best Explanation" (IBE) (technically designated *abduction*). It is a mode of reasoning that infers the truth of a situation by means of comparing different solutions to ascertain which offers the best explanation of the greatest amount of evidence relevant to the case. Thus, for example, in

---

37. I realize that this paragraph about homosexuality and transgenderism is inadequate as a convincing response to the current cultural conflict on the nature of human sexuality; it is simply intended in this context as an illustration of a significant cultural shift in thinking about human being. I have written at much greater length on the subject in a forthcoming book, with the title *The Abuse of Language and the Language of Abuse*, which deals with the rhetorical misappropriation of key words like "tolerance/intolerance," "equality," "fundamentalist," "justice," "rights" and "homophobia," and them being currently hoisted on the populace without sufficient analytical vigor.

38. This last section of the whole study is taken from the conclusion of my research on the current epistemological predicament of the West; see Kirk, *Christian Mission as Dialogue*, 129, 131–32.

the medical sciences, a particular diagnosis of an illness is confirmed in a preliminary way, because it offers the best explanation (cause) of the symptoms manifested.

IBE is a tool, used by reason, for settling the truth of a matter. It is evidence-based: beginning with the information available to us, we infer what would, if true, provide the *best* explanation of that information (*best* implies the most persuasive among possible alternative explanations).

Now, it is legitimate to claim that IBE is the most adequate way yet devised of engaging in dialogue between conflicting beliefs. It proceeds in a way similar to the proceedings of the law courts, with the aim of establishing the truth of the matter relating to a particular crime (the motive, the opportunity, the nature of the crime itself, and the likely perpetrator) "beyond all reasonable doubt."

In the case of being human, the theory's explanatory power is measured by its success in accounting for the data of personal experience, observation, historical witness, and conduct. It is also fruitful in its predictive ability with regard to human behavior, as in the case of being able to explain why children, who are deprived of proper care, security, and affection by a male and female parent, will suffer destructive consequences for their emotional stability. It is based on evidence that is open to being rationally assessed and empirically tested. It is open for anyone to participate in its conversational method. As it is applicable to many disciplines, it commands wide acceptance as a method of checking truth claims. It avoids begging questions about whether basic beliefs have to be agreed upon prior to any dialogue taking place; even though they may be disputed, they can still be brought into any discussion as potential explanations of human life. Discussions about truth are essentially examinations of the nature of a reality of which everyone is a part. It avoids an immediate appeal to subjective experience, which is always hard to assess, and which may not be easily communicable.

So IBE offers an excellent, tried-and-tested method for rationally considering all claims to know the ultimate reality that lies behind involvement in being human. Its process is one of advocacy, in a courteous manner, in which alternative explanations of the great questions of existence are promoted, discussed, evaluated, and accepted or rejected.

If the apprehension of truth is the most fundamental issue that always confronts us, then IBE is concerned with offering the most comprehensive and intellectually and existentially compelling evaluation of the realities of existence. Its pragmatic value lies in its ability to distinguish between truth and error, fact and fantasy. There is no question that lies outside its purview. It is, therefore, equally applicable to scientific research, moral debate, and religious claims, each of which, in its own way, appeals to a transcendental realism.

In spite of the skepticism of postmodern thinking, human beings, to fulfill their self-understanding, need to situate their lives within a discourse that offers a metainterpretation of their experience. This has been called "a grand narrative," an account of life that links together all the fragmentary parts into a plausible whole. Human beings can be seen to flourish best when they can make sense of the past, present, and future. In the West, there are still only two major grand narratives that offer this kind of interpretation: modernity in its current form of liberal, secular humanism, and Christian faith.[39]

I argue, toward the end of the inquiry, that liberal secular humanism gives an inadequate account of reality in a number of crucial areas. It is unable to explain why the conditions necessary for the scientific enterprise to function exist perfectly. It cannot offer grounds adequate enough for knowledge to be possible—the total coherence between subject and object, the observer and the observed. It is forced to be reductionist in its attempts to explain the rich experience of human life, for on the basis of a naturalist, evolutionary account of the rise of human life, it fails to account for the existence of consciousness, the self, rationality, the inherent dignity of the human species, moral duty, and aesthetic appreciation. In a meaningless world, it is hard pressed to offer an explanation as to why human beings wish to invest their lives with meaning. This would seem to suggest a poor adaptive strategy, since there is an apparent incoherence between reality (senselessness) and what human beings long for (significance and value). A neo-Darwinian evolutionary account of the history of the universe makes the world both impersonal and hostile. Secular humanism is committed to continuing the myth that the worlds of science and faith have to be confrontational. It appears to operate on

---

39. I acknowledge that there are a number of other grand narratives represented today in Europe: Islam, Buddhism, Hinduism, the remnants of Marxism, and a resurgent fascism. I also am aware of the fact that adherents of a postmodern reading of culture disclaim any notion of grand-narratives. In the former cases, religions other than Christianity, or ideological beliefs have not had the same impact yet on Western culture, although most of them certainly offer alternatives to the two main protagonists. In the latter case, postmodernity cannot escape so easily from the accusation that it too offers a grand-narrative, for, in spite of its relativistic rhetoric, it certainly stands for a number of universal values.

the basis that they are incompatible alternatives. As a result, it converts itself into a kind of pseudoreligion: methodological naturalism translates into metaphysical naturalism.

Fortunately, IBE is available as an effective, heuristic means of arriving at the greatest possible approximation to the truth, for it has the ability to overcome subjective partialities. IBE can be productive in the rational consideration of all claims to know the ultimate reality that lies behind the experience of being human. No claim to know the ultimate meaning of life is excluded *ab initio*. All can be part of the dialogue, which proceeds by way of testing the claims against one another and against the stubborn facts of human life in the world. Naturally, there is no final human arbiter. Each person or group has to decide for itself how far its intuition, common sense, philosophy of life (homespun or borrowed), ideology, or religion is best able to make sense of the widest spread of the reality of life. The process is one of advocacy in which alternative explanations are promoted, discussed, and judged. It is assumed that where there are conflicting claims, they cannot both be valid, though they could both be false.

When it comes to knowledge in the realm of human self-awareness, where there are numerous conflicting interpretations, IBE is almost certainly the best way of arriving at an understanding of how and why things are as they are. This is a nondogmatic, bottom-up approach. If alternative explanations are treated fairly, on the basis of mutual respect and consideration, the most favorable condition for arriving at a knowledge of the truth can prevail.[40] The method, in its application to the means of attaining justified, true belief, can heal the breach between knowledge of facts and mere opinions, between public truth and private beliefs.

It is exemplified in a book by Keith Ward,[41] in which he concludes by arguing that, as an explanation of human experience in the universe, materialism as an alternative to theism is deficient in its ability to explain a number of ultimate questions: the final basis of matter, consciousness, moral sensibility, the universal longing for a sense of purpose, the com-

---

40. In *Theory of Communicative Action*, Jurgen Habermas offers an analysis of the conditions necessary for interpersonal communication to be governed by the ideal of rational discourse, such as sincerity, truth-telling, and rational warrant. He refers to this as an ideal speech situation. He hoped that these rules would enable people to conduct the discussion of disagreements in a way most likely to promote understanding of all the issues involved; see also Putnam, *Collapse of the Fact/Value Dichotomy*, 113–17.

41. Ward, *God Conclusion*; see ch. 11: "Materialism and its Discontents."

mitment to rational thinking and the existence of the universe. These are precisely the questions, and there are others (such as aesthetic appreciation and the intrinsic dignity of human beings) which are unanswerable unless the means of arriving at truth are generally agreed upon.

It is curious, however, that a theistic worldview (rejected by metaphysical naturalism) gives a perfectly adequate, rational explanation for each one of these questions. It is perhaps not surprising that some atheists are prepared to concede that, although in their opinion theism is false, human beings nevertheless function better on the supposition that it is true. This, of course, though not a demonstration of its truth, may be a reliable indication.

Questions

1. This lengthy study ends up by discussing a distinction between Christian theism and secular humanism as the two main existing alternative explanations of what it means to be human. Do you think this is a fair conclusion of the state of the debate in the Western world?

2. In your opinion, what are the chief challenges to these two metanarratives that might put their principal conclusions in jeopardy?

3. In light of the discussion so far, what evidence can you see for holding an optimistic view for human progress in the future? To what extent would you see such a view as realistic?

4. The final section promotes "inference to the best explanation," within "an ideal speech situation," as a method of rational engagement most likely to produce the best understanding amongst people who hold deeply conflicting views. How far would you agree or disagree with such a proposition?

Bibliography

Acampora, Christa Davis. "Beholding Nietzsche: *Ecce Homo*, Fate, and Freedom." In *The Oxford Handbook of Nietzsche*, edited by Ken Gemes and John Richardson, 363–85. Oxford: Oxford University Press, 2013.

Anchor, Robert. *The Enlightenment Tradition*. Berkeley: University of California Press, 1967.

Archibald, Peter. *Marx and the Missing Link: Human Nature*. Basingstoke, UK: Macmillan, 1989.

Avineri, Shlomo. *The Social and Political Thought of Karl Marx*. Cambridge: Cambridge University Press, 1968.

Baier, Annette C. *The Pursuits of Philosophy: An Introduction to the Life and Thought of David Hume*. Cambridge, MA: Harvard University Press, 2011.

Barrett, Paul H., et al., eds. *Charles Darwin's Notebooks*. Cambridge: Cambridge University Press, 1987. http://darwin-online.org.uk/.

Beauchamp, Tom L., ed. *David Hume: An Enquiry Concerning Human Understanding*. Oxford: Oxford University Press, 1999.

Behler, Ernst. "Nietzsche in the Twentieth Century." In *The Cambridge Companion to Nietzsche*, edited by Bernard Magnus and Kathleen M. Higgins, 281–322. Cambridge: Cambridge University Press, 1996.

Berdyaev, Nicholas. *The Origin of Russian Communism*. Ann Arbor, MI: University of Michigan Press, 1960.

Bishop, Paul, ed. *A Companion to Friedrich Nietzsche*. Rochester, NY: Camden, 2015.

Bloch, Ernst. "Man and Citizen According to Marx." In *Socialist Humanism: An International Symposium*, edited by Erich Fromm, 220–27. NY: Doubleday, 1965.

Bloom, Harold, ed. *Sigmund Freud (Modern Critical Views)*. London: Chelsea, 1985.

Bloom, Paul. *Just Babies: The Origins of Good and Evil*. New York: Broadway, 2014.

Bottomore, Tom, et al., eds. *A Dictionary of Marxist Thought*. 2nd ed. Oxford: Blackwell, 1991.

Brecher, Bob. "The Politics of Humanism." In *Debating Humanism*, edited by Dolan Cummings, 108–16. Exeter, UK: Societas, 2006.

Bremner, Geoffrey. *Order and Chance: The Patterns of Diderot's Thought*. Cambridge: Cambridge University Press, 1983.

Brotton, Jerry. "Myth of the Renaissance in Europe." www.bbc.co.uk/history/british/tudors/renaissance_europe_01.shtml

———. *The Renaissance: A Very Short Introduction*. Oxford: Oxford University Press, 2006.

Browne, Janet. "Introduction." In *The Descent of Man, and Selection in Relation to Sex*, by Charles Darwin, ix–xxv. Ware, UK: Wordsworth Classics, 2013.
Brumfitt, John Henry. *The French Enlightenment*. Basingstoke, UK: Macmillan, 1972.
Buber, Martin. *Paths in Utopia*. Syracuse, NY: Syracuse University Press, 1995.
Burckhardt, Jacob. *The Civilization of the Renaissance in Italy*. Reprint. Harmondsworth, UK: Penguin, 1990.
Burke, Peter. *The Italian Renaissance: Culture and Society in Italy*. 3rd ed. Cambridge, UK: Polity, 2014.
Burnham, Douglas. *Nietzsche Dictionary*. London: Bloomsbury Academic, 2015.
Burns, William. *The Enlightenment: History, Documents and Key Questions*. Crossroads in World History. Santa Barbara, CA: ABC-CLIO, 2016.
Butler, Melissa. "Early Liberal Roots of Feminism: John Locke and the Attack on Patriarchy." In *The Selected Political Writings of John Locke*, edited by Paul E. Sigmund, 379–85. New York: Norton, 2005.
Caferro, William. *Contesting the Renaissance*. Oxford: Wiley-Blackwell, 2011.
Carroll, John. *Humanism: The Wreck of Western Culture*. New York: Fontana, 1993.
Cast, David J. *The Ashgate Research Companion to Giorgio Vasari*. Farnham, UK: Ashgate, 2014.
Cave, Peter. *Humanism: A Beginner's Guide*. Oxford: One World, 2009.
Chappell, Vere. "Locke on Freedom of the Will." In *Locke's Philosophy: Content and Context*, edited by G. A. J. Rogers, 101–22. Oxford: Clarendon, 1994.
Cheah, Fook Meng. "A Review of Luther and Erasmus: Free Will and Salvation." www.prca.org/prtj/nov95b.html.
Clark, Maudemarie. *Nietzsche on Ethics and Politics*. Oxford: Oxford University Press, 2015.
Clifford, William K. *Lectures and Essays*. London: Macmillan, 1879.
Cohen, Gerald. *Karl Marx's Theory of History: A Defence*. Princeton: Princeton University Press, 1978.
Cohn, Samuel. *The Black Death Transformed: Disease and Culture in Early Renaissance Florence*. London: Arnold, 2003.
Conquest, Robert. *Where Marx went Wrong*. Ann Arbor, MI: University of Michigan Press, 1970.
Cook, Alexander, et al., eds. *Representing Humanity in the Age of Enlightenment*. London: Pickering and Chatto, 2013.
Cooper, David E. *World Philosophies: An Introduction*. Oxford: Blackwell, 1996.
Copson, Andrew. "Humanism and Faith Schools." In *Debating Humanism*, edited by Dolan Cummings, 75–83. Exeter, UK: Societas, 2006.
Cummings, Dolan, ed. *Debating Humanism*. Exeter, UK: Societas, 2006.
Darwin, Charles. *The Descent of Man, and Selection in Relation to Sex*. Ware, UK: Wordsworth Classics, 2013.
———. *On Natural Selection*. London: Penguin, 2004.
———. *The Origin of Species by Means of Natural Selection*. 6th ed. Oxford: Benediction Classics, 2011.
Davies, Tony. *Humanism: The New Critical Idiom*. 2nd ed. Abingdon, UK: Routledge, 2008.

Dawkins, Richard. *The Blind Watchmaker*. London: Norton, 1986.
———. *River Out of Eden*. New York: Basic, 1995.

de Waal, Frans. *Are We Smart Enough to Know How Smart Animals are?* New York: Norton, 2016.

Degler, Carl. *In Search of Human Nature: The Decline and Revival of Darwinism in American Social Thought.* New York: Oxford University Press, 1991.

de las Casas, Bartolome. *Obras Completas.* Madrid: Alianza Editorial, 1992.

Dembski, William. *Being as Communion: A Metaphysics of Information.* Farnham, UK: Ashgate, 2014.

Dembski, William, ed. *Uncommon Dissent: Intellectuals Who Find Darwinism Unconvincing.* Wilmington, DE: ISI, 2004.

Denton, Michael. *Evolution: Still a Theory in Crisis.* Seattle: Discovery Institute, 2016.

d'Holbach, Baron. *The System of Nature: Laws of the Physical World and of the Moral World.* Translated by Balraj Joshi. Self-published: Xlibris, 2016.

Diderot, Denis. "Letter on the Blind for the Use of Those Who See." In *Diderot's Early Philosophical Works,* edited by Margaret Jourdain, 68–142. Neuilly sur Seine: Ulan, 2012.

———. *Rameau's Nephew and Other Works.* Translated by Ralph H. Bowen. Indianapolis: Hackett, 2001.

Dufresne, Todd. *The Late Sigmund Freud: Or, the Last Word on Psychoanalysis, Society, and All the Riddles of Life.* Cambridge: Cambridge University Press, 2017.

Dupre, Louis. *Religion and the Rise of Modern Culture.* Notre Dame: University of Notre Dame Press, 2008.

Dyson, Anthony, and Bernard Towers. *Evolution, Marxism and Christianity: Studies in the Teilhardian Synthesis.* Atlantic Highlands, NJ: Humanities Press International, 1967.

Engels, Friedrich. *Origin of the Family, Private Property and the State.* London: Penguin Classics, 2010.

Erasmus, Desiderius, and Martin Luther. *Discourse on Free Will.* London: Bloomsbury, 2013.

———. *The Education of Children.* Perfect Library Edition. Create Space, 2015.

———. *In Praise of Folly.* London: Penguin, 1971.

———. *Praise of Folly.* 2nd ed. Harmondsworth, UK: Penguin, 1993.

———. *Praise of Folly.* Translated by Marciano Guerrero. New York?: MaryMarc Translations, 2013.

Erwin, Edward A. *A Final Accounting: Philosophical and Empirical Issues in Freudian Psychology.* Cambridge, MA: MIT Press, 1996.

Etienne, Balibar. *Identity and Difference: John Locke and the Invention of Consciousness.* London: Verso, 2013.

Evans, Dylan. "Secular Fundamentalism." In *Debating Humanism,* edited by Dolan Cummings, 12–21. Exeter, UK: Societas, 2006.

Farr, James. "So Vile and Miserable an Estate: The Problem of Slavery in Locke's Political Thought." In *The Selected Political Writings of John Locke,* edited by Paul E. Sigmund, 374–79. New York: Norton, 2005.

Ferrone, Vincenzo, and Elisabetta Tarantino. *The Enlightenment: History of an Idea.* Princeton: Princeton University Press, 2015.

Feuerbach, Ludwig. *The Essence of Christianity.* Translated by Elisabetta Tarantino. New York: Harper, 1957.

Fisher, Seymour, and Roger P. Greenberg. *Freud Scientifically Reappraised: Testing the Theories and Therapy.* Boston: Wiley & Sons, 1996.

Forster, Michael. "Hegel's Dialectical Method." In *The Cambridge Companion to Hegel*, edited by Frederick C. Beiser, 130–70. Cambridge: Cambridge University Press, 1993.
Fowler, James. *New Essays on Diderot*. Cambridge: Cambridge University Press, 2011.
Frazer, James. *Totemism and Exogamy: A Treatise on Certain Early Forms of Superstition and Society*. Hamburg: Severus, 2011.
Freud, Sigmund. *An Autobiographical Study*. [s.l.]: Saphis, 2017.
———. *Beyond the Pleasure Principle and Other Writings*. Translated by John Reddick. Harmondsworth, UK: Penguin, 2003.
———. *Introductory Lectures on Psychoanalysis*. Harmondsworth, UK: Penguin, 1973.
Freud, Sigmund, and Carl Jung. *The Freud/Jung Letters*. Cambridge, MA: Harvard University Press, 1988.
Fromm, Eric. *Fear of Freedom*. London: Routledge and Paul, 1960.
———. *Marx's Concept of Man*. 3rd ed. London: Continuum, 2004.
———. *Socialist Humanism: An International Symposium*. Garden City, NY: Doubleday, 1965.
Fukuyama, Francis. *The End of History and the Last Man*. London: Hamish Hamilton, 1992.
Furedi, Frank. *On Tolerance: A Defence of Moral Independence*. London: Continuum, 2011.
Gardner, Sebastian. *Kant and the Critique of Pure Reason*. London: Routledge, 1999.
Gaskin, John C. A. "Hume on Religion." In *The Cambridge Companion to Hume*, edited by David F. Norton, 480–514. Cambridge: Cambridge University Press, 1993.
Gay, Peter. *The Enlightenment: A Comprehensive Anthology*. New York: Simon & Schuster, 1973.
———. *The Freud Reader*. New York: Norton, 1995.
Gayon, Jean. "From Darwin to Today in Evolutionary Biology." In *The Cambridge Companion to Darwin*, edited by Jonathan Hodge and Gregory Radick, 277–301. Cambridge: Cambridge University Press, 2009.
Geisler, Norman. *Is Man the Measure? An Evaluation of Contemporary Humanism*. Eugene, OR: Wipf & Stock, 2005.
Gemes, Ken, and John Richardson, eds. *The Oxford Handbook of Nietzsche*. Oxford: Oxford University Press, 2013.
Geras, Norman. *Marx and Human Nature: Refutation of a Legend*. 3rd ed. London: Verso, 2016.
Girardi, Giulio. *Marxism and Christianity*. Dublin: Gill and Son, 1968.
Golomb, Jacob. "Will to Power: Does it Lead to the 'Coldest of all Cold Monsters?'" In *The Oxford Handbook of Nietzsche*, edited by Ken Gemes and John Richardson, 525–50. Oxford: Oxford University Press, 2013.
Gonzalez, Ondina E., and Justo L. Gonzalez. *Christianity in Latin America: A History*. Cambridge: Cambridge University Press, 2008.
Goodman Anthony, and Angus Mackay. *The Impact of Humanism on Western Europe*. London: Longman, 1990.
———. *Philosophy: A Guide through the Subject*. Oxford: Oxford University Press, 1995.
Grant, Michael, and John Hazel. *Who's Who in Classical Mythology*. London: Routledge, 1994.

Grayling, Anthony C. *The God Argument: The Case against Religion and for Humanism.* London: Bloomsbury, 2013.
———. "Humanism, Religion and Ethics." In *Debating Humanism*, edited by Dolan Cummings, 47–54. Exeter, UK: Societas, 2006.
Grayling, Anthony, ed. *Philosophy: A Guide through the Subject.* Oxford: Oxford University Press, 1995.
Habermas, Jurgen. *The Theory of Communicative Action.* Translated by Thomas McCarthy. Boston: Beacon, 1984.
Hanrahan, James, and Siofra Pierse, eds. *The Dark Side of Diderot.* Bern, Switzerland: Lang, 2016.
Harris, James A. *Hume: An Intellectual Biography.* Cambridge: Cambridge University Press, 2015.
Hause, Steven, and William Maltby. *A History of European Society: Essentials of Western Civilization, Vol. 2.* Belmont, CA: Thomson, 2001.
Hayes, Dennis. "Re-humanising Education." In *Debating Humanism*, edited by Dolan Cummings, 84–92. Exeter, UK: Societas, 2006.
Hegel, Georg Wilhelm Friedrich. *Phenomenology of Spirit.* Translated by A. V. Miller. Oxford: Oxford University Press, 1977.
Helvetius. *A Treatise on Man: His Intellectual Faculties and His Education.* [s.l.]: Palala, 2018.
Herrick, Jim. *Humanism: An Introduction.* Amherst, NY: Prometheus, 2005.
Hibben, John Grier. *The Philosophy of the Enlightenment.* San Diego: Didactic, 2015.
Hobbes, Thomas. *Leviathan.* Edited by J. C. A. Gaskin. Oxford: Oxford University Press, 1996.
Hobson, Theo. *God Created Humanism: The Christian Basis of Secular Values.* London: SPCK, 2017.
Hodge, Jonathan, and Gregory Radick. *The Cambridge Companion to Darwin.* Cambridge: Cambridge University Press, 2009.
Hollingdale, Reginald J. "The Hero as Outsider." In *The Cambridge Companion to Nietzsche*, edited by Bernard Magnus and Kathleen M. Higgins, 71–89. Cambridge: Cambridge University Press, 1996.
———. *Nietzsche: The Man and His Philosophy.* 2nd ed. Cambridge: Cambridge University Press, 1992.
Hollingdale, Reginald J., ed. *A Nietzsche Reader.* London: Penguin, 1977.
Holmes, George. *The Florentine Enlightenment: 1400–1450.* 2nd ed. Oxford: Clarendon, 1992.
Hook, Sidney. *From Hegel to Marx: Studies in the Intellectual Development of Karl Marx.* New York: Columbia University Press, 1994.
Horkheimer, Max, and Theodor Adorno. *Dialectic of Enlightenment: Philosophical Fragments.* Stanford: Stanford University Press, 2002.
Hosle, Vittorio, and Christian Illies. *Darwinism and Philosophy.* Notre Dame: Notre Dame University Press, 2005.
Hume, David. *An Enquiry Concerning Human Understanding.* Edited by Tom Beauchamp. Oxford: Oxford University Press, 1999.
———. *A Treatise on Human Nature.* Charles Town, WV: Jefferson, 2015.
Hunter, Michael, and David Wootton. *Atheism from the Reformation to the Enlightenment.* Oxford: Oxford University Press, 1992.

Huntington, Samuel P. *The Clash of Civilizations and the Remaking of World Order.* London: Simon & Schuster, 1997.

Huxley, Julian. *Evolution: The Modern Synthesis.* Cambridge, MA: MIT Press, 2010.

Isbister, J. N. *Freud: An Introduction to his Life and Work.* Cambridge, UK: Polity, 1985.

Israel, Jonathan I. *Democratic Enlightenment: Philosophy, Revolution and Human Rights, 1750–1790.* Oxford: Oxford University Press, 2011.

Jackson, Roy. *Nietzsche: A Complete Introduction.* London: Hodder and Stoughton, 2014.

Janaway, Christopher. "The Gay Science." In *The Oxford Handbook of Nietzsche*, edited by Ken Gemes and John Richardson, 252–71. Oxford: Oxford University Press, 2013.

Jordan, Stuart. *The Enlightenment Vision: Science, Reason and the Promise of the Future.* New York: Prometheus, 2012.

Julian of Norwich. *Revelations of Divine Love.* Edited and translated by John Skinner. New York: Doubleday, 1997.

Kahn, Michael. *Basic Freud.* New York: Basic, 2002.

Kamenka, Eugene. *The Ethical Foundations of Marxism.* Abingdon, UK: Routledge and Paul, 1972.

Kant, Immanuel. *An Answer to the Question: What is Enlightenment?* London: Penguin, 2009.

Katsafanas, Paul. "Nietzsche's Philosophical Psychology." In *The Oxford Handbook of Nietzsche*, edited by Ken Gemes and John Richardson, 727–55. Oxford: Oxford University Press, 2013.

Kaufmann, Walter. *Nietzsche: Philosopher, Psaychologist, AntiChrist.* 4th ed. Princeton: Princeton University Press, 1974.

Kaufmann, Walter, ed. *The Basic Writings of Nietzsche.* New York: Random House, 2000.

———. *The Portable Nietzsche.* London: Penguin, 1976.

Kirk, John Andrew. *Christian Mission as Dialogue: Engaging the Current Epistemological Predicament of the West.* Nijmegen, Netherlands: Nijmegen Institute for Mission Studies, 2011.

———. *The Church and the World: Understanding the Relevance of Mission.* Milton Keynes, UK: Paternoster, 2014.

———. *Civilisations in Conflict?: Islam, the West and Christian Faith.* Oxford: Regnum, 2011.

———. *The Future of Reason, Science and Faith: Following Modernity and Post-Modernity.* Aldershot, UK: Ashgate, 2007.

———. *Liberation Theology: An Evangelical View from the Third World.* Basingstoke, UK: Marshall, Morgan and Scott, 1979.

———. *The Meaning of Freedom: A Study of Secular, Muslim and Christian Views.* Carlisle, UK: Paternoster, 1998.

Kirkpatrick, Betty, ed. *Cassell's Concise English Dictionary.* London: Cassell, 1993.

Kitcher, Philip. *Life after Faith: The Case for Secular Humanism.* New Haven, CT: Yale University Press, 2014.

Klyce, Brig. "Neo-Darwinism: The Current Paradigm." www.panspermia.org/neodarw.htm.

Knobe, Joshua, and Brian Leiter. "The Case for Nietzschean Moral Psychology." In *Nietzsche and Morality*, edited by Brian Leiter and Neil Sinhababu, 83–109. Oxford: Oxford University Press, 2007.
Knott, Sarah, and Barbara Taylor, eds. *Women, Gender and Enlightenment*. Basingstoke, UK: Palgrave Macmillan, 2005.
Koch, Hans-Gerhard. *The Abolition of God: Atheistic Ideology in Relation to the Christian Faith*. London: SCM, 1963.
Kramer, Matthew H. *John Locke and the Origins of Private Property: Philosophical Explorations of Individualism, Community and Equality*. Cambridge: Cambridge University Press, 1997.
Kramnick, Isaac, ed. *The Portable Enlightenment Reader*. Harmondsworth, UK: Penguin, 1995.
Kurtz, Paul. *What is Secular Humanism?* Amherst, NY: Prometheus, 2005.
Lamont, Corliss. *The Philosophy of Humanism*. 5th ed. New York: Philosophical Library, 1949.
Landes, Joan. "The History of Feminism: Marie-Jean-Antoine-Nicolas de Caritat, Marquis de Condorcet." https://plato.stanford.edu/entries/histfem-condorcet/.
Lane, Nick. *The Vital Question: Why is Life the Way It Is?* London: Profile, 2015.
Lasch-Quinn, Elisabeth. "Morality and the Crisis of Secularization." In *Debating Humanism*, edited by Dolan Cummings, 30–38. Exeter, UK: Societas, 2006.
Latham, Anthony. *The Naked Emperor: Darwinism Exposed*. London: Jason, 2005.
Law, Stephen. *Humanism: A Very Short Introduction*. Oxford: Oxford University Press, 2011.
Lear, Jonathan. *Freud*. 2nd ed. Abingdon, UK: Routledge, 2015.
Le Fanu, James. "Doubts about Darwin." http://thomasmoreinstitute.org.uk/papers/doubts-about-darwin/.
Lefebre, Georges. "The Declaration of the Rights of Man as the Essence of the Enlightenment." In *The Coming of the French Revolution*. Princeton: Princeton University Press, 1947.
———. *Dialectical Materialism*. Minneapolis: University of Minnesota Press, 2008.
Lehmann, Paul. "Christian Theology in a World in Revolution." In *Openings for Marxist-Christian Dialogue*, edited by Thomas Ogletree, 98–138. Nashville: Abingdon, 1969.
Lenin, Vladimir. *What Is to Be Done? Burning Questions of Our Movement*. London: Aziloth, 2017.
Leiter, Brian. *Nietzsche on Morality*. 2nd ed. Abingdon, UK: Routledge, 2014.
Lenin, Vladimir. *Collected Works*. Vol. IV. New York: International, 1929.
Leopold, David. *The Young Karl Marx: German Philosophy, Modern Politics and Human Flourishing*. Cambridge: Cambridge University Press, 2007.
Levy, Bernard-Henri, and Michel Houellebecq. *Public Enemies: Duelling Writers Take on Each Other and the World*. New York: Random House, 2011.
Lichtheim, George. *Marxism: An Historical and Critical Study*. London: Routledge and Kegan Paul, 1964.
Locke, John. "Epistle to the Reader." In *An Essay Concerning Human Understanding, Complete and Unabridged*, 9–21. ftp://ftp.dca.fee.unicamp.br/pub/docs/ia005/humanund.pdf.
———. *An Essay Concerning Human Understanding, Complete and Unabridged*. S.l.: WLC, 2009.

———. *A Paraphrase and Notes on the Epistles of St Paul*. Edited by Arthur Wainwright. Oxford: Clarendon, 1987.

———. *The Reasonableness of Christianity* Edited by L. T. Ramsey. Stanford, CA: Stanford University Press, 1958.

———. *The Selected Political Writings of John Locke*. Norton Critical Edition. New York: Norton, 2005.

Lockyer, Roger. *Hapsburg and Bourbon Europe: 1470–1720*. Harlow, UK: Longman, 1974.

Losonsky, Michael. "Locke on Meaning and Signification." In *Locke's Philosophy: Content and Context*, edited by G. A. J. Rogers, 123–41. Oxford: Clarendon, 1994.

Lowe, E. Jonathan. *Locke on Human Understanding*. London: Routledge, 1995.

Lowith, Karl. *From Hegel to Nietzsche: The Revolution in Nineteenth Century Thought*. 2nd ed. New York: Columbia University Press, 1991.

Lukes, Steven. "Article Morals." In *A Dictionary of Marxist Thought*, edited by Tom Bottomore, 387–89. 2nd ed. Oxford: Blackwell, 1991.

MacIntyre, Alasdair. *After Virtue: A Study in Moral Theory*. Notre Dame: Notre Dame Press, 1981.

Mack, Eric. *John Locke: Vol. 2 of Major Conservative and Liberal Thinkers*. Edited by John Meadowcroft. London: Continuum, 2009.

Magnus, Bernard, and Kathleen Higgins, eds. *The Cambridge Companion to Nietzsche*. Cambridge: Cambridge University Press, 1996.

———. "Nietzsche's Works and Their Themes." In *The Cambridge Companion to Nietzsche*, edited by Bernard Magnus and Kathleen M. Higgins, 21–68. Cambridge: Cambridge University Press, 1996.

Makari, George. *Soul Machine: The Invention of the Modern Mind*. New York: Norton, 2015.

Margulis, Lynn. *Symbiotic Planet: A New Look at Evolution*. New York: Basic, 1999.

Maritain, Jacques. *True Humanism*. 4th ed. London: Geoffrey Bles, 1946.

Martin, Michael. *Atheism, Morality and Meaning*. New York: Prometheus, 2002.

Marx, Karl. *Selected Works*. New York: International, 1968.

Mason, John Hope, and Robert Wokler, eds. *Diderot: Political Writings*. Cambridge: Cambridge University Press, 1992.

Mayr, Ernst. *Toward a New Philosophy of Biology*. Cambridge, MA: Harvard University Press, 1988.

McGrath, Alister. *Darwinism and the Divine: Evolutionary Thought and Natural Theology*. Oxford: Wiley-Blackwell, 2011.

McLellan, David. *Marx's Grundrisse*. Basingstoke, UK: Macmillan, 1973.

———. *The Thought of Karl Marx*. Basingstoke, UK: Papermac, 1995.

Michael, Martin. *Atheism, Morality and Meaning*. New York: Prometheus, 2002.

Michelet, Jules. *History of France*. Translated by W. K. Kelly. Neuilly sur Seine: Ulan, 2012.

Milton, Richard. *Shattering the Myths of Darwinism*. Rochester, VT: Park Street, 1997.

Moltmann, Jurgen. *On Human Being: Christian Anthropology in the Conflicts of the Present*. 2nd ed. Minneapolis: Fortress, 2009.

Morley, John. *Diderot and the Encyclopedists*. 2 vols. Neuilly sur Seine: Ulan, 2018.

Nagel, Thomas. *Mind and Cosmos: Why the Materialist Neo-Darwinian Conception of Nature is Almost Certainly False*. Oxford: Oxford University Press, 2012.

Naskar, Abhijit. *Principia Humanitas*. Self-published, Amazon, 2017.

BIBLIOGRAPHY

Nauert, Charles. *Historical Dictionary of the Renaissance*. Lanham, MD: Scarecrow, 2003.
Neu, Jerome, ed. *The Cambridge Companion to Freud*. Cambridge: Cambridge University Press, 1994.
Niebuhr, Reinhold. *Moral Man and Immoral Society: A Study of Ethics and Politics*. Louisville: Westminster/John Knox, 2002.
———. *The Nature and Destiny of Man: Volume I, Human Nature*. London: Nisbet, 1941.
Nietzsche, Friedrich. *The Antichrist: Curse on Christianity*. Self-published: Create Space, 2015.
———. "Introduction to the Later Writings." In *The Nietzsche Reader*, edited by Keith Pearson and Duncan Large, 297–310. Oxford: Blackwell, 2006.
Norton, David F., ed. *The Cambridge Companion to Hume*. Cambridge: Cambridge University Press, 1993.
Nuovo, Victor. *John Locke: Writings on Religion*. New York: Oxford University Press, 2002.
O'Hara, Kieron. *The Enlightenment: A Beginner's Guide*. London: One World, 2010.
Ollman, Bertell. *Alienation: Marx's Conception of Man in Capitalist Society*. 2nd ed. Cambridge: Cambridge University Press, 1976.
Outram, Dorinda. *The Enlightenment: New Approaches to European History*. 3rd ed. Cambridge: Cambridge University Press, 2013.
Ozment, Steven. *The Age of Reform: 1250–1550: An Intellectual and Religious History of Late Medieval and Reformation Europe*. New Haven, CT: Yale University Press, 1980.
Pagden, Anthony. *The Enlightenment and Why It Still Matters*. Oxford: Oxford University Press, 2013.
Paine, Thomas. "The Rights of Man." In *The Portable Enlightenment Reader*, edited by Isaac Kramnick, 469–72. Harmondsworth, UK: Penguin, 1995.
Paley, William. *Natural Theology: Or, Evidences of the Existence and Attributes of the Deity*. London: Faulder, 1809.
Pearson, Keith. *A Companion to Nietzsche*. Oxford: Blackwell, 2006.
Pearson, Keith, and Duncan Large. *The Nietzsche Reader*. Oxford: Blackwell, 2006.
Penelhum, Terence. "Fideism." In *A Companion to the Philosophy of Religion*, edited by Philip L. Quinn and Charles Taliaferro, 376–82. Oxford: Blackwell, 1997.
Pennock, Robert T., ed. *Intelligent Design Creationism and Its Critics: Philosophical, Theological and Scientific Perspectives*. Cambridge, MA: MIT Press, 2001.
Phillips, Adam, ed. *The Penguin Freud Reader*. London: Penguin, 2006.
Pico della Mirandola, Giovanni. *Oration on the Dignity of Man (1486)*. Cambridge: Cambridge University Press, 2012.
———. *Oration on the Dignity of Man*. Translated by Charles Wallis. London: Optimistbooks.com, 2018.
Pierse, Siofra. "Subversive Scepticism: Diderot and Narrative Doubt." In *The Dark Side of Diderot*, edited by James Hanrahan and Siofra Pierse, 57–84. Bern, Switzerland: Lang, 2016.
Pippin, Robert B. "Nietzsche's Alleged Farewell: The Premodern, Modern and Postmodern Nietzsche." In *The Cambridge Companion to Nietzsche*, edited by Bernard Magnus and Kathleen M. Higgins, 252–78. Cambridge: Cambridge University Press, 1996.

Plamenatz, John. *Karl Marx's Philosophy of Man*. Oxford: Oxford University Press, 1975.
Poellner, Peter. "Nietzsche's Metaphysical Sketches: Causality and Will to Power." In *The Oxford Handbook of Nietzsche*, edited by Ken Gemes and John Richardson, 675–700. Oxford: Oxford University Press, 2013.
Pojman, Louis. "On Equal Human Worth: A Critique of Contemporary Egalitarianism." In *Equality: Selected Readings*, edited by Louis Pojman and Robert Westmoreland, 282–99. Oxford: Oxford University Press, 1997.
Polyani, Michael. *Personal Knowledge: Towards a Post-Critical Philosophy*. Chicago: University of Chicago Press, 1958.
———. *The Tacit Dimension*. Chicago: University of Chicago Press, 1966.
Pope, Alexander. "An Essay on Man." In *The Portable Enlightenment Reader*, edited by Isaac Kramnick, 255–56. Harmondsworth, UK: Penguin, 1995.
Popper, Karl. *Conjectures and Refutations*. London: Routledge & Paul, 1963.
———. *The Logic of Scientific Discovery*. London: Hutchinson, 1959.
———. *The Open Society and its Enemies*. Routledge Classics. 6th ed. Abingdon, UK: Routledge, 2011.
———. *The Poverty of Historicism*. Abingdon, UK: Routledge, 2002.
———. *Unended Quest: An Intellectual Autobiography*. La Salle, IL: Open Court, 1976.
Popple, William. "To the Reader, (Preface to Locke, John, A Letter Concerning Toleration)." In *The Selected Political Writings of John Locke*, edited by Paul E. Sigmund, 125–26. New York: W. W. Norton, 2005.
Putnam, Hilary. *The Collapse of the Fact/Value Dichotomy*. Cambridge: Harvard University Press, 2004.
Quinodoz, Jean-Michel. *Sigmund Freud: An Introduction*. Abingdon, UK: Routledge, 2018.
Rand, Ayn. *The Virtue of Selfishness*. New York: Signet, 1964.
Randall, John Herman. *The Career of Philosophy: From the Middle Ages to the Enlightenment*. New York: Columbia University Press, 1962.
———. "David Hume: Radical Empiricist and Pragmatist." In *The Career of Philosophy: From the Middle Ages to the Enlightenment*. New York: Columbia University Press, 1962.
Ree, Jonathan, and Urmson, J. O. Urmson, eds. *The Concise Encyclopedia of Western Philosophy and Philosophers*. London: Routledge, 1989.
Reed, Langford. *The Complete Limerick Book*. London: Jarrolds, 1925.
Reginster, Bernard. "The Psychology of Christian Morality: Will to Power as Will to Nothingness." In *The Oxford Handbook of Nietzsche*, edited by Ken Gemes and John Richardson, 701–26. Oxford: Oxford University Press, 2013.
Richards, Robert J. "Darwin on Mind, Morals and Emotions." In *The Cambridge Companion to Darwin*, by Jonathan Hodge and Gregory Radick, 96–119. Cambridge: Cambridge University Press, 2009.
Richardson, John. "Nietzsche on Life's Ends." In *The Oxford Handbook of Nietzsche*, edited by Ken Gemes and John Richardson, 756–83. Oxford: Oxford University Press, 2013.
Richardson, John, and Brian Leiter, eds. *Nietzsche*. Oxford Readings in Philosophy. Oxford: Oxford University Press, 2001.
Ricoeur, Paul. *Freud and Philosophy*. New Haven, CT: Yale University Press, 1969.
Rizzuto, Ana-Maria. *Why did Freud Reject God? A Psychodynamic Interpretation*. New Haven, CT: Yale University Press, 1998.

Robertson, John. *Enlightenment: A Very Short Introduction*. Oxford: Oxford University Press, 2015.
Rockmore, Tom. *Marx after Marxism: The Philosophy of Karl Marx*. Oxford: Blackwell, 2002.
Rogers, G. A. J. *Locke's Philosophy: Content and Context*. Oxford: Clarendon, 1994.
Ruggiero, Guido. *The Renaissance in Italy: A Social and Cultural History of the Renascimiento*. New York: Cambridge University Press, 2015.
Rupp, E. Gordon, and Philip S. Watson, eds. *Luther and Erasmus: Free Will and Salvation*. London: SCM, 1969.
Salome, Lou. *Nietzsche*. Redding Ridge, CT: Black Swan, 1988.
Sandford, Stella. "Introduction: The Incomplete Locke: Balibar, Locke and the Philosophy of the Subject." In *Identity and Difference: John Locke and the Invention of Consciousness*, by Etienne Balibar, xi–xxxix. London: Verso, 2013.
Sartre, Jean-Paul. *Existentialism is a Humanism*. New Haven, CT: Yale University Press, 2007.
Sayers, Sean. *Marxism and Human Nature*. Abingdon, UK: Routledge, 1998.
Schacht, Richard. "Nietzsche's Genealogy." In *The Oxford Handbook of Nietzsche*, edited by Ken Gemes and John Richardson, 323–43. Oxford: Oxford University Press, 2013.
———. "Nietzsche's Kind of Philosophy." In *The Cambridge Companion to Nietzsche*, edited by Bernard Magnus and Kathleen M. Higgins, 151–79. Cambridge: Cambridge University Press, 1996.
Schaff, Adam. *Marxism and the Human Individual*. New York: McGraw-Hill, 1970.
Schneewind, Jerome B., ed. *Moral Philosophy from Montaigne to Kant*. Cambridge: Cambridge University Press, 2003.
Scott-Kakures, Dion, et al., eds. "David Hume." In *History of Philosophy*, edited by Dion Scott-Kakures et al., 208–35. New York: Harper Collins, 1993.
———. "Hume's Moral Theory." In *History of Philosophy*, edited by Dion Scott-Kakures et al., 296–303. New York: Harper Collins, 1993.
Sedgwick, Peter. *Nietzsche: The Key Concepts*. Abingdon, UK: Routledge, 2009.
Segundo, Juan Luis. *Evolution and Guilt*. Dublin: Gill & Macmillan, 1980.
———. *Grace and the Human Condition*. Dublin: Gill & Macmillan, 1980.
———. *A Theology for Artisans of a New Humanity*. Dublin: Gill and Macmillan, 1980.
Seward, Albert C. *Darwin and Modern Science*. Cambridge: BiblioBazaar, 2006.
Shanahan, Timothy. *The Evolution of Darwinism: Selection, Adaptation and Progress in Evolutionary Biology*. Cambridge: Cambridge University Press, 2004.
Sichel, Edith. *The Renaissance*. New York: Holt, 1914.
Sigmund, Paul E. "Equality, Legitimacy and Majority Rule in Locke." In *The Selected Political Writings of John Locke*, edited by Paul E. Sigmund, 306–13. New York: Norton, 2005.
Sigmund, Paul E., ed. *The Selected Political Writings of John Locke*. New York: Norton, 2005.
Simmons, John. "From the Lockean Theory of Rights." In *The Selected Political Writings of John Locke*, edited by Paul E. Sigmund, 286–90. New York: Norton, 2005.
Smith, Robertson. *The Religion of the Semites: First Series*. New York: Meridian Library, 1956.
———. *The Religion of the Semites: Second and Third Series*. Sheffield, UK: Sheffield Academic Press, 1995.

Smoker, Barbara. *Humanism for Enquiring Minds.* London: Foote, 2017.
Sober, Elliott. "Metaphysical and Epistemological Issues in Modern Darwinian Theory." In *The Cambridge Companion to Darwin*, by Jonathan Hodge and Gregory Radick, 302–19. Cambridge: Cambridge University Press, 2009.
Solomon, Robert C. "Nietzsche ad hominem: Perspectivism, Personality and Ressentiment." In *The Cambridge Companion to Nietzsche*, edited by Bernard Magnus and Kathleen M. Higgins, 180–222. Cambridge: Cambridge University Press, 1996.
Spellman, W. W. "Locke and Original Sin." In *The Selected Political Writings of John Locke*, edited by Paul E. Sigmund, 363–65. New York: Norton, 2005.
Stalin, Josef. *The Foundations of Leninism.* LaPorte, IN: Marx, Engels, Lenin Press, 2015.
Stawson, Galen. *Locke on Personal Identity: Consciousness and Concernment.* Princeton: Princeton University Press, 2011.
Stenmark, Mikael. *How to Relate Science and Religion: A Multi-Dimensional Model.* Grand Rapids: Eerdmans, 2004.
Stern, Robert. *Hegel and the Phenomenology of Spirit.* London: Routledge, 2002.
Storr, Anthony. *Freud: A Very Short Introduction.* Oxford: Oxford University Press, 2001.
Strachey, James, ed. *Standard Edition of the Complete Psychological Works of Sigmund Freud.* 24 vols. London: Hogarth Press, 1986.
Strawson, Galen. *Locke on Personal Identity: Consciousness and Concernment.* Princeton: Princeton University Press, 2011.
Strugnell. *Diderot's Politics: A Study of the Evolution of Diderot's Political Thought.* Hague: Nijhoff, 1973.
Suprenant, Celine. *Freud: A Guide for the Perplexed.* London: Continuum, 2008.
Symonds, John Addington. "The Beginning and Progress of the Renaissance: Fourteenth to Sixteenth Century." http://history-world.org/Beginning%20And%20Progress%20Of%20The%20Renaissance.htm.
———. *Renaissance in Italy.* 7 vols. N.p.: Hall, 2009.
———. *Renaissance in Italy: The Age of the Despots.* Whitefish, MO: Kessinger, 2018.
Tanner, Michael. *Nietzsche: A Very Short Introduction.* Oxford: Oxford University Press, 2000.
Tauber, Alfred I. *Freud: The Reluctant Philosopher.* Philadelphia: Princeton University Press, 2010.
Taylor, Barbara. *Mary Wollstonecraft and the Feminist Imagination.* Cambridge: Cambridge University Press, 2003.
Taylor, Charles. *A Secular Age.* Cambridge: Harvard University Press, 2007.
———. *The Sources of the Self.* Cambridge: Cambridge University Press, 1989.
Temple, William. *Nature, Man and God.* London: Macmillan, 1935.
Teresi, Dick. "Discover Interview: Lynn Margulis Says She's Not Controversial, She's Right." http://discovermagazine.com/2011/apr/16-interview-lynn-margulis-not-controversial-right.
Thompson, Harry. *This Thing of Darkness.* London: Headline, 2005.
Thomson, Garrett. *On Locke.* Belmont, CA: Thomson, 2001.
Thornton, Stephen P. "Sigmund Freud." www.iep.utm.edu/freud.
Thurschwell, Pamela. *Sigmund Freud.* 2nd ed. Abingdon, UK: Routledge, 2009.
Todorov, Tzvetan. *Imperfect Garden: The Legacy of Humanism.* Princeton: Princeton University Press, 2002.

Towers, Bernard., ed. *Evolution, Marxism and Christianity*. London: Humanities Press International, 1968.
Tracy, James D. *Erasmus: The Growth of a Mind*. Geneva: Libraire Droz, 1972.
Trigg, Roger. *Equality, Freedom and Religion*. Oxford: Oxford University Press, 2012.
Tucker, Robert C. *The Marx-Engels Reader*. New York: Norton, 1972.
Tully, James. "The Two Treatises and Aboriginal Rights." In *Locke's Philosophy: Content and Context*, edited by G. A. J. Rogers, 165–97. Oxford: Clarendon, 1994.
United Nations. *Universal Declaration of Human Rights*. http://www.un.org/en/universal-declaration-human-rights/.
Vasari, Giorgio. *Lives of the Most Excellent Painters, Sculptors and Architects*. Modern Library Edition. New York: Random House, 2006.
von Tevenar, Gudrun. "Zarathustra: That Malicious Dionysian." In *The Oxford Handbook of Nietzsche*, edited by Ken Gemes and John Richardson, 272–97. Oxford: Oxford University Press, 2013.
Vranicki, Predrag. "Socialism and the Problem of Alienation." In *Socialist Humanism: An International Symposium*, edited by Fromm, Erich, 299–313. Garden City, NY: Doubleday, 1965.
Waldron, Jeremy. "God, Locke and Equality." In *The Selected Political Writings of John Locke*, edited by Paul E. Sigmund, 313–23. New York: Norton, 2005.
Ward, Keith. *The Evidence for God: The Case for the Existence of the Spiritual Dimension*. London: Darton, Longman & Todd, 2014.
———. *The God Conclusion: God and the Western Philosophical Tradition*. London: Darton, Longman & Todd, 2009.
Watson, Kirk. *Philosophical Thoughts and Other Texts: Denis Diderot*. Self-published, 2018.
Webb, Nick, and Peter Elmer, eds. *The Renaissance in Europe: An Anthology*. Milton Keynes, UK: Open University, 2000.
Webster, Richard. *Why Freud was Wrong: Sin, Science and Psychoanalysis*. New York: Basic, 1995.
Whitebrook, Joel. *Freud: An Intellectual Biography*. Cambridge: Cambridge University Press, 2017.
Wilson, Andrew N. *Charles Darwin: Victorian Mythmaker*. London: John Murray, 2017.
Wollstonecraft, Mary. *A Vindication of the Rights of Woman*. London: Penguin, 2004.
Wolterstorff, Nicholas. *John Locke and the Ethics of Belief*. Cambridge: Cambridge University Press, 1996.
Young, Julian. *Nietzsche's Philosophy of Religion*. Cambridge: Cambridge University Press, 2006.

Index

abduction, 170, 380–383
Adorno, Theodor, 95
aesthetics, 9
Alberti, 42–43
Amerindians, the case of, 68–71
Anabaptists, 298
Apollo, 376
art, visual, of the "High Renaissance," 24–26
assumption, materialist, 15,16
Augustine, of Hippo, 348
    Confessions, 348
Avila, Theresa of, 34

Bacon Roger, 28
Bayle, Pierre, 94, 111–112
beauty, the sense of, 184–185
beliefs, fundamental, viii–ix
Berdyaev, Nicholas, 157
Berkeley, George, 112
Bloch, Ernst, 159
Bloom, Paul, 374
    Just Babies: The Origins of Good and Evil, 374
Bonhoeffer, Dietrich, 331
Bradwardine, Thomas, 28
Brotton, Jerry, 27
Burckthardt, Jacob, 27
Burke, Peter, 28

Cabala, mystical tradition of, 46–47
Caferro, William, 28
Capitalism, 164–165
Casas, Bartolome, de las, 32, 298
Charron, Pierre, 109

Christian faith, 91–92, 107, 152, 211, 218, 223, 224–226, 270–271, 276, 284, 300
church, separation from the state, 74
civilization, western, 1
civilizations, clash of, 3
class-struggle, the, 162–163
Common Life, Brethren of the, 48
Communism, 2, 259, 326, 327–328,
complexity, theory of, 14
Condorcet, Nicolas de, 94, 97, 98, 100, 127
conscience, 8
consciousness, 8–9, 79–81, 184, 272
culture, western, vii

Darwin, Charles, 12, 101, 166–193, 304
    The Descent of Man, 174–179
    The Origin of Species, 174, 361–364
Darwinism-Neo, 12–13, 268
Dawkins, Richard, 16–17, 168
"Death Black," 30, 365
deism, 105, 129
Dembski, William, 14–15
"Design Intelligent," 14–15
destiny, manifest, 2
dialogue, 379–383
Diderot, Denis, 102, 127–136
    Jacques le fataliste, 137
    Le Neveu de Rameau, 137
    Le Reve de d'Alembert, 132
    Lettre sur les aveugles, 129
    Pensees philosophiques, 128

Diderot, Denis (continued)
   Pensees sur l'interpretation de la nature, 130
   Promenade du sceptique 129
   Refutation d'Helvetius, 135
Dionysus, 234, 259, 354, 376
disability, mental, 9
Djilas, Milovan, 160
Donatello, 38

Empire, Holy Roman, 1
   Ottoman, 23, 25
Encyclopedie, 127
Enlightenment, the, 93–114, 210, 234, 350
equality, 67–68, 89
Erasmus, Desiderius, 47–54
   De libero arbitro, 50–52
   Enchiridion, 48
   In Praise of Folly, 49, 365
   On the Purity of the Tabernacle, 54
Este, Isabelle d', 34
evil, 373–377
evolution, "chance," 12–13, 166
   critique of theory, 173, 306
   Neo-Darwinian thesis, 171–172, 177
   "theistic," 15–17, 172
existentialism, 291

faith, religious, 82–87
fallacy, the deontic, 188
   the genetic, 228–230
   the naturalistic, 305–308
Feuerbach, Ludwig, 145–146, 152, 164, 350–351
Ficino, Marsilio, 40–42
fideism, 88
freedom, to choose, 47
   political, 158
freewill, 53–54, 55–56, 76–78, 91, 122–123, 132, 270, 335–336
Freud, Sigmund, 236–274, 325, 346
   and scientific method, 238–239, 241–242, 263, 267–269
   anthropology, 271–274
   Beyond the Pleasure Principle, 240
   civilization, 257–260
   Civilization and its Discontents, 240
   Dream analysis, 248–252
      repression, 251
   The Future of an Illusion, 240, 241
   guilt, 260–261, 268
   hysteria, 244
   Id, Ego and Superego, 252–254, 342
   infantile sexuality, 245–246
   libido, 377
   major themes of his writings, 239,
   Moses and Monotheism, 240
   Oedipus complex, the, 246–248, 260, 261, 268
   pleasure principle and death wish, 254–257, 273–274
   religion, 242–243, 261–263, 269–272
   therapeutic methods, 243–245
   Totem and Taboo, 261
   world-view, 264–266
Fromm, Eric, 270

golden rule, the, 295
Goldmann, Lucien, 160
Grayling, Anthony, 295, 296–297

Habermas, Jurgen, 230, 382
Hegel, Georg, 101, 141–144
   theory of history, 142–144, 164
Hegelians, the young, 145
Helvetius, Claude Adrien, 106, 110–111, 368
heritage, Christian, 3
"hidden hand," the, 96
Hobbes, Thomas, 73
Holbach, Baron d', 105–106, 108
   Systeme de la nature, 130
Horkheimer, Max, 95
human, distinguishing features of, 6–11, 180–192
   origin of, 12–20,

science of, 126
social existence, 185–186, 366
humanism, secular, 3, 234, 275–309, 324, 367
   Christian, 367
   exclusive, 106–107, 277
   foundational belief, 277–278
      and a religious world-view, 295–299
      anthropology, 285–289
      assumptions, 278–281
      characteristics, 281–285
      ethical theories, 289–295
      faith, act of 302–304
      internal critiques, 301–302
      wager, the humanist, 302
   of Marx, 164
   of the Renaissance, 21–56, 365, 366
Hume, David, 115–127
   An Enquiry Concerning Human Understanding, 115–127
   An Enquiry Concerning the Principles of Morals, 119–121
   A Treatise of Human Nature, 116
Hutcheson, Francis, 108
Huxley, Julian, 364
   Evolution: the Modern Synthesis, 362

idealism, 112, 162, 163, 337
Ideal Observer Theory, 293–294
ideal speech situation, 382
ideas, innate, 74
identity, personal, 78–81, 90–91, 377–379
individualism, 102, 134, 159
interventionism, western, 2

Julian of Norwich, 346
Jung, Carl, 238, 265–266

Kant, Immanuel, 98, 102, 111, 299

labor, 150–151
Lane, Nick, 17
language,
   development of, 183–184
   origin of, 183–184
Laplace, Pierre-Simon, 104
learning, 6–8
Lefebre, Georges, 103
Lehmann, Paul, 156
Lenin, Vladimir, 156–158, 161
life, purpose of, 263
Lincoln, Abraham, 96
Locke, John, 57–92, 276
   An Essay concerning Human Understanding, 60–65
   Second Treatise of Government, 66–76
   The Reasonableness of Christianity, 82–85
Lopez-Silva, Pablo, xi
love, giving and receiving, 9–10
Luther, Martin, 47, 354
   De servo arbitrio, 52
   On the Babylonian Captivity of the Church, 50
Luxemburg, Rosa, 158

MacIntyre, Alasdair, 291
Maritain, Jacques, 323–330
   Christendom, secular, 326, 328–330
   critique of secular humanism, 338–339
   evil, source and resolution, 326–327
   the human condition, 325
   humanism, integral, 325–330
Marx, Karl, 101, 140–165, 262, 268
   and morality, 153–156
   critique of theistic anthropology, 152–153
   The German Ideology, 162
   Manifesto of the Communist Party, 147
   The Poverty of Philosophy, 162
   theory of alienation, 148, 155
   theory of history, 144–148
   theory of negation, 162
   vision of human being, 149–151
materialism, 130–132
Mendel, Gregor, 12,

mental capacity, 180–183,
Mettrie, La, 104, 112
Michelangelo, 38–39
Michelet, Jules,
mind, reality of, 16
miracles, 124, 125–126
Mirandola, Pico della, 43–47, 365
Moltmann, Jurgen, 347–354
    anthropology, 348–351
        sin, original, 350
    The Coming of God, 348
    emigration, inward, 352
    God in Creation, 348
    Jesus, death of, 353–354
    On Human Being: Anthropology in the Conflicts of the Present, 348
    romanticism, 352–353
    salvation, 351–354
    utopia, 353
morality, 8–9, 71–72, 81–82, 108–109, 132–134, 186–190, 317–323, 367–373
    "the golden rule," 188
    origin of, 292–293
    relation to empirical facts, 189–190
motion, matter in, 129–130

Nagel, Thomas, 363
Naskar, Abhijit, 288–289
naturalism, methodological, 15, 171, 173
    philosophy of, 337
nature, state of, 68–69
Naziism, 1
Niebuhr, Reinhold, 330–339
    anthropology, 331–332, 335–339
    evil and sin, cause and resolution, 332–335,
    Moral Man and Immoral Society: A Study of Ethics and Politics, 331
    The Nature and Destiny of Man: A Christian Interpretation, 331
Nietzsche, Friedrich, 194–235, 262, 325, 351, 354

    Christian faith, and, 224–226
    drives, psychological, 215–216
    Ecce Homo, 224
    freedom of the will, 217–219, 231–233
    Human, All Too Human, 217
    human nature, 219–221
    intentions in writing, 197–198
    life, pursuit of, 212–213
    metaphysics, 224–226
    morality 201–211, 213
        ascetic ideal, the, 205–207
        conventional 201–202
        noble, 207–209
        resentment, 203–205
        revaluation of all values, 209–211
        slave, 203
    On the Genealogy of Morals, 205–207
    perspectivism, 221–223
    philosophical assumptions, 198–201
    reason, approach to, 230–231
    Thus Spoke Zarathustra, 234
    The Twilight of the Idols, 209–210
    Ubermensch, the, 214–216, 376
    the will to power, 213–214
    writing style, 194–196

Paine, Thomas, 103–104, 105
Paul, apostle, 342–343, 375
philosophy, natural, 46
    political, 66–76
physicalism, non-reductive, 278
Plekhanov, Georgi, 156, 161
Pope, Alexander, 109
Popper, Karl, 160, 163–164, 304
postmodernity, 381
Prevost, Antoine, 113
Priestley, Joseph, 97, 127
progress, 100–101
property, private, 150, 154, 258
psychoanalysis, 342

questions, fundamental, 5, 19

Rand, Ayn, 288
rationalism, 113
reason, use of, 9, 122,
    and faith, 82–87, 89
Reformation, the, 1, 366
Reid, Thomas, 112
religion, 124–127, 138
    origin of, 125, 190–192
Renaissance, the, vii, 1, 324, 336–337, 350
    characteristics of, 22–31
    humanism of, in art, 35–39
    humanism of, in literature, 39–54
    social and political context, 31–34
    stages of, 29–31
Revisionists, Marxist, 158
Revolution, French, 94, 141
Ricouer, Paul, 342
rights, human, 1, 11, 71–73, 159, 298, 299
    Declaration of, 102–103
    of private property, 69–70
    Universal Declaration of, 5, 307, 323
romanticism, 113, 338
Ruggiero, Guido, 30
rule-utilitarianism, 82

Sade, Marquis de, 133
Salamanca, University of, 298
Sartre, Jean-Paul, 285–286, 291, 340–341, 357
Schaff, Adam, 159
sciences, natural, 1
    nature of, 169–171, 193, 280
scientism, 323
Segundo, Juan Luis, 339–347
    evil, 342–345
        guilt, 344
    Evolution and Guilt, 340
    grace, 340
    Grace and the Human Condition, 340
    human condition, the, 340–34
    liberation, 346–347
sensationalism, 105

sensibility, nature of, 135–136,
sin, original, 270, 325
slave-trade, 71
Smith, Adam, 96, 112
socialists, utopian, 154
Spirit, the absolute, 143–144
spirituality, 278
Stenmark, Mikael, 17
Symonds, John, 28

Taylor, Charles, 106
Temple, William, 271, 312–323
    anthropology, 315–317
    Christian belief, characteristics of, 314–315
    dialogue, invitation to, 313–314
    moral thought and action, 317–323
        evil, problem of, 318–320
        evil, resolution of, 320–323
    theology, definition of, 313
    Nature, Man and God, 312–323
theism, 124–125, 276
Toderov, Tzvetan, 357
toleration, 73–76, 90
transcendence, sense of, 10–11, 152–153, 367
Trigg, Roger, 76

universe, origin of, 130

Vasari, Giorgio, 22
Voltaire, Francois-Marie, 94, 105, 112
Vinci, Leonardo da, 24

war, first world, 1–2
    justification of, 71
    second world, 2
Ward, Keith, 10, 16, 383
Wilson, A.N., 167, 363
    Charles Darwin: Victorian Mythmaker, 167
wisdom, the gaining of? 356–383
    assumptions, 358–362
        materialism, 359–362
        theism, 358–359
    values, the revaluation of, 360–361

wisdom, the gaining of (continued)
    dialogue in the context of truth, 379–383
    evil, origin, reality and overcoming, 373–377
    human identity, 377–379
    humanism, 364–367
    morality, 367–373
    origin of species, the, 361–364
women, rights of, 99–100
Wollstonecraft, Mary, 99
worldview, naturalistic, 3
    Christian, 20, 312

www.ingramcontent.com/pod-product-compliance
Lightning Source LLC
Chambersburg PA
CBHW071228290426
44108CB00013B/1336